THE LEGALITY AND ACCOUNTABILITY OF AUTONOMOUS WEAPON SYSTEMS

By adopting a multi-disciplinary approach, this book provides a comprehensive analysis of the legality of the use of autonomous weapons systems under international law. It examines different arguments presented by States, roboticists and scholars to demonstrate the challenges such systems will create for the laws of war. This study examines how technology of warfare seeks to increase the dissociation of risk and communication between weapons and their human operators. Furthermore, it explains how algorithms might give rise to 'errors' on the battlefield that cannot be directly attributed to human operators. Against this backdrop, Dr Seixas-Nunes examines three distinct legal frameworks: the distinction between the legality of weapons and the laws of targeting; different mechanisms of individual accountability and the importance of recovering the category of 'dolus eventualis' for programmers and technicians and, finally, State responsibility for violations of the laws of war caused by weapons' software errors.

Afonso Seixas-Nunes, Jesuit Priest, graduated in Law, Philosophy (Vitorino Sousa Alves Award) and Theology, and holds an Mst in Human Rights from the London School of Economic and a PhD from the University of Essex. He was a visiting scholar at the Oxford Institute for Ethics, Law and Armed Conflict and since July 2021 he joined the University of St Louis School of Law (SLU-Law).

The Legality and Accountability of Autonomous Weapon Systems

A HUMANITARIAN LAW PERSPECTIVE

AFONSO SEIXAS-NUNES
University of Oxford

CAMBRIDGE
UNIVERSITY PRESS

CAMBRIDGE
UNIVERSITY PRESS

Shaftesbury Road, Cambridge CB2 8EA, United Kingdom

One Liberty Plaza, 20th Floor, New York, NY 10006, USA

477 Williamstown Road, Port Melbourne, VIC 3207, Australia

314–321, 3rd Floor, Plot 3, Splendor Forum, Jasola District Centre, New Delhi – 110025, India

103 Penang Road, #05–06/07, Visioncrest Commercial, Singapore 238467

Cambridge University Press is part of Cambridge University Press & Assessment, a department of the University of Cambridge.

We share the University's mission to contribute to society through the pursuit of education, learning and research at the highest international levels of excellence.

www.cambridge.org
Information on this title: www.cambridge.org/9781009088381

DOI: 10.1017/9781009090001

First published 2022
First paperback edition 2026

A catalogue record for this publication is available from the British Library

Library of Congress Cataloging-in-Publication data
NAMES: Seixas-Nunes, Afonso, author.
TITLE: The legality and accountability of autonomous weapon systems : a humanitarian law perspective / Afonso Seixas-Nunes, University of Oxford.
description: Cambridge, United Kingdom ; New York, NY : Cambridge University Press, 2022. | Includes index.
IDENTIFIERS: LCCN 2021041350 (print) | LCCN 2021041351 (ebook) | ISBN 9781316514832 (hardback) | ISBN 9781009090001 (ebook)
SUBJECTS: LCSH: Autonomous weapons systems (International law) | Humanitarian law.
CLASSIFICATION: LCC KZ5645.5.A98 S45 2022 (print) | LCC KZ5645.5.A98 (ebook) | DDC 341.6/3–dc23/eng/20211028
LC record available at https://lccn.loc.gov/2021041350
LC ebook record available at https://lccn.loc.gov/2021041351

ISBN 978-1-316-51483-2 Hardback
ISBN 978-1-009-08838-1 Paperback

To my mother. . ..

To Casa do Casal, *Cabeceiras de Basto*

Contents

Acknowledgements

I would firstly like to express my sincere gratitude to Professors Noam Lubell and Wayne Martin, my supervisors, who accepted the tiresome task of supervising my research, offering invaluable guidance and support in good and bad times. Above all, I would like to thank them for believing in me and in my work.

Among others, I would also like to express my gratitude to Professor Azeredo Lopes, my first international public law teacher at the Faculty of Law, Catholic University of Portugal, Porto, and to Professor Claire Moon, Dr Ayça Çubukçu and Dr Devika Hovell, my teachers at the London School of Economics, for enticing me to embrace the adventure of a PhD and specifically the world of international humanitarian law (IHL). I only hope that one day I will be able to encourage future international lawyers as all these teachers encouraged me.

Last but not least, I thank Professor Dapo Akande from the Oxford Institute of Ethics, Law and Armed Conflict (ELAC), Professor Charles Garraway, Fellow of the University of Essex, Major General Timothy Cross CBE from the British Army, Professor Rain Liivoja from the University of Queensland, and Dr Russell Buchan from the University of Sheffield for their insights and advice while I was dealing with what, at that time, seemed to be autonomous weapons systems' insurmountable challenges.

To my friends at the School of Law of the University of Essex: Anil, Daragh and Nathan; to my friends at the ELAC at the University of Oxford: Antonio Coco, Harry Begg, Talita de Souza Dias, Zachary Vermeer; to my fellow Jesuits: Carlos Carneiro, Duarte, João, Manuel, Michael Barnes, Michael Holman, Pedro and Rob Marsh; to all my friends, especially those who supported me in the course of these five years: Ana Cabral, os 'Super-Costas', Frith Hooton, Gonçalo e Mariana Noronha Andrade, Ines e Marco

Frazao; Mariana e Tiago Lopes Pinto; Ana e ZeZe Cardoso da Costa, Teresa e Rodrigo Lourenço; Santólicos, Sofia and ZB Fraga, Vera e Gonçalo Diniz Vieira I thank you from my heart.

A special word to Tio José Fraga and Zé Pedro Anacoreta for their example and to the British Province of the Society of Jesus for granting all the support I needed during these last five years.

Finally, I want to thank my family, my father and cousins, for being always so supportive with their unwavering love. I would like to dedicate this book in a special way to the *Casa do Casal*, in Cabeceiras de Basto, the place on earth where I always find myself.

Abbreviations

AGI	artificial general intelligence
AI	artificial intelligence
AMW Manual	Manual on International Law Applicable to Air and Missile Warfare
API	First Additional Protocol to the 1949 Geneva Conventions, relating to the Protection of Victims of International Armed Conflicts (1977)
APII	Second Additional Protocol to the 1949 Geneva Conventions, relating to the Protection of Non-International Armed Conflicts (1977)
ARSIWA	Draft Articles on the Responsibility of States for Internationally Wrongful Acts
AWS	autonomous weapons system
CCF	continuous combat function
CCM	Convention on Cluster Munitions
CCW	Convention on Prohibitions or Restrictions on the Use of Certain Conventional Weapons Which May Be Deemed to Be Excessively Injurious or to Have Indiscriminate Effects
CDEM	collateral damage estimate methodology
DARPA	United States Defense Advanced Research Projects Agency
DoD	United States Department of Defense
DPH	direct participation in hostilities
EBO	effects-based operation
EG	AWS ethical governor
EU	European Union

Final Report 2021	United States National Security Commission on AI Final Report 2021
GDPR	General Data Protection Regulation
GEE	Group of Governmental Experts at the CCW
GGE 2019 Report	Report of the 2019 session of the Group of Governmental Experts on Emerging Technologies in the Area of Lethal Autonomous Weapons Systems (25–29 March and 20–21 August 2019)
GOFAI	good old-fashioned artificial intelligence
GPS	global positioning systems
HBI	human-based intelligence
House of Lords Report	2018 House of Lords Report on Artificial Intelligence
HRW	Human Rights Watch
ICC	International Criminal Court
ICC Statute	1998 Rome Statute of the International Criminal Court
ICJ	International Court of Justice
ICL	international criminal law
ICRAC	International Committee for Robots Arms Control
ICRC	International Committee of the Red Cross
ICTR	International Criminal Tribunal for Rwanda
ICTY	International Criminal Tribunal for the Former Yugoslavia
IHL	international humanitarian law
IHRC	Harvard International Human Rights Clinic
IHRL	international human rights law
ILC	International Law Commission
Interpretative Guidance	ICRC Interpretative Guidance on the Notion of Direct Participation in Hostilities under International Humanitarian Law
JIT	joint investigation team
JURI	European Parliament's Committee on Legal Affairs
LOAC	Law of Armed Conflict
LOW	Laws of war
LWM	United States Department of Defense Law of War Manual

MHC	meaningful human control
MoD	United Kingdom Ministry of Defence
NATO	North Atlantic Treaty Organization
NGO	non-governmental organisation
OPLAN	operational plan
Oslo Manual	Oslo Manual on Select Topics of the Law of Armed Conflict
OTP	Office of the Prosecutor
PGM	precise guided munitions
PTSD	post-traumatic stress disorder
Roadmap 2013–2018	Unmanned Systems integrated Roadmap: FY2013–2038
ROE	rules of engagement
RPE	ICC Rules of Procedure and Evidence
Sanremo Handbook	*Sanremo Handbook on Rules of Engagement* (2009)
SAWS	supervised autonomous weapon systems
SCO	Shanghai Cooperation Organisation
SI	swarm intelligence
STL	Special Tribunal for Lebanon
Tallinn Manual	Tallinn Manual 2.0 on International Law Applicable to Cyber Warfare
Task Force Report	2012 Task Force Report: The Role of Autonomy in DoD Systems
UK JDN 2/11	United Kingdom Approach to Unmanned Aircraft Vehicles, 2011
UK JDP 0–30.2	Joint Doctrine Publication 0–30.2 Unmanned Aircraft Systems
UN Charter	Charter of the United Nations of 26 June 1945, as amended on 17 December 1963, 20 December 1965 and 20 December 1971
UNIDIR	United Nations Institute for Disarmament Research
USA DoD	United States Department of Defence
UWI	unified web-intelligence
WSO	weapon system officer
XAI	explainable AI

Introduction

Increasing progress in the field of Artificial Intelligence (AI) and greater understanding of its many potential applications in warfare have, for some time now, given rise to much heated international debate. While drone technology has already demonstrated that modern weapons of war can be 'uninhabited' (no human operator is to be found inside the drone) and remotely controlled, current research on AI has begun investigating the feasibility of producing *autonomous weapon systems*.[1] Seducing some and scaring others, weapon systems capable of *identifying, selecting and engaging military targets without human intervention* could in the not too distant future be deployed on the battlefield.

The debate became demanding, as well as confusing, when NGOs, states, scholars and roboticists began raising questions about whether the behaviour of future AWS would be sufficiently predictable to be safe, or indeed lawful. AWS tend to evoke in the public consciousness such robots as *The Terminator*, no longer existing merely as science fiction horrors, but in reality; and with this comes the terrifying corollary that humankind could become enslaved by its own inventions.[2] It has even been suggested that if such machines were to replace human soldiers, able to gather their own data, make their own deductions and take lethal targeting decisions without human intervention, it would constitute a 'third revolution in military affairs'.[3]

1 Alex Leveringhaus, *Ethics and Autonomous Weapons* (Palgrave Pivot 2016) 47–49; PAX, 'Slippery Slope. The Arms Industry and Increasingly Autonomous Weapons' (PAX International 2019) ch 2 <https://paxforpeace.nl/what-we-do/publications/slippery-slope>

2 Neil M Richards and William D Smart, 'How Should the Law Think About Robots?' [2013] SSRN 1, 1–2; PW Singer, *Wired for War: The Robotics Revolution and Conflict in the 21st Century* (Reprint edn, Penguin 2011); Mark A Lemley and Bryan Casey, 'You Might Be a Robot' [2019] *Cornell Law Review* 1, 7; Yonah Jeremy Bob, 'Scientists Warn AI Control of Nukes Could Lead to "Terminator-Style" War' *The Jerusalem Post* (25 December 2019) <www.jpost.com/International/Nuke-scientists-warn-AI-control-could-lead-to-Terminator-style-nuke-war-612123>.

3 Future of Life, 'Open Letter on Autonomous Weapons' (28 July 2015) <https://futureoflife.org/open-letter-autonomous-weapons/>; Future of Life, 'An Open Letter to the United Nations

Notwithstanding the gravity of the questions prompted by the emergence of AWS, the topic has been surrounded, and to a certain extent adversely affected, by the plethora of terms coined to describe the systems, and the snowstorm of policy documents all desperately trying to come to terms with the implications of introducing lethal weapons that are, to all intents and purposes, capable of making their own decisions and acting of their own volition. Will it still be realistic to categorise them as weapons, or might they rather, as some experts have suggested, become a new and independent quasi-agent on the battlefield? Some authors are of the opinion that autonomous systems already exist; in their view, AWS are just more sophisticated weapons than any we have seen hitherto. Others sternly defend the opposing argument that, because of their capacity for machine learning and independent decision-making, AWS must inherently be unpredictable – and therefore unlawful. These advisers urge all the states concerned to call for a total, pre-emptive ban on the study, development and acquisition of such systems.[4]

The aim of this thesis is to explore and understand the challenges to the rule of International Humanitarian Law (IHL) that would surely follow the introduction of AWS into the battlespace. These 'autonomous' weapons, as a subject of study and discourse, can be approached from a number of perspectives and divergent fields of knowledge; this aspect of the matter has certainly proved to be one of the most fascinating and complex issues with which this research has had to grapple.

There is no doubt that AWS would deliver enormous advantages in the theatre of war. First and foremost, they would guarantee the physical and psychological distancing of soldiers from lethal risk on the battlefield. Second, the increasing sophistication of modern communication technology means that computers can access and process high-quality data in quantity, and at a speed that would simply be impossible for any human operator. Thus, AWS promise to be safer, faster, and more efficient than human personnel.[5] The

Convention on Certain Conventional Weapons' (21 August 2017) <https://futureoflife.org/autonomous-weapons-open-letter-2017/>.

4 Metdi Haji-Janev and Kiril Hristovski, 'Beyond the Fog of War: Autonomous Weapons Systems in the Context of International Law of Armed Conflicts' (2017) 57 *Jurimetrics* 325, 326, 330–332; Kenneth Anderson and Mathew C Waxman, 'Debating Autonomous Weapon Systems, Their Ethics, and Their Regulation Under International Law' in Roger Brownsword, Eloise Scotford and Karen Yeung (eds), *The Oxford Handbook of Law, Regulation, and Technology* (Oxford University Press 2017) 1098–1100 <https://papers.ssrn.com/sol3/papers.cfm?abstract_id=2978359>; Simon Chesterman, 'Artificial Intelligence and the Problem of Autonomy' (2020) 1 *Notre Dame Journal on Emerging Technologies* 211, 229.

5 The Russian Federation, '2019 Group of Governmental Experts: Potential Opportunities and Limitations of Military Uses of Lethal Autonomous Weapons Systems' (2019) CCW/GGE.1/

problems, for those who question the legitimacy of AWS, all relate to the potential consequences of employing weapon systems that are no longer supervised by human operators.[6]

The entire debate was initiated by the release of two very different documents: one published in the United States, *USA Department of Defence Directive 3000.09*, in 2012, and one in the United Kingdom, the *Joint Doctrine Publication 0–30.2 Unmanned Aircraft Systems*, in 2017.[7] While the US directive defines AWS as 'weapon systems that operate without human intervention', the UK's definition is 'weapon systems that operate without human control'. Moreover, in the 2011 directive, the *UK Approach to Unmanned Aircraft Vehicles*, the UK's policy was to regard AWS as 'self-aware' systems.[8] Thus, even a factor as fundamental as the role of human operators at the human–machine interface has been, from the beginning, subject to misinterpretation and disagreement, rather than providing common grounds for a consensual and productive debate.

In 2013, an international agreement was reached among all states privy to the Convention on Certain Conventional Weapons (CCW), which would come to be the most appropriate international forum in which states could investigate, analyse and debate the many questions and interests surrounding AWS.[9] In the same year, Special Rapporteur Christof Heyns called all states 'to declare and implement national moratoria' until an international agreement on the future of AWS was reached.[10] In 2016, at the CCW meeting it was

https://reachingcriticalwill.org/images/documents/Disarmament-fora/ccw/2019/gge/Documents/GGE.2-WP1.pdf.

6 Yonah Jeremy Bob, 'The Future of AI in Warfare and Counterterrorism' *The Jerusalem Post* (23 January 2020) <www.jpost.com/Jpost-Tech/The-future-of-AI-in-warfare-and-counterterrorism-615112>.

7 Anderson and Waxman, 'Debating Autonomous Weapon Systems, Their Ethics, and Their Regulation Under International Law' (n 4) 1097–1098; US Department of Defense, 'DoD 3000.09. Autonomy in Weapon Systems' (21 November 2012) <www.hsdl.org/?abstract&did=726163>; UK Ministry of Defence, 'Joint Doctrine Publication 0–30.2 Unmanned Aircraft Systems' (2017) <https://assets.publishing.service.gov.uk/government/uploads/system/uploads/attachment_data/file/673940/doctrine_uk_uas_jdp_0_30_2.pdf>.

8 UK Ministry of Defence, 'The UK Approach to Unmanned Aircraft Vehicles, JDN 2/11' (2011) <https://assets.publishing.service.gov.uk/government/uploads/system/uploads/attachment_data/file/644084/20110505-JDN_2-11_UAS_archived-U.pdf>.

9 Vincent Boulanin and Maaike Verbruggen, 'Mapping the Development of Autonomy in Weapon Systems' (Sipri – Stockholm International Peace Research Institute 2017) 1 <www.sipri.org/sites/default/files/2017-11/siprireport_mapping_the_development_of_autonomy_in_weapon_systems_1117_1.pdf>.

10 Christof Heyns, 'Report of the Special Rapporteur on Extrajudicial, Summary or Arbitrary Executions, Christof Heyns' (Human Rights Council 2013) A/HRC/23/47 <www.ohchr.org/Documents/HRBodies/HRCouncil/RegularSession/Session23/A-HRC-23-47_en.pdf>.

decided that a Group of Governmental Experts (GGE) should be appointed to look at all aspects of the debate, identify problematic issues and point out which questions demanded legal responses.[11] At the time of writing, the GGE has met five times: first in August 2017, and more recently in August 2019 and September 2020.[12] To date, however, little consensus has been achieved.[13] Until today, consensus was achieved in what concerns the CCW as 'the most appropriate forum to discuss emerging technologies in the area of Lethal Autonomous Weapons Systems',[14] and that 'International Humanitarian Law (IHL) fully applies to existing and emerging weapons systems and that states remain responsible and accountable for their development, deployment and use in situations of armed conflict'.[15]

Considering the proliferation of reviews, opinions and debates that have now been aired between engineering and robotics experts, NGOs, scholars and State representatives, there is still a lack of common agreement on the precise definition, the true nature and the legal status of an AWS. Most worrying of all is the question that has now been raised as to whether the deployment of AWS might, in legal terms, open the doors to a disastrous 'responsibility gap'.[16] Although these machines are expected

[11] 'Fifth Review Conference of the High Contracting Parties to the Convention on Prohibitions or Restrictions on the Use of Certain Conventional Weapons Which May Be Deemed to Be Excessively Injurious or to Have Indiscriminate Effects (CCW/Conf.V/10)' (2016) <www.unog.ch/80256EDD006B8954/(httpAssets)/B80134C5E97FB90AC125814F0047CCB1/$file/FinalDocument_FifthCCWRevCon.pdf>.

[12] Group of Governmental Experts on Emerging Technologies in the Area of Lethal Autonomous Weapons System, 'Report of the 2019 Session of the Group of Governmental Experts on Emerging Technologies in the Area of Lethal Autonomous Weapons Systems' (2019) CCW/GGE.1/2019/3, para 2 <https://undocs.org/en/CCW/GGE.1/2019/3>. The GGE Meetings in 2020, due to the COVID-19 pandemic, have only made available recording of the ten State members' meetings. '2020 Convention on Certain Conventional Weapons – Group of Governmental Experts on Lethal Autonomous Weapons Systems Recordings' (2020) <https://meetings.unoda.org/section/ccw-gge-2020_reports_10635_press-releases_10640/>.

[13] 'UN Talks on Killer Robots End in a Stalemate' (*NEWEUROPE*, 25 November 2019) <www.neweurope.eu/article/un-talks-on-killer-robots-end-in-a-stalemate/>.

[14] Israel, 'Group of Experts Meeting on Lethal Autonomous Weapons Systems Convention on Certain Conventional Weapons (CCW) 2018' (United Nations 2018).

[15] '2019 EU Statement. 5(a) An Exploration of the Potential Challenges Posed by Emerging Technologies in the Area of Lethal Autonomous Weapons Systems to International Humanitarian Law' (2019) <www.unog.ch/80256EDD006B8954/(httpAssets)/EA84B3C2340F877DC12583CB003727F3/$file/ALIGNED+-+LAWS+GGE+EU+statement+IHL.pdf>; 'Final Report. National Security Commission on Artificial Intelligence' (2021) 91 <www.nscai.gov/wp-content/uploads/2021/03/Full-Report-Digital-1.pdf>.

[16] Andreas Matthias, 'The Responsibility Gap: Ascribing Responsibility for the Actions of Learning Automata' (2004) 6 *Ethics and Information Technology* 175; Marc Champagne and Ryan Tonkens, 'Bridging the Responsibility Gap in Automated Warfare' (2015) 28 *Philosophy & Technology* 125; Cortney Weinbaum, 'The Ethics of Artificial Intelligence in Intelligence

to be capable of gathering their own data, evaluating the data and selecting targets – sometimes involving lethal force – based on their own deductions, without human oversight, no one has yet found a satisfactory way of apportioning blame should IHL violations result. These are the concerns that have determined the structure of this thesis, which now, modestly, seeks to provide some clarity, articulate the questions that need to be discussed. In light of the aforementioned discussion, Chapter 1 deals with the scientific and technological elements that facilitate the design and construction of AWS: the author believes, as a necessary precursor to any discussion of the weapons themselves, that a rigorous understanding of AWS is required. Concepts such as 'dissociation of risk' and 'dissociation of communication' become vitally important to explain modern weapon systems, as they develop from those with inbuilt deterministic algorithms to a new model of machine 'deep learning'. According to this shift, algorithms are designed and programmed to 'learn' and to 'adapt' to rapidly changing circumstances, always in accordance with a pre-established goal.[17]

The concept of AWS and its specific machine–human interface is crucial to determine the status of such systems. Some scholars have argued that AWS blur the distinction between 'combatants' and 'weapons', hypothesising the advent of 'new agents' on the battlefield.[18] Such a possibility would have an enormous impact on IHL, but the understanding in this thesis is that an AWS will operate according to an algorithm designed and programmed by human operators *for the mission*. In a nutshell, AWS should be deployed to accomplish a preset human goal.

In order to understand how an *algorithm for the mission* operates, it is important to consider the steps involved in carrying out a military mission: the collection, evaluation and selection of data; the organising and planning of the mission; and, finally, the attack. Thus, it is argued that, amidst the complexity of a military operation, the *algorithm for the mission* can usefully be viewed as a tripartite structure: the *algorithm for situation assessment*, the

Agencies' (*National Interest*, 18 July 2016) <https://nationalinterest.org/blog/the-buzz/the-ethics-artificial-intelligence-intelligence-agencies-17021>.

17 '2019 EU Statement. 5(a) An Exploration of the Potential Challenges Posed by Emerging Technologies in the Area of Lethal Autonomous Weapons Systems to International Humanitarian Law' (n 15).

18 Hin-Yan Liu, 'Refining Responsibility: Differentiating Two Types of Responsibility Issues Raised by Autonomous Weapons Systems' in Nehal Bhuta and others (eds), *Autonomous Weapons Systems: Law, Ethics, Policy* (Cambridge University Press 2016) 327; Heyns, 'Report of the Special Rapporteur on Extrajudicial, Summary or Arbitrary Executions, Christof Heyns' (n 10) para 38; Lemley and Casey (n 2) 7.

selection algorithm and *the algorithm for situation management*, each algorithm being 'responsible' for a stage of the targeting process.

Once the way in which an AWS operates has been explored, the author will be in a better position to analyse the current state of the debate; this will be done in Chapter 2. The first step is to look at the different definitions of AWS that have been put forward by some of the states involved, for example Ireland, the Netherlands, the Russian Federation, the United Kingdom and the United States, and gain an understanding of how widely their approaches towards AI and AWS diverge. The second step is to examine all the arguments (legal, ethical and political) promulgated by those who advocate a total ban and/or try to prevent states from investing in further research and development and, above all, from arming themselves with AWS.

Chapter 3 will address the way in which confusion about the concept of 'autonomy' has been at the heart of the arguments for and against AWS as expressed by scholars and NGOs – and illustrated by the two policy documents mentioned earlier. But the main question that has to be addressed is 'what does "autonomy" mean when applied in the context of weapons technology?' Chapter 3 will confirm the definition of what will be called 'functional autonomy'.

An agreed interpretation of 'autonomy' will provide a platform from which to address questions relating to the status of AWS, and avoid the introduction of emotive terms such as 'quasi-agents', 'independent actors' and 'new agents on the battlefield', albeit favoured by some authors. Once the meaning of 'autonomy' has been determined, it will be proposed that AWS constitute a new type of weapon system, designed, programmed and developed to perform autonomously at all stages of a selection-making and targeting process. This will be examined in the context of what is known as the 'OOSA Loop', an adaptation of the 'OODA Loop', the well-known cycle observe–orient–decide–act, developed by military strategist and US Air Force Colonel John Boyd.

Chapter 4 deals with the long- and well-established legal principles of IHL regarding the use of weapons and the laws of targeting. Since AWS are expected to carry out their operations without human intervention, two sets of these rules are of particular relevance. First, there are those concerning the freedom of states to legitimately develop new weapons technology (covered by Articles 35 and 36 of the API). Second, there are the precautionary measures (enshrined in Article 57 API) that must in law be respected by those who 'plan and decide upon an attack', namely the Principle of Distinction and the Principle of Proportionality. Our approach will be to examine the complexities and requirements of those rules – complexities that are, in themselves, frequently the object of contentious debate. It will indeed be a considerable challenge for their champions to provide convincing proof that AWS can comply with these rigorous and far-reaching legal requirements.

Finally, Chapter 5 will look in detail at the problems of accountability and the implications of the 'responsibility gap' alluded to earlier. In order to approach the problem, it is necessary to consider the multifarious factors that may contribute to a violation of IHL. In this connection, it will be important to clearly distinguish between situations resulting from 'system malfunction', from 'accidents' and from 'errors'. After the distinctions between these causal factors are made, it will become clear that human operators should be held responsible only for 'accidents' because these, and only these, can be traced back to human fault.

It will be posited that 'malfunctions' and 'errors' do not result from human fault, but rather from unexpected causes, and, therefore, the customary and conventional forms of individual accountability are not applicable. Malfunctions will not constitute a new problem: just like any other weapon or weapon system, AWS will be, on occasion, susceptible to technical and hardware failure, and this is an issue that has already been addressed by the academy.[19] The true novelty, and the source of all the ensuing legal complexities, is the potential for the system to make its *own errors* – situations, that is, in which an AWS, through misinterpretation of incoming data or any other cause, subverts the pre-given mission and initiates events that cause violations of IHL. In this chain of causation there is no link whatsoever with human behaviour, but with the system's 'reasoning' process. As Thompson Chengeta argues, 'the possibility of AWS acting in an unpredictable manner, they may represent an unresolved challenge as far as the establishment of the accused person's *mens rea* is concerned'.[20]

In light of the aforementioned discussion, looking at the complexity of AWS and at the situations in which those systems might be involved, it should be a legal requirement that designers, programmers, technicians and commanders take on a higher level of responsibility. If there is human fault at the level of designing, programming or maintenance that results in an IHL violation (*accident*), human operatives will have to be prepared to be held accountable. This obligation will necessitate an examination of different levels of *mens rea*

19 Ian Henderson, Patrick Keane and Josh Liddy, 'Remote and Autonomous Warfare Systems: Precautions in Attack and Individual Accountability' in Jens David Ohlin (ed), *Research Handbook on Remote Warfare* (Edward Elgar Press 2016).

20 Thompson Chengeta, 'Accountability Gap: Autonomous Weapon Systems and Modes of Responsibility in International Law' (2016) 45 *Denver Journal of International Law and Policy* 1, 3.

to establish an appropriate link of causation between unlawful outcomes and AWS' human operators.

In cases of 'error', it will be impossible to identify any human operative to be held accountable. However, there is no reason to posit a 'responsibility gap', because in these cases State responsibility would be invoked. There are ample grounds, already entrenched in Conventional and Customary International Law, to sustain the argument that the AWS' deploying State bears direct responsibility for violations of IHL caused by system failures ('errors').

In order for the distinctions just discussed to be clear, to guarantee the transparency of the operation and to determine the appropriate form of accountability, it will be necessary for the factors according to which an AWS has selected its course of action to be clearly identifiable at the end of the operation. As will be explained, '*factual algorithms*', that is, algorithms that provide clear information about which factors the system has weighed in the balance in making its decisions, will need to be designed and installed at the time of programming the system. Only in this way will a court of law be able to ascertain with certainty *who* or *what* has caused a violation: *how* to achieve this will be the next challenge.

1

Introducing Autonomous Systems of War

The Challenges of Artificial Intelligence

1.1 AUTONOMOUS WEAPON SYSTEMS: THE MULTIDISCIPLINARY NATURE OF THE *THIRD REVOLUTION OF MILITARY AFFAIRS*

The past few years have seen a marked escalation in international debate about the deployment and activation of weapons systems imbued with artificial intelligence (AI), known as autonomous weapon systems (AWS).[21] These weapons, once programmed, will be dependent on AI to adapt to different circumstances on the battlefield and to identify, select and engage military targets without the need for human intervention. For some, AWS might represent a shift of paradigm in terms of weapons and human control and become the 'third revolution of military affairs',[22] from instruments to new agents on the battlefield.[23] For many, AWS are an inevitable reality, whilst for

[21] Aviv Gaon and Ian Stedman, 'A Call to Action: Moving Forward with the Governance of the Artificial Intelligence in Canada' (2019) 56 *Alberta Law Review* 1137, 1139.

[22] Stuart J Russell, 'Take a Stand on AI Weapons' (2015) 521 *Nature* 415 <www.nature.com/polopoly_fs/1.17611!/menu/main/topColumns/topLeftColumn/pdf/521415a.pdf>; Singer (n 2) 203–204; Anthony Cullen, 'The Characterization of Remote Warfare under International Humanitarian Law' in Jens David Ohlin (ed), *Research Handbook on Remote Warfare* (Edward Elgar Press 2017) 123 <http://eprints.mdx.ac.uk/20259/>; Rain Liivoja, Koby Leins and Tim McCormack, 'Emerging Technologies of Warfare' in Rain Liivoja and Tim McCormack (eds), *Routledge Handbook of the Law of Armed Conflict* (Routledge 2016) 662 <https://papers.ssrn.com/sol3/papers.cfm?abstract_id=2679669>; '2017 LAWS GGE Australian Statement – General Exchange of Views' (2017) <https://geneva.mission.gov.au/gene/Statement783.html>.

[23] ICRC, 'International Humanitarian Law and the Challenges of Contemporary Armed Conflicts. Recommitting to Protection in Armed Conflict on the 70th Anniversary of the Geneva Conventions' (2019) 29–31 <www.icrc.org/sites/default/files/document/file_list/challenges-report_new-technologies-of-warfare.pdf>; Jeffrey S Thurnher, 'Examining Autonomous Weapon Systems from a Law of Armed Conflict Perspective' in Robert McLaughlin and Hitoshi Nasu

others they are only a sci-fi hypothesis.[24] A possible explanation for such opposing perspectives might result from the lack of acceptance that AWS are an *engineering reality*. Thus, before it becomes a question for legal analysis, it is important to understand why states are interested in developing AWS and how these systems become possible. Thus, the aim of this chapter is to provide some clarification about the advantages AWS might bring to the battlefield and the technical achievements of AI, such as enabling decision-making processes to take place without human intervention, which will undoubtedly entail deep reflection for international lawyers.

Autonomous technology is emerging in every area of human life, proving to have an outstanding potential for accelerating discoveries – not only for transforming medical and health care, labour, services, entertainment and law enforcement but also for suggesting new ways in which war can be conducted.[25] Warfare technology is just one of the areas that AI is challenging with a number of controversial developments. Thus, the aim of this work is to deal with the specific questions that will emerge at the heart of International Humanitarian Law (IHL) if states decide to deploy AWS in armed conflicts.

(eds), *New Technologies and the Law of Armed Conflict* (Asser Press Springer 2014) <https://papers.ssrn.com/sol3/papers.cfm?abstract_id=2271158>; Hin-Yan Liu, 'Categorization and Legality of Autonomous and Remote Weapons Systems' (2012) 94 *International Review of the Red Cross* 627, 628.

24 Vincent C Muller and Thomas W Simpson, 'Killer Robots: Regulate, Don't Ban' (Blavatnik School of Government – BSG Pilocy Memo November 2014) <www.researchgate.net/publication/283513768_Killer_robots_Regulate_don't_ban>; Benjamin Haas, '"Killer Robots": AI Experts Call for Boycott over Lab at South Korea University' *The Guardian* (Seoul, 15 April 2018) <www.theguardian.com/technology/2018/apr/05/killer-robots-south-korea-university-boycott-artifical-intelligence-hanwha>.

25 Ashley Deeks, Noam Lubell and Daragh Murray, 'Machine Learning, Artificial Intelligence, and the Use of Force by States' (2019) 10(1) *Journal of National Security Law & Policy* 1; Christof Heyns, 'Human Rights and the Use of Autonomous Weapons Systems (AWS) during Domestic Enforcement' (2016) 38 *Human Rights Quarterly* 350; Patrick Lin, 'Introduction to Robot Ethics' in Patrick Lin, Keith Abney and George A Bekey (eds), *Robot Ethics* (MIT Press 2012) 5–8; cf Jennifer Rankin, 'Artificial Intelligence: €20bn Investment Call from EU Commission' *The Guardian* (Brussels, 25 April 2018) <www.theguardian.com/technology/2018/apr/25/european-commission-ai-artificial-intelligence>; 'Artificial Intelligence (AI) Robots Market by Robot Type (Service, Industrial), Offering (GPU, MPU), Technology (Machine Learning, Computer Vision), Application (Public Relations, Stock Management), and Geography – Global Forecast to 2023' (*CISION PR Newswire*, 23 March 2018) <www.prnewswire.com/news-releases/artificial-intelligence-ai-robots-market—global-forecast-to-2023-market-to-grow-at-a-cagr-of-2878-300618740.html>; Lemley and Casey (n 2) 13–15; 'Artificial Intelligence Summit Focuses on Fighting Hunger, Climate Crisis and Transition to "Smart Sustainable Cities"' (*United Nations News*, 29 May 2019) <https://europeansting.com/2019/05/29/artificial-intelligence-summit-focuses-on-fighting-hunger-climate-crisis-and-transition-to-smart-sustainable-cities/>.

Controversy arises at the very beginning. In order to present and define AWS, a range of terms has been suggested by academics, non-governmental organisations (NGOs) and states in their policy documents, all of which are attempting to grapple with the unique characteristics of these new systems. A sample of such terms includes 'killer robots',[26] 'autonomous robotic soldiers',[27] 'autonomous military robots',[28] 'autonomous weapons systems',[29] 'fully autonomous weapons',[30] 'lethal autonomous weapon systems',[31] 'autonomous military systems',[32] 'weaponised autonomous systems'[33] and 'lethal autonomous robots'.[34] A bundle of terms, all of which, in fact, essentially try to describe the same reality since all include the term *autonomy* to qualify a specific category of weapons.[35] For the purposes of this book, these systems will be identified as 'autonomous weapon systems' (AWS), in order to

26 Armin Krishnan, *Killer Robots: Legality and Ethicality of Autonomous Weapons* (Routledge 2016); Thompson Chengeta, 'Are Autonomous Weapon Systems the Subject of Article 36 of Additional Protocol I to the Geneva Conventions?' (2016) 23 *University of California, Davis* 66, 81.

27 Peter Asaro, 'How Just Could a Robot War Be?' in P Brey, A Briggle and K Waelbers (eds), *Current Issues in Computing and Philosophy* (IOS Press 2008) 1.

28 Maciej Zalac and Wojciech J Bober, 'Autonomous Military Robots – Critical Topography of Possible Reactions to Upcoming Technological Revolution' (2017) 110 *Zeszyty Naukowe Politechniki Slaskiej* 201, 202.

29 Peter Asaro, 'On Banning Autonomous Weapon Systems: Human Rights, Automation and the Dehumanization of Lethal Decision Making' (2012) 94 *International Review of the Red Cross* 687, 690.

30 Noel Sharkey, 'Robot Wars Are a Reality' *The Guardian* (Brussels, 18 August 2007) <www.theguardian.com/commentisfree/2007/aug/18/comment.military>; Human Rights Watch and International Human Rights Clinic, 'Losing Humanity: The Case against Killer Robots' (2012) <www.hrw.org/sites/default/files/reports/arms1112ForUpload_0_0.pdf>.

31 Several countries have adopted this designation in the context of the CCW negotiations since 2014 (Australia, Austria, Croatia, India, Ireland, the UK, among others) cf 'Statements to the 2014 CCW Meeting of Experts' (*Reaching Critical Will*, 2014) <https://reachingcriticalwill.org/disarmament-fora/ccw/2014/meeting-experts-laws/statements>; Tetayana Krupiy, 'Regulating a Game Changer: Using a Distributed Approach to Develop an Accountability Framework for Lethal Autonomous Weapon Systems' (2018) 50 *Georgetown Journal of International Law* 46; Muller and Simpson (n 24).

32 Tim McFarland, 'Factors Shaping the Legal Implications of Increasingly Autonomous Military Systems' (2015) 97 *International Review of the Red Cross* 1313, 1315.

33 LtCol Atur Kuptel and Andrew Williams, 'Policy Guidance Autonomy in Defence Systems' (Multinational Capability Development Campaign (MCDC) 2013–14 29 October 2014) 8–9 <www.academia.edu/9347371/Policy_Guidance_Autonomy_in_Defence_Systems>.

34 Ronald C Arkin, *Governing Lethal Behavior in Autonomous Robots* (Chapman & Hall Book 2009) 37; Heyns, 'Report of the Special Rapporteur on Extrajudicial, Summary or Arbitrary Executions, Christof Heyns' (n 10).

35 The problem of terminology is common to 'maritime autonomous vehicles'. cf Natalie Klein, 'Maritime Autonomous Vehicles within the International Law Framework to Enhance Maritime Security' (2019) 95 *International Law Studies* 244, 248.

differentiate them from other weapons systems, to recognise their characterising features and to address the concerns that are emerging among different voices in the international community.

The development of AWS has been characterised, and gravely affected, as has been pointed out by many scholars, by the lack of a set of industry-wide, tested and agreed definitions.[36] This deficit has resulted in confusion and rushed decisions affecting the future of AWS, simply because academics and roboticists are addressing different conceptual realities.[37] Therefore, as this book begins, the author cannot stress too strongly the crucial importance of recognising the dangers inherent in the proliferation of definitions and opposing interpretations of AWS among scholars, civilians, NGOs and the militaries of different states. What, exactly, do the different groups expect from the 'third revolution in military affairs'?

Roboticists and engineers believe they have a mission to 'engineer ideas into reality'. Thus, the long-expected days of machine supremacy may be arriving, and AWS will replace humans in the context of hostilities.[38] In technical terms, 'the difference between a machine that can do all these things and "assist in attack decisions" and one that makes its own "attack decision" would be just a matter of programming'.[39] Programs will become so sophisticated that enthusiasts foresee a new cultural paradigm they are hailing as 'techno sapiens'. The convergence of robotics and neuroscience, it is thought, could lead to the creation of robots with higher cognitive capabilities than their makers.[40] In the words of the US National Security Commission on Artificial Intelligence 2021 Final Report (hereinafter Final Report 2021), 'the sources of battlefield advantage will shift from traditional factors like force size and levels of armaments to factors like superior data collection and assimilation, connectivity, computing power, algorithms, and system security'.[41]

36 Haji-Janev and Hristovski (n 4) 329; Henderson, Keane and Liddy (n 19) 337.
37 Philip Alston, 'Lethal Robotic Technologies: The Implications for Human Rights and International Humanitarian Law' (2012) 21 *Journal of Law, Information & Science* 35, 50; ICRC, 'International Humanitarian Law and the Challenges of Contemporary Armed Conflicts. Recommitting to Protection in Armed Conflict on the 70th Anniversary of the Geneva Conventions' (n 23).
38 Singer (n 2) 27.
39 Thomas K Adams, 'Future Warfare and the Decline of Human Decisionmaking (Reprint)' (2011) 41 *Parameters* 1.
40 Wendell Wallach, 'From Robots to Techno Sapiens: Ethics, Law and Public Policy in the Development of Robotics and Neurotechnologies' (2011) 3 *Law, Innovation and Technology* 185, 186, 203.
41 'Final Report. National Security Commission on Artificial Intelligence' (n 15) 22.

Lawyers, however, believe that, as promising as a future of autonomous systems might appear, it should not be assumed that these systems will be beyond scrutiny just because they will be technically achievable and available for deployment by states. AWS must not be accepted just because they are intended to be more efficient;[42] the scope of the questions and concerns arising in connection with AWS goes well beyond any question of efficiency. There are long-held and well-established norms of international law concerning the deployment of new technologies of warfare, with which AWS will have to comply in order to be accepted as a new technology of warfare.

The task, however, is not an easy one. Apart from the different terms used, and the different definitions offered, exactly what is expected from an AWS may also be the subject of debate and perplexity. In this regard, it is useful to analyse briefly how the USA and the UK – until now the only two states with internal directives on the matter – have addressed the reality of AWS.

According to USA Department of Defense Directive 3000.09 (DoD 3000.09), 2012, an AWS is 'a weapon system that, once activated, can select and engage targets without further intervention by a human operator'.[43] Generally speaking, it can be said that an AWS is, first and foremost, a *weapon* that, due to the sophisticated level of the AI embedded in its system, has the capacity to identify and engage military targets *without requiring human supervision or intervention*. The possibility of future systems of war being able to select and engage military targets *without the intervention* of human operators raises the question of whether AWS are not, in fact, an ontological revolution: a radical development that will see such weapons becoming, in effect, a new type of agent on the battlefield. Such a possibility would have the most serious legal implications for how 'agency', 'weapons' and 'accountability' have been understood.

As surprising and 'science fictional' as this scenario may seem, this would appear to be the future contemplated in 'The UK Approach to Unmanned Aircraft Vehicles', 2011 (UK JDN 2/11).[44] According to this directive, an autonomous system must not only 'be capable of achieving the same *level of situational understanding as a human*' but also be '*self-aware*'. As the UK JDN 2/11 clarifies, 'as computing and sensor capability increases, it is likely that many systems [. . .] will appear and be described as autonomous systems, but as

42 Asaro, 'How Just Could a Robot War Be?' (n 27) 55–56.

43 US Department of Defense, 'DoD 3000.09. Autonomy in Weapon Systems' (n 7).

44 UK Ministry of Defence, 'The UK Approach to Unmanned Aircraft Vehicles, JDN 2/11' (n 8) (our emphasis).

long as it can be shown that the system logically follows a set of rules or instructions and is not capable of human levels of situational understanding, then they should only be considered to be *automated*'.[45] *Automated systems* follow pre-established rules and are designed and programmed by humans. However, to postulate that autonomous systems would become *intentional self-aware systems of warfare* is a totally different and radical proposition.[46]

In August 2017, however, the UK Ministry of Defence published a new directive – the 'Joint Doctrine Publication 0–30.2, Unmanned Aircraft Systems' (hereinafter UK JDP 0–30.2) – which replaces JDN 2/11.[47] In UK JDP 0–30.2 it is pointed out that 'particular care should be taken with the terms "automated" and "autonomous", which differ considerably between countries and equipment manufacturers. The way *the UK defines these terms is important as they are tied to the UK policy on autonomous weapons and our interpretation of International Law*.'[48] If the notion of automated systems has not suffered changes under this new directive, no reference is now made to autonomous systems as 'self-aware', or that the systems should be 'capable of achieving the same level of situational understanding as a human'.[49] Indeed, UK JDP 0–30.2 goes further, stating that the 'UK does not possess armed autonomous aircraft systems and it has no intention to develop them. The [...] operation of UK weapons will always be under human control as an absolute guarantee of human oversight, authority and accountability.'[50]

The fact that the UK has amended its position regarding AWS does not mean that all the problems have been solved. As the House of Lords Report on AI (hereinafter House of Lords Report) clarifies the UK policy of qualifying an autonomous system as one 'capable of understanding higher-level intent and direction', 'is clearly out of step with the definitions used by most other governments [...] [limiting the UK's ability] to take an active role as a moral

45 ibid 2–4 (our emphasis).

46 Some authors identify both directives as equal. Cesáreo Gutierrez Espada and Maria Jose Cervell Hortal, 'Autonomous Weapons Systems, Drone and International Law' (2013) 2 *Revista del Instituto Español Estratégicos* 2–9 <http://revista.ieee.es/index.php/ieee/article/viewFile/86/89>. For a distinction between automatic and automated systems, see Tim McFarland, *Autonomous Weapon Systems and the Law of Armed Conflict: Compatibility with International Humanitarian Law* (Cambridge University Press 2020) 41.

47 UK Ministry of Defence, 'Joint Doctrine Publication 0–30.2 Unmanned Aircraft Systems' (n 7).

48 ibid 2 (our emphasis).

49 UK Ministry of Defence, 'The UK Approach to Unmanned Aircraft Vehicles, JDN 2/11' (n 8).

50 UK Ministry of Defence, 'Joint Doctrine Publication 0–30.2 Unmanned Aircraft Systems' (n 7).

and ethical leader on the global stage in this area'.[51] Indeed, other countries (e.g. India, the USA and Russia) have different policies towards the development and deployment of AWS and, therefore, those policies must be considered.[52] At the 2019 Group of Governmental Experts meetings (GGE), however, the UK seems to have distanced itself from its previously held concept of 'autonomous systems' by arguing that:

> 'autonomy' is often used by participants to describe systems with agency and independent decision-making powers. Arguably this description is reserved for systems which can understand and act on intent. The UK does not envisage a scenario in which machines with high-order autonomy will exercise complete self-determination: all weapon systems will function because of some human decision to deploy the system in order to achieve a specific outcome.[53]

Thus, it can be concluded that UK policy now recognises a third type of system, that is, weapon systems with *low-order autonomy*.

The multidisciplinary confusion surrounding AWS is not reduced to the engineering challenges or the aforementioned questions. An autonomous system poses, first of all, a question for the philosophy of law. Many roboticists have long been advancing the possibility of the future existence of artificial agents, describing them as 'third existence entities', able to perform not only better but 'more ethically than human soldiers are capable of'.[54] Philosophers, on the other hand, have been cautious in classifying AWS and have tended to assign them to a 'grey area'.[55] Peter Asaro points out that as 'robots begin to

51 House of Lords Select Committee on Artificial Intelligence, 'AI in the UK: Ready, Willing and Able?' (2018) 2017–2019 <https://publications.parliament.uk/pa/ld201719/ldselect/ldai/100/100.pdf>.

52 R Shashank Reddy, *India and the Challenge of Autonomous Weapons* (Carnegie Endowment for International Peace 2016). Aside from the public statements of India and their desire to invest in AWS, China, Israel, Russia, South Korea and the USA have invested heavily in the study and development of AWS. cf Bonnie Docherty, 'We're Running out of Time to Stop Killer Robot Weapons' *The Guardian* (Brussels, 11 April 2018) <www.theguardian.com/commentisfree/2018/apr/11/killer-robot-weapons-autonomous-ai-warfare-un>.

53 '2019 United Kingdom of Great Britain and Northern Ireland Statement. Agenda Item 5(b): "Characterization of the Systems under Consideration in Order to Promote a Common Understanding on Concepts and Characteristics Relevant to the Objectives and Purposes of the Convention"' (*Reaching Critical Will*, 25 March 2019) <https://reachingcriticalwill.org/disarmament-fora/ccw/2019/laws/statements>.

54 Arkin, *Governing Lethal Behavior in Autonomous Robots* (n 34) 31–32.

55 Yueh-Husuam Weng, Chien-Hsun Chen and Chuen-Tsai Sun, 'Towards the Human-Robot Co-Existence Society: On Safety Intelligence for Next Generation Robots' (2009) 1 *International Journal of Social Robotics* 267, 275; Robert Sparrow, 'Killer Robots' (2007) 24 *Journal of Applied Philosophy* 62–64.

approach more sophisticated human-like performances [...] they might be treated as *quasi-agents or quasi-persons* by the law, enjoying only partial rights and duties'.[56] Is this perspective applicable to AWS?

At this level, it is interesting to note that the resolution approved by the European Parliament in 2017 – the General Data Protection Regulation (GDPR) – although excluding AWS from its objects of analysis, envisages 'applying electronic personality to cases where robots make autonomous decisions or otherwise interact with third parties independently'.[57] At the same time, however, AI experts, computer scientists and law professors, among others, have addressed a letter to the European Commission arguing that granting legal personhood to autonomous systems would not be appropriate from the legal and ethical point of view.[58]

The same controversy is found among lawyers. Some authors do not consider AWS problematic as regards IHL, while others, in spite of looking favourably at AWS, recognise their impossibility in that these systems will not be able to exercise the required level of discretion or the subtleties of human judgement that the battlefield demands.[59] At the other extreme, still others suggest that the introduction of AWS will lead to an unacceptable 'responsibility gap'.[60] In line with this reasoning and looking at the problems that AWS seem to represent, a dramatic solution is proposed by the campaigns promoted

56 As the author explains, it is possible that a robot might be considered one day a legal person because the concept of personhood is directed linked with the concept of agency. Once the type of agency is determined it is possible to understand the kind of person and liability system that can be applied. Peter Asaro, 'Robots and Responsibility from a Legal Perspective' [2007] *IEEE* <www.peterasaro.org/writing/asaro%20legal%20perspective.pdf>, considering 'lethal autonomous robots as "quasi-agents"', Heather M Roff, 'Killing in War: Responsibility, Liability and Lethal Autonomous Robots' in Fritz Allhoff, Nicholas G Evans and Adam Henschke (eds), *Routledge Handbook of Ethics and War: Just War Theory in the Twenty-First Century* (Routledge 2013) <www.academia.edu/2606840/Killing_in_War_Responsibility_Liability_and_Lethal_ Autonomous_Robots>.

57 European Parliament, 'Civil Law Rules on Robotics European Parliament Resolution of 16 February 2017 with Recommendations to the Commission on Civil Law Rules on Robotics (2015/2103(INL))' (2017) <www.europarl.europa.eu/sides/getDoc.do?pubRef=-//EP//NONSGML+REPORT+A8-2017-0005+0+DOC+PDF+V0//EN>.

58 Janosch Delcker, 'Europe Divided over Robot "Personhood"' (*POLITICO*, 12 April 2018) <www.politico.eu/article/europe-divided-over-robot-ai-artificial-intelligence-personhood/>. Loukia Papadoloupos, 'Experts Denounce EU Proposal Granting Robots Personhood' (*Interesting Engineering*, 15 April 2018) <https://interestingengineering.com/experts-denounce-eu-proposal-granting-robots-personhood>.

59 Jack M Beard, 'Autonomous Weapons and Human Responsibilities' (2014) 45 *Georgetown Journal of International Law* 617; Leveringhaus (n 1) 102–104.

60 Matthias (n 16); Ryan Calo, 'Robotics and the Lessons of Cyber-Law' (2015) 103 *California Law Review* 513.

by NGOs, which call for a pre-emptive ban of AWS on account of their unpredictable nature and the absence of human control.[61]

Be that as it may, AI will undoubtedly become a principal factor in warfare systems, and the capabilities of AI could well lead to a 'dehumanisation of war' and 'dehumanisation of IHL': a possible scenario of war in which the necessity for a human presence might disappear because lawful outcomes can be made perfectly by machines.[62] The progressive dehumanisation of war, envisaged by many – and especially by Austria, Costa Rica, the Holy See and Pakistan, among others – raises several legal and ethical questions.[63] For example, if autonomous systems (defined by UK JDP 0–30.2 as systems capable of understanding higher-level intent and direction) become a reality, what will remain of the power of human operators to change the course of action, or, hypothetically, to deactivate the system if the circumstances on the battlefield change?[64] For instance, the 2019 accident involving a Boeing 737 Max model is enough to raise questions about the necessity for human operators

61 Human Rights Watch and International Human Rights Clinic, 'Losing Humanity: The Case against Killer Robots' (n 30); Human Rights Watch and International Human Rights Clinic, 'Mind the Gap: The Lack of Accountability for Killer Robots' (2015) 4 <www.hrw.org/report/2015/04/09/mind-gap/lack-accountability-killer-robots>; 'Killing by Machine: Key Issues for Understanding Meaningful Human Control' (*Article* 36, 2015) 36 <www.article36.org/wp-content/uploads/2013/06/KILLING_BY_MACHINE_6.4.15.pdf>.

62 Asaro, 'On Banning Autonomous Weapon Systems: Human Rights, Automation and the Dehumanization of Lethal Decision Making' (n 29) 694–695.

63 Campaign to Stop KILLER ROBOTS, 'Country Views on Killer Robots' (2018) <www.stopkillerrobots.org/wp-content/uploads/2018/11/KRC_CountryViews22Nov2018.pdf>; Holy See, 'Statement by the Permanent Mission of the Holy See to the United Nations and Other International Organizations in Geneva at the 2018 Group of Governmental Experts on Lethal Autonomous Weapons Systems (LAWS)' (*Reaching Critical Will*, 27 August 2018) <https://reachingcriticalwill.org/images/documents/Disarmament-fora/ccw/2018/gge/statements/27August_HolySee.pdf>; Austria, 'General Exchange of Views Statement Austria. Group of Governmental Experts on Lethal Autonomous Weapon Systems Geneva, 9–13 April 2018' (*Reaching Critical Will*, April 2018) <https://reachingcriticalwill.org/images/documents/Disarmament-fora/ccw/2018/gge/statements/9April_Austria.pdf>; Austria, Brazil and Chile, '2018 Proposal for a Mandate to Negotiate a Legally binding Instrument That Addresses the Legal, Humanitarian and Ethical Concerns Posed by Emerging Technologies in the Area of Lethal Autonomous Weapons Systems (LAWS)' (2018) <www.unog.ch/80256EDD006B8954/(httpAssets)/3BDD5F681113EECEC12582FE0038B22F/%24file/2018_GGE+LAWS_August_Working+paper_Austria_Brazil_Chile.pdf>.

64 Heather M Roff and Richard Moyes, 'Meaningful Human Control, Artificial Intelligence and Autonomous Weapons' (*Article* 36, April 2016) <www.article36.org/wp-content/uploads/2016/04/MHC-AI-and-AWS-FINAL.pdf>; Carol Glatz, 'Killer Robots Will Make War Even More Inhumane, Vatican Official Says' (*Crux*, 12 April 2018) <https://cruxnow.com/vatican/2018/04/killer-robots-will-make-war-even-more-inhumane-vatican-official-says/>; Markus Wagner, 'The Dehumanization of International Humanitarian Law: Legal, Ethical, and Political Implications of Autonomous Weapon Systems' (2014) 47 *Vanderbilt Journal of Transnational Law* 1371.

to be able to override automated, let alone autonomous, systems. According to the official investigation, the crash of Ethiopian Airlines Flight 302 was caused by the automated flight control system.[65]

It can be concluded that perspectives adopted and questions asked about AWS will have serious legal implications. However, before addressing legal matters, it is important, first, to consider how to explain the advent of AWS. For the purposes of this book, two key elements have contributed to the current situation in terms of war technology. First, the 'dissociation of risk', that is, the distancing of human combatants from the field and from one another, which is an inevitable trend as technology of war becomes progressively more automated. Second, increasingly complex and sophisticated information systems contribute to a progressive 'dissociation of communication', that is, distancing human operators from the decision-making process and from one another.[66] Both elements will be further examined as this chapter proceeds, but it is important to consider how those factors enable systems to operate without human intervention.

1.2 FROM THE INSTRUMENTALIST PARADIGM TO THE 'DISSOCIATION OF RISK': THE CASE FOR THE DEPLOYMENT OF AWS

The nature of military life demands that military commanders and soldiers take risks – risks that they might have to pay for with their lives. With soldiers being regarded as 'fallible beings', subject to stress, liable to make unwise decisions under duress and vulnerable to post-traumatic stress disorder (PTSD) (a mental health disorder that can be developed by soldiers after the traumatic experience of the battlefield),[67] efforts have been made by psychologists and psychiatrists to explain the causes of the psychiatric traumas suffered by soldiers.[68] However,

65 Andrew J Hawkins and Jon Porter, 'Preliminary Report into 737 Max Crash Clears Pilots, Suggests Anti-Stall Tech to Blame' (*The Verge*, 4 April 2019) <www.theverge.com/2019/4/4/18294317/boeing-737-max-ethiopian-airlines-crash-report>; Aaron C Davis, Luz Lazo and Paul Schemm, 'Additional Software Problem Detected in Boeing 737 Max Flight Control System, Officials Say' *Washington Post* (Washington, 4 April 2019) <www.washingtonpost.com/world/africa/ethiopia-says-pilots-performed-boeings-recommendations-to-stop-doomed-aircraft-from-diving-urges-review-of-737-max-flight-control-system/2019/04/04/3a125942-4fec-11e9-bdb7-44f948cc0605_story.html?utm_term=.a4533e90c924>.

66 Linell A Letendre, 'Lethal Autonomous Weapon Systems: Translating Geek Speak for Lawyers' (2020) 96 *International Law Studies* 274, 278.

67 Dave Grossman, *On Killing – The Psychological Cost of Learning to Kill in War and Society* (Open Road Media 2014).

68 Christopher Coker, *Future Wars* (Polity Press 2015) 57–60; Asaro, 'On Banning Autonomous Weapon Systems: Human Rights, Automation and the Dehumanization of Lethal Decision Making' (n 29) 703.

the complexity of that topic goes well beyond this study; it is just interesting to note, for the record, that human soldiers begin to show signs of 'combat exhaustion' after as little as twenty-five days of combat.

Fatigue, confusional states, conversion hysteria, anxiety states, obsessional and compulsive states and character disorders are some of the manifestations of psychiatric stresses that make soldiers unable to fight, and all are indicative of PTSD. There are some measures, such as training, experience, leadership and good equipment, that can reduce the risk of psychiatric problems, providing what has become known as 'psychological inoculation'.[69]

As Dave Grossman explains, 'there is a direct relation between the empathic and physical proximity of the victim, and the resultant difficulty and trauma to kill', which explains why developing a physical distance between the attacker and the victim has become, since the very beginning, the central principle of technology of warfare.[70] The distance, however, cannot be merely physical. There is also an emotional distance that is vital to justify and reinforce acts of killing or destruction of the military forces of the enemy. Aspects such as cultural distance, moral distance and social distance are equally important 'in permitting the killer to deny that he is killing a human being'.[71] This process of promoting a distance is what is going to be called, in this work, the *dissociation of risk*, a process that envisages creating physical and emotional mechanisms of protection for soldiers. It should not be difficult to accept that the State has a moral duty to protect the members of its armed forces called to serve the country on the battlefield, and, therefore, *dissociation of risk* should be taken as a moral imperative for any State party to an armed conflict.[72]

Looking at the history of weapons from the first artillery pieces – the non-torsion crossbows developed by Syracusan engineers in the fourth century BC – there has always been an intent to create the maximum physical and emotional distance between attacker and attacked. The classic example is the attempt by the Lateran Council in 1137 to ban the crossbow not only for its asymmetric nature – a foot soldier could now threaten an armoured knight – but also for

69 ibid 81–82; Edgar Jones and Simon Wessely, *Shell Shock to PSTD. Military Psychiatry from 1900 to the Gulf War* (Psychology Press 2005).

70 Grossman (n 67) 97.

71 ibid 158–160.

72 Jones and Wessely (n 69) 185. For the problems that dissociation of risk might entail looking to modern systems of warfare and their compliance with IHL, Cullen (n 22) 128. Frank Nicholas Kelly, 'Analyzing the Potential for Universal Disarmament of Autonomous Weapons Systems Or How I Learned to Stop Worrying and Love the Killer Robot' (2018) 44 *Brooklyn Journal of International Law* 381, 395–397.

humanitarian reasons in view of the injuries that the crossbow could inflict.[73] Each successive invention of new weapons and methods of warfare has been followed by discussions regarding the associated moral and legal implications. Gunpowder and, especially, nuclear power (the first and second revolutions in military technology) did not escape such debate, and the latter is still a source of hot international controversy.[74] Clearly, autonomous weapons will be subject to the same questions and concerns, but it is important to understand the specificities of AWS and why they are cause for extreme and opposing considerations on the part of roboticists, scholars and states.[75]

Until today, the two advantages of the dissociation of risk – invulnerability to physical harm and more precision on the battlefield – have never led to any suggestion that the battlefield be considered as anything other than a 'human space', where all decisions are made by humans and *even the most sophisticated weapon has always been an instrument* to enhance 'our ability to throw things at enemies we could see and hear'.[76]

The instrumental character of technology was explored in the study developed by J.W. Clark in the late 1960s for the *New Scientist*, 'Remote Control in Hostile Environments'. The author explores precisely the practicalities pertaining to dissociation of risk. According to the author, there are two possible ways of tackling hostile environments: either placing a machine or placing a protected man there.[77] The main aims include not only physical protection but also greater accuracy. Thus, Clark describes the development of machines that would allow 'of manipulation at a distance – "telechirics machines"' (from the Greek *tele* meaning 'distance' and *kheir* meaning 'hand') – so that humans no longer have to expose themselves to danger. An interesting element, important to consider, is Clark's emphasis on the fact that the remoteness of the system would depend on the capacity of the human operator 'to identify him/herself' with his/her remotely controlled machine. *Telechirics* machines

73 Christopher Greenwood, 'Historical Development and Legal Basis' in Dieter Fleck (ed), *The Handbook of International Humanitarian Law* (2nd edn, Oxford University Press 2008) 18, para 109; Cullen (n 22) 111–113.

74 Jakob kellenberger, 'International Humanitarian Law and New Weapon Technologies, 34th Round Table on Current Issues of International Humanitarian Law, San Remo, 8–10 September 2011 Keynote Address by Dr Jakob Kellenberger, ICRC President, and Conclusions by Dr Philip Spoerri, ICRC Director for International Law and Cooperation' (2012) 94 *International Review of the Red Cross* 809.

75 Mary Ellen O' Connell, 'Banning Autonomous Killing – The Legal and Ethical Requirement That Humans Make Near-Time Lethal Decisions' in Matthew Evangelista and Henry Shue (eds), *The American Bombing – Changing Ethical and Legal Norms from Flying Fortresses to Drones* (Cornell university Press 2014).

76 Adams (n 39) 1.

77 Gregoire Chamayou, *Drone Theory* (Penguin Special 2013) 21.

would create the opportunity for clearer judgement because the operator would be in a 'safe zone' outside the 'danger zone'; this would render the human element 'invulnerable'.[78] But, these technological devices would still be regarded as 'extensions of our own humanity'.[79]

In the light of the above, it is easy to understand why drone technology, still comparatively new, has excited so much public interest. Designed to be used in a wide range of differing military domains (sea, land and air), drones are also known as 'unmanned vehicles', or 'remote-piloted aircraft', and have introduced the novelty of being 'uninhabited weapons'.[80] Pilots situated thousands of miles from their military hardware are able, by means of sophisticated sensors, and with the aid of an unprecedented range of relevant data, to create an 'augmented reality'. These technical features most certainly have legal implications.[81] Drone pilots can identify and refine targets, providing a much more detailed knowledge of the battlefield than was possible using only the natural human senses, establish 'pattern of life analysis' and choose the most appropriate weapon indicated. But, more importantly, technically drones allow for an increased compliance with the laws of targeting.[82] As the UN Special Rapporteur on Extrajudicial, Summary or Arbitrary Executions for the Office of the High Commissioner for Humans Rights, Professor Philip Alston (hereafter Special Rapporteur P. Alston) had the wisdom to highlight that new technologies of war bring insurmountable risks but also bring with them the important positive effect of 'saving the lives of civilians by making the targeting of combatants more accurate and reducing collateral damage'.[83]

Apart from all the advantages that can be enumerated, the use of drone technology does not escape legal and technical controversy.[84] It would be impossible here to cover all those aspects, but one factor that it is important to bear in mind is that drones facilitate effective physical invulnerability for the

78 ibid 21; Coker, *Future Wars* (n 68) 79.

79 Coker, *Future Wars* (n 68) 73.

80 Leveringhaus (n 1) 48; US Department of Defense, 'Unmanned Systems Integrated Roadmap: FY2013–2038' <www.dtic.mil/dtic/tr/fulltext/u2/a592015.pdf>; Yoram Dinstein and Arne Willy Dahl, *Oslo Manual on Select Topics of the Law of Armed Conflict. Rules and Commentary* (Springer 2020) Rule 36.

81 Liivoja, Leins and McCormack (n 22) 611–612.

82 Coker, *Future Wars* (n 68) 57; Michael N Schmitt, 'Unmanned Combat Aircraft Systems and International Humanitarian Law: Simplifying the Oft Benighted Debate' (2012) 30 *Boston University International Law Journal* 595; Chamayou (n 77) 42–45; UK Ministry of Defence, 'Joint Doctrine Publication 0–30.2 Unmanned Aircraft Systems' (n 7) 39–40, paras 4.1–4.4.

83 Alston, 'Lethal Robotic Technologies: The Implications for Human Rights and International Humanitarian Law' (n 37); cf Heyns, 'Report of the Special Rapporteur on Extrajudicial, Summary or Arbitrary Executions, Christof Heyns' (n 10).

84 Chamayou (n 77) chs 4 and 18.

attacker.[85] However, the same cannot be said about the other aspect of the dissociation of risk: psychological invulnerability.[86] According to studies carried out by the US Defence Department and a number of American scholars, drone pilots seem to experience mental health problems such as depression and anxiety and develop PTSD symptomology at the same rate as pilots of manned aircraft who are deployed to Iraq and Afghanistan.[87]

The proposal here is that the features mentioned earlier should be regarded as the first steps towards future AWS. There would no longer be a requirement for human soldiers to fight, whether on the battlefield or remotely, resulting in a true *dissociation of risk*.[88] If to 'human invulnerability' it is possible to add information systems able to gather and process accurate information according to a pre-established human goal, the second requirement for a truly AWS is fulfilled. Military missions would be carried out, in effect, by operating algorithms with very little, if any, human supervision.[89] It is precisely this point upon which, according to some authors, discussions around AWS must focus. The argument is that the progressively increasing physical and temporal distancing of humans from lethal decisions should be restricted, pending appropriate deliberation, because the current legal framework is built around an assumption of human involvement.[90]

85 ibid 163; Markus Wagner, 'Taking Humans Out of the Loop: Implications for International Humanitarian Law' (2011) 21 *Journal of Law, Information & Science* 1.

86 Christof Heyns, 'Autonomous Weapon Systems: Living a Dignified Life and Dying a Dignified Death' in Nehal Bhuta and others (eds), *Autonomous Weapons Systems: Law, Ethics, Policy* (Cambridge University Press 2016) 4.

87 Annie Brookman-Byrne, 'There Is a Spectrum of Responses to Killing Far-off Enemies' (*The Psychologist… the British Psychological Society*, February 2020) <https://thepsychologist.bps.org.uk/volume-33/february-2020/there-spectrum-responses-killing-far-enemies>; Wayne L Chappelle and others, 'Symptoms of Psychological Distress and Post-Traumatic Stress Disorder in United States Air Force "Drone" Operators' (2014) 179 *Military Medicine* 63; Sarah McCammon, 'The Warfare May Be Remote But the Trauma Is Real' (*npr*, 24 April 2017) <www.npr.org/2017/04/24/525413427/for-drone-pilots-warfare-may-be-remote-but-the-trauma-is-real>; Pratap Chatterjee, 'Drone Pilots Are Quitting in Record Numbers' (*MotherJones*, 5 March 2015) <www.motherjones.com/politics/2015/03/drone-pilots-are-quitting-record-numbers/>; Heather Linebaugh, 'I Worked on the US Drone Program. The Public Should Know What Really Goes On' *The Guardian* (Brussels, 29 December 2013) <www.theguardian.com/commentisfree/2013/dec/29/drones-us-military>; James Dao, 'Drone Pilots Are Found to Get Stress Disorders Much as Those in Combat Do' *The New York Times* (23 February 2013) <www.nytimes.com/2013/02/23/us/drone-pilots-found-to-get-stress-disorders-much-as-those-in-combat-do.html>.

88 US Department of Defense, 'Unmanned Systems Integrated Roadmap: FY2013–2038' (n 80) 20, para 3.1.

89 James G Bellingham and Kanna Rajan, 'Robotics in Remote Hostile Environments' (2007) 318 *Science* 1098.

90 O' Connell, 'Banning Autonomous Killing – The Legal and Ethical Requirement That Humans Make Near-Time Lethal Decisions' (n 75) 228.

1.2.1 *The Development of Systems of Information of War: An Introduction to Machine Learning Algorithms*

As the development of the autonomous weapon industry prompts us to question the need for a human presence on the battlefield, it is legitimate to ask whether, in the near future, the battlefield will become a realm of 'digital minds'.[91] However, before further questions are asked, it is important to understand what underpins autonomous technology.

The late 1970s is known as the time of third industrial revolution: the information era, and specifically the way in which information (*data*) is processed. The full impact of this era is far off being wholly comprehended, but one aspect of this revolution goes without mentioning: the fact that ours is a computerised society. It would be very hard to imagine any area of modern life that does not depend on computer and data analytics.[92] Thus, it does not seem difficult to envisage a revolution in military affairs, one characterised by a preponderance of autonomous computerised systems. It is imperative, notwithstanding, to bear in mind that computers are not self-created objects but are dependent on programs, which are executed through algorithms. A definition of 'algorithm' is not always self-evident even amongst computer scientists.[93] For the purposes of this work, an algorithm is 'a sequence of instructions' or a 'simply very detailed recipe – a sequence of small steps a computer has to give to obtain a specific result'.[94] In similar vein, *JDP 0–30.2* defines an algorithm as 'a series of instructions for performing a calculation or solving a problem, especially with a computer. They form the basis for everything a computer can do and are therefore a fundamental aspect of all AI systems.'[95]

Considering the aforementioned discussion, the challenge that AI represents is not so much the definition of 'algorithm' but rather the system's level of openness to the environment. If the algorithm is open to data collected after its programming, it is fair to question the certainty and predictability of

91 Arlindo Oliveira, *The Digital Mind, How Science Is Redefining Humanity* (MIT Press 2017) 8.

92 ibid 3; Brent Mittelstadt and others, 'The Ethics of Algorithms: Mapping the Debate' (2016) 3 *Big Data & Society* 1, 3.

93 Mittelstadt and others (n 92) 6.

94 Pedro Domingos, *The Master Algorithm – How to Quest for the Ultimate Learning Machine Will Remake Our World* (Allen Lane 2015) 1–6; Oliveira (n 91) 6–7.

95 UK Ministry of Defence, 'Joint Doctrine Publication 0–30.2 Unmanned Aircraft Systems' (n 7) 2.

its outcome.[96] Machine learning algorithms, for example, will define their own processes, unfolding step by step when confronted with new inputs, making it difficult, if not impossible, to predict with certainty the outcomes.[97]

In order to grasp the acuteness of the challenge, it is very important to bear in mind the different nature of 'deterministic' and 'machine learning' algorithms. Beginning with the former, they are those proper to automated systems – as *JDN 2/11* and *JDP 0–30.2* define them – that are 'programmed to logically follow a predefined set of rules in order to provide an outcome' – also called *deterministic*. Then there are those algorithms – and these are at the core of our attention – that are able to learn, to be *adaptive*, to new data collected from the environment, and are designed to replicate human decision-making processes.[98] It is not difficult to accept that while in the case of deterministic algorithms it is possible to understand the mathematical structure, with adaptive algorithms the situation might be the inverse. As Pedro Domingos explains, in the AI subfield of machine learning the structure of the algorithm is not that *data* → *algorithm* → *outcome* but rather $\textit{algorithm}_1$ *(collected data)* → $\textit{algorithm}_2$ *[(data* $\textit{algorithm}_2$*)]* → $\textit{algorithm}_3$ *[*$\textit{algorithm}_2$ *new data]* → *outcome*, ending up with computers reprogramming themselves, creating new algorithms according to the new data collected.[99]

From what can be seen as a simple development in the continuum of computer science, an immediate question emerges: could machine learning algorithms operate without human control/human intervention? Will it be possible for algorithms to be transparent, if accessibility to and comprehensibility of the data may be highly compromised?[100] This question is at the core of such new regulations as the *GDPR* and the recent House of Lords Report.

96 Mittelstadt and others (n 92) 17–19.

97 Wendell Wallach, *A Dangerous Master. How to Keep Technology from Slipping Beyond Our Control* (Basic Books 2015) 34–38.

98 This distinction was at the centre of the distinction between automated and autonomous systems in *JDN 2/11* but was abandoned by *JDP 0–30.2*. The last only says that 'autonomous systems' have a higher level of intent and direction to state that the United Kingdom will not have 'fully autonomous systems'. cf UK Ministry of Defence, 'The UK Approach to Unmanned Aircraft Vehicles, JDN 2/11' (n 8); UK Ministry of Defence, 'Joint Doctrine Publication 0–30.2 Unmanned Aircraft Systems' (n 7) 2; House of Lords Select Committee on Artificial Intelligence (n 51) paras 335–337. See Gaon and Stedman (n 21) 1139; Letendre (n 66) 286.

99 Domingos (n 94) 6–10.

100 Mittelstadt and others (n 92) 21.

1.3 MACHINE LEARNING AND THE DISSOCIATION OF COMMUNICATION

1.3.1 *AI: From Machine Learning to Artificial General Intelligence (AGI)*

The intention here is not to offer a comprehensive account of all that can be known about machine learning as a specific field of AI applied to AWS. It is, however, crucial to establish some understanding of how roboticists conceive of autonomous decision-making processes for AWS, and the direction in which AI appears to be heading.

Science fiction writers like to depict robots as autonomous machines capable of making their own decisions and expressing their own personalities, but the reality is quite different. Up until the present time, weapons systems, such as they are, have been 'things' that belong to owners who dictate to them how and when to engage pre-chosen military targets. Any outcome that goes beyond the expected outcome must be the result either of technical/mechanical/electronic malfunction or an operator's fault. But what if systems replace human decision-making processes or even if AWS would be able to replicate human cognitive capacities?[101]

The terms '*neural network*', '*deep learning*' and '*computational AI*' are all metaphors referring to the most recent paradigm of AI, which tries to recreate in computer software the complexity of the internal processes of the human brain in order to emulate the way in which that organ analyses information and, in consequence, adopts a decision-making process.[102] Humans can think abstractly, communicate complex thoughts, and accumulate cultural information over the generations far better than any other species on the planet.[103] Until today humans have also been, as defined by philosophy and law, the only species of 'fully autonomous agent', that is, they possess a capacity for self-awareness and self-critical analysis. Human actions are chosen to further certain ends, according to the human being's capacity to reason on the basis of his/her own past experience, and this is a reality that has not changed.[104]

101 Kyle Bowyer, 'Robots Rights: At What Point Should an Intelligent Machine Be Considered a "Person"?' (*The Conversation – Academic Rigour Journalistic Flair*, 6 February 2017) <http://theconversation.com/robot-rights-at-what-point-should-an-intelligent-machine-be-considered-a-person-72410>.

102 Eric Postma, 'Deep Learning: The Third Wave Neural Network Wave' (*Tilburg University – Cognitive and Artificial Intelligence Group*, February 2016) <www.tilburguniversity.edu/research/institutes-and-research-groups/data-science-center/blogs/data-science-blog-eric-postma/>.

103 Nick Bostrom, *SuperIntelligence: Paths, Dangers, Strategies* (Oxford University Press 2014) 27–29.

104 Sparrow, 'Killer Robots' (n 55) 65; John Christman, *The Politics of Persons: Individual Autonomy and Socio-Historical Selves* (Reissue edn, Cambridge University Press 2011) 134–142.

However, human capabilities have enabled humans to develop increasingly efficient productive technologies, and those technologies have in turn increased the rate of innovation.[105] This has led to the widely popularised idea of a coming *technological singularity*, a concept used to convey the possibility of an intelligence explosion or, more precisely, an explosion of machine superintelligence, culminating in the creation of 'minds' that are much faster and more efficient than those with which we are biologically endowed. If this becomes reality, it does seem likely to change everything: it would be a technological innovation that promised to question what it means to be human.[106]

Looking briefly at the history of AI, the Dartmouth Summer Project (1956) at Dartmouth College is often regarded as the foundation event of AI.[107] However, what exactly should be understood by 'AI' is subject to debate, and the question is most of the time avoided by scholars. For that reason and for the purposes of this work, the definition given by the House of Lords Report will be adopted: '*technologies with the ability to perform tasks that otherwise require human intelligence, such as visual perception, speech recognition, and language translation*'.[108]

Since the late 1950s, the research and development of AI has been through periods of high expectation, alternating with periods of setback and disappointment. However, by the 1990s, new techniques seemed to offer an alternative to the traditionalist logical and deductive paradigm often referred to as 'good old-fashioned artificial intelligence' (GOFAI).[109] The new techniques entail machine learning.[110] Machine learning has proved to be a powerful technique in creating and refining algorithms capable of producing

105 Gregor Noll, 'War by Algorithm: The End of Law?' in Max Liljefors, Gregor Noll and Daniel Steuer (eds), *War and Algorithm* (Rowman & Littlefield 2019) 85.

106 Callum Chace, *Surviving AI: The Promise and Peril of Artificial Intelligence* (Three Cs 2015) 18.

107 Konstantine Arkoudas and Selmer Bringsjord, 'Philosophical Foundations' in Keith Frankish and William M Ramsey (eds), *The Cambridge Handbook of Artificial Intelligence* (Cambridge University Press 2014) 39–41; Oliveira (n 91) 87.

108 House of Lords Select Committee on Artificial Intelligence (n 51) 14, para 10. A slightly different definition is the one used by computer scientists, according to which the field IA research defines itself as the 'study of 'intelligent agents': any device that perceives its environment and takes actions that maximise its chance of success at some goal. AI is mostly vertical: it is excellent in doing one thing as compared to the versatility of the human intelligence that we could call horizontal and apt to manifold of tasks', cf Giovanni Comande, 'Multilayered (Accountable) Liability for Artificial Intelligence' in Sebastian Lohsse, Reiner Schulze and Dirk Staudenmayer (eds), *Liability for Artificial Intelligence and the Internet of Things* (Nomos Hart 2019) 167.

109 Margaret A Boden, 'GOFAI' in Keith Frankish and William M Ramsey (eds), *The Cambridge Handbook of Artificial Intelligence* (Cambridge University Press 2014) 93–96; Bostrom (n 103) 27; Letendre (n 66) 292–293.

110 Chace (n 106) 78; Bostrom (n 103) 9; Weng, Chen and Sun (n 55) 268–269.

conclusions based on data without being explicitly programmed to do so. When the system is provided with the accurate data, machine learning algorithms can *make predictions and solve problems*.[111] This, in turn, depends on other modern computational techniques, such as the capacity of computers to establish *pattern recognition*, *statistical machine learning techniques* and *data mining*, discovering links and properties in large data sets which were previously undetectable.

These techniques have allowed a major development in one of the main areas of machine learning: known as *deep learning*, which is inspired by the internal working of parts of the human brain.[112] Essentially, deep learning crunches vast quantities of data and uses colossal amounts of computing power (*Big Data*).[113] With the pioneer work of Frank Rosenblatt, the first steps were taken towards the '*neural network wave*', that is learning algorithms that are modelled upon human neurons and their adaptive connections.[114] These techniques involve *neural networks* that can learn from experience, find natural ways of generalising from examples and discover hidden statistical patterns in their input.[115]

Another important detail about machine learning is *Probabilistic Reasoning in Intelligent Systems*, or the *Bayesian Network*. The Bayesian element makes probabilistically optimal use of the information available.[116] When provided with data, structured, for example, by neural networks, the Bayesian rule allows for the determination of the probability of hypotheses given that data.[117] This factor is crucial to understanding the problem of the *unpredictable nature* of modern algorithms and autonomous systems embedded with machine learning algorithms. Looking only at the Bayesian rule, algorithms would be in some ways more transparent on inspection owing to the probabilistic mathematical formulas, but when applied to 'neural networks', it is almost impossible to know what and how data will be processed.[118] These

111 House of Lords Select Committee on Artificial Intelligence (n 51) 14, para 12.

112 Bostrom (n 103) 188; Oliveira (n 91) 89, 95–97.

113 Comande (n 108) 168.

114 Krupiy (n 31) 75–76.

115 Bostrom (n 103) 13; 'The Return of the Machinery Question' *The Economist* (2016) 1, 3; Oliveira (n 91) 103–110; Noll (n 105) 82.

116 Bostrom (n 103) 9; Stuart J Russell and Peter Norvig, *Artificial Intelligence: A Modern Approach* (3rd edn, Pearson 2010).

117 David Danks, 'Learning' in Keith Frankish and William M Ramsey (eds), *The Cambridge Handbook of Artificial Intelligence* (Cambridge University Press 2014) 154–157; Oliveira (n 91) 110–115.

118 Nick Bostrom and Elizer Yudkowsky, 'The Ethics of Artificial Intelligence' in Keith Frankish and William M Ramsey (eds), *The Cambridge Handbook of Artificial Intelligence* (Cambridge University Press 2014) 319.

algorithms will not look to the intrinsic properties of data but to the structural features presented by that data (i.e. location; some configuration; some pattern of behaviour).[119] Fundamentally, in deep learning, the algorithms use several layers of gathered data, each taking data from previous layers and passing an output to the next layer, a process known as *connectionism*, based on the structural features of collected data.[120]

In light of the observations made earlier, the main advantage of machine learning, as compared with traditional programming, is its capacity to analyse data so that humans do not have to explicitly define either the problem or the solution. The machine is designed, instead, to improve its knowledge through experience, offering solutions to potential data connections.[121] Now, not all systems engaged in machine learning present the same level of complexity. It is important to distinguish three separate layers of '*intelligence action function*' that a system can deploy.

The first layer, '*action intelligence*', comprises a system capable of situating itself within an environment, observing aspects of that environment and drawing conclusions. Unlike less sophisticated systems, it does more than just gather and store data according to pre-established rules. The second layer is known as the '*autonomous intelligence*'. This layer comprises systems capable of solving problems that require behaviour-pattern recognition, having the ability to schedule and plan according to prior experience. Systems with 'autonomous intelligence' are able to be adaptive on the battlefield when their 'past experience' equips them to 'recognise' the terrain. Questions of predictability may emerge, however, when the system is confronted with battlespace data that it has never processed before. At this point it is very important to avoid the temptation of being misled by science fiction scenarios. The layers of intelligence or 'computational AI', described earlier, involve human designing and programming, and there is by no means even a suggestion of any kind of 'conscious behaviour'.

The third layer is categorised as *human-based intelligence* (HBI), also known as *artificial general intelligence* (AGI) or *Strong AI*.[122] The latter is indeed the kind of AI that excites more concern and discussion among scholars

119 Danks (n 117) 160.

120 Neural Networks can detect subtle features of input data. However, the result depends very much on rules established for the different weight that should be given to the input data. cf 'The Return of the Machinery Question' (n 115) 4, 10; Bostrom (n 103) 10; Oliveira (n 91) 108.

121 Machine learning algorithms can indeed produce unexpected solutions and explore the interconnectedness of things and of humans. cf Comande (n 108) 165.

122 Bostrom (n 103) 22; Boden (n 109) 102–103; Arkoudas and Bringsjord (n 107) 35–36; Cathy Burke, 'AI Crisis: Pentagon Grappling with Future of Weapons That "Make Their Own Decisions"' (*NewsMax*, 11 April 2018) <www.newsmax.com/us/department-of-defense-pentagon-artificial-intelligence-ai/2018/11/04/id/889293/>.

than any other. Whatever the term chosen, HBI is characterised by the ability to replicate natural learning methods, enabling the systems not only to interact with their environment, create their own set of values and options and also able to adapt their behaviour to any changes that might result from that interaction. The outcomes can be considered '*original*', in the sense that human programming only provides the tools for the system to obtain an outcome. The originality results only from the connections established by the algorithms between the collected data, which will be unknown, a priori, to the operator.[123]

The last two types of machine 'intelligence' would deal better than 'traditional' artificial intelligence with non-logical problems, with the uncertainty and unpredictability of the battlefield, for example. At the same time, however, it might prove problematic when dealing with pre-established rules. In the situation of HBI systems, the systems have their own rules and what might be called a degree of 'self-awareness', at least enough to create their own values and make decisions.[124] This last possibility is considered totally unrealistic by many, engendering in some members of the community a degree of premature hysteria about the uncertainty of the future.[125]

In fact, to reach this stage of evolution in AI would require that intelligence explosion touched upon earlier, which is currently not much more than a motivational ideal with a way to go.[126] For others, the new technologies associated with HBI pose unsurmountable challenges to humanity as a whole, because it will not be possible to predict and assess the 'subjectivity' of these systems. To agree to the continuation of research that could result in the creation of self-aware machines would be very much a case, according to Elon Musk, of 'summoning the demon'.[127]

123 The design and programming of 'intelligent machines' can be traced back to the Alan Turing project. Turing, facing the impossibility of defining 'machine' and 'think' created the 'imitation game', which entailed delegating to individual judges the task of recognising whether an answer, provided in response to the posing of a specific case or problem, was given by a computer or by a human. At the point where that distinction became impossible, machines would have achieved a level on a par with the 'intelligent answer' of a human. Lemley and Casey (n 2) 10–11; Oliveira (n 91) 92.

124 Weng, Chen and Sun (n 55) 275.

125 'The Return of the Machinery Question' (n 115) 11.

126 Weng, Chen and Sun (n 55) 11–12; Bostrom (n 103) 13.

127 Wallach, 'From Robots to Techno Sapiens: Ethics, Law and Public Policy in the Development of Robotics and Neurotechnologies' (n 40) 205; Future of Life, 'Autonomous Weapons: An Open Letter from AI & Robotics Researchers' <https://futureoflife.org/open-letter-autonomous-weapons/>; Samuel Gibbs, 'Musk, Wozniak and Hawking Urge Ban on Warfare AI and Autonomous Weapons' *The Guardian* (Brussels, 27 July 2015) <www.theguardian.com/technology/2015/jul/27/musk-wozniak-hawking-ban-ai-autonomous-weapons>; Samuel Gibbs, 'Elon Musk: Artificial Intelligence Is Our Biggest Existential Threat' *The Guardian* (Brussels,

It is important, however, in order to proceed with the argument of this thesis, to establish what AI has achieved and what can be regarded as feasible in the near future. It is imperative, at the same time, to leave aside the notion of a situation in which systems become their own creators and masters, because such a development is still at the stage of theoretical hypothesis.

In support of this line of thought, Nick Bostrom offers a tremendous contribution to the understanding of the present stage of research, of what can be envisaged, and also of its perils. In essence, until today AI has succeeded in every area that requires 'thinking', that is, in all operations subject to logic, be they deductive or inductive. However, it has failed to do what humans and animals do 'without thinking', naturally performing deductions that cannot be translated into mathematical rules, for example analysing visual scenes and recognising objects. So far, AI has failed at controlling the behaviour of any system in environments that challenge logic owing to their unstructured nature or tendency to operate according to 'common sense'.[128] Artificial Intelligence, to be qualified as HBI, would very much need a 'whole brain prosthesis' resulting in 'conscious digital minds', a concept which has been characterised as a kind of *an algorithm soup*.[129] In fact, HBI would be 'extremely alien' to human intelligence, having entirely different goals.[130] It should not be expected that an HBI system, that is, a system designed to deliver maximum efficiency by means of the manipulation of pre-established parameters, should evince love, compassion or any other human sentiment.[131]

In light of the aforementioned observation, a more plausible scenario, according to Pedro Domingos and Nick Bostrom, is to accept that the internet will accumulate improvements through the work of many people over many years, collecting an incalculable quantity of data. The work of roboticists and engineers will be to create more powerful information-filtering algorithms, better autonomous software agents and more effective efficiency protocols to govern the *interactions (connections) between the different layers in AI systems*, if they are to obtain optimum results. In essence, what can be expected in the years to come is a '*unified web intelligence*' (UWI), allowing systems to operate in swarm and invisibly.[132]

27 October 2014) <www.theguardian.com/technology/2014/oct/27/elon-musk-artificial-intelligence-ai-biggest-existential-threat>.

128 Bostrom (n 103) 14.

129 ibid 55.

130 Oliveira (n 91) 88.

131 Bostrom (n 103) 35, 55.

132 ibid 60; Domingos (n 94) 45; Tim Stevens, 'Cyberweapons: Power and the Governance of the Invisible' (2018) 55 *International Politics* 482, 491; McFarland, *Autonomous Weapon Systems*

While HBI is still in the stage of development, successful results have been achieved in terms of UWI. In the late 1980s, the term *swarm intelligence* (SI) was coined to refer to a collection of robotic systems deliberately coordinated, able to interact in an environment and to strike from all directions, by means of a sustainable pulsing force.[133] However, in recent years, SI has developed to the point of being able to design 'intelligent multi-agent systems' with the ability to be flexible, robust and self-organised like a swarm of insects.[134] These capabilities will allow systems *to quickly adapt* to a changing environment and, in military terms, as Chris Jenks argues, this can allow commanders to plan decentralised attacks, creating confusion or discomfort on the battlefield, as a swarm of bees or ants are able to cause to any person's daily life.[135] But, as the author adds, nothing would exclude the possibility of swarm technology deploying lethal force, first, for defensive purposes and then for offensive purposes.[136]

and the Law of Armed Conflict: Compatibility with International Humanitarian Law (n 46) 54.

133 Francis Grimal and Jae Sundaram, 'Combat Drones: Hives, Swarms, and Autonomous Action?' (2018) 23 *Journal of Conflict & Security Law* 105, 112; McFarland, *Autonomous Weapon Systems and the Law of Armed Conflict: Compatibility with International Humanitarian Law* (n 46) 45, 54–56. See Dinstein and Dahl (n 80) Rule 40.

134 Yueh-Ming Huang and Chien-Hung Liu, 'Applying Adaptive Swarm Intelligence Technology with Structuration in Web-Based Collaborative Learning' (2009) 52 *Computers & Education* 789, 790; Timothy Chung, 'OFFensive Swarm-Enabled Tactics (OFFSET)' (*DARPA – Defense Advanced Research Projects Agency*) <www.darpa.mil/program/offensive-swarm-enabled-tactics>; Matt Williams, 'The DARPA Robotics Challenge' (*Hero X*) < www.herox.com/crowdsourcing-news/148-the-darpa-robotics-challenge>; Grimal and Sundaram (n 133) 112. As an example of swarm technology, on 16 September 2011, British warplanes fired two dozen Brimstone missiles at a group of Libyan tanks that were shelling civilians. cf John Markoff, 'Fearing Bombs That Can Pick Whom to Kill' *The New York Times* (11 November 2014) <www.nytimes.com/2014/11/12/science/weapons-directed-by-robots-not-humans-raise-ethical-questions.html>.

135 It is important to note the Russian Federation claims that had been a target of a drone swarm in 2018. A group of small armed unmanned aircraft were launched at a Russian airbase in Syria, and China has developed performed tests of swarms with more than 1,200 units, although the swarm was dependent on deterministic algorithms instead of inter-drone communication. Michael Safi, 'Are Drone Swarms the Future of Aerial Warfare?' *The Guardian* (Brussels, 4 December 2019) <www.theguardian.com/news/2019/dec/04/are-drone-swarms-the-future-of-aerial-warfare>; Scott N Romaniuk and Tobias Burgers, 'China's Swarms of Smart Drones Have Enormous Military Potential' (*The Diplomat*, 3 February 2018) <https://thediplomat.com/2018/02/chinas-swarms-of-smart-drones-have-enormous-military-potential/>; Anna de Courcy Wheeler, 'Swarms. Discussion Paper for the Convention on Certain Conventional Weapons (CCW)' (*Article 36*, March 2019) <www.article36.org/wp-content/uploads/2019/06/swarms.pdf>; Zachary Kallenborn, 'The Era of the Drone Swarm Is Coming, and We Need to Be Ready for It' (*Modern War Institute at West Point*, 25 October 2018) <https://mwi.usma.edu/era-drone-swarm-coming-need-ready/>.

136 Chris Jenks, 'The Gathering Swarm: The Path to Increasingly Autonomous Weapons Systems' (2017) 57 *Jurimetrics* 341, 345, 351–354. For the complexity of SWARM Architecture, Grimal and

1.3.2 *The Mission and the Dissociation of Communication*

Machine learning and recent advances in the manufacture of hardware create the perfect technological environment for the development of AWS, but this will not come about without challenges and difficulties.[137] Whilst, on the one hand, it clearly offers a number of advantages in terms of the autonomous technology of warfare (physical and psychological distance from the battlefield; more precise and faster organisation of data, among others), on the other hand, it may be impossible to follow the operations of these algorithms. As roboticists Danny Zhu and Manuela Veloso explain, the lifecycle of an algorithm, in the context of an autonomous system, is unique in the sense that it can run multiple times per second, each run contributing a tiny factor affecting the behaviour of the system. If protocols for communicating with the system do not exist, the results cannot be understood solely by watching the system operating.[138]

Before the era of machine learning, an algorithm was designed expressly to achieve a pre-established outcome, according to a self-contained set of rules. In these situations, human operators analysed and selected the relevant data in order to give an order/instruct a system that an individual/tank/building be targeted. In such cases, the human operator was said to be *in-the-loop* operating the weapon as an extension of him/herself.

Completely different is the situation of neural networks, governed by the Bayesian rule, analyse data, exploit structural relations within that data and infer outcomes that are not necessarily pre-given to the system in order to perform its mission, that is, a preset human goal (e.g. a system determines that *y* is an individual and, according to data collected by that system, that he/she has a *continuous combat function* [CCF] and therefore can be legitimately targeted). Another aspect is, if swarm technology is borne in mind, that data will not necessarily come from the same source and there can be a truly decontextualisation that algorithms will have to make sense of it.[139]

In light of the aforementioned discussion, it can be said that there is an emergent *dissociation of communication* between the system and humans in

Sundaram (n 133) 112–116. Jack Richardson, 'The Coming Drone Swarm' (*Defence Procurement International*, 16 February 2017) <www.defenceprocurementinternational.com/features/air/drone-swarms>; Wheeler (n 135); 'Final Report. National Security Commission on Artificial Intelligence' (n 15) 23.

137 Boulanin and Verbruggen (n 9) 23.

138 Danny Zhu and Manuela Veloso, 'Virtually Adapted Reality and Algorithm Visualization for Autonomous Robots' (20th Robocup International Symposium, Germany 2016) <www.ais.uni-bonn.de/robocup.de/2016/papers/RoboCup_Symposium_2016_Zhu.pdf>.

139 Comande (n 108) 166.

terms of control of the main operations of decision-making. With machine learning algorithms, human operators will find themselves *on-the-loop* – that is the human operator has the capacity to supervise and intervene – or even *out-of-the-loop*, which is the case in which no human intervention is possible, and the system operates exclusively in accordance with the embedded algorithms' rules. For this reason, some authors have argued that systems run by deep neural networks operate like '*black-box systems*'.[140] It is important, for the purposes of this work, to remember that 'black-box system' has two possible interpretations. The term is sometimes used to refer to a *recording device*, such as the data-monitoring systems in planes, trains and cars. The meaning adopted in this thesis, however, is 'a system whose workings are carried out unbeknownst to its human operators or military commanders', that is the *inputs* and *outputs* are observable but the processes that take place between (the structural interrelations amongst the data) are invisible.[141]

These considerations will be extremely important when it comes to dealing with the problems of accountability. If AWS do not allow human intervention, human operators can only be found liable for what was established *before* the AWS was deployed. However, the fact that the AWS' inner workings take place in a black-box system means that access to the information of *what or who* caused the IHL violations might be highly compromised.

Considering the aforementioned discussion, the phenomenon of dissociation of communication associated with AI brings with it two consequences. First, human control (available and selected data; constrains in how data should be processed; criteria for targeting) will necessarily be reserved to a phase which precedes the deployment of that system. Second, AWS will not be regarded as *reliable* but as *predictable* systems (*probabilistic systems*).[142] The system will choose the course of action that will most *probably* accomplish the preset human goal. These consequences will be present wherever AWS are deployed and, as a result, it is necessary to analyse what types of algorithms will be in operation and how unpredictable they might be considered to be.

140 Ben Taylor, 'Artificial Intelligence and Robotics: Who's Liable for the Decisions Made?' (*ITProPortal*, 20 March 2017) <www.itproportal.com/features/artificial-intelligence-and-robotics-whos-liable-for-the-decisions-made/>; 'The Return of the Machinery Question' (n 115) 13; Boulanin and Verbruggen (n 9) 24; Chesterman (n 4) 239–240.

141 Frank Pasquale, *The Black Box Society: The Secret Algorithms That Control Money and Information* (Harvard University Press 2015) 4. For the complexity of the matter of black box systems already in the civil society, cf Chapter 3; Tom Simonite, 'AI Experts Want to End "Black Box" Algorithms in Government' (*WIRED*, 18 October 2017) <www.wired.com/story/ai-experts-want-to-end-black-box-algorithms-in-government/>.

142 Markoff (n 134).

1.3.3 *The Importance of the Mission. Algorithm Trilogy: Situation Assessment, Selection Algorithm and Situation Management*

Perhaps one of the difficulties around the legal implications of the use of AWS in future armed conflicts is the excessive attention that has been given to the technical aspects of these systems, what a system can and cannot do. This emphasis can only lead lawyers into a realm of speculation and raise questions that are impossible to answer. The argument chosen for the thesis, because it is a more accurate way of approaching the issue, is to look at the centrality of *the mission* that is to be entrusted to modern systems of war. This is for two sets of reasons. First, no State is interested in studying and developing AWS with uncertain capabilities or that could turn against the State's own interests as a result of some kind of 'machine free will'.[143] For that reason it is in states' own interest to ensure that such technologies are subjected to thorough tests and legal reviews (Article 36 API). These examinations will, however, be impossible to carry out without a clear understanding of the mission(s) that the systems might be required to perform. Second, in the context of military operations, those who plan or decide upon an attack (Article 49 API) need to do everything feasible 'to verify that the objectives to be attacked are neither civilians nor civilian objects and are not subject to special protection but are military objectives' and to 'take all feasible precautions in the choice of means and methods of attack with a view to avoiding, and in any event to minimising, incidental loss of civilian life, injury to civilians and damage to civilian objects' (Article 57(2)(a)(i)(ii) API). Precautions can only be taken, however, when those in charge have a clear knowledge of the situation in which an AWS is to be deployed. Thus, AWS will only be used for missions where no risk of violating IHL is envisaged. It is, therefore, the mission that will govern the degree according to which AWS can be deployed and be autonomous.[144]

143 Major Kathleen McKendrick, 'Banning Autonomous Weapons Is Not the Answer' (*Chatham House – The Royal Institute of International Affairs*, 2 May 2018) <www.chathamhouse.org/expert/comment/banning-autonomous-weapons-not-answer#>; Elsa Kania, 'China's Strategic Ambiguity and Shifting Approach to Lethal Autonomous Weapons Systems' (*Lawfare*, 17 April 2018) <www.lawfareblog.com/chinas-strategic-ambiguity-and-shifting-approach-lethal-autonomous-weapons-systems#>; Dan Saxon, 'A Human Touch: Autonomous Weapons, DoD Directive 3000.09 and the Interpretation of "Appropriate Levels of Human Judgement over the Use of Force"' in Nehal Bhuta and others (eds), *Autonomous Weapons Systems: Law, Ethics and Policy* (Cambridge University Press 2016); Robin Geiss, 'The International Law Dimension of Autonomous Weapons Systems' (2015) 6 <http://library.fes.de/pdf-files/id/ipa/11673.pdf>; 'Final Report. National Security Commission on Artificial Intelligence' (n 15) 10–11, 133.

144 Kelly Cass, 'Autonomous Weapons and Accountability: Seeking Solutions in the Law of War' (2015) 48 *Loyola of Los Angeles Law Review* 1017, 1042.

In light of the aforementioned discussion, the *mission* is the guiding principle for the design and programming of an AWS's algorithm, so that will be named the *algorithm for the mission*. The centrality and the importance of the *algorithm for the mission* helps to understand the reason why some states prefer to designate the advent of AWS as an 'algorithmic', 'mosaic' or 'intelligentised' warfare.[145] However, before addressing the different types of algorithm that a mission performed by an AWS entails, some observations will be made about what is understood by 'mission'. In the course of this thesis, the term refers to 'those military operations, developed in the context of an armed conflict, that involve the deployment of lethal force'. Thus, *enforcement operations* (i.e. military enforcement pursuant to Chapter VII of the UN Charter) and *self-defence operations* that rise to the level of armed conflict (i.e. the right of a state, according to Customary International Law and pursuant to Article 51 UN Charter, to respond individually or collectively to an illegal armed attack directed against its territory, citizens, military vessels, aircraft, or installations, abroad or located in international sea or airspace) will be taken into account since in these cases IHL is fully applicable.[146]

The two kinds of military operations mentioned earlier require concrete 'plans' or 'orders' to prepare the military operation according to the specific circumstances prevailing in that specific armed conflict. While an *operation plan* (OPLAN) refers to a group of operations planned well in advance, the term *order* or *operational order* is used when the plan is put into effect.[147] These terms shall not be confused with the *Rules of Engagement* (hereinafter ROE), which are lawful commands issued by competent authorities, namely military commanders, to circumscribe the 'circumstances and limitations within which military forces may be employed to achieve their objectives'.[148] Clearly, ROE will reflect IHL rules and principles regarding the use of force in an armed conflict.

Looking now at the specific situation of AWS, the *operational order* is particularly important, since it will be the responsibility of the commander to decide whether the OPLAN can be totally or partially executed by one/several AWS. This decision will have three important implications: first, the

145 'Final Report. National Security Commission on Artificial Intelligence' (n 15) 79.

146 Terry D Gill and Dieter Fleck (eds), *The Handbook of the International Law of Military Operations* (2nd edn, Oxford University Press 2015) 5.01 and 11.01. Peace enforcement operations will not be considered since they usually do not involve use of force rising to the level of an armed conflict. cf ibid para 70.

147 ibid para 77.

148 ibid para 86; International Institute of Humanitarian Law, *Sanremo Handbook on Rules of Engagement* (US Naval War College edn, 2009) pt I, para 3 <www.iihl.org/wp-content/uploads/2017/11/ROE-HANDBOOK-ENGLISH.pdf>.

OPLAN can be a 'multiple operational order' or 'an individual operational order'. According to the first, the mission entrusted to the system can include multiple operations (e.g. a village siege); according to the second, the system is entrusted with an individual targeting operation (e.g. to target *x*). Second, the different levels of the operational order will determine the way that the *algorithm for the mission* is designed and programmed. Finally, the 'operational order' is the order to activate an AWS in the battlespace. An important question now emerges, that is 'how should the ROE be set for AWS?'

According to the *Sanremo Handbook*, ROE should be continually assessed by commanders so that they remain consistent the *operational mission*.[149] As can now be seen, updating the ROE once the AWS is activated will be impossible since no human intervention is allowed once the system is operating. It is at this point that machine learning can be a revolutionary tool, enabling the system to adapt to fast-changing circumstances. Taking into account that an OPLAN can pinpoint at least three crucial moments – *situation assessment*, the *selection of military targets* and *situation management* (the final engagement of the target) – the *algorithm for the mission* can be divided into three different algorithms, each encoding the ROE appropriate to it according to the OPLAN, and able to adapt in action without human intervention.

Applying this structure to AWS, it is proposed that these three stages correspond with the three types of algorithm: the *algorithm for situation assessment*, the *selection algorithm* and the *algorithm for situation management*.

The *algorithm for situation assessment* gathers and processes the relevant data. At this stage humans can exercise control, selecting what data is to be considered relevant to the *selection algorithm*. In this case, the situation is one of *supervised learning algorithms*. As David Danks explains, in this type of algorithm *some known values (x) determine how the algorithm will proceed*.[150] The *selection algorithm* will be designed based on this true variable and the *algorithm for situation management* will act accordingly. Another possibility is of an *open algorithm*. Looking at a possible example, if the *algorithm for situation assessment* can identify common patterns of individuals likely to be civilians or combatants, the human operator can choose which elements should be regarded as 'ground truth' for the *selection algorithm* and the *algorithm for situation management* will execute the mission, taking into

149 International Institute of Humanitarian Law (n 148) Appendix 1 to Annex A, para 8.
150 Danks (n 117).

account new relevant data collected on the battlefield that will be unknown to the operator (open algorithm).

Bearing in mind that AWS are systems that operate without human intervention, both situations are acceptable in the sense that the outcome will always be produced by an algorithm. Notwithstanding this, the *algorithm for situation management* is in itself dependent on new data collected from the battlefield and, therefore, can only be predictable. The possible advent of HBI would necessarily change this scenario. It would give place to 'unsupervised learning algorithms',[151] algorithms would have a higher level of unpredictability and validation of the outcomes produced will be almost impossible, since the *selection algorithm* will be a product of the system and not subjected to human constrains. However, both situations, although different, are examples of the 'dissociation of communication' inherent in modern technology.

1.3.4 AWS: *Reliable or Predictable Systems? The Causes of Unpredictable Outcomes*

The dissociation of communication is pointed out by Robert Sparrow, among others, as being the main problem associated with AWS.[152] In order to avoid unpredictable results on the battlefield, it is understood that there will be a need for a human operator to exercise control over what, how and when military targets are to be engaged.[153] However, if a system is open to communication (has a machine–human interface), it must introduce an interval, however brief, when action is halted whilst the system 'waits for approval'; this could be viewed as a safety valve, but also as a technical weakness.[154] It is a difficult balance indeed. The openness of a system makes it vulnerable (e.g. to adverse environmental factors) but, at the same time, machine learning algorithms introduce precisely the advantage of being capable of learning

151 'A Guide to Using Artificial Intelligence in the Public Sector' (Office for Artificial Intelligence, Government Digital Service 2020) 7, 11 <www.gov.uk/government/publications/a-guide-to-using-artificial-intelligence-in-the-public-sector>.

152 Sparrow, 'Killer Robots' (n 55) 68; Justin McClelland, 'The Review of Weapons in Accordance with Article 36 of Additional Protocol I' (2003) 85 *International Review of the Red Cross* 397, 405.

153 ICRC, 'ICRC Statement. Agenda Item 5(b) – Further Consideration of the Human Element in the Use of Lethal Force; Aspects of Human-Machine Interaction in the Development, Deployment and Use of Emerging Technologies in the Area of Lethal Autonomous Weapon Systems' (*Reaching Critical Will*, 2019) <https://reachingcriticalwill.org/images/documents/Disarmament-fora/ccw/2019/gge/statements/26March_ICRC5b.pdf>; Christof Heyns, 'Autonomous Weapons in Armed Conflict and the Right to a Dignified Life: An African Perspective' (2017) 33 *South African Journal of Human Rights* 46, 48.

154 Bostrom (n 103).

from the environment and being able to adapt the mission to meet the circumstances in the battlespace (i.e. *selection algorithm algorithm for situation management*).

This tension is recognised by the *United States Air Force Unmanned Aircraft Systems Flight Plan 2009–2047*.[155] The report states that it is crucial to ensure uninterrupted communication between systems and control stations, in order to prevent undesirable outcomes, but at the same time draws attention to the difficulties faced by communications planners in guaranteeing the necessary level of communication 'without exposing either the sender or receiver to possible hostile interception'.[156] Thus, it seems fair to conclude that it is not possible to theorise all the possible circumstances surrounding the deployment of an AWS, but it is possible to design an algorithm for the mission that sets filters and value criteria to posterior data collected by the system. In other words, the designers and programmers have to encode all the relevant information for the mission entrusted to the system.[157] However, as the CCW Chair, in 2019, had occasion to state: 'setting operational constraints on systems, regarding tasks, target profiles, time-frame of operation, scope of movement over an area and operating environment, could increase predictability and thereby assist with compliance with IHL, *but, in general, would not alone be sufficient to ensure IHL compliance*'.[158]

Taking the mission entrusted to the system as the centre of analysis, according to some roboticists and scholars, AWS will do precisely what is entrusted to them and, theoretically, will also produce better outcomes and, potentially, be more efficient than human soldiers.[159] However, a problem emerges

155 United States Air Force, 'United States Air Force Unmanned Aircraft Systems Flight Plan 2009–2047' (2009) <https://fas.org/irp/program/collect/uas_2009.pdf>.

156 ibid.

157 McFarland, *Autonomous Weapon Systems and the Law of Armed Conflict: Compatibility with International Humanitarian Law* (n 46) 57–58.

158 Ljupco Jivan Gjorgjinski, '2018 Draft Conclusions – Chair's Non-Paper' (*Reaching Critical Will*, 7 May 2019) s C, para V <https://reachingcriticalwill.org/images/documents/Disarmament-fora/ccw/2019/gge/Documents/GGE.2-Chair-Non-Paper.pdf>; ICRC, 'ICRC Statement. Agenda Item 5(b) – Further Consideration of the Human Element in the Use of Lethal Force; Aspects of Human-Machine Interaction in the Development, Deployment and Use of Emerging Technologies in the Area of Lethal Autonomous Weapon Systems' (n 153).

159 Arkin, *Governing Lethal Behavior in Autonomous Robots* (n 34); Ronald C Arkin, 'The Case for Ethical Autonomy in Unmanned Systems' (2010) 9 *Journal of Military Ethics* 332; Charles J Dunlap Jr., 'Accountability and Autonomous Weapons: Much Ado about Nothing Autonomous Legal Reasoning: Legal and Ethical Issues in the Technologies in Conflict' (2016) 30 *Temple International & Comparative Law Journal* 63; William D Smart, Cindy M Grimm and Woodrow Hartzog, 'An Education Theory of Fault for Autonomous Systems' (2021) 33 *Notre Dame Journal on Emerging Technologies* 35, 36–38; Jenks (n 136) 343.

in situations when flexibility is required from the AWS to adapt to fast-changing circumstances.[160] As *JDP 0–30.2* clarifies, 'predictability is likely to be inversely proportional to mission and environment complexity';[161] therefore, an adaptive system will necessarily be *unpredictable* for two sets of reasons. First, the system is called upon to adapt to unknown circumstances in the battlefield and, second, AWS will depend on highly complex and sophisticated algorithms, with several programs running at the same time ('algorithm soup') and the complexity of the battlefield can sometimes be more than the available systems can handle.[162]

Charles Dunlap argues that an AWS acting in an unforeseeable way is 'obviously wrong because deploying a weapon that is expected to launch attacks "unforeseeably" is itself punishable and a breach of the responsibilities of commanders, operators, and the nations they represent'.[163] However relevant this consideration might be, it is important not to confuse what is proper to *reliable* systems and what is proper to *predictable* systems.[164]

The system is considered *reliable* when it is trustworthy, performing consistently within the rules with which it was programmed. In short, a reliable system is a controlled and closed-in system that will function as intended, that is, without failures or unintended effects.[165] Looking at the present models of defensive systems deployed by states (Samsung Sentris, Iron Dume, AEGIS and the Brimstone Missile, among others), it is easy to conclude that what is missing is the characteristic of 'generality': the algorithms are deliberately designed to work in a single, restricted domain, identifying a specific type of target, not necessarily directly related to the circumstances on the battlefield. For example, none of these systems, once activated, is able to distinguish the

160 Paul Scharre, 'A Security Perspective: Security Concerns and Possible Arms Control Approaches' *UNODA Occasional Papers* (United Nations, 2017).

161 UK Ministry of Defence, 'Joint Doctrine Publication 0–30.2 Unmanned Aircraft Systems' (n 7) 2.

162 Danks (n 117); ICRC, 'ICRC Statement. Agenda Item 5(b) – Further Consideration of the Human Element in the Use of Lethal Force; Aspects of Human-Machine Interaction in the Development, Deployment and Use of Emerging Technologies in the Area of Lethal Autonomous Weapon Systems' (n 153).

163 Dunlap Jr. (n 159) 71.

164 ICRC, 'ICRC Statement. Agenda Item 5(b) – Further Consideration of the Human Element in the Use of Lethal Force, Aspects of Human Machine Interaction in the Development, Deployment and Use of Emerging Technologies in the Area of Lethal Autonomous Weapon Systems' (n 153); Vincent C Muller, 'Autonomous Killer Robots Are Probably Good News' in Ezio Di Nucci and Filippo Santoni De Sio (eds), *Drones and Responsibility: Legal, Philosophical and Socio-Technical Perspectives on the Use of Remotely Controlled Weapons* (Routledge 2016) 68.

165 Neil Davison, 'A Legal Perspective: Autonomous Weapon Systems under International Humanitarian Law' *UNODA Occasional Papers* (United Nations, 2017).

presence of civilians. Unlawful outcomes can be caused by malfunctions or accidents.[166]

This scenario necessarily changes when more complex algorithms (neural networks) operate based on probabilities and in contexts that are unforeseeable in all their extension.[167] Thus, predictability can be compromised, and it cannot be asked from commanders, as Dunlap suggests, to know more that is reasonable to foresee at the time the *algorithm for the mission* is programmed.[168] It is true that new technology of warfare will be routinely tested according to different possible scenarios of warfare, but the openness of the algorithms prevents us from saying that '*semantic and syntactic errors*' will not occur.[169]

The unconventional nature of modern armed conflicts makes it almost impossible to accurately translate every possible situation into software. Interpretation of the workings of warfare is dependent on human background knowledge that is not only technical but also cultural and subjective. There is, therefore, the risk of *semantic error* every time a situation turns out to be not as predicted or is inadequately translated into software.[170] The other cause of unpredictability is a natural consequence of the first: '*syntactic errors*'. These errors are the result of the failure or incapacity of the system to correctly identify properties of the physical world. A perfect example is furnished by the Tesla autopilot crash on 7 May 2016, when J. Brown's tragic death was caused, in part, because one of the sensors read a truck as a cloud.[171]

Following the aforementioned discussion, it is impossible to follow Tim McFarland's argument that AWS 'are not fundamentally distinct from simpler types of automated or manually operated weapon systems'.[172] In fact, the same author recognises that 'the ability to predict how an AWS will behave in a given situation is limited by complexity arising from various sources, and

166 cf Chapter 5, Section 5.3.2.2.

167 Bostrom and Yudkowsky (n 118) 318.

168 Smart, Grimm and Hartzog (n 159) 14–15, 25; Dunlap Jr. (n 159) 69–70.

169 ICRC, 'ICRC Statement. Agenda Item 5(b) – Further Consideration of the Human Element in the Use of Lethal Force; Aspects of Human-Machine Interaction in the Development, Deployment and Use of Emerging Technologies in the Area of Lethal Autonomous Weapon Systems' (n 153).

170 Smart, Grimm and Hartzog (n 159) 17–21.

171 Jack Stewart, 'Tesla Car That Crashed and Killed Driver Was Running on Autopilot, Firm Says' (*WIRED*, 30 March 2018) <www.wired.com/story/tesla-autopilot-self-driving-crash-california/>; Danny Yadron and Dan Tynan, 'Tesla Driver Dies in First Fatal Crash While Using Autopilot Mode' *The Guardian* (Brussels, 1 July 2016) <www.theguardian.com/technology/2016/jun/30/tesla-autopilot-death-self-driving-car-elon-musk>.

172 McFarland, *Autonomous Weapon Systems and the Law of Armed Conflict: Compatibility with International Humanitarian Law* (n 46) 40.

that is that is almost impossible to avoid software errors'.[173] Furthermore, McFarland introduces the concept of brittleness – referring to the commonly encountered problem of systems failing when faced with challenges for which they were not designed – which is particularly relevant 'where flexibility and adaptability are expected or required' from weapon systems.[174]

The aforementioned does not exclude that 'unit tests' can be performed by engineers to prevent the occurrence of errors (semantic and syntactic), but it will become harder to provide guarantees of predictability when it comes to AWS.[175] It may become impossible to establish a link of direct causation between the programming level and the outcome, because the best that can be said is that a military *mission is probable* (Bayesian rule) and that it is possible to predict a lawful outcome from the deployment of an AWS.[176]

1.4 CLARIFYING TERMINOLOGY: ROBOTS, AWS, LAWS, LARS AND FULLY AUTONOMOUS WEAPON SYSTEMS

One of the terms often used when referring to an AWS is, as noted earlier, '*robot*'. This term seems to be quite an obvious one, but there is still a lack of consensus among roboticists on how they define the object that is the main focus of their own profession.[177] In general terms robots were thought of as physical, 'telechiric' machines, since they would be able to perform some human tasks but only in compliance with a deterministic algorithm. However, as Riza points out, current industrial robots do not illustrate what modern engineers mean when they talk of robots. The incorporation of AI has the potential, more specifically through embedded supervised learning algorithms, to enable weapons systems to access a vast amount of data and to identify and to *select*

173 ibid 60.
174 ibid 63.
175 ibid 62–64; Chengeta, 'Are Autonomous Weapon Systems the Subject of Article 36 of Additional Protocol I to the Geneva Conventions?' (n 26) 87.
176 Ludovic Righetti, 'Emerging Technology and Future Autonomous Weapons' (ICRC Expert Meeting – Autonomous Weapon Systems. Implications of Increasing Autonomy in the Critical Functions of Weapons, Versoix, Switzerland, 15 March 2016); Smart, Grimm and Hartzog (n 159).
177 George A Bekey, 'Current Trends in Robotics' in Patrick Lin, Keith Abney and George A Bekey (eds), *Robot Ethics: The Ethical and Social Implications of Robotics* (MIT Press 2012) 17. The word itself comes from a Czech play entitled *R.U.R.* (Rossum's Universal Robots), by Karel Capek. In the play, the 'robots' are artificial humans who work as slaves in a factory. The term 'roboticist' instead was coined by I. Asimov in 1948. cf Richards and Smart (n 2) 5; Lemley and Casey (n 2) 8–9.

a course of action and *act* within its environment.[178] These are the capabilities that qualify a system as 'autonomous'; however, it is hard to predefine or pre-establish what AWS will look like.[179] Thus, the term chosen for the purposes of this work – *Autonomous Weapons System(s)* – illustrates precisely the capacity of a system to carry out, independent of a physical presence on the battlefield, a *technical* autonomous decision-making process.

In the discussions between state representatives at the 1980 United Nations Convention on Certain Conventional Weapons (hereinafter CCW) held in Geneva in 2013, the term chosen was LAWS (*Lethal Autonomous Weapons Systems*) or LARS (*Lethal Autonomous Robots*). However, these terms are understood in completely different ways; for example China, Sweden and the United Kingdom understand LAWS to be *fully* AWS. On the other hand, France and the United States believe that LAWS stands for weapon systems that have certain autonomous functions, because it is impossible to think of a system completely without human intervention.[180]

Chapter 3, will explore the meaning of 'autonomy', and examine the ontological problems raised by some of the terminologies used. For now, it is important to bear in mind that AWS will *act* on the battlefield, using supervised learning algorithms based upon a 'ground truth' that is given to the system. It will depend on a *mission* assigned by human operators and designed to operate in compliance with the rules of engagement for a specific conflict within the constraints of IHL.

What are known as '*fully autonomous weapon systems*', however, will not depend on designed machine learning algorithms but onHBI. Those systems will have the capacity to produce outcomes based on reasons that will be responsive to the internal states – desires, beliefs and values – of the system

178 M Shane Riza, *Killing without Heart: Limits on Robotic Warfare in an Age of Persistent Conflict* (Potomac Books 2013) 15–17.

179 Bekey (n 177).

180 China, 'Group of Governmental Experts of the High Contracting Parties to the Convention on Prohibitions or Restrictions on the Use of Certain Conventional Weapons Which May Be Deemed to Be Excessively Injurious or to Have Indiscriminate Effects. Position Paper Submitted by China' (*Reaching Critical Will*, 2018) CCW/GGE.1/2018/WP.7 <https://reachingcriticalwill.org/images/documents/Disarmament-fora/ccw/2018/gge/documents/GGE.1-WP7.pdf >; France, '2016 France Statement at Convention on Certain Conventional Weapons. Elements d'Intervention – Debat General' (*Reaching Critical Will*, 2016) <www.reachingcriticalwill.org/images/documents/Disarmament-fora/ccw/2016/meeting-experts-laws/statements/11April_France.pdf>; United States of America, '2017 United States of America Working Paper "Characteristics of Lethal Autonomous Weapons Systems"' (*Reaching Critical Will*, 10 November 2017) <www.reachingcriticalwill.org/images/documents/Disarmament-fora/ccw/2017/gge/documents/WP7.pdf>.

itself.[181] These systems are termed by roboticists *teleological* systems. Their capabilities have justified claims to 'self-awareness' (e.g. *UK JDN 2/11*), whilst some authors draw a direct analogy with human soldiers.[182]

The opportunity afforded by these arguments will be thoroughly explored throughout this work, but what is important to retain for now is that the eventual development of deliberative artificial agents still lies a long way in the future, as is acknowledged even by their most fiercely enthusiastic advocates. The challenges that such systems might present to IHL, therefore, go well beyond the scope of this thesis. Rather, we will focus on the current challenges posed by AWS.

1.5 CONCLUSION

In Chapter 1, we have reviewed and analysed the concept of AWS as the 'third revolution of military affairs', which has gripped the attention of the international community over the past few years. If there is one certain conclusion to be taken from this chapter, it is that the whole concept of AWS is surrounded by confusion – confusion concerning the terms used to designate autonomous systems of war, confusion about what is expected from these systems and, above all, confusion regarding the notion of 'autonomy'.

The topic is surrounded by a fog of sci-fi literature heralding the advent of new autonomous agents on the battlefield. Up until now this possibility has belonged in the theatre of speculation. The question of what *fully autonomous weapon systems* might actually be is not, however, our concern here; this work will focus exclusively on the probable future of AWS. Fully autonomous systems are dependent on the evolution and maturing process of HBI, which at the time of writing is still making its first steps.

As stated at the beginning of this chapter, the aim was to provide a concise explanation of the development of AI, namely 'autonomous intelligence', and how AWS become a technical possibility. Machine learning algorithms (neural networks) have the potential to facilitate a better and more thorough 'perception' of the reality of the battlefield for those in charge of military operations. In this regard, it is crucially important to understand that the

181 Sparrow, 'Killer Robots' (n 55) 65.

182 ibid; UK Ministry of Defence, 'The UK Approach to Unmanned Aircraft Vehicles, JDN 2/11' (n 8); Rebecca Crootof, 'Weapon, Combatant, Child, Animal: They're All Insufficient Analogies for Autonomous Weapon Systems' (*Just Security*, 6 September 2016) <www.justsecurity.org/32748/weapon-combatant-child-animal-inappropriate-analogies-autonomous-weapon-systems/> Rebecca Crootof, 'Autonomous Weapon Systems and the Limits of Analogy' (2018) 9 *Harvard National Security Journal* 51.

algorithm for the mission will encapsulate the *mission* entrusted to an AWS. In order to explain the different levels in which a system can be considered to be autonomous is important to distinguish the *algorithm for situation assessment*, *selection algorithm* and the *algorithm for situation management*. Looking at the possibility of swarm technology, each of the algorithms mentioned can be inbuilt in different systems that operate together in network.

AWS can also introduce several advantages on the battlefield. In continuity with the history of technology of warfare, AWS will be able to keep soldiers, physically and emotionally, invulnerable to the hardships of war. At the same time, if these systems are to be more precise, they can promote humanitarian values.

Systems like these seem to put the traditional instrumentalist paradigm, as idealised by Clark, at risk. AWS slowly evolve from being instruments to acquiring some level of 'functional autonomy' on the battlefield, assessing conditions and selecting the best course of action most likely to optimise a pre-given mission, progressively challenging the paradigm of the *man-in-the-loop*.

The efficiency that AWS can introduce to the battlefield does not come, however, without its downsides. The fact that neural networks will be open to the changing features of the battlespace in itself makes these systems unpredictable, in the sense that it is impossible to guarantee what the outcome of a given course of action will be. Because AWS will operate without human intervention, it is possible to envisage a situation in which there is no human causal link. In this case, a legal classification such as 'individual liability', currently standing as the cornerstone of IHL, can find itself abruptly challenged. The problem is exacerbated because the *algorithm for the mission* will operate within a 'black box', and there will be no opportunity to observe its workings, observe how the 'decision-making' process is made or ascertain, after the event, *how* the system operated.[183]

[183] ICRC, 'ICRC Statement. Agenda Item 5(b) – Further Consideration of the Human Element in the Use of Lethal Force; Aspects of Human-Machine Interaction in the Development, Deployment and Use of Emerging Technologies in the Area of Lethal Autonomous Weapon Systems' (n 153).

2

AWS

The Current State of the AWS Debate and of State Policy

The purpose of this chapter is to examine how the advent of AWS has been addressed by the international community and to explain different state policies towards this new technology of warfare. As will be shown, the topic is surrounded by multiple opposing definitions, contradictory considerations and arguments that might well lead the most committed reader into despair. Thus, the aim of this chapter is to provide the necessary clarity of discourse, pointing out, at the same time, the vital importance of analysing, before any other question, a definition of AWS. Without a clear understanding of what an AWS means, any debate about its pros and cons will most certainly be fruitless.

2.1 THE CURRENT STATE OF THE INTERNATIONAL DEBATE

During the last twenty years, questions surrounding AI and its implications for society have been hotly debated. However, it was not until 2007 that Noel Sharkey, emeritus professor of artificial intelligence at the University of Sheffield, called attention to the possible introduction of AWS onto the battlefield. In an article published in *The Guardian*, the author pointed out the dangers of 'fully autonomous robots'. According to Sharkey, the deployment of robots in the Iraq war was the first step towards a dangerous new precedent involving the deployment of '*robots able to decide who, where and when to kill*' on the battlefield.[184] The international debate ignited immediately following the release of the report 'Losing Humanity: The Case against Killer Robots', co-authored by Harvard's International Human Rights Clinic and Human Rights Watch.[185] Following this line of thought, a global coalition

[184] Sharkey, 'Robot Wars Are a Reality' (n 30) (our emphasis). See Chesterman (n 4) 230–231.

[185] Human Rights Watch and International Human Rights Clinic, 'Losing Humanity: The Case against Killer Robots' (n 30); Alan L Schuller, 'At the Crossroads of Control: The Intersection

of NGOs, individuals[186] and states has, since 2013, supported the call for a *pre-emptive ban* on 'fully autonomous weapon systems', and this has met with widespread acceptance.[187] In March 2018, the UN Secretary-General voiced the pre-emptive ban by stating 'imagine the consequences of an autonomous

of Artificial Intelligence in Autonomous Weapons Systems with International Humanitarian Law' (2017) 8 *Harvard National Security Journal* 379, 382.

186 In June 2018, thousands of Google's employees signed a petition urging the company to cease involvement in Project Maven – a contract with the United States Department of Defense (DoD) to develop artificial intelligence for analysing drone footage. Google subsequently announced its decision not to renew its contract for Project Maven and vowed not to 'design or deploy AI . . . [for] technologies that cause or are likely to cause overall harm'. In July 2018, over 200 organisations and 3,000 individuals (including Elon Musk, Google DeepMind's founders and CEOs of various robotics companies) followed suit, pledging to 'neither participate in nor support the development, manufacture, trade, or use of lethal autonomous weapons'. In light of these events, the DoD tasked the Defense Innovation Board with developing ethical principles to guide the DoD's use of AI in military weapons and operations. Hayley Evans and Natalie Salmanowitz, 'Lethal Autonomous Weapons Systems: Recent Developments' (*Lawfare*, 7 March 2019) <www.lawfareblog.com/lethal-autonomous-weapons-systems-recent-developments>.

187 By Algeria, Argentina, Bolivia, Brazil, Chile, Costa Rica, Cuba, Ecuador, Egypt, Ghana, Guatemala, the Holy See, Iraq, Mexico, Nicaragua, Pakistan, the State of Palestine, Panama, Peru, Uganda, Venezuela and Zimbabwe. cf Human Rights Watch, 'Support Grows for New International Law on Killer Robots' (*Stop Killer Robots*, 17 November 2017) <www.stopkillerrobots.org/2017/11/gge/>. More recently Austria has also called for a ban. cf Austria, 'General Exchange of Views Statement Austria. Group of Governmental Experts on Lethal Autonomous Weapon Systems Geneva, 9–13 April 2018' (*Reaching Critical Will*, April 2018) <https://reachingcriticalwill.org/images/documents/Disarmament-fora/ccw/2018/gge/statements/9April_Austria.pdf>. As far as the European Union is concerned, the European Parliament adopted a resolution by a vote of 534/49 calling for a ban on the 'development, production and use of fully autonomous weapons which enable strikes to be carried out without human intervention'. On killer robots, the resolution calls on the European Union (EU) member states, the Council of Ministers of the EU and the EU's High Representative for Foreign Affairs and Security Policy, Baroness Catherine Ashton, to 'ban the development, production and use of fully autonomous weapons which enable strikes to be carried out without human intervention' (2.(d)). cf European Parliament, 'European Parliament Resolution of 27 February 2014 on the Use of Armed Drones' (2014) <www.europarl.europa.eu/sides/getDoc.do?pubRef=-//EP//NONSGML+TA+P7-TA-2014–0172+0+DOC+PDF+V0//EN>. In February 2014, Dutch NGO PAX (formerly IKV Pax Christi) issued a new report listing eight objections to fully autonomous weapons. PAX, 'Deadly Decisions: 8 Objections to Killer Robots' (PAX International 2014) <www.paxforpeace.nl/stay-informed/news/stop-killer-robots-while-we-still-can>. In August 2017, more than 100 of the world's leading robotics and AI pioneers, in an open letter to the international community, called on the UN to ban the development and use of killer robots. cf Future of Life, 'Autonomous Weapons: An Open Letter from AI & Robotics Researchers' (n 127). For more details regarding institutions, scholars and roboticists supporting a ban on AWS, cf Dr Stephen Goose and Mary Wareham, 'The Growing International Movement against Killer Robots' (*Human Rights Watch*, 2017) <www.hrw.org/news/2017/01/05/growing-international-movement-against-killer-robots>; Campaign to Stop KILLER ROBOTS, 'Country Views on Killer Robots' (n 63).

system that could, by itself, target and attack human beings. I call upon states to ban these weapons, which are politically unacceptable and morally repugnant.'[188]

In light of discussions held among different groups and of the uncertainty surrounding the physical realisation of AWS, the UN Special Rapporteur on extrajudicial, summary or arbitrary executions for the Office of the High Commissioner for Human Rights, Professor Christof Heyns (hereafter Special Rapporteur C. Heyns), presented, in May 2013, a report to the Human Rights Council. This report questioned whether the deployment of AWS would be legitimate or not according to IHL rules, calling 'on all States to declare and implement national moratoria on at least the testing, production, [. . .] deployment and use of LARS until such time as an internationally agreed upon framework on the future of LARS has been established'.[189]

In 2013, an international agreement was reached that the 1980 United Nations Convention on Certain Conventional Weapons (CCW) – which regulates weapons that may be deemed to have an excessively injurious or indiscriminate effect – would be the most appropriate international forum to undertake this role, with its ability to comprehend and regulate the diverse diplomatic, legal, ethical, civil and military interests at stake.[190] Consequently, in May 2014, representatives from eighty states, United Nations agencies, civil society and other international and transnational organisations attended the first Meeting of Experts on Lethal Autonomous Weapons Systems to discuss the possibility of a complete ban on such weaponry.[191]

The CCW State Parties agreed on a lethal autonomous weapons systems (LAWS) mandate in 2013 and held Experts' Meetings to discuss LAWS in 2014, 2015 and 2016 with the aim of drafting 'Protocol VI' for presentation to the

188 Axel Bugge, 'U.N.'s Guterres Urges Ban on Autonomous Weapons' (*Reuters World News*, 5 November 2018); Evans and Salmanowitz (n 186); Chesterman (n 4) 234.

189 Heyns, 'Report of the Special Rapporteur on Extrajudicial, Summary or Arbitrary Executions, Christof Heyns' (n 10) para 113.

190 'Convention on Prohibitions or Restrictions on the Use of Certain Conventional Weapons Which May Be Deemed to Be Excessively Injurious or to Have Indiscriminate Effects' (1980) <www.un.org/disarmament/the-convention-on-certain-conventional-weapons/>.

191 All CCW State Parties meet annually at a *Meeting of the States parties* (or at a review conference – every five years) to review the status and operation of the Convention and its protocols (I – Non Detectable Fragments; II – Mines, Booby Traps and Other Devices; III – Incendiary Weapons; IV – Blinding Laser Weapons; and V – Explosive Remnants of War) and to consider the work done by the *Group of Governmental Experts* (GGE) which was established in 2001. The States parties might also decide on the mandate of the GGE and its meetings of military and technical experts, which may be to negotiate a new protocol or to study a specific problem or weapon, as well as on the number of sessions per year it may need to fulfil its mandate.

Convention.[192] The Experts' Meeting held in 2016 produced a non-binding recommendation to the CCW Fifth Review that an open-ended group of governmental experts should be formally established. The 2016 Fifth Review Conference, in agreement, decided to form the Group of Governmental Experts (hereinafter GGE) on LAWS. The first session took place in August and the second in November 2017. The GGE, chaired by Ambassador Amandeep Singh Gill of India, met again in August 2018. In the 2018 GGE Final Report, the recommendation was made that 'the group of Governmental Experts [...] shall meet for a duration of ten days in 2019 in Geneva in accordance with Decision 1 of the Fifth Review Conference of the High Contracting Parties to the Convention'.[193] The first meeting took place from 25 to 29 March 2019 and the second meeting took place in August 2019.[194]

At the 2018 GGE meeting, the Republic of Korea pointed out that 'the active exchange of views in the last informal meetings not only helped us understand the complexity of the issue and identify critical subjects *but also reminded us how much we diverge on this complicated and ever evolving issue*'.[195] Although some progress was made in the discussion as far as it related to AWS, the matter is still surrounded by the very challenging contentions that have been put forward by all parties involved. As a step forward, all states' representatives agreed that IHL should be applied at every stage of the study, development and deployment of AWS.[196]

A number of states (among them China, the European Union, the Russian Federation, Sri Lanka, Sweden, Switzerland and the United Kingdom), however, insist that there is still no clearly defined classification of AWS. The United States, on the other hand, maintains that a lack of clarity over the classification of AWS need not prevent further discussion.[197] Whereas some

192 Marco Sassoli, 'Autonomous Weapons and International Humanitarian Law: Advantages, Open Technical Questions and Legal Issues to Be Clarified' (2014) 90 *International Legal Studies* 308, 309.

193 'Report of the 2018 Session of the Group of Governmental Experts on Emerging Technologies in the Area of Lethal Autonomous Weapons Systems' (*Reaching Critical Will*, 2018) CCW/GGE.1/2018/3 7, para 32 <https://reachingcriticalwill.org/images/documents/Disarmament-fora/ccw/2018/gge/documents/final-report.pdf>.

194 UNOG – The United Nations Office in Geneva, 'Background on LAWS in the CCW' <www.un.org/disarmament/the-convention-on-certain-conventional-weapons/background-on-laws-in-the-ccw/>.

195 Republic of Korea, 'Group of Governmental Experts on Lethal Autonomous Weapons Systems. Statement by H. E. Ambassador Inchul KIM' (9 April 2018) (emphasis not in original) <https://docs-library.unoda.org/Convention_on_Certain_Conventional_Weapons_-_Group_of_Governmental_Experts_(2018)/2018_LAWSGeneralExchange_RoK.pdf>.

196 Evans and Salmanowitz (n 186).

197 Michael W Meier, '2016 CCW Informal Meeting of Experts on Lethal Autonomous Weapon Systems. U.S.A. Delegation Opening Statement' (2016) <https://geneva.usmission.gov/2016/04/11/laws/>.

states (France, Germany[198] and Switzerland[199]) argue that a non-binding political declaration to validate a common understanding should be put in place as a possible immediate solution, others, the Non-Aligned Movement[200] and Pakistan, for example, insist that such a declaration 'can only be an interim step toward a legally binding instrument'.[201] At the other extreme, Estonia considers unnecessary any binding declaration since IHL is a 'robust and dynamic regulatory regime [and] it is capable of dealing with a range of emerging or new technologies'.[202]

In light of the previous discussion it is possible to put the differing parties into distinct groups. First, an increasing number of states, NGOs and individuals believe there is a need for an *emergency brake*;[203] for this group, the only possible solution is a pre-emptive ban. The reasons diverge among the different protagonists of a ban but AWS are considered to be unpredictable or incompatible with IHL compliance (raising the spectre of an accountability vacuum), or simply unethical because their operation will be beyond human control.

Most states, however, have declared that they are not yet prepared to discuss a ban as they are still in the process of working out what repercussions the deployment of AWS might have, and, until this is known, are not willing to

198 'H. E. Ambassador Michael Biontino Permanent Representative of Germany to the Conference on Disarmament and Ambassador for Global Disarmament Affairs' (*Reaching Critical Will*, November 2017) <www.reachingcriticalwill.org/images/documents/Disarmament-fora/ccw/2017/gge/statements/13Nov_Germany.pdf>.

199 '2017 Switzerland. Statement S. E. Mme Sabrina Dallafior Représentante Permanent de La Suisse Auprès de La Conférence Du Désarmement' (*Reaching Critical Will*, 13 November 2017) <https://reachingcriticalwill.org/images/documents/Disarmament-fora/ccw/2017/gge/statements/13Nov_Switzerland.pdf>.

200 The Non-Aligned Movement, 'Group of Governmental Experts of the High Contracting Parties to the Convention on Prohibitions or Restrictions on the Use of Certain Conventional Weapons Which May Be Deemed to Be Excessively Injurious or to Have Indiscriminate Effects' (*Reaching Critical Will*, 2018) CCW/GGE.1/2018/WP.1 <https://reachingcriticalwill.org/images/documents/Disarmament-fora/ccw/2017/gge/documents/WP10.pdf>.

201 Pakistan, '2018 Pakistan Statement at Group of Governmental Experts of the High Contracting Parties to the Convention on Prohibitions or Restrictions on the Use of Certain Conventional Weapons Which May Be Deemed to Be Excessively Injurious or to Have Indiscriminate Effects' (*Reaching Critical Will*, 2018) <https://reachingcriticalwill.org/images/documents/Disarmament-fora/ccw/2018/gge/statements/9April_Pakistan.pdf>.

202 Estonia, '2018 Estonia Statement at Group of Governmental Experts on Emerging Technologies in the Area of Lethal Autonomous Weapons Systems' (*Reaching Critical Will*, 2018) <https://reachingcriticalwill.org/images/documents/Disarmament-fora/ccw/2018/gge/statements/10April_Estonia.pdf>.

203 Gabi Siboni and Yoni Eshpar, 'Dilemmas in the Use of Autonomous Weapons' (2014) 16 *The Institute for National Security Studies – Strategic Assessment* 75, 89. Opting instead for the term 'Global Ban Approach', see Zalac and Bober (n 28) 208.

take up a final stand.[204] The majority of states (Brazil, Ireland and Portugal among them) are settling for a position of '*wait and see*'.[205] AWS, in any case, are considered to be a phenomenon of the future, and the fact is that any attempt to regulate them would be so speculative that it might well lead to more harm than good. In fact, it could even be argued that, if technology is indeed able to provide systems that can identify military targets more quickly and accurately than humans while at the same time respecting the imperatives of IHL, there could be no sensible justification for such a ban.[206] At the other extreme, we find those states (among them Estonia, India, the Netherlands, the Russian Federation, the United Kingdom and the United States) that recognise the *legitimacy* and have indicated their acceptance of AWS.[207]

However straightforward this may sound, it can be a struggle to come to grips with all the different perceptions of AWS – even among their supporters. Apart from the different concepts of AI held by different states, none of the statements they have put forward about AWS and LAWS agree.[208] In order to grasp some of the contrasting points of view, the next three sections will look, first, at the arguments developed by those who advocate the introduction of an 'emergency brake'; second, at the different positions and definitions adopted by states in support of the further development of autonomous systems; and, finally, a new definition of AWS will be proposed that, it is hoped, will render further discussion about this new technology of warfare more fruitful.

2.2 THE NON-ADMISSIBILITY ARGUMENTS

In the previous sections, there was opportunity to make reference to some of the concerns regarding the possible deployment of AWS on the battlefield.

204 Boulanin and Verbruggen, 'Mapping the Development of Autonomy in Weapon Systems' (n 9) 1–3.

205 Siboni and Eshpar (n 203) 83; Brazil, 'Group of Governmental Experts of the High Contracting Parties to the Convention on Prohibitions or Restrictions on the Use of Certain Conventional Weapons Which May Be Deemed to Be Excessively Injurious or to Have Indiscriminate Effects' (*Reaching Critical Will*, 2018) <https://reachingcriticalwill.org/images/documents/Disarmament-fora/ccw/2018/hcp-meeting/statements/21Nov_Brazil5.pdfireka>; Ireland, 'Group of Governmental Experts Lethal Autonomous Weapons Systems Convention on Certain Conventional Weapons Geneva' (*Reaching Critical Will*, 2018) <https://reachingcriticalwill.org/images/documents/Disarmament-fora/ccw/2018/hcp-meeting/statements/21Nov_Ireland.pdf>. Some authors call this position 'Enforced Restrictions Approach', Zalac and Bober (n 28) 210.

206 Coker, *Future Wars* (n 68) 13.

207 This position is also known as 'Laissez Faire Approach', Zalac and Bober (n 28) 206.

208 Corinne Cath and others, 'Artificial Intelligence and the "Good Society": The US, EU, and the UK Approach' (2017) 24 *Science and Engineering Ethics* 505.

The most compelling of these have come from the pro-ban advocates and have, for the purposes of discussion, been dubbed as the 'non-admissibility arguments'. The aim of this section is just to introduce those arguments, alongside the difficulties they might expect to encounter. The non-admissibility arguments fall into two main categories: the first is endorsed by legal arguments, and the second is supported by considerations relating to the *ethos* and morality of war.

A prohibition on AWS would not be a novelty in terms of war technology. Up until now, six types of weaponry have been internationally banned: poison gas, biological weapons, chemical weapons, blinding lasers, antipersonnel landmines and cluster munitions.[209] However, it has to be said, only 'blinding lasers' were the object of pre-emptive ban.[210] In the belief that AWS will never comply with the principles of IHL (distinction, proportionality and precaution), HRW's campaign presses for a total international prohibition rather than any other kind of regulation. It is important, however, to note that the 2012 report produced by HRW and the Harvard International Human Rights Clinic (hereinafter IHRC) does not aim to ban all autonomous technology. Its purpose is to call for a ban on those systems of warfare in which the human operator would be out-of-the-loop or on-the-loop, with limited potential for oversight or veto.[211]

Another matter of concern is the 'accountability vacuum' that it has been suggested as consequent upon the use of AWS and, finally, that AWS could become the perfect tool of repression for 'autocrats seeking to strengthen or retain power' and also for non-state actors and armed groups who 'do not care about regulations and could turn off programming designed to regulate a robot's behaviour'.[212] These concerns were shared by the majority of the

209 Goose and Wareham (n 187).

210 In October 1995, the Protocol on Blinding Laser Weapons was adopted by the Review Conference of the Parties to the CCW. The Protocol prohibits weapons 'specifically designed, as their sole combat function or as one of their combat functions, to cause permanent blindness to unenhanced vision' (Article 1, Protocol IV to the CCW). Burrus M Carnahan and Marjorie Robertson, 'The Protocol On "Blinding Laser Weapons": A New Direction for International Humanitarian Law' (1996) 90 *American Journal of International Law (Unbound)* 484, 485–488; Yorum Dinstein, *The Conduct of Hostilities under the Law of International Armed Conflict* (5th edn, Cambridge University Press 2007) 72–73; William Boothby, *Weapons and the Law of Armed Conflict* (Oxford University Press 2016) 202; William Boothby, *Conflict Law: The Influence of New Weapons Technology, Human Rights and Emerging Actors* (Springer 2014) 5 (footnote 5).

211 Human Rights Watch and International Human Rights Clinic, 'Fully Autonomous Weapons: Questions and Answers' (2013) 9–10 <www.hrw.org/sites/default/files/supporting_resources/10.2013_killer_robots_qa.pdf>.

212 ibid 7. For the specific questions of the access of non-state actors to AWS, see Sasha Radin and Jason Coats, 'Autonomous Weapon Systems and the Threshold of Non-International Armed Conflict' (2016) 117 *Temple International & Comparative Law Journal* 133, 137–150.

states present at the 2017, 2018 and 2019 GGE meetings, but, for most of them, those concerns are not reason enough for a ban; they are, however, the reason for further consideration. For now, the aim of proceeding sections is not to examine each issue exhaustively, since they will be addressed in later chapters, but just to present them in order to give a complete picture of the arguments.

2.2.1 *The Problem of Qualitative Legal Assessments on the Battlefield: The Rules of Precaution, the Principles of Distinction and Proportionality*

The rules of precaution and the IHL principles of distinction and proportionality are of crucial importance in the context of armed conflicts. According to many authorities, compliance with these principles will always involve an element of human judgement that cannot be translated into an algorithm, even of the most sophisticated type.[213]

Questions about the requirements of precaution, distinction and proportionality will be further developed in Chapter 4. For now, it is important to remember that the rules of precaution, as enshrined in Article 57 API, require complex subjective analysis of a situation, an assessment of the means and methods of combat required and an assurance that all 'feasible precautions' are taken. To be able to assess the value of military necessity and the concrete and direct advantage of any course of action, a judgement – currently entrusted to those who plan and decide an attack – requires the 'context-dependent, value-based judgment of a commander'.[214] AWS will not be moral agents, capable of critical reflection, and they will not, therefore, be able to comply with the Rules of Precaution.

According to the principle of distinction, as enshrined in Article 48 API, 'the parties to the conflict shall at all times distinguish between the civilian population and combatants and between civilian objects and military objectives and accordingly shall direct their operations only against military objects'. An AWS's inability to comprehend context would render it incapable of distinguishing a combatant from anyone else on the battlefield, and it would have equal difficulty in recognising when someone was wounded and hors de combat or when soldiers were in the process of surrendering.[215] Such a subtle

[213] Heyns, 'Report of the Special Rapporteur on Extrajudicial, Summary or Arbitrary Executions, Christof Heyns' (n 10) para 72; Human Rights Watch and International Human Rights Clinic, 'Losing Humanity: The Case against Killer Robots' (n 30) 4; Cullen (n 22) 124.

[214] Human Rights Watch and International Human Rights Clinic, 'Losing Humanity: The Case against Killer Robots' (n 30) 34.

[215] ibid 30.

level of discrimination would demand much more sophisticated sensory and processing capabilities than those with which AWS are equipped at present.[216]

The principle of distinction also requires that civilian objects be distinguished from military objects. For example, an AWS is called upon to distinguish between objects of military significance and those of a civilian nature that do not 'offer a definite military advantage' (Article 52(2) API). The principle of distinction also applies to those objects that are considered to be 'indispensable to the survival of the civilian population' (Article 54 API), those that form part of the natural environment (Article 55 API) and those 'installations containing dangerous forces' (Article 56 API).[217]

The principle of proportionality prohibits the launching of attacks where the incidental injury to civilians and collateral damage to civilian objects would be considered *excessive* in relation to the concrete and direct military advantage anticipated (Articles 51 (5)(b) and 57(2)(iii) API).[218] Proportionality is believed to be highly contextual and, therefore, requires a fairly wide margin of appreciation. Even if algorithms can (in theory) estimate the potential collateral damage balance, by means, for example, of collateral damage estimate methodology (CDEM), it is still difficult to envisage a design into which the parameters of every unforeseeable situation are programmed. It is even more difficult to imagine that any algorithm will, one day, be able to master 'human reason'.[219]

2.2.2 *The Problems of Accountability and 'Meaningful Human Control', Critical Functions and Human Intervention*

The problem of accountability has commanded the attention of every scholar, military body, international organisation and, more specifically, the 2015 HRW report 'Mind the Gap. The Lack of Accountability for Killer Robots'.[220]

216 Human Rights Watch, 'Making the Case: The Dangers of Killer Robots and the Need for a Preemptive Ban' (Harvard International Human Rights Clinic 2016) 5 <www.hrw.org/report/2016/12/09/making-case/dangers-killer-robots-and-need-preemptive-ban>.

217 Wagner, 'Taking Humans Out of the Loop: Implications for International Humanitarian Law' (n 85) 6; Noam Lubell, *Extraterritorial Use of Force against Non-State Actors* (Oxford University Press 2011) 135–136; Boothby, *Weapons and the Law of Armed Conflict* (n 210) 65–68.

218 Wagner, 'Taking Humans Out of the Loop: Implications for International Humanitarian Law' (n 85) 7.

219 ibid 9; Human Rights Watch, 'Making the Case: The Dangers of Killer Robots and the Need for a Preemptive Ban' (n 216) 7; Maziar Homayounnejad, 'Ensuring Lethal Autonomous Weapon Systems Comply with International Humanitarian Law' (2017) Paper 85/2017 TLI Think! 1, 14–25.

220 Human Rights Watch and International Human Rights Clinic, 'Mind the Gap: The Lack of Accountability for Killer Robots' (n 61); Cullen (n 22) 124–125.

To envisage AWS in action – whichever concept of them is adopted – will always entail the assumption of an outcome produced without the aid of a human operator's selection process. Leaving aside the case of fully autonomous systems, until today, at least, no more than a theoretical hypothesis, the mission of an AWS is pre-established by a human operator, and the question of legal responsibility for any malfunction or error resulting in a violation of IHL on the battlefield remains to be answered. Reports such as those issued by HRW tend to focus on the potential 'responsibility vacuum' that might result from the deployment of AWS, assuming that personal responsibility could become diluted to the point where unlawful outcomes could not be imputed to the actions of those who deployed the systems.[221]

In spite of the importance of this question of liability, it is difficult to identify which AWS are the object of greatest concern. In the report 'Losing Humanity', HRW defines 'fully autonomous weapons' as 'weapons that could select and engage targets without human intervention'.[222] In a more recent report, HRW defines 'fully autonomous systems' in a different way, namely as those that 'would select and engage targets without *meaningful human control*' (MHC).[223] Although no definition of MHC is given in the report, in the memorandum to the CCW – 'Killer Robots and the Concept of Meaningful Human Control' – MHC 'signifies control over the selection and engagement of target, that is, the "critical functions" of a weapon', adding that 'critical functions' refer to systems that 'would make their own determinations about the use of lethal force'.[224] So, the conclusion is that all systems having the capacity to select and engage targets without human intervention should be banned because without a 'man in charge', any breach of the law becomes a 'faceless crime'.[225] However, if this criterion is applied, AWS would not be the only weapons to be banned but many other already employed by states. Second, the terms used – without human intervention, meaningful human

221 Markus Wagner, 'Beyond the Drone Debate: Autonomy in Tomorrow's Battlespace' (2012) 106 *ASIL Annual Meeting Proceedings* 80, 83; Matthias (n 16) 177.

222 Human Rights Watch and International Human Rights Clinic, 'Losing Humanity: The Case against Killer Robots' (n 30) 1.

223 Human Rights Watch and International Human Rights Clinic, 'Mind the Gap: The Lack of Accountability for Killer Robots' (n 61) 5.

224 Human Rights Watch, 'Killer Robots and the Concept of Meaningful Human Control: Memorandum to Convention on Conventional Weapons (CCW) Delegates' (2016) 1 <www.hrw.org/news/2016/04/11/killer-robots-and-concept-meaningful-human-control>. Sharing the HRW's perspective Chengeta, 'Are Autonomous Weapon Systems the Subject of Article 36 of Additional Protocol I to the Geneva Conventions?' (n 26) 90–91, 99.

225 Heyns, 'Autonomous Weapon Systems: Living a Dignified Life and Dying a Dignified Death' (n 86) 13–14; Chengeta, 'Accountability Gap: Autonomous Weapon Systems and Modes of Responsibility in International Law' (n 20) 4, 34.

control, critical functions – form a slippery slope into vagueness which does nothing to further understanding of the arguments put forward.[226]

As far as automatic defensive systems are concerned – those systems that automatically identify an incoming military threat but have a human operator present who accepts or overrides the action suggested by the system – they are acceptable because 'they seem to present less danger to civilians because they are stationary and defensive weapons that are designed to destroy munitions, not launch offensive attacks'.[227] At the same time, these systems could be seen as problematic if they were to lead to 'an automation bias', that is, if a human operator fails to question the plan of action presented by the system, becoming, in effect, an *automatic operator.*[228] As Gregor Noll argues, AI reconfigures decision-making processes in such a way 'that human study only begins once the system has already made a decision'.[229]

However, malfunctions and accidents may happen with automatic systems, leading to loss of civilian lives: *Iran Flight* 655 and the *Petrov Case* provide perfect examples, among others.[230] In the former, a missile fired unfortunately resulted in the tragic deaths of innocent civilians, whilst in the latter, if it had not been for the presence of a human operator, millions of innocent citizens would have been killed.

Today's technology is so sophisticated and accurate that 'automation bias' has become an inherent risk pertaining to all modern systems of war. Is there any way to avoid this risk? Is a ban the right legal instrument to prevent

226 Deeks, Lubell and Murray (n 25) 16.

227 Human Rights Watch and International Human Rights Clinic, 'Losing Humanity: The Case against Killer Robots' (n 30) 12; See Chesterman (n 4) 230.

228 For the context and problems of 'automation bias' in the context of *Jus ad Bellum*, Deeks, Lubell and Murray (n 25) 17–18.

229 Noll (n 105) 78.

230 The *Iran flight* 655 *Case* refers to an Iranian Flight, in July 1988, which took off from Bandar Abbas Airport towards Dubai when the US-guided missile cruiser Vincennes fired two missiles at the plane. The US Aegis system was not able to monitor civilian radio channels and detected flight 655 as an Iranian Air Force f-14 a military aircraft, killing 290 civilians on board. David Akerson, 'The Illegality of Offensive Lethal Autonomy' in Dan Saxon (ed), *International Humanitarian Law and the Changing Technology of War* (Martinus Nijhoff 2013) 74. The *Petrov Case* refers to a situation that occurred in September 1983, when the Soviet Oko nuclear early-warning system malfunctioned and reported an incoming US missile strike launched from Montana. The system's mistake was correctly identified by the duty officer at the command centre, Deputy Chief for Combat Algorithms Stanislav Petrov, avoiding what could have instigated World War III. Bostrom (n 103) 357 (ch 10, footnote 12). Other examples include Air France Flight 447 in 2009, the 2011 Fukushima Daiichi meltdown, the 2015 AC-130 bombing in Afghanistan, cf Paul Scharre, 'Autonomous Weapons and Operational Risk: Ethical Autonomy Project' (*Center for a New American Security*, 2016) <www.cnas.org/publications/reports/autonomous-weapons-and-operational-risk>.

'automation bias'? It may seem impossible to reverse the progress of technology, and the situation becomes even more complex in view of the fact that Deputy Chief Petrov was given an official reprimand for failing to follow protocol and was duly demoted.[231] The military structure strongly calls into question the likelihood that human operators will intervene according to their own discernment because the level of trust in technology is now so high that it is difficult to envisage humans questioning the outcomes produced by artificial systems.

2.2.3 *State Responsibility*

As was observed, the question of the attribution of responsibility for violations of IHL is absolutely crucial, as a 'responsibility gap' would render any legal system powerless. As McFarland states, 'perceived difficulties in attributing AWS actions to the State, or to individuals, are the basis of the supposed "accountability gap" which is often cited as a factor rendering the use of AWS inherently illegal'.[232] However, it is possible to question the responsibility of any individual only within the limits of his/her own activity and authority.[233] It is precisely this problem that, according to Sparrow, puts AWS in a 'grey area'; it is difficult to envisage how anyone can be held liable for actions which are beyond the limits of his/her authority.[234]

The determination to identify an appropriate source to attribute violations of IHL caused by AWS has been compelling, so much so that many scholars have expended an enormous amount of effort trying to prove that AWS should, from a deontological and consequentialist point of view, be banned altogether.[235] Such ethical considerations, however valid, should not be allowed to blind us to the fact that a whole universe of legal mechanisms is available for use in the case of IHL violations. Among these is state responsibility.

In putting forward arguments advocating a pre-emptive ban on AWS, HRW invokes the concept of a 'responsibility vacuum' from a legal perspective. Its analysis is based exclusively on individual responsibility and argues that

231 Ian Morris, *War, What Is It Good For?* (Profile Books 2014) 5.

232 McFarland, *Autonomous Weapon Systems and the Law of Armed Conflict: Compatibility with International Humanitarian Law* (n 46) 134.

233 Michael Walzer, *Just and Unjust Wars: A Moral Argument with Historical Illustrations* (4th edn, Basic Books 1977) 304.

234 Sparrow, 'Killer Robots' (n 55) 65; Noll (n 105) 94.

235 Sparrow, 'Killer Robots' (n 55) 67; Daniele Amoroso and Guglielmo Tamburrini, 'The Convergence of Deontological and Consequentialist Reasons for Banning Autonomous Weapons Systems' [2016] *Universita degli Studi di Napoli Federico II Open Archive* 1, ss 1, 5.

existing modalities of liability for violations of IHL and ICL are both ineffective and inadequate as regards securing accountability for 'crimes' committed by fully autonomous systems.[236] Regarding these questions, Special Rapporteur C. Heyns pointed out that 'a stronger emphasis on State as opposed to individual responsibility may be called for, except in respect of its use by non-state actors'.[237] Although the HRW report recognises 'state responsibility', it 'focuses on personal accountability, for either natural or legal persons, which punishes the conduct of a specific offender rather than the State'.[238] The *Mind the Gap* report goes on to assert, and rightly so, that 'such accountability is required by international law', but it fails to explain why state responsibility cannot be a suitable legal mechanism to regulate the deployment of AWS.[239]

The question of state responsibility cannot simply be excluded or ignored since states are bound to respect, and to ensure respect for, the customary and conventional rules of IHL. Both Common Article 1 to GC, 1949, and Article 1 of API state that those responsible for ensuring compliance with IHL, in all circumstances, are the 'High Contracting Parties'.[240] The ICC Statute states clearly that individual responsibility shall not affect the 'responsibility of States under international law' (Article 25(4) ICC Statute). Thus, if AWS are designed in such a way as to eliminate human intervention, the responsibility of states for ensuring that AWS comply with IHL standards is clear. In accordance with this reasoning, some states at the 2018 GGE meetings (e.g. the European Union, the Russian Federation and Switzerland) pointed out that states should be held accountable for the development and use of AWS in armed conflicts. As the Russian Federation working paper suggests, the human

236 Human Rights Watch, 'Making the Case: The Dangers of Killer Robots and the Need for a Preemptive Ban' (n 216) 10.

237 Heyns, 'Report of the Special Rapporteur on Extrajudicial, Summary or Arbitrary Executions, Christof Heyns' (n 10) para 81; Human Rights Watch and International Human Rights Clinic, 'Mind the Gap: The Lack of Accountability for Killer Robots' (n 61) 11. As an example of the concern of some states regarding the access of non-state actors, Israel has carried out two strikes in Syria to prevent weapons transfers between Iran and the paramilitary group Hezbollah. David Daoud, 'Israel Carries Out Two Strikes against Assad Regime, Hezbollah Targets in Syria' (*FDD's Long War Journal*, 21 March 2017) <www.longwarjournal.org/archives/2017/03/israel-carries-out-two-strikes-against-assad-regime-hezbollah-targets-in-syria.php?utm_source=feedburner&utm_medium=email&utm_campaign=Feed%3A+LongWarJournalSiteWide+%28FDD%27s+Long+War+Journal+%28Site-Wide%29%29>.

238 Human Rights Watch and International Human Rights Clinic, 'Mind the Gap: The Lack of Accountability for Killer Robots' (n 61) 13.

239 ibid 2.

240 SJ Afonso Seixas-Nunes, 'Autonomous Weapons Systems and the Procedural Accountability Gap' (2021) 46 *Brooklyn Journal of International Law* s 2.1.

operator should be responsible *only* for the decision to use an AWS. It is therefore fair to conclude that the human operator would only be responsible for the unlawful results caused by the decision to use an AWS, excluding individual accountability for unlawful unpredictable outcomes.

2.3 NON-LEGAL ARGUMENTS: IS IT THE END OF 'WAR' AND THE END OF 'JUSTICE'?

This section will address the three main arguments usually put forward against research into manufacture and deployment of AWS. The arguments are considered here not so much from the point of view of their legal significance, but rather of the ethically unacceptable consequences associated in the public mind with any future deployment of AWS on the battlefield. The first argument is that, as a result of increased dissociation of risk, the threshold at which a state might take the decision to go to war might be lowered. The second argument concerns the impossibility of 'delegating' certain key decisions to artificial systems, and the third centres on the potential legal value of the *Martens Clause* enshrined in Article 1 (2) API.

2.3.1 *War Would No Longer Be War*

The rules governing *resort to force* form a central element, known as *jus ad bellum*, within international law. The principle behind this is an internationally agreed determination to minimise and regulate the legitimacy with which states may turn to the use of armed force.

The starting point for any examination of the law on the use of force is the prohibition enshrined in Article 2(4) of the UN Charter, according to which 'all members shall refrain in their international relations from the threat or use of force against the territorial integrity or political independence of any State, or in any other manner inconsistent with the Purposes of the United Nations'. The International Court of Justice (ICJ) in the *Nicaragua Case* had occasion to consider that although 'the United Nations Charter [...] by no means covers the whole area of the regulation of the use of force in international relations', the prohibition stands not only as a treaty obligation but also as customary law and even *jus cogens*,[241] that is, 'a norm accepted and recognised by the international community of States as a whole as a norm from which no derogation is permitted and which can be modified only by a subsequent

[241] *Military and Paramilitary Activities in and against Nicaragua (Nicaragua v United States of America)* (ICJ (Judgement)) paras 176, 188, 199.

norm of general international law having the same character'.[242] In spite of its peremptory tone, Article 2(4) of the UN Charter is subject to exceptions. These are laid down in two other provisions of the Charter: collective measures taken with the authorisation of the Security Council under Chapter VII, and in self-defence (Article 51 UN Charter).[243] Closely allied to the principle of the prohibition of the use of armed force are the principles of non-intervention in the free choices of a country, and the principle of respect for the sovereignty of states.[244]

It is true, however, that over the last seventy years the UN Charter scheme has never been implemented in the manner that a literal reading of the text might suggest. Notwithstanding this, armed interventions have always been a matter for discussion in the Security Council and in the international arena. It is almost impossible for armed conflict to start up anywhere in the world without international organisations being fully aware of it, right down to the types of weapon deployed.[245]

One of the arguments presented by advocates of an AWS ban is related not so much to doubts about the capacity of AWS to comply with IHL rules but focuses, rather, on how AWS might be an inducement for political leaders to go to war since 'their own troops would not face death or injury'.[246] The introduction of AWS into the battlespace distances, both physically and psychologically, the actuality of conflict from its instigators. The 'normal' distressing consequences of war would be reduced, even perhaps eliminated: there would be no shedding of blood, no bodies being returned home and no post-traumatic stress disorder (PTSD) among the survivors. The human and financial costs of a war would probably be lower. Together, all these factors could well lead to a state of affairs that would call into question the concept of 'war'. Until now generally understood to be a 'last resort', it would become

242 'The 1969 Vienna Convention on the Law of Treaties' (Article 53) <http://legal.un.org/ilc/texts/instruments/english/conventions/1_1_1969.pdf>.

243 Christine Gray, *International Law and the Use of Force* (3rd edn, Oxford University Press 2008) 6–25; Malcolm N Shaw, *International Law* (6th edn, Cambridge University Press 2008) 1123–1124.

244 *Military and Paramilitary Activities in and against Nicaragua (Nicaragua v United States of America)* (n 241) paras 14, 108; Shaw (n 243) 1174–1188.

245 The most recent attacks in Syria using chemical weapons are a perfect example. Michael R Gordon, 'Worst Chemical Attack in Years in Syria; U.S. Blames Assad' *The New York Times* (4 April 2017) <www.nytimes.com/2017/04/04/world/middleeast/syria-gas-attack.html?_r=0.>; 'Convention on the Prohibition of the Development, Production, Stockpiling and Use of Chemical Weapons and on Their Destruction' (1993) <www.opcw.org/chemical-weapons-convention/download-the-cwc/>.

246 Human Rights Watch and International Human Rights Clinic, 'Losing Humanity: The Case against Killer Robots' (n 30) 4.

merely an 'option' among others. It has also been suggested that this distancing might lead to the (extremely dangerous) development, on the part of those launching the weapons, of what has been termed a 'play station mentality' towards the use of force.[247]

Some scholars, however, have recently called attention to the fact that 'machine learning raises the possibility of *automated self-defense systems* in a much wider variety of contexts, systems that could draw on the resources of the entire armed forces and possess the capacity to launch counter-attacks' in response to cyber-attacks, for example, among other threats.[248] Notwithstanding the sphere of possibility that machine learning will undoubtedly open up in the context of the battlefield, it will surely require a very thorough debate to establish at which level a state might commit and rely its entire national defence to AWS.

Indeed, war would not only become one option among others, it would become something of a different nature entirely. That AWS effect a total dissociation of risk is only true for those parties to the conflict who have access to such systems. According to Special Rapporteur C. Heyns, this factor would have grave consequences, since 'there is a qualitative difference between reducing the risk that armed conflict poses to those who participate in it, and the situation where one side is no longer a "participant" [...] as its combatants are not exposed to any danger'.[249] In this scenario, AWS could easily become politically instrumental, in the hands of the powerful, threatening to destroy that balance which is crucial to the principle of the sovereignty of states. It has also been pointed out that once states enter into conflict, there could be a danger of its becoming not only protracted but also hidden, because there would no longer be the casualties that make conflict so painfully visible.[250]

As regards the arguments sketched out earlier, they do not so much concern International Law as International Politics. However, they are not unworthy of consideration. First, the argument that the option of deploying AWS might potentially undermine states' perception of war as a last resort, reducing it to merely one choice among others, implies some kind of carte blanche allowing states to go to war. Without going into depth here about the concept of

247 Heyns, 'Report of the Special Rapporteur on Extrajudicial, Summary or Arbitrary Executions, Christof Heyns' (n 10) paras 57–58; Philip Alston, 'Report of the Special Rapporteur on Extrajudicial, Summary or Arbitrary Executions, Philip Alston. Addendum - Study on Targeted Killings' (Human Rights Council 2010) para 79 <https://digitallibrary.un.org/record/685887/files/A_HRC_14_24_Add-6-EN.pdf>.

248 Deeks, Lubell and Murray (n 25) 2.

249 Heyns, 'Report of the Special Rapporteur on Extrajudicial, Summary or Arbitrary Executions, Christof Heyns' (n 10) para 60. F.

250 Wagner, 'Beyond the Drone Debate: Autonomy in Tomorrow's Battlespace' (n 221) 83.

a 'just war', especially in its traditional form, the question of its being a last resort is not the only criterion. Alongside stand another five: *just cause*, *legitimate authority*, *right intention*, *proportionality* and *prospect of success*.[251] Therefore, even if war becomes a more attractive option for states, it does not mean that they can freely override the international system, in particular the authority of the Security Council.

Second, it is very difficult to conceive of a situation in which the decision to initiate an armed attack is left to an autonomous system without any human input. It is one thing to envisage defensive systems which are activated once a military target is identified, but quite another to imagine that these systems will ever be allowed to engage in war on their own initiative, according to their own criteria, without legitimate authorisation and a specific mission entrusted to the system.[252]

War will remain war, and it may be legitimate and justified, although this is not to overlook the terrible evils attendant upon any type of armed conflict. However, one reason why a state might consider it wiser not to intervene in legitimate situations susceptible to armed intervention might be for financial considerations or lack of manpower. If we are to reject *pacifism*, it is important to bear in mind that non-action also has its own consequences. The intervention in Kosovo in 1999, for example, was certainly illegal but most probably legitimate in the light of the prevailing international commitment to human rights.[253]

2.3.2 *The Morality of War and Delegation of Justice*

The two arguments about to be presented concern the ethics of war, and they are explained here in order to highlight certain points of interest that help us to appreciate as broad an overview as possible of the arguments made against the deployment of AWS.

The first argument has been developed by authors such as Paul W. Kahn, and concerns the consequences of 'riskless warfare'. Although Kahn does not explore all the problems connected with the emergence of AWS, a view is expressed that technology is transforming armed conflict into 'riskless warfare' when the scenario may in fact be one of 'extreme asymmetry' (i.e. when the

251 Nigel Biggar, *In Defence of War* (Oxford University Press 2013) 3.

252 Sassoli, 'Autonomous Weapons and International Humanitarian Law: Advantages, Open Technical Questions and Legal Issues to Be Clarified' (n 192) 315–316.

253 Biggar (n 251) 33. T Franck stresses that a strict legal positivist interpretation of the Charter leads to a '*reductio ad absurdum*' and that a bilateral relationship between law and the 'common sense of values' should always be promoted. Thomas Franck, 'Lessons of Kosovo' (1999) 93 *American Journal of International Law (Unbound)* 857–860, 857; Thomas Franck, *Recourse to Force: State Action against Threats and Armed Attack* (Cambridge University Press 2002) 139–169, 175–177.

combatant parties are not equal in terms of wealth and power, the deployment of AWS could aggravate that inequality), instead of 'reciprocal imposition of risk'.[254] In such a situation, war might be said to give place to a kind of police enforcement, under which the principle of distinction would no longer make sense.[255] Indeed, even today it can be hard to determine what, exactly, constitutes a 'civilian', when civilians participate directly in hostilities and, in particular, when a state of 'continuous combat function' blurs the clarity of who is who. An 'unbalanced society' risks falling into extreme asymmetry, dependent upon what is termed its 'Leviathan' or 'Globocop'.[256]

Notwithstanding the legitimacy of the author's conclusion about extreme asymmetry, Kahn focuses his analysis on the exclusive presence of a 'single heavyweight', the United States. However, the reality is, first, that the balance of power in modern international society, together with advances in the weapons industry, means that the United States is not necessarily the *only* Leviathan with surveillance policies – see Russia, China and the United Kingdom, for example.[257] Second, it is the circumstances governing the new type of conflict that will dictate the choice of weapon used on the battlefield, not the other way around. That the principle of distinction has become so difficult to apply results precisely from the changing nature of the circumstances surrounding outbreaks of modern conflict.

Dissociation of risk, together with improvements in modern systems of communication, has facilitated novel ways of going to war – those that have been dubbed, for example, 'riskless warfare' and 'cyberwarfare'. These may undermine the opportunity combatants formerly had to exercise the principle of distinction, but, arguably, although war is being redefined, one surety is that the principle of humanity stands a chance of being reinforced by the deployment of AWS owing

254 Paul W Kahn, 'The Paradox of Riskless Warfare' (2002) 22 *Philosophy & Public Policy Quarterly* 2, 4–5.

255 ibid 8.

256 Morris (n 231) 338. The author analyses how modern societies give up the model of a Leviathan, geographically circumscribed, in favour of a 'globocop' that has a more international scope.

257 Christof Heyns and others, 'The International Law Framework Regulating the Use of Armed Drones' (2016) 65 *International and Comparative Law Quarterly* 791, 793; Michael Pearson, 'Russia's Resurgent Drone Program' (CCN, 16 October 2015) <https://edition.cnn.com/2015/10/16/world/russia-drone-program/index.html>; Malte Humpert, 'Canada and Russia Looking to Deploy Surveillance Drones in the Arctic' (*High North News*, 22 February 2019) <www.highnorthnews.com/en/canada-and-russia-looking-deploy-surveillance-drones-arctic>; Nick Whigham, 'China Looks to Bolster Surveillance Network with Birdlike Drones' (*news.com.au*, 25 June 2018) <www.news.com.au/technology/innovation/inventions/china-looks-to-bolster-surveillance-network-with-birdlike-drones/news-story/fbef8af0169a08cb64ebddbf6cf44981>.

to their newly powerful information-gathering systems. These facilitate better compliance with the principle of distinction because the information they provide is, for the most part, better than the intelligence gleaned by other means.

The second problem is raised by Peter Asaro around what is termed the 'Delegation of Justice'. This argument, although not strictly of a legal nature, is possibly the one upon which the future of AWS will depend. According to Asaro's reasoning, the key element underpinning the system of justice is human judgement. The entire legal system is conceived by humans and, concomitantly, its entire framework is based upon the human capacity to understand and interpret the challenges of the battlefield in the spirit of the law. IHL rules, as the principles of distinction and proportionality demonstrate, are quite clear, but their application in the specific context of hostilities can call for different types of answer. Is it conceivable that a system will perform that well? According to Asaro, 'it will be difficult or impossible to design systems capable of dealing with the fog and friction of war'.[258]

Asaro's argument goes beyond technicality, beyond even the fact that these systems may perform better than human operators. For all the undoubted precision of a modern weapons system, there is still that elusive dimension of moral responsibility, which remains with humans alone. It is a moral imperative, he asserts, 'to prevent the delegation of lethal authorisation to unsupervised non-human systems' and, therefore, 'any automated system that can initiate lethal force without the specific, conscious and deliberate decision of a human operator, controller or supervisor' should be banned.[259] However, as Robert Hart points out, an effective ban cannot be measured by its possible practical value. The fact that an approved ban exists does not mean, unfortunately, that it will be effective – the use of chemical weapons in the conflict in Syria in 2017 provides a telling example of how a ban will never be watertight. The condemnation needs always to rest on moral grounds.[260]

In the light of these arguments, it appears that it is not only those systems in which human operators are out-of-the-loop that need to be examined, but also those involving humans on-the-loop. A lethal decision-making process is a deliberative one and therefore *must not be delegated* whatever the circumstances.

258 Asaro, 'On Banning Autonomous Weapon Systems: Human Rights, Automation and the Dehumanization of Lethal Decision Making' (n 29) 692.

259 ibid 689, 695–696; O' Connell, 'Banning Autonomous Killing – The Legal and Ethical Requirement That Humans Make Near-Time Lethal Decisions' (n 75) 231; Heyns, 'Human Rights and the Use of Autonomous Weapons Systems (AWS) during Domestic Enforcement' (n 25) 351, 355.

260 Robert Hart, 'The Case for Banning Autonomous Weapons Rests on Morality, Not Practicality' (*Bulletin of the Atomic Scientists*, 2017) <https://thebulletin.org/2017/04/the-case-for-banning-autonomous-weapons-rests-on-morality-not-practicality/>.

In essence, two conditions are required: a human operator and also that the 'human decision-maker be allowed sufficient time to be deliberative, be suitably trained and well informed'.[261] This author argues that the planned level of investment and research in AWS should be redirected towards the development of resources that will enhance the ethical performance of human decision-makers.[262]

As important as this is, it is also essential to ask if a machine should ever be allowed to make the *decision* to engage a target. If it is accepted that these machines are capable of being designed and programmed according to IHL principles and ROE requirements, it might further be asked whether the system could, perhaps, be programmed to recognise military targets only, rather than to distinguish as military any unidentified object in the environment. As Marco Sassoli points out, the decision to target, in the context of hostilities, is not a judgement made about a person being innocent or guilty, but about his/her status (combatant/civilian) and/or the objective impression resulting from their conduct (direct participation in the hostilities). It is not difficult then to think about the capabilities of machine learning to classify modes of conduct. Of course, the question is whether AI will ever be able to achieve this level of accuracy, especially in the unpredictable circumstances of an armed conflict. But another question can also be asked: as AWS become progressively more precise, and as a result become instrumental in reducing collateral damage, is it so impossible to hypothesise that these systems could be more 'efficient', in terms of compliance with IHL rules and, more specifically, of the imperative to protect the civilian population and objects at all times?

2.3.3 *The Martens Clause: Foundation for a Ban on AWS*

The *Martens Clause* was first unveiled at the Hague Convention (II) on the Laws and Customs of War on Land of 1899, and is enshrined, in its modern version, in Article 1 (2) API, 1977:

> In cases not covered by this Protocol or by any other international agreements, civilians and combatants remain under the protection and authority of the principles of international law derived from established custom, from the principles of humanity and from the dictates of public conscience.

The very same clause is enshrined in paragraph 5 of the CCW Preamble, using in both texts an abridged version of the language in the Preamble to the

261 Asaro, 'On Banning Autonomous Weapon Systems: Human Rights, Automation and the Dehumanization of Lethal Decision Making' (n 29) 695.

262 ibid 689.

Hague Convention IV 1907.[263] Thus, it was recognised, even before World War I, that 'elementary considerations of humanity' and 'public conscience' provide a protective and balancing counterforce to war; that the Martens Clause continues to be cited in more recent documents serves to re-emphasise its value within the IHL framework.[264]

A relatively narrow interpretation of the Martens Clause suggests that the body of IHL is not exhaustive and that, as a discipline, it cannot be isolated from developments in other fields of International Law. This position finds support in the 1996 ICJ *Advisory Opinion on the Legality of the Threat and Use of Nuclear Weapons* (hereinafter the 1996 Advisory Opinion), which states that the Martens Clause 'proved to be an effective means of addressing the rapid evolution of military technology'.[265] This argument has been echoed in HRW reports and by other commentators.[266] More recently it was also invoked, for example, by the Sri Lankan Government at the 2018 GGE Meetings and by Australia and Brazil at the 2019 GGE Meetings.[267]

263 Convention (IV) Respecting the Laws and Customs of War on Land, para 5, in Adam Roberts and Richard Guelff, *Documents on the Laws of War* (3rd edn, Oxford University Press 2000) 70; Boothby, *Weapons and the Law of Armed Conflict* (n 210) 94; '1980 Convention on Certain Conventional Weapons (CCW)' (1980) para 5 <www.un.org/disarmament/publications/more/ccw/>.

264 Nina HB Jorgensen, *The Responsibility of States for International Crimes* (Oxford University Press 2000) 119. In para 17 (g) of the 2019 GGE report is stated that 'lethal autonomous weapons systems not covered by the CCW and its annexed Protocols or by other international agreements, the civilian population and the combatants shall at all times remain under the protection and authority of the principles of international law derived from established custom, from the principles of humanity and from the dictates of public conscience'. cf Group of Governmental Experts on Emerging Technologies in the Area of Lethal Autonomous Weapons System (n 12).

265 *ICJ, Advisory Opinion on the Legality of the Threat and Use of Nuclear Weapons, Judgment* (1996) para 78.

266 In 2018 HRW report the Martens Clause is considered to be the 'unique provision in IHL that establishes a baseline protection for civilians and combatants when no specific treaty law on topic exists'. Although the report recognises the debatable value of the Martens Clause, it states that 'the clause provides key factors for States to consider as they evaluate emerging weapons technology'. Human Rights Watch, 'Heed the Call: A Moral and Legal Imperative to Ban Killer Robots' (2018) 1 <www.hrw.org/sites/default/files/report_pdf/arms0818_web.pdf>; Akerson (n 230) 93.

267 Sri Lanka, 'General Exchange of Views 9–13 April 2018 – Geneva Statement by Sri Lanka' (*Reaching Critical Will*, 2018) <https://reachingcriticalwill.org/images/documents/Disarmament-fora/ccw/2018/hcp-meeting/statements/21Nov_SriLanka.pdf>; Brazil, '2019 GGE on Laws. Challenges to IHL Item 5(a)' (*Reaching Critical Will*, 2019) <https://reachingcriticalwill.org/images/documents/Disarmament-fora/ccw/2019/gge/statements/26March_Brazil5a.pdf>; Australia, '2018 Group of Governmental Experts of the High Contracting Parties to the Convention on Prohibitions or Restrictions on the Use of Certain Conventional Weapons Which May Be Deemed to Be Excessively Injurious or to Have Indiscriminate Effects. The Australian Article 36 Review Process' (2018) CCW/GGE.2/2018/WP.6 <https://docs-library.unoda.org/Convention_on_Certain_Conventional_Weapons_-_Group_of_Governmental_Experts_(2018)/2018_GGE%2BLAWS_August_Working%2Bpaper_Australia.pdf>.

According to these observers, the Martens Clause was ratified by the ICJ as 'influenc[ing] the discussions and debates preceding the development of CCW Protocol IV on Blinding Lasers', which pre-emptively banned the use of laser weapons, 'specifically designed [...] to cause permanent blindness to unenhanced vision' (Article 1, CCW, Protocol IV).[268] However, as the ICJ in 1996 *Advisory Opinion* also recognised, difficulties and lack of consensus regarding its interpretation hindered resolution of the many controversies surrounding the Martens Clause.[269] In spite of the indisputable value that is generally accorded to the document, it is generally accepted by scholars, and by the jurisprudence, that the Martens Clause does not possess the standing of an independent source of International Law. The ICJ in the 1996 *Advisory Opinion* stated that the Martens Clause has become part of International Customary Law,[270] but as the ICTY clarified in the *Kupreškić Case*, 'this Clause may not be taken to mean that the "principles of humanity" and the "dictates of public conscience" have been elevated to the rank of independent sources of International Law, for this conclusion is belied by international practice'.[271]

It is true that the Martens Clause was invoked throughout the negotiations of Protocol IV of CCW. However, HRW omits to examine satisfactorily the fundamental differences between Protocol IV, concerned with blinding lasers – the potential of which to cause 'superfluous injury or unnecessary suffering' has, from the start, been clearly recognised – and AWS.[272] The latter, unlike blinding lasers, might have the potential to comply with the principles of distinction and proportionality, perhaps better than any human operator will ever be able to do.[273]

268 Human Rights Watch, 'Making the Case: The Dangers of Killer Robots and the Need for a Preemptive Ban' (n 216) 17; Hart (n 260).

269 Iain Scobbie, 'The Approach to Customary International Law in the Study' in Elizabeth Wilmshurst and Susan Breau (eds), *Perspectives on the ICRC Study on Customary International Humanitarian Law* (Chatham House 2007) 18. The debate surrounding the meaning of the Marten's Clause was acknowledged by the CCW GGE meetings by the Chair in 2019. cf Gjorgjinski (n 158) para 1 (iii); Chesterman (n 4) 232–233.

270 *ICJ, Advisory Opinion on the Legality of the Threat and Use of Nuclear Weapons, Judgment* (n 265) para 84.

271 *Kupreškić et al* [2000] ICTY Trial Chamber IT-95-16 [525].

272 Dinstein (n 210) 72–73; Pablo Kalmanovitz, 'Judgment, Liability and the Risks of Riskless Warfare' in Nehal Bhuta and others (eds), *Autonomous Weapons Systems: Law, Ethics, Policy* (Cambridge University Press 2016) 148; McFarland, *Autonomous Weapon Systems and the Law of Armed Conflict: Compatibility with International Humanitarian Law* (n 46) 139.

273 Talal Husseini, 'US Army Clarifies Rules on Autonomous Armed Robots' (*Army Technology*, 13 March 2019) <www.army-technology.com/digital-disruptions/us-army-armed-robots/>; Gert-Jan Lokhorst and Jeroen van den Hoven, 'Responsibility for Military Robots' in Patrick Lin, Keith Abney and George A Bekey (eds), *Robot Ethics: The Ethical and Social Implications* (Massachusetts Institute of Technology 2012) 148.

The comparison is not between like objects, and in this context Protocol IV can be presented only as an example of one pre-emptive ban amongst others.

A second problem with the line of argument discussed earlier is that surveys are presented as revealing *elementary principles of humanity*, or of *public conscience*.[274] Such terminology is intended to illustrate the role of public morality in the development of International Law, especially in relation to those hideous transgressions known as 'crimes against humanity'. In essence, this terminology brings internationally shared values to the forefront, any violation of which would threaten the very core of international society. As the Australian Government had the opportunity to highlight in 2018 and 2019, the Martens Clause can be applied 'in the narrow sense of preserving customary international law. That is, the Martens Clause "*prevents the assumption that anything which is not explicitly prohibited by the relevant treaties is therefore permitted*"', but it cannot be considered an independent source of international law.[275]

In conclusion, it can hardly be argued that AWS would, in themselves, constitute a rupture of international values. Surely it is, rather, the idea of delegating powers of decision-making to a machine that will cause reverberations in our concept of human dignity. It is at this level that advocates of a ban can present a solid line of reasoning, explaining and offering instances of how delegation to AWS would call into question the concept of what it means to be human, and demonstrating the ways in which human judgement conjures a sine qua non of a far higher order than technological accuracy and efficiency.

2.4 STATES CONCEPTUALISATION OF 'AUTONOMOUS WEAPON SYSTEMS' (AWS)

The inspiration for this section's title arises from the truth enshrined in the 2018 Russian Federation working paper, which points out that the major problem 'lies with the speculative discussions divorced from reality owing to the lack of both actually operating LAWS and general understanding with regard to their working definition and basic functions at the moment' and from the Israeli Government stating that in late 2018 'there are still differences of opinion. One of them is the definition or characterization of LAWS'.[276] In order to avoid the opacity of the current debate, some states, among them, Ireland, the Netherlands, the Russian

274 Human Rights Watch, 'Europe Poll Supports Killer Robots Ban Failing Diplomatic Talks Show Need for a Different Path Print' (13 November 2019) <www.hrw.org/news/2019/11/13/europe-poll-supports-killer-robots-ban>.

275 Australia (n 267) para 15, e, footnote 20 (our emphasis).

276 The Russian Federation, 'Group of Governmental Experts of the High Contracting Parties to the Convention on Prohibitions or Restrictions on the Use of Certain Conventional

Federation, the United Kingdom and the United States, have suggested their own definitions of AWS.

In Chapter 1, a reference was made to the definitions of AWS that have been put forward by the United Kingdom and the United States. It is now important to compare them with those emanating from the Netherlands and the Russian Federation and, more recently, the Republic of Ireland. From the organisational point of view, all the definitions include AWS features and information about human operators–AWS interface.

Some CCW states (e.g. China, Italy and the Russian Federation) have insisted that the debate focus exclusively on *fully autonomous weapons*, but no country has yet explained satisfactorily exactly what they mean by this. Looking at the definitions set out in Table 2.1, it can be seen that still more acute problems may emerge. First, the Netherlands Statement at the GGE in 2018 uses the terms 'AWS' and 'LAWS' indiscriminately, prompting the question of whether they refer to the same systems. In this regard, the Irish Statement points out that never before has it been necessary to add 'lethal' to the description of any weapon system and that it is thus necessary to ask if 'AWS' excludes non-lethal autonomous systems.[277] According to the definition provided by the Irish Government that seems to be the accurate interpretation.

The definition presented by the United Kingdom seems to introduce nuances not hitherto raised.[278] The 2018 GGE UK Statement first asserts that the definition of 'autonomous systems' applies to LAWS, but adds that those systems 'do not currently exist', and then goes on to say that 'the UK has no intention of ever developing lethal systems that could select and engage targets without human control'.[279] For the United Kingdom,

Weapons Which May Be Deemed to Be Excessively Injurious or to Have Indiscriminate Effects' (*Reaching Critical Will*, 2018) CCW/GGE.1/2018/WP.6 <https://reachingcriticalwill.org/images/documents/Disarmament-fora/ccw/2018/gge/documents/29August_Russia_Definition.pdf>; Israel (n 14).

277 The Government of Ireland emphasised the problem of non-lethal weapons in 2019, questioning whether the term 'AWS' should or should not include less lethal or non-lethal weapon systems. Ireland (n 205); '2019 Statement by Ireland. Agenda Item 5(b): Characterization of the Systems under Consideration in Order to Promote a Common Understanding on Concepts and Characteristics Relevant to the Objectives and Purposes of the Convention' (*Reaching Critical Will* 2019) <https://reachingcriticalwill.org/images/documents/Disarmament-fora/ccw/2019/gge/statements/25March_Ireland5b.pdf>; 'Report of the 2018 Session of the Group of Governmental Experts on Emerging Technologies in the Area of Lethal Autonomous Weapons Systems' (n 193) Annex III, para 3.

278 The Netherlands (n 278).

279 '2018 United Kingdom of Great Britain and Northern Ireland. Statement for the General Exchange of Views at the Meeting of the Group of Government Experts on Lethal Autonomous Weapons Systems' (*Reaching Critical Will*, 2018) <https://reachingcriticalwill.org/images/documents/Disarmament-fora/ccw/2018/gge/statements/9April_United-Kingdom.pdf>.

TABLE 2.1 *States definitions of AWS*

Country	Definition
Republic of Ireland[280]	A weapon system which can act autonomously in delivering lethal effects to a target and may also act autonomously in detection and target selection prior to engagement of the target. The level of autonomy can vary from basic levels of automation through a spectrum of an increasing number of autonomous functions and decreasing human control up to and including fully autonomous systems which can operate across a range of functions without direct human control.
The Netherlands[281] (CCW/GGE.1/2017/WP.2)	A weapon that, without human intervention, selects and engages targets matching certain predefined criteria, following a human decision to deploy the weapon on the understanding that an attack, once launched, cannot be stopped by human intervention.
Russian Federation[282] (CCW/GGE.1/2018/WP.6)	A) Autonomous weapon system – an unmanned piece of technical equipment that is not a munition and is designed to perform military and support tasks under

However, it should be noted that in 2019 the UK MoD awarded £2.5 million to Blue Bear Systems Research in order to develop drone swarm technology with the capability of 'explosive ordinance detection and disposal'. According to Ian Williams-Wynn, Managing Director of Blue Bear Systems, 'the ability to deploy a swarm of low-cost autonomous systems delivers a new paradigm for battlefield operations. During this project we will deploy next generation autonomy, machine learning, and AI to reduce the number of operators required, the time it takes to train them, and the cognitive burden on any operator during active operations.' The question of how a single operator will be able to exercise supervision or 'control' over such swarms was left unanswered. cf UK Ministry of Defence, '£2.5 million Injection for Drone Swarms – Press Release' (28 March 2019) <www.gov.uk/government/news/25m-injection-for-drone-swarms>; Wheeler (n 135).

280 Ireland (n 205).

281 The Netherlands, '2017 Netherlands Group of Governmental Experts of the High Contracting Parties to the Convention on Prohibitions or Restrictions on the Use of Certain Conventional Weapons Which May Be Deemed to Be Excessively Injurious or to Have Indiscriminate Effects' (*Reaching Critical Will*, 13 November 2017) <https://reachingcriticalwill.org/images/documents/Disarmament-fora/ccw/2017/gge/documents/WP2.pdf>.

282 The Russian Federation, 'Group of Governmental Experts of the High Contracting Parties to the Convention on Prohibitions or Restrictions on the Use of Certain Conventional Weapons Which May Be Deemed to Be Excessively Injurious or to Have Indiscriminate Effects' (n 276). In GGE Meeting in 2019, the Russian Federation argued that the discussion should be 'limited to fully autonomous weapons, for which propose the following definition: "unmanned technical means others than ordnance that are intended for carrying out combat and support missions. Without any involvement of the operator"'. cf The Russian Federation, '2019 Group of Governmental Experts: Potential Opportunities and Limitations of Military Uses of Lethal Autonomous Weapons Systems' (n 5) para 5.

TABLE 2.1 *(continued)*

Country	Definition
	remote control by an operator, autonomously or using the combination of these methods. B) Semi-autonomous weapon system – type of robotic military equipment requiring involvement of the operator.
United Kingdom[283] (JDP 0–30.2)	An autonomous system is capable of understanding higher-level intent and direction. From this understanding and its perception of its environment, such a system is able to take appropriate action to bring about a desired state. It is capable of deciding a course of action, from a number of alternatives, without depending on human oversight and control, although these may still be present. Although the overall activity of an autonomous unmanned aircraft will be predictable, individual actions may not be.
United States[284] (*DoD 3000.09*)	A weapon system that, once activated, can select and engage targets without further intervention by a human operator. This includes human-supervised autonomous weapon systems that are designed to allow human operators to override operation of the weapon system, but can select and engage targets without further human input after activation.

compliance with fundamental IHL principles and evaluation of the risks attendant upon the use of lethal force 'can only be assessed and applied by a human'.[285] This could imply that the United Kingdom is implicitly suggesting a ban on AWS in general. However, the UK Statement declares that 'the UK does not support a pre-emptive ban on LAWS' and that it is 'important that this GGE shall discuss the characteristics of LAWS, and give further consideration to the human element in the use of lethal force'.[286] From a combined reading of *JDN 2/11*, *JDP 0–30.2* and the 2018 UK Statement, it might be concluded that the United Kingdom will

283 UK Ministry of Defence, 'Joint Doctrine Publication 0–30. UK Air and Space Doctrine' (2013) 13.

284 US Department of Defense, 'DoD 3000.09. Autonomy in Weapon Systems' (n 7).

285 '2018 United Kingdom of Great Britain and Northern Ireland. Statement for the General Exchange of Views at the Meeting of the Group of Government Experts on Lethal Autonomous Weapons Systems' (n 284).

286 ibid.

accept autonomous systems only on the condition that they operate under human supervision. In short, what the United States defines as 'human-supervision autonomous weapon systems', the Russian Federation calls 'semi-autonomous weapon systems'. Indeed, *JDP 0–30.2* defines a remote and automated system as 'a system comprising the platform, control and sensor equipment, the supporting network, information processing system and associated personnel where the platform may be operated remotely and/or have automated functionality'.[287] However, both the United States and the United Kingdom exclude remote and automated systems from the 'autonomous system' category.[288] Therefore, it is legitimate to conclude that, for the United Kingdom, there are just two categories of system: 'autonomous systems' – characterised by their capability of understanding higher-level intent and direction – and 'automated systems'. As pointed out in *JDN 2/11*, if a system 'is not capable of human levels of situational understanding, then it should only be considered automated'.[289]

Considering the aforementioned discussion, the definition given by the Republic of Ireland leads to a clearer definitional platform. In contrast with *JDP 0–30.2*, autonomy is presented not in terms of 'black and white' (automated versus autonomous systems) but rather as a continuum, suggesting that it is possible to find systems with different levels of autonomy. The Irish definition of an autonomous system includes the observation that a system can autonomously engage military targets and 'may also act autonomously in detection and target selection prior to engagement of the target'. Indeed, this definition admits the possibility of systems for situation assessment, target selection and target engagement, all operating autonomously. The difficulty with the Irish definition is not that there is a need to clarify what is to be understood by 'fully autonomous systems' which can operate 'without *direct* human control'. It is rather the need to ask, 'would these systems be at the end of the autonomy spectrum or do they exist?' The question is relevant as so many current weapon systems already operate without human intervention.[290]

287 UK Ministry of Defence, 'Joint Doctrine Publication 0–30.2 Unmanned Aircraft Systems' (n 7) 2.

288 ibid 13; US Department of Defense, 'DoD 3000.09. Autonomy in Weapon Systems' (n 7) 4 (c)(1).

289 UK Ministry of Defence, 'The UK Approach to Unmanned Aircraft Vehicles, JDN 2/11' (n 8); UK Ministry of Defence, 'Joint Doctrine Publication 0–30.2 Unmanned Aircraft Systems' (n 7) 2; '2018 United Kingdom of Great Britain and Northern Ireland. Statement for the General Exchange of Views at the Meeting of the Group of Government Experts on Lethal Autonomous Weapons Systems' (n 284).

290 cf Chapter 2, Section 2.5.3.3.

A completely different approach is taken by the United States. It is important to bear in mind that *DoD 3000.09* emerges as the latest of several previous documents, the 'Roadmaps for unmanned Weapon Systems' produced between 2005 and 2011, and is complemented by a posterior document *Unmanned Systems Integrated Roadmap, FY 2013–2038* (hereinafter the *Roadmap FY 2013–2038*).

Since 2016, the United States has taken the position that there is no advantage in providing a definition of LAWS. In 2017, one of the working papers presented by the United States explained that the definition given in *DoD 3000.09* is not intended to outline the sophistication of a weapon but, rather, its capacity to select and engage military targets autonomously, which is relevant in terms of IHL and embodies the true novelty of LAWS.[291] This is possible because 'machine learning can facilitate and enhance the implementation of IHL, including the principles of distinction and proportionality'.[292]

Looking now to the operator–AWS interface, the *UK JDP 0–30.2* and the Irish definition have their focus on the capabilities of weapons systems, while the Netherlands' definition focuses rather on the presence or absence of 'human intervention'. At CCW meetings on LAWS since 2016, the problem of 'human–machine interaction' or 'meaningful human control' has been raised.[293] Indeed, the Netherlands clarifies in its working paper that although

291 United States of America, '2017 Group of Governmental Experts of the High Contracting Parties to the Convention on Prohibitions or Restrictions on the Use of Certain Conventional Weapons Which May Be Deemed to Be Excessively Injurious or to Have Indiscriminate Effects. US Opening Statement. Autonomy in Autonomous Systems' (2017) <https://reachingcriticalwill.org/images/documents/Disarmament-fora/ccw/2017/gge/documents/WP6.pdf>; Tomg Ong, 'US Govt Panel: Don't Ban AI-Powered Autonomous Weapons' (*The Defense Post*, 28 January 2021) <www.thedefensepost.com/2021/01/28/us-panel-ai-autonomous-weapons/>.

292 United States of America, '2017 Group of Governmental Experts of the High Contracting Parties to the Convention on Prohibitions or Restrictions on the Use of Certain Conventional Weapons Which May Be Deemed to Be Excessively Injurious or to Have Indiscriminate Effects. US Opening Statement. Autonomy in Autonomous Systems' (n 291).

293 In 2016, Austria, ICRC, the Netherlands, Poland, South Africa, Sweden, the United Kingdom, the United States. cf UNOG – The United Nations Office in Geneva, '2016 Meeting of Experts on LAWS' (*Reaching Critical Will*, 11 April 2016) <www.reachingcriticalwill.org/disarmament-fora/ccw/2016/laws/statements>. In 2017, Brazil, Cuba, China, the Netherlands. cf UNOG – The United Nations Office in Geneva, '2017 Group of Governmental Experts on Lethal Autonomous Weapons (LAWS)' (10 November 2017). In 2018, China, European Union, Italy, Pakistan, Spain, Sri Lanka, Switzerland, the United Kingdom, the Netherlands. Opposing the criteria of MHC, Russian Federation. cf UNOG – The United Nations Office in Geneva, '2018 Group of Governmental Experts on Lethal Autonomous Weapons Systems (LAWS)' (*Reaching Critical Will*, April 2018) <https://reachingcriticalwill.org/disarmament-fora/ccw/2019/laws/statements>.

in the case of truly autonomous systems there will be no 'human intervention' over specific attacks, human operators will

> play a prominent role in (a) programming the characteristics of the targets that are to be engaged, (b) the consideration of aspects such as target selection, weapon selection and implementation planning (time and space) and assessment of potential collateral damage, (c) the decision to deploy the weapon, and (d) the Battle Damage Assessment (BDA) after the attack, in which commanders can be held accountable for the effects of 'their' LAWS. Under these circumstances, humans are involved in the 'wider loop' of the decision-making process. This means that humans continue to play a crucial role in the wider targeting process and exercise meaningful human control.[294]

In light of this, it might be concluded that the Netherlands distinguishes 'human control' from 'human intervention'. Once an AWS is activated, 'human intervention' is no longer expected, but this does not prevent human operators from being involved in the design and programming of the system and in the moment of activation of an AWS. Another factor that deserves attention is the way accountability seems to be addressed. According to the Dutch Statement, 'there is no (legal) accountability gap as long as humans exercise meaningful human control in the wider loop of the decision-making process for deploying autonomous weapon systems. Under such conditions, the existing legal regime is adequate to hold offenders accountable, as there is no change in the accountability of commanders, subordinates [...] Likewise, state responsibility remains unchanged in the event of deployment of autonomous weapon systems under meaningful human control.'[295] However, this proposition raises some legal concerns. First, the Dutch Government seems to exclude the possibility of AWS's software making errors of their own when selecting and engaging military targets. Second, it accepts state responsibility for AWS 'under meaningful human control' but what to make its situations in which violations of IHL cannot be attributed to human fault?

If questions remain to be answered concerning the Netherlands' definition, harder still to disentangle is that offered by the Russian Federation. The latter clearly states that it does not include munitions but only *the platforms* from which the munitions will be released. Those platforms can be controlled by human operators or operate autonomously. Without further explanation, it is

294 The Netherlands (n 278).
295 ibid.

almost impossible, in these statements, to distinguish autonomous systems from semi-autonomous systems since remote human control features in both. However, by express reference, the working paper excludes drone technology, asserting that although 'UAVs represent a particular group of the available war systems with a high autonomy degree', the definition of autonomous weapons should not be restricted to target identification and hit command functions, but should go beyond those functions to the point where 'we "forget" that the automated aim identification and hit command functions are set to the machine by the human through certain algorithms'.[296]

The Russian Federation's definition does not clarify what those 'extra functions' would be, although there is a suggestion that they may be the systems' capabilities to adapt to the specific circumstances of the battlefield, since 'an improved autonomy use could contribute to more accurate guidance of weapons directed against military assets which would contribute to the reduced risk of unintentional strikes against civilians and civil facilities'.[297] Notwithstanding the difficulties to envisage what exactly an AWS would be, more serious problems emerge as far as accountability is concerned. The Russian Federation defends that those extra autonomous functions should rely on states' own standards because 'attempts to develop certain universal parameters of the so called critical functions [. . .] can hardly give practical results'.[298] At the same time, the Russian working paper states that the 'legal responsibility issue should be addressed by both States and individuals that use weapon systems with autonomous functions'.[299] Although no explanation is given about state responsibility, the document adds that 'an autonomous system cannot perform its functions without a human behind it. Hence, the responsibility [. . .] should be with the human who operates or programs the robot system and orders to use LAWS',[300] which allows the conclusion that unlawful outcomes that are not caused by human fault should depend on state responsibility. However, the fact the Russian Federation supports the development of states' own standards might well compromise the international rules for individual and state responsibility.

296 The Russian Federation, 'Group of Governmental Experts of the High Contracting Parties to the Convention on Prohibitions or Restrictions on the Use of Certain Conventional Weapons Which May Be Deemed to Be Excessively Injurious or to Have Indiscriminate Effects' (n 276).
297 ibid para 9.
298 ibid para 9.
299 ibid para 11.
300 ibid para 11.

The US *DoD 3000.09* does not accept 'meaningful human control' as a key criterion but instead refers to 'appropriate levels of human judgment'.[301] The US at the 2016 CCW meeting in Geneva argued that the latter concept would be more helpful for the discussion, 'because [the] human/machine relationship extends throughout the development and employment of a system and is not limited to the moment of a decision to engage a target'.[302] The United States also remarked that 'the United States Delegation intends to provide further clarification [. . .] on this subject during the appropriate session' (but that clarification was not in the event provided). Given the lack of further clarification, Dan Saxon suggested that a reasonable interpretation would be to assume that the level of human judgement would vary according to the circumstances.[303] In other words, the complexity of the mission would dictate the level of human judgement required to guarantee compliance with IHL. In Chapter 1, it was noted that the *mission* was central to any consideration of how an autonomous system would function but, as the *Roadmap: FY 2013–2038* (hereinafter *2013–2038 Roadmap*) states,

> [t]he future of autonomous systems is characterized as a movement beyond autonomous *mission execution to autonomous mission performance*. The difference between execution and performance is that the former simply executes a preprogrammed plan whereas performance is associated with mission outcomes that can vary even during a mission and require deviation from pre-programmed tasks.[304]

It follows, therefore, that an autonomous system is self-directed by choosing the behaviour it follows to reach a human-directed goal. Throughout all the Group of Experts Meetings promoted by the CCW since 2014, all state parties have expressed their concern regarding the 'human element', 'meaningful human control', 'human–machine interaction' and, finally, 'appropriate levels of human judgement'.[305] Indeed, for some states (among them Belgium, China, the Netherlands), 'fully autonomous weapon systems' means a system in which any human intervention, after the system is launched,

301 US Department of Defense, 'DoD 3000.09. Autonomy in Weapon Systems' (n 7).

302 Meier, '2016 CCW Informal Meeting of Experts on Lethal Autonomous Weapon Systems. U.S.A. Delegation Opening Statement' (n 197).

303 Saxon (n 143) 200–208.

304 US Department of Defense, 'Unmanned Systems Integrated Roadmap: FY2013–2038' (n 80) 66–67, para 4.6 (our emphasis).

305 As examples: Republic of China, European Union, Italy, the Netherlands, Pakistan, Spain, Sri Lanka, Switzerland, the United Kingdom, among others. cf UNOG – The United Nations Office in Geneva, '2018 Group of Governmental Experts on Lethal Autonomous Weapons Systems (LAWS)' (n 293).

would be impossible – a fully autonomous system would not even be supervised by human operators.[306] Norway, however, warned that 'a robot or an algorithm is obviously precluded from any moral and legal accountability', arguing that removing humans from the OODA Loop would lead to an 'accountability vacuum'.[307] The fact that there would be a human presence at the moment of designing the algorithm for the mission was not considered sufficient.[308]

2.4.1 *Some Considerations about States' Policies*

Looking at the several statements issued by states, and at the working papers and contributions put forward by scholars and NGOs, it seems that the range of problems has certainly been narrowed down. Among the most relevant remain the need for a clear definition of what constitutes an AWS, the issue of human intervention in the decision-making process (known as the OODA Loop) and, above all, the question of accountability. As it has been observed, the focus allotted to each of these problems varies from state to state. All states have emphasised their agreement that autonomous systems have to be able to comply with IHL imperatives, and this, at least, represents common ground for all states. The statement presented by Spain goes as far as stating that there is a '*Jus Cogens* principle, an imperative to all members of the international community, according to which all weapon systems need to operate in compliance with IHL and International Law and Human Rights (ILHR), as well as the Principles of Distinction, Proportionality, Military Necessity and Precaution'.[309]

Apart from a certain element of confusion in the Spanish statement, it is fair to note that none of the states considered IHL to be a relic of the past, not fit for purpose when it comes to dealing with emerging technologies. Even the states that recommend a binding (or non-binding) political declaration do not call into question the applicability of IHL as the appropriate legal framework for the development of AWS. However, throughout the discussions, states have paid little attention to the problem of how to articulate the

[306] ibid.

[307] OODA Loop stands for *observe, orient, decide and act*, a representation of human decision-making process developed by J Boyd. Frans PB Osinga, *Science, Strategy and War: The Strategic Theory of John Boyd* (Routledge 2007) 3–9.

[308] UNOG – The United Nations Office in Geneva, '2017 Group of Governmental Experts on Lethal Autonomous Weapons (LAWS)' (n 293).

[309] UNOG – The United Nations Office in Geneva, '2018 Group of Governmental Experts on Lethal Autonomous Weapons Systems (LAWS)' (n 293).

current potentialities of AI with the definitions as confused as they currently are, and have opted to just point out legal problems without addressing their complexity.

To sum up, it is important to bear in mind that AWS depend on AI or, more specifically, on machine learning for the 'mission performance', as rightly explained by the United States.[310] These types of algorithms raise questions about their operationality on the battlefield. To believe – as seems to be the case with the Netherlands – that the process of selection and engagement of military targets can be pre-defined is in line with the capabilities of machine learning algorithms. However, it seems to fall short of what is expected from AWS' capabilities, such as autonomous selection. As is made clear in the document presented by Regina Surber at the 2018 GGE meeting, the relevance of autonomous technology is crucial in the 'what-to-do-next' situation in which human operators cannot foresee all the relevant data. Indeed, the problem of machine learning algorithms is that it *is impossible to know what we do not know*. Thus, neural networks 'could independently do something that may resemble free will', because the systems are not designed to deal with data not previously anticipated.[311] If, on the other hand, the entire process were pre-defined and pre-established by human operators, AWS would be reliable, but this would have to be characterised as a movement towards 'mission execution' rather than 'mission performance', in opposition to the US perspective.

Some of the problems touched upon, such as what it means for a system to be 'autonomous', will be revisited and thoroughly discussed in later chapters. However, it is important at this stage to clarify the definition and delimitate AWS in comparison with previous weapon systems.

2.5 DEFINING AUTONOMOUS WEAPON SYSTEMS

To offer a definition is always a complex task. In the case of AWS this task is even more complex due to the fields of knowledge that are involved: computer science, law and robotics. For the purposes of discussion, however, a definition may be useful first to delimitate the systems that can be considered

[310] US Department of Defense, 'Unmanned Systems Integrated Roadmap: FY2013–2038' (n 80) 66–67.

[311] Regina Surber, 'Artificial Intelligence: Autonomous Technology (AT), Lethal Autonomous Weapons Systems (LAWS) and Peace Time Threats' (*ICT4Peace Foundation and the Zurich Hub for Ethics and Technology*, 21 February 2020) <http://ict4peace.org/wp-content/uploads/2018/02/2018_RSurber_AI-AT-LAWS-Peace-Time-Threats_final.pdf>.

autonomous, establish how they differ from earlier technologies (automatic systems and automated systems)[312] and what they are not (fully autonomous systems). Second, a definition will provide a platform for further discussions to be held by the international community regarding the contours of new technologies of warfare, avoiding alarming scenarios such as 'inscrutable killer robots, over which we do not have control'.[313]

Considering the aforementioned factors, some authors have already ventured to offer definitions.[314] Rebecca Crootof defines an AWS as 'a weapon system that, based on conclusions derived from gathered information and preprogramming constraints, is capable of independently selecting and engaging targets'.[315] The author goes on to add that AWS

> might operate in structured or unstructured environments; they may be mobile or stationary; they may have rudimentary artificial intelligence, be capable of in-field learning, or even have human-level reasoning; they may be supervised or entirely uncontrollable.[316]

[312] The author takes here the definitions presented by Tim McFarland, according to which an *automatic system* 'refers to very simple devices which perform well-defined tasks and may have pre-set responses to external disturbances' and an *automated system*, that can sometimes overlap with automatic systems, 'but are likely to follow more complex sets of rules in normal operation and in responding to disturbances, such that they can perform more complex tasks or operate in more complex environments'. cf McFarland, *Autonomous Weapon Systems and the Law of Armed Conflict: Compatibility with International Humanitarian Law* (n 46) 41.

[313] Lokhorst and Hoven (n 273) 153. At the 2019 GGE Meeting, Germany, however, stated that 'having an exact joint definition of the systems under consideration is not a necessary prerequisite for moving the work of this group forward'. Ireland, on the other hand, stated that 'reaching a common understanding on the concepts and characteristics relevant to LAWS will aid in our consideration of the most suitable response for addressing the humanitarian and international security challenges posed by LAWS'. Thus, the states' delegations at the GGE are still struggling to find a common definition of AWS. cf '2019 Germany Statement. Statement by Germany – On Agenda Item 5(d) Characterization of the Systems under Consideration in Order to Promote a Common Understanding on Concepts and Characteristics Relevant to the Objective and Purpose of the Convention' (2019). cf '2020 Chairperson's Summary' (19 April 2021) 46–47; '2019 Statement by Ireland. Agenda Item 5(b): Characterization of the Systems under Consideration in Order to Promote a Common Understanding on Concepts and Characteristics Relevant to the Objectives and Purposes of the Convention' (n 282); 'Report of the 2018 Session of the Group of Governmental Experts on Emerging Technologies in the Area of Lethal Autonomous Weapons Systems' (n 193) Annex III, para 22.

[314] McFarland, *Autonomous Weapon Systems and the Law of Armed Conflict: Compatibility with International Humanitarian Law* (n 46) 42.

[315] Rebecca Crootof, 'The Killer Robots are Here: Legal and Policy Implications' (2015) 36 *Cardozo Law Review* 1837, 1854.

[316] Rebecca Crootof, 'War Torts: Accountability for Autonomous Weapons' (2016) 164 *University of Pennsylvania Law Review* 1347 (our emphasis).

Crootof seems to include in her definition any kind of system capable of operating without a human presence,[317] adding that 'their capacity for *self-determined action* makes them uniquely effective and uniquely unpredictable'.[318] It is imperative to comment on these considerations. First, Crootof's definition has not been adopted by subsequent policy documents, see *DoD 3000.09*, *JDN 2/11*, *JDP 0–30.3*, and every report issued by the states that attended the CCW GGE's meetings in 2017, 2018 and 2019.[319] As Paul Scharre and Michael Horowitz have pointed out, before reaching any conclusions 'useful definitions must precisely distinguish between [...] existing uses of autonomy (many of which date back to World War II) and future weapons that would search over wide areas for targets then decide whether to destroy them completely on their own'.[320]

Second, to suggest that an AWS has the 'capacity for self-determined action' is to postulate a technological revolution by questioning the conventional paradigm of what a weapon is or should be.[321] It is one thing to use the term 'decide' – with due caution – when speaking of an AWS capable of choosing the most advantageous from among several available courses of action, but a completely different thing to state that these systems are capable of 'self-determined actions'. To achieve that level of independence, the system would have to be provided with representational structures such as *goals*, *beliefs* and *plans*, proper to *multi-level autonomous systems* (teleological systems), a level of sophistication that is well beyond the reach of AI research at present.[322] However, Crootof has not been the only author to subtly suggest an ontological move. According to Hin-Yan Liu, the capacity for an autonomous decision-making process 'may elevate advanced weapons systems from the category of passive military material towards that of the active combatant'.[323]

317 Crootof, 'The Killer Robots are Here: Legal and Policy Implications' (n 315) 1864.

318 Crootof, 'War Torts: Accountability for Autonomous Weapons' (n 316) 1349 (our emphasis).

319 US Department of Defense, 'DoD 3000.09. Autonomy in Weapon Systems' (n 7) 6; UK Ministry of Defence, 'The UK Approach to Unmanned Aircraft Vehicles, JDN 2/11' (n 8).

320 Paul Scharre and Michael C Horowitz, 'Ban or No Ban, Hard Questions Remains on Autonomous Weapons' (*IEEE Spectrum*, 20 August 2015) <https://spectrum.ieee.org/automaton/robotics/military-robots/ban-or-no-ban-hard-questions-remain-on-autonomous-weapons>.

321 Lucas Kello, *The Virtual Weapon and International Order* (Yale University Press 2018) 96.

322 Giovanni Sartor and Andrea Omicini, 'The Autonomy of Technological Systems and Responsibilities for Their Use' in Nehal Bhuta and others (eds), *Autonomous Weapons Systems: Law, Ethics, Policy* (Cambridge University Press 2016) 51–58.

323 Liu, 'Categorization and Legality of Autonomous and Remote Weapons Systems' (n 23) 632 (our emphasis).

The majority of scholars, however, tend to simply adopt the definition given by *DoD 3000.09*.[324] This definition was already the object of attention, but it is now important to understand if it defines accurately the reality of AWS. As has been seen, according to that directive an AWS is

> [a] weapon system that, once activated, can select and engage targets without further intervention by a human operator. This includes human-supervised autonomous weapon systems that are designed to allow human operators to override operation of the weapon system, but can select and engage targets without further human input after activation.[325]

The definition given by *DoD 3000.09* presents great advantages – but also some problems. To begin with, it opens by depicting an AWS as a 'weapon system', and that continues to be its status throughout the directive.[326] Second, describing its functions, for example, 'selecting' and 'engaging targets', is helpful to delineate the novelty of AWS. Third, it provides for a possible *safe clause* for *Supervised Autonomous Weapon Systems* (hereinafter SAWS): in the case of such systems, a human operator will always have the option of interrupting the course of action selected by the system.

A closer look into the definitions and explanations given by scholars, however, soon leads to the conclusion that some aspects of the definition can be problematic.[327] For one thing, the definition seems to include two different types of autonomous systems. The first sentence presents AWS, and the second introduces SAWS. The difference between the two, according to the definition, is whether or not a system allows human intervention once it is activated. It is important, however, to bear in mind that both types of systems can operate without human intervention but only SAWS afford opportunities for human operators to intervene. Thus, it might seem unclear and become

324 Guglielmo Tamburrini, 'On Banning Autonomous Weapons Systems: From Deontological to Wide Consequentialist Reasons' in Nehal Bhuta and others (eds), *Autonomous Weapons Systems: Law, Ethics, Policy* (Cambridge University Press 2016) 125; Kalmanovitz (n 272) 146; Sarah Knuckey, 'Autonomous Weapons Systems and Transparency: Towards an International Dialogue' in Nehal Bhuta and others (eds), *Autonomous Weapons Systems: Law, Ethics, Policy* (Cambridge University Press 2016) 166; Kenneth Anderson and Mathew C Waxman, 'Law and Ethics for Autonomous Weapon Systems: Why a Ban Won't Work and How the Laws of War Can' (2013) American University WCL Research Paper 2013-11, Columbia Public Law Research Paper 13-351 1, 11–12.

325 US Department of Defense, 'DoD 3000.09. Autonomy in Weapon Systems' (n 7).

326 With a completely different approach to autonomous systems, cf UK Ministry of Defence, 'The UK Approach to Unmanned Aircraft Vehicles, JDN 2/11' (n 8).

327 For a full account of DoD 3000.09, cf Mark Gubrud, 'Killer Robots and Laser-Guided Bombs: A Reply to Horowitz & Scharre' (*gubrud.net*, 4 December 2014) <http://gubrud.net/?=398>; cf Saxon (n 143) 185–189.

a source of confusion when authors, such as Michael Schmitt, when commenting on US *DoD 3000.09*, argue that 'the crux of autonomy is a capability to identify, target and attack a person or object without human interface. Although a human operator may retain the ability to take control of the system, it can operate without any control being exercised.'[328] Considering the fact that an AWS's operation will, at least in part, take place within a 'black box', and that their reaction time is way faster than that of human operators, it is legitimate to ask if there will be any real possibility of exercising human control, especially when there is no temporal or geographical gap between the operational system and the release of AWS' munition.[329] A separate question is whether AWS can be designed to include a 'kill-switch', allowing human operators to abort the mission if necessary, or self-destruct mechanisms, whenever the circumstances on the battlefield no longer require the mission to be carried because there is a perceived risk of violating IHL.

Another problematic point is that the definition recognises that AWS 'select and engage targets' without further human intervention but leaves open the question of whether the authors have or have not in mind systems that replicate human cognitive skills (fully autonomous systems). Lastly, the *safe clause* can be a factor of diversion in relation to the risks attendant upon *dissociation of communication*. Even if a weapon system can be deactivated that does not guarantee that the human operator will be able to intervene in time to avoid violations of IHL. This part of the definition seems to correspond more with the concept of a semi-autonomous system than a true AWS, but a question must be asked: will a system's 'autonomy', by definition, exclude a 'kill-switch'? Looking at an AWS' inbuilt capabilities would suggest it does – both Belgium and China are clearly of this understanding.[330] However, if a commander, looking at the specific circumstances of the battlefield, considers that a particular mission is no

328 Michael N Schmitt, 'Autonomous Weapon Systems and International Humanitarian Law: A Reply to the Critics' [2013] *Harvard National Security Journal Feature* 1, 4; Michael N Schmitt and Jeffrey S Thurnher, '"Out of the Loop": Autonomous Weapon Systems and the Law of Armed Conflict' (2013) 4 *Harvard National Security Journal* 231, 235.

329 Heyns, 'Report of the Special Rapporteur on Extrajudicial, Summary or Arbitrary Executions, Christof Heyns' (n 10) paras 53, 88. As Comandé explains 'machine learning process is classified as "non-interpretable" (by humans), for instance because the machine learned scheme is assessing thousands of variables, there will be not human intervention or a meaningful explanation of why a specific outcome is reached'. cf Comande (n 108) 166; Krupiy (n 31) 66.

330 Belgium, 'Group of Governmental Experts of the High Contracting Parties to the Convention on Prohibitions or Restrictions on the Use of Certain Conventional Weapons Which May Be Deemed to Be Excessively Injurious or to Have Indiscriminate Effects. Position Paper Submitted by Belgium' (2017) CCW/GGE.1/2017/WP.3 <http://undocs.org/ccw/gge.1/2017/WP.3>; China (n 180).

longer necessary, it seems unreasonable that he/she would be without the means to deactivate the system. Thus, it is possible to identify two different situations: SAWS, which can operate without human intervention but are at the same time designed to allow human operators to intervene in order to conduct the system to a specific outcome, and AWS, whose operators cannot intervene directly in the system's operations but can abort a mission if circumstances so require. This solution, as will be explained further, is compatible with the rules of Precaution (Article 57 API), although it does not accommodate a commander's intervention in the operations of an autonomous system.

Considering the aforementioned discussion, it is suggested that the best way to define an AWS *is as a weapon system designed and programmed for a mission to be adaptive and to identify, select and engage military targets, without human intervention*.

2.5.1 *A Weapon System*

Undeniably, a great deal of time and effort has gone into the study of weapons yet, almost without exception, scholars have stopped short of asking the most basic question: 'what exactly is a weapon?' Looking first to the history of military technology, as Robert O' Connell points out, a weapon is always the product of an inevitable process of evolution where, sometimes, there is no clear path of investigation.[331] Military theory and the organisation, tactics and strategy of war have changed more slowly than the technology – innovations at the technological level are always ahead in time – but whatever AWS turn out to be, in reality, war technology has a history. This prompts us to ask: in what way, exactly, will AWS be revolutionary comparing to other weapon systems?

Interestingly, ethicists and lawyers have directed little attention to the concept of 'weapon'; according to many the process of defining a weapon is 'a relatively straightforward process'.[332] Ethicists and lawyers are more concerned with the use of force and its effects than with exactly what constitutes a weapon.[333] A quotation from Seneca that Schmitt uses in one of his articles provides a clear example: 'a sword is never the killer, it is a tool in the killer's hands'.[334]

331 Robert L O' Connell, *Of Arms and Men: A History of War, Weapons and Aggression* (Oxford University Press 1989) 10–13.

332 McClelland (n 152) 404.

333 Boothby, *Weapons and the Law of Armed Conflict* (n 210) 4; James D Fry, 'Contextualized Legal Reviews for the Methods and Means of Warfare: Cave Combat and International Humanitarian Law' (2006) 44 *Columbia Journal of Transnational Law* 453.

334 Schmitt, 'Autonomous Weapon Systems and International Humanitarian Law: A Reply to the Critics' (n 328) 1.

However, if it is true that AWS will be capable of autonomous decision-making, this clearly challenges the accepted notion of 'weapon' as a 'tool'. As Justin McClelland rightly points out, the impact of the new capabilities of an already-existing weapon might well cause it to be classified as a 'new weapon', specifically designed to bridge a particular 'capability gap'.[335] But AWS, as a new weapon, may blur the distinction between weapons and combatants.[336] The status of AWS will be thoroughly discussed in Chapter 3. For now, it is sufficient to argue that AWS should be understood as a new 'weapon system'.[337]

In light of the aforementioned discussion, according to the *Manual on International Law Applicable to Air and Missile Warfare* (hereafter the AMW *Manual*), 'means of warfare' suggests 'weapons, weapon systems or platforms employed for the purpose of attack'. The AMW *Manual* goes on to explain that weapons 'are instruments used to cause, in the course of an armed conflict, (i) injury to, or death of, persons; or (ii) damage to, or destruction of, objects'.[338]

The definition presented by the AMW *Manual* deserves some clarification. First, it draws attention to the fact that 'means of warfare' are those applied in the context of an attack, specifically designed to 'injure or kill the enemy or damage, or destroy objects'. Accordingly, it can be stated that the defining feature of a weapon is that it is an object designed to be used in an attack.[339] Thus, as Leveringhaus stresses, the intended behaviour of a weapon is its ability to inflict harm. That it is intended to inflict harm is the attribute which differentiates a weapon from other objects (stone, scissors, etc.), which, whilst they might be used to cause harm, are not *specifically designed* to do so.[340] However, it cannot be forgotten that a weapon can also be used to 'prevent damage',[341] see for example current supervised autonomous systems

335 McClelland (n 152) 401.

336 Heyns, 'Report of the Special Rapporteur on Extrajudicial, Summary or Arbitrary Executions, Christof Heyns' (n 10) para 28; Chengeta, 'Are Autonomous Weapon Systems the Subject of Article 36 of Additional Protocol I to the Geneva Conventions?' (n 26) 77; McFarland, *Autonomous Weapon Systems and the Law of Armed Conflict: Compatibility with International Humanitarian Law* (n 46) 67–68, 73.

337 For the full discussion concerning the nature of AWS, see Chapter 3, Section 3.5. A completely different view is argued by Thompson Chengeta. cf Chengeta, 'Are Autonomous Weapon Systems the Subject of Article 36 of Additional Protocol I to the Geneva Conventions?' (n 26) 77–78.

338 HPCR, *Manual on International Law Applicable to Air and Missile Warfare* (The program on Humanitarian Policy and Conflict Research at Harvard University, Cambridge University Press 2013) 31, Rule 1 (t).

339 ibid Rule 1 (t), para 4.

340 Leveringhaus (n 1) 35.

341 O' Connell, *Of Arms and Men: A History of War, Weapons and Aggression* (n 331) 14.

such as the Aegis Combat System, among other defensive systems.[342] Thus, designing a 'weapon machine' requires starting from a functional specification describing the machine's general intended behaviour.[343] In the case of AWS, design will assume a special importance when it comes to categorisation. It is advisable to ask: 'what is the intentionality, the purpose for which AWS are to be designed and programmed?'

A second key element is that the description includes the concept of 'weapon systems'. Although a definition is not given, an illustrative example is provided: 'an aircraft used to conduct an attack together *with associated systems integral to the execution of the attack constitutes a means of warfare*'.[344] Similarly, a ground-based target designator used to guide a weapon to its target qualifies as a component part of a 'means of warfare'.[345] In this context, 'system' refers to any piece of hardware and/or software, any component considered indispensable and integral to the accomplishment of a military task. Modern technologies are likely to be integrated into military hardware and software that would not normally be classified as weaponry; however, as means necessary to the development of an attack operation, they are not considered in their individuality but as part of a 'means of warfare'.[346]

Finally, another relevant aspect of the definition is that within the term 'means of warfare' are included 'non-kinetic systems', such as those used in electronic warfare (EW) and computer network attacks (CNAs). This would mean that the computers, the software codes and all associated equipment would also be classified as 'means of warfare', but it is important to describe the specificity of AWS in this capacity.

2.5.2 *Designed and Programmed for a Mission*

Two central ideas: (1) the design and programming of the AWS *must* be IHL compliant, and (2) the design and programming *must* be carried out in accordance with the specific mission in hand.

342 'Aegis Combat System' (*Lockheed Martin*) <www.lockheedmartin.com/us/products/aegis.html>.

343 Nicola Bezzo and others, 'RobMakers: The Future of Digital Rapid Design and Fabrication of Robots' (2015) 22 *IEEE Robotics & Automation Magazine* 27, 28–29.

344 HPCR (n 338) 31 (t), para 3 (our emphasis).

345 ibid 31, Rule 1(t).

346 McFarland, 'Factors Shaping the Legal Implications of Increasingly Autonomous Military Systems' (n 32) 1315. With an opposite view, classifying AWS as a new method of warfare, see Chengeta, 'Are Autonomous Weapon Systems the Subject of Article 36 of Additional Protocol I to the Geneva Conventions?' (n 26) 74–77.

The *DoD 3000.09* definition and the discourse surrounding AWS focus on the possibility of systems' independently targeting military objects. However, before considering the legality and acceptability of such systems, it is crucial to remember the requirement that all states party to the API must subject new weapons to legal reviews (Article 36 API) and, according to the *ICRC Commentary*, 'if these measures are not taken, the State will be responsible in any case for any wrongful damage ensuing'.[347]

The problems of legal review will be addressed in Chapter 4, but it is important to highlight here that whatever the challenges are, one thing is certain: AWS can only emerge if there are significant improvements in the design of both software and hardware. Thus, weapon systems and their degree of autonomy are to be shaped by the factors considered relevant by their designers and programmers. It will not be a function of the system to choose its own values, missions or courses of action as fully autonomous weapon systems would be expected to do. The truth is that whilst autonomy may represent a technological enhancement, it is *dependent* on the relationship between designer, programmer and machine. As McFarland states, 'the controller of an autonomous system consists of the hardware and software that manages the vehicle, weapon or other device according to a program provided by a developer'.[348]

The mission entrusted to the system will establish the framework, the *area of competence*, of a certain AWS, in accordance with which its autonomous capabilities will be designed and programmed.[349] An AWS will be optimised to perform specific tasks, and will not function at all in a different context – take for example an autonomous ground vehicle: it clearly will not be competent to operate underwater or in the air. Having said this, it is correct to argue that there will always be a level of human control that, in the case of AWS, is made a priori, at the level of design and programming. However, the system's software will have the capability to operate *autonomously*, without direct human intervention.[350] According to the *Oslo Manual on Select Topics of the Law of Armed Conflict* (Oslo Manual), what differentiates autonomous

347 International Committee of the Red Cross, *Commentary on the Additional Protocols of 8 June 1977 to the Geneva Conventions of 12 August 1949* (Jean Pictet and others eds, International Committee of the Red Cross 1987) para 1466.

348 McFarland, *Autonomous Weapon Systems and the Law of Armed Conflict: Compatibility with International Humanitarian Law* (n 46) 32.

349 Remus Titiriga, 'Autonomy of Military Robots: Assessing the Technical and Legal ("Jus in Bello") Thresholds' (2016) 32 *The John Marshall Journal of Information Technology & Privacy Law* 57.

350 McFarland, 'Factors Shaping the Legal Implications of Increasingly Autonomous Military Systems' (n 32) 1325–1326; Leveringhaus (n 1) 48.

technology 'is its ability to apply what perhaps can most accurately be described as "human-like reasoning"'.[351]

2.5.3 *To Be Adaptive and to Identity, Select and Engage Military Targets*

This part of the definition encompasses two technical capabilities which will be essential to the realisation of AWS: the system will have to be *adaptive* and equipped with technology that enables it to *identify*, *select* and *engage* military targets.

2.5.3.1 Adaptive Systems

DoD 3000.09 establishes that autonomous and semi-autonomous systems will go through rigorous tests and evaluations to ensure that those systems:

a) function as anticipated in realistic operational environments against adaptive adversaries;
b) complete engagements in a time frame consistent with commander and operator intentions and, if unable to do so, terminate engagements or seek additional human operator input before continuing the engagement;
c) are sufficiently robust to minimise failures that could lead to unintended engagements or to loss of control of the system to unauthorised parties.

These points highlight three major concerns relating to autonomous systems:

d) The system demonstrates *a capacity to adapt to the dynamics both of the battlefield and the enemy*.
e) The system has sufficient 'assertiveness', that is, capacity to 'obey' in order to ensure that the purpose for which it was designed and programmed is fulfilled.
f) The system should be able to produce predictable results and be protected from external attack.[352]

Whereas an AWS is designed and programmed to fulfil a specific military purpose (this forming, so to speak, the *rigid element* of the system), it must also be provided with a *fluid element*, since it needs to be capable of adapting to the dynamic circumstances of the battlefield. It is this latter element that precisely

[351] Dinstein and Dahl (n 80) Rule 38, para 3.
[352] US Department of Defense, 'DoD 3000.09. Autonomy in Weapon Systems' (n 7) 2, para 4 'Policy' (our emphasis).

distinguishes the type of algorithm that enables a system to be autonomous in the true sense of the word.[353]

Scholars have reinforced the centrality of these factors, arguing that a weapons system exhibits three features that require analysis. First, the frequency with which a human operator needs to interact with the system in order for it to successfully perform its mission (this frequency, in the case of an AWS, would have to be minimal); second, *adaptability*, that is, the system's capacity to adapt to uncertain and unpredictable environments and, third, *assertiveness*, the ability to change its operating plan, without the guidance of a human operator, in order to complete its mission.[354]

It has been asseverated that *assertiveness* and *adaptability* are two sides of the same coin. As Giovanni Sartor and Andrea Omicini explain, 'an adaptive system needs to have a feedback mechanism, which keeps the system focused on its objective by changing its internal state as the environment changes'.[355] However, both features – *adaptability* and *assertiveness* – require the AWS to possess some level of decision-making ability, some ability to make a 'choice in action' and the capacity to 'independently' pursue pre-given military goals.[356] As Markus Wagner points out, the system is required to make 'discretionary decisions' in order to adapt to the mutable circumstances of the battlefield.[357]

Benjamin Kastan uses an analogy to help us envisage the adaptability of an AWS: just because a pilot is 'autonomous' does not mean that he/she can operate without orders. Similarly, even an AWS would have to follow orders from a higher authority but, according to Kastan's analogy, 'fully autonomous

353 Some authors, when referring to autonomous systems, tend to apply the term 'automated'. As an example, among others, Lucy Suchman and Jutta Weber define AWS as 'weapon systems in which the identification of targets, and the initiation of fire is automated in ways that preclude deliberative human intervention'. However, an autonomous system is characterised and distinguished for its ability to adapt the course of action in order to comply with the algorithm for the mission. Automated functions are proper to deterministic algorithms or for standard and automatic processes (cf Chapter 3, Section 3.4.1). Lucy Suchman and Jutta Weber, 'Human-Machine Autonomies' in Nehal Bhuta and others (eds), *Autonomous Weapons Systems: Law, Ethics, Policy* (Cambridge University Press 2016) 76; Deeks, Lubell and Murray (n 25) 3, 8–9, 17–18, 21.

354 William Marra and Sonia McNeil, 'Understanding "The Loop": Regulating the Next Generation of War Machines' (2013) 36 *Harvard Journal of Law and Public Policy* 1140, 1150–1155; McFarland, 'Factors Shaping the Legal Implications of Increasingly Autonomous Military Systems' (n 32) 1135; McFarland, *Autonomous Weapon Systems and the Law of Armed Conflict: Compatibility with International Humanitarian Law* (n 46) 37–40.

355 Sartor and Omicini (n 322) 49.

356 Marra and McNeil (n 354) 1151.

357 Wagner, 'The Dehumanization of International Humanitarian Law: Legal, Ethical, and Political Implications of Autonomous Weapon Systems' (n 64) 1383.

systems would largely take the role of the pilot or vehicle operator'.[358] Thus, as would any 'pilot', an AWS will have a mission, and will have to respect IHL norms, but it should be able to adapt its own system to the circumstances encountered on the battlefield.[359]

The comparison with a human pilot is relevant as far as the type of algorithms upon which an AWS will depend are concerned. These algorithms (neural networks) do not perform rule-based calculations as do most computers. Instead, they learn by exposure to data, analyse it and generate outputs favourable in terms of the pre-given objectives of the mission. Having said this, it is important to remember that neural networks operate in a 'black box'. Not only can this preclude human understanding of the decision-making process but, as is known, neural networks can also fail and make errors – especially *counterintuitive* errors. In a study of visual classification, neural networks interpreted images (images that, to the human eye, looked like static or abstract wavy lines) as animals or other objects, and asserted greater than 99.6 per cent confidence in their interpretations.[360]

In sum, to assert that an AWS is capable of 'discretionary decisions' recalls the undesirability of using anthropomorphic language in connection with autonomous systems.[361] However, it also recalls that unpredictability is a feature of adaptable systems.

2.5.3.2 Identify, Select and Engage Military Targets

The discourse of autonomous weapons technology is normally associated with unmanned aerial vehicles, or 'drones'. These were first used solely in surveillance roles (e.g. during the war in Kosovo), but increasingly drones have taken

358 Benjamin Kastan, 'Autonomous Weapons Systems: A Coming Legal "Singularity"?' (2014) 2013 *Journal of Law, Technology & Policy* 45, 50.

359 Although it is not an autonomous system, the C-130 Hercules is an example of an adaptable system due to its capacity to use prepared or unprepared runways for take-offs and landings. 'NZ Military Announces Upgrade of Hercules Aircraft Fleet, Worth $661 Million' (*GlobalSecurity.org*, 11 June 2019) <www.globalsecurity.org/military/library/news/2019/06/mil-190611-sputnik04.htm?_m=3n%252e002a%252e2597%252emtoa008t5t%252e2e7v>.

360 Scharre, 'Autonomous Weapons and Operational Risk: Ethical Autonomy Project' (n 230) 14–15; National Science and Technology Council, 'The National Artificial Intelligence Research and Development Strategic Plan' (Executive Office of the President of the United States 2016) 24 <www.nitrd.gov/pubs/national_ai_rd_strategic_plan.pdf>; Comande (n 108) 167.

361 The 2018 Chair non-paper at the CCW states that 'in crafting potential policy measures, emerging technologies in the area of lethal autonomous weapons systems should not be anthropomorphized. IHL imposes obligations on States and individuals, not machines.' cf Gjorgjinski (n 158) s G, para ii.

on combat roles as evidenced in Afghanistan, Yemen and Pakistan.[362] However, as Leveringhaus notes, these systems should be qualified as *uninhabited* rather than unmanned systems, because their innovative ability is that of facilitating the selection and engagement of military targets without physical contact with the battlefield.[363] But while a drone is directly controlled by a human operator, AWS promise to be systems where the human operator will be *out-of-the-loop*.

Notwithstanding the presence of human decision-makers, the truth is that a degree of 'autonomy' is already used in a variety of military tasks performed by drones, including identifying, tracking, selecting, prioritising, signalling targets and indicating the precise time at which a weapon is to be fired.[364] This sort of activity can establish the 'pattern of life' of an individual, identify precisely the location of objects of military significance and monitor conditions on the battlefield. Bearing in mind the idea of 'weapon system', there is no reason why an AWS could not have access to data collected by a drone or drones in order to identify, locate and select a target; a variety of fundamental operations could be congregated in one single system.

This understanding is espoused by the ICRC, which, in its document entitled *International Humanitarian Law and the Challenges of Contemporary Armed Conflicts*, suggests that AWS should be an 'umbrella term', able to include any kind of weapon, whether operating in the air, on land or at sea, that is autonomous in respect of its 'critical functions', that is *select* (search for, detect, identify, track and select) and *engage* (use force against, neutralise, damage or destroy) any military target. Weapon systems would use their sensors, programming and weapon(s) to carry out the sort of targeting process that would ordinarily be directed and controlled by human operators.[365]

362 For the overall controversy regarding the use of Drone Technology and its capabilities, see Oren Gross, 'The New Way of War: Is There a Duty to Use Drones?' (2015) 67 *Florida Law Review* 1; Susanne Krasmann and Jutta Weber (eds), 'Game Changer? On the Epistemology, Ontology and Politics of Drones' (2015) 8 *Behemoth A Journal on Civilisation* 3; Markus Wagner, 'Autonomy in the Battlespace: Independently Operating Weapon Systems and the Law of Armed Conflict' in Dan Saxon (ed), *International Humanitarian Law and the Changing Technology of War* (Martinus Nijhoff 2013) 102–103; Stuart Casey-Maslen, 'Pandora's Box? Drone Strikes under Jus Ad Bellum, Jus in Bello, and International Human Rights Law' (2012) 94 *International Review of the Red Cross* 597; Cullen (n 22) 114–121; Heyns and others (n 257) 792.

363 Leveringhaus (n 1) 49.

364 Paul Scharre and Michael C Horowitz, 'An Introduction to Autonomy in Weapon Systems' (Centre for a New American Security 2015) 3 <www.files.ethz.ch/isn/188865/Ethical%20Autonomy%20Working%20Paper_021015_v02.pdf>.

365 ICRC, 'International Humanitarian Law and the Challenges of Contemporary Armed Conflicts. Recommitting to Protection in Armed Conflict on the 70th Anniversary of the Geneva Conventions' (n 23).

Following the same line of reason, the US National Science and Technology Council noted, in its 2016 Strategic Plan, that 'integrated data from perception forms situational awareness to provide AI systems with the comprehensive knowledge and a model of the state of the world necessary to plan and execute tasks effectively and safely'.[366] In this context, it is useful to allude to the distinction made by the Oslo Manual between a *highly automated system* and an *autonomous system*. While the former is a weapon system 'constrained by algorithms that determine its responses by imposing rules of engagement and setting mission parameters which limit its ability to act independently', the latter is 'programmed to apply human-like reasoning to determine *whether an object or person is a target, whether it should be attacked and if so, how and when*'.[367]

Though the capabilities of some information technology may still be challenged, the fact is that with increasingly sophisticated and accurate systems it will soon be possible to monitor and track everything of military significance on Earth. Such systems include global military communications, 'global positioning systems' (GPS) and systems with intelligence, reconnaissance and surveillance capabilities. Still more significant are systems such as the video capture system *Gorgon Stare*, which enables drones to keep entire populations under surveillance, and *biometrics* and *facial recognition systems*, such as that deployed across Moscow (which can scan ten million images in less than seven seconds).[368]

In spite of all this current and potential technical progress, the identification, selection and engagement of military targets has to be made under the scrutiny of *Jus in Bello*. This is probably one of the most important questions to ask roboticists: how will AWS technology comply with the well-established customary and conventional norms of IHL? Ronald Arkin advances a preliminary answer, stating that an AWS must be able to 'adhere to its moral standards within the situations that it has been designed for, in

366 National Science and Technology Council (n 360) 18.

367 Dinstein and Dahl (n 80) Rules 37 and 38 (our emphasis).

368 Armin Krishnan, 'Mass Surveillance, Drones, and Unconventional Warfare' (2015) 8 *Behemoth A Journal on Civilisation* 12, 14–22; Michael A Newton, 'Back to the Future Reflections on the Advent of Autonomous Weapons Systems' (2015) 47 *Case Western Reserve Journal of International Law* 5, 21; Tyler Rogoway, 'Drones in Afghanistan Have the Most Advanced Aerial Surveillance Ever' (2015) *Jalopnik* <https://jalopnik.com/drones-in-afghanistan-have-the-most-advanced-aerial-sur-1695912540>; 'Identity Dominance: The U.S. Military's Biometric War in Afghanistan' (*Public Intelligence*, 2014) <https://publicintelligence.net/identity-dominance/>; 'Standoff Technology Integration and Demonstration Program: Biometric Optical Surveillance System Tests' (US Department of Homeland Security 2012) <www.dhs.gov/sites/default/files/publications/privacy_pia_008a_s%26t_dec2012.pdf>; Carly Kind, 'Nowhere to Hide' (*The World Today*, March 2020) <www.chathamhouse.org/publications/twt/living-ai>.

this case *specific battlefield missions and not in a more general sense*'.[369] Thus, it becomes rather difficult to accept the argument promulgated by some authors, among them Crootof, that 'an autonomous weapon system could either *operate with no constraints* or with pre-programmed boundaries'.[370] The specificity of a military mission will, indeed, set its own boundaries and constraints long before the effective engagement of the target. It will determine which data should be collected and how they should be organised in order to establish the optimal course of action to engage a legitimate target. The problem, however, does not seem to be so much the *selection algorithm* and its rules, but rather the *algorithm for situation management*. The latter will have to be open to the environment and adapt to changing circumstances without losing its assertiveness towards the *algorithm for the mission*, as is confirmed by *JDP 0–30.2*.[371] Thus, it seems likely that most problems will stem from the interaction of the AWS with uncontrollable events unfolding in the battlespace.

2.5.3.3 Without Human Intervention – Humans in-, on- and out-of-the-Loop

This part of the definition is certainly the one that causes more concern among scholars, ethicists and lawyers than any other.[372] What does it mean for a weapon system to operate without human intervention? This is a very important question to all parties involved. Since 2014, all states party to the CCW have flagged up the question of human control; at the 2018 GGE Meeting only the United States failed to mention the problem of how to establish a human operator–AWS interface, looking towards the humanitarian implications of introducing AWS.[373] As was explained

369 Arkin, *Governing Lethal Behavior in Autonomous Robots* (n 34) 69.

370 Crootof, 'The Killer Robots are Here: Legal and Policy Implications' (n 315) 1857 (our emphasis).

371 UK Ministry of Defence, 'Joint Doctrine Publication 0–30.2 Unmanned Aircraft Systems' (n 7) 13.

372 Human Rights Watch and International Human Rights Clinic, 'Losing Humanity: The Case against Killer Robots' (n 30) 2; Human Rights Watch and International Human Rights Clinic, 'Mind the Gap: The Lack of Accountability for Killer Robots' (n 61); Wagner, 'Taking Humans Out of the Loop: Implications for International Humanitarian Law' (n 85) 4; Marra and McNeil (n 354) 1144–1155; Kalmanovitz (n 272) 154–158; Geoffrey S Corn, 'Autonomous Weapons Systems: Managing the Inevitably of "Taking the Man out of the Loop"' in Nehal Bhuta and others (eds), *Autonomous Weapons Systems: Law, Ethics, Policy* (Cambridge University Press 2016) 214.

373 United States of America, 'Human-Machine Interaction in the Development, Deployment and Use of Emerging Technologies in the Area of Lethal Autonomous Weapons Systems' (*Reaching Critical Will*, 2018) CCW/GGE.1/2018/WP.4 <https://reachingcriticalwill.org/images/documents/Disarmament-fora/ccw/2018/gge/documents/GGE.2-WP4.pdf>.

before, states tend to use 'human intervention' or 'human control' somewhat inattentively, without distinguishing one from the other. However, it is proposed here that the former should be seen as just one of the possible expressions of the latter.

The assertion that AWS will be capable of operating 'without human intervention' is intended to emphasise that – whatever the level of autonomy – AWS will always be designed and programmed to work towards certain human goals. AWS will be tested, evaluated in order to be used by humans and for human purposes. Thus, there will always be a certain level of human control and coordination at the time of testing, evaluating, designing and programming an AWS.

In order to determine the level of human intervention in a targeting decision-making process, a common and traditional approach has been to distinguish between weapon systems with a human ***in-the-loop, on-the-loop*** or ***out-of-the-loop***.[374] In this situation, *the loop* refers to a decision-making process known as the *DOODA Loop*, that is the OODA loop (*Observation, Orientation, Decision* and *Action*) preceded by 'D' to represent the *dynamic nature* of the battlefield. In this context, we can identify four situations:

1) A human operator selects a target and initiates an attack. In this case, the entire decision-making process is entrusted to a human operator who is *in-the-loop* of an *automated* weapon system (to quote *JDN 2/11*) or of a *semi-autonomous weapon* (to quote *DoD 3000.09*). The system uses autonomy to engage individual targets or specific groups of targets that a human has decided are to be engaged. The algorithm is, therefore, designed to function in accordance with fixed rules.

In light of the aforementioned discussion, some weapons can be included in the *in-the-loop* group, for example guided munitions, whether they be *signature-guided munitions* or *go-onto-location-in-space guided munitions*, commonly known as *Precise Guided Munitions* (*PGM*). Both categories have in common the fact that the human operator launching these weapons knows what specific targets will be engaged. In the case of *signature-guided munitions*, some use 'passive sensors', merely sensing signals from the environment to close in on a target, others use 'active sensors', such as radar, that send out signals and track the target's return signal. There are also weapons

374 Eric Talbot Jensen, 'The Future of the Law of Armed Conflict: Ostriches, Butterflies, and Nanobots' (2014) 35 *Michigan Journal of International Law* 253, 294; Dinstein and Dahl (n 80) Rule 39.

with the capacity to *lock on* to the target before the launch, and others that lock on after launching – the latter are first launched and then their sensors are activated. *Go-onto-location-in-space guided munitions* are designed to hit a target not by recognising its signature, but rather by being directed to the specific geographic area where the target is known to be located. This type includes GPS-guided bombs, like the Brimstone.[375] This is a fire-and-forget, radar-guided missile that can seek and destroy armoured targets at long range. It is programmable to adapt to particular mission requirements, and is loaded with targeting data by the weapon systems officer (WSO) prior to launch. Such weapons are equipped with a capability that includes, essentially, the ability to find targets within a certain area (such as those near friendly forces), and to self-destruct if it is *unable* to find a target within the designated area. It can operate in *indirect mode* when the position of the target is not visible to the pilot, and the missile can lock on before launch, using its on-board navigation system to head for the target and searching, using its radar, to find pre-selected targets.[376]

2) Another type of system is that where the human is ***on-the-loop***. These systems, once activated, can identify, select and engage targets without human intervention, but they are designed and programmed to allow human operators to intervene and terminate engagements at any stage. The human operator is kept *on-the-loop* in order to avoid any kind of damage or unlawful results. These systems are called *human-supervised autonomous weapons systems* by *DoD 3000.09* and are still included in the category of *automated systems* according to *JDN 2/11* and *JDP 0–30.2*.[377] As in the case of *semi-autonomous systems*, the task of identifying the target is allotted to the system. The only difference is the position of the human operator, who supervises the system's operation in real time and can intervene if necessary, reversing the course of action taken by the system.

These systems have been deployed by many states as defensive mechanisms, where the reaction time required for engagement is so short that it would be

375 Scharre and Horowitz, 'An Introduction to Autonomy in Weapon Systems' (n 364) 9.

376 'Brimstone Advance Anti Armour Missile' (*Army Technology*, 2021) <www.army-technology.com/projects/brimstone/>.

377 UK Ministry of Defence, 'The UK Approach to Unmanned Aircraft Vehicles, JDN 2/11' (n 8) 2–3; UK Ministry of Defence, 'Joint Doctrine Publication 0–30.2 Unmanned Aircraft Systems' (n 7) 2–9; US Department of Defense, 'DoD 3000.09. Autonomy in Weapon Systems' (n 7) 14.

'physically impossible for a human to remain "in the loop" *and take positive action before each engagement and still defend effectively*'.[378] In this group are included air-defence systems such as the *AEGIS Combat System*[379] (deployed by Australia, Japan, Norway, South Korea, Spain and the United States), the *Goalkeeper CIWS*[380] (deployed by the Netherlands, Portugal, Qatar, South Korea, the United Arab Emirates and the United Kingdom), the *MK Phalanx Close-in Weapon System*[381] (deployed by Australia, Bahrain, Canada, Egypt, India, Israel, Japan, New Zealand, Pakistan, Poland, Portugal, Saudi Arabia, South Korea, Taiwan, the United Kingdom and the United States), the *Patriot Missile*[382] (deployed by Egypt, Germany, Greece, Israel, Japan, Kuwait, the Netherlands, Saudi Arabia, South Korea, Spain, Taiwan, the United Arab Emirates and the United States) and the *SeaRam Anti-Ship Missile Defence System*[383] (deployed by Japan and the United States).[384] In this group should finally be included the *Brimstone* when operating in *direct mode*. In this situation, the human operator eventually has the ability to laser-guide, using a sighting system to select the target.[385]

3) Finally, there is the type of system in which the human operator is *out-of-the-loop*. It has to be recalled here that, according to *DoD 3000.09*, autonomous weapon systems are those that 'once activated, can select and engage targets without further intervention by a human operator'.[386] This directive, however, as Mark Gubrud argues, employs the ancient rhetorical strategy of '*equivocation*' and, by exploiting ambiguities, it omits to draw a line between 'semi-autonomous' and 'fully autonomous'

378 Scharre and Horowitz, 'An Introduction to Autonomy in Weapon Systems' (n 364) 12. According to Scharre and Horowitz, at least thirty nations employ or have in development at least one system of this type, including Australia, Bahrain, Belgium, Canada, Chile, China, Egypt, France, Germany, Greece, India, Israel, Japan, Kuwait, the Netherlands, New Zealand, Norway, Pakistan, Poland, Portugal, Qatar, Russia, Saudi Arabia, South Africa, South Korea, Spain, Taiwan, the United Arab Emirates, the United Kingdom and the United States.

379 'Aegis Combat System' (n 342).

380 'GoalKeeper – Close-in Weapon System (CIWS)' <www.thalesgroup.com/en/goalkeeper-close-weapon-system>.

381 'PHALANX Close-in Weapon System' <www.raytheon.co.uk/capabilities/products/phalanx/>.

382 'Patriot Missile' <(www.army-technology.com/projects/patriot/>.

383 'SeaRam Anti-Ship Missile Defense System' <www.raytheon.com/capabilities/products/searam/>.

384 Scharre and Horowitz, 'An Introduction to Autonomy in Weapon Systems' (n 364) 22–23. The document also gives details about defensive ground systems which are in use or in development.

385 'Brimstone Advance Anti Armour Missile' (n 376).

386 US Department of Defense, 'Unmanned Systems Integrated Roadmap: FY2013–2038' (n 80).

weapons systems.[387] Indeed, what does it actually mean to say a weapon system 'can select'? Does it mean that it also identifies the target? Or that in some circumstances it cannot select autonomously?[388] Another important factor is that *DoD 3000.09* includes two radically different types of system in the category of 'autonomous systems'. As the Netherlands' definition clearly states: an AWS 'selects and engages targets [...] on the *understanding that an attack, once launched, cannot be stopped by human intervention*'.[389] This last point is vitally important as it distinguishes AWS from systems that allow 'dynamic diligences' between the system and the human officer or operators, that is, assessments of specific system operations.[390] The opposite happens in the case of AWS: operators are *out-of-the-loop* of the decision-making process. However, the fact that human operators cannot intervene in the 'inner world' of a system does not preclude some human control over the system. There are two options. First, the algorithm for situation management includes a *self-destruction mechanism* that activates if the AWS detects that the mission cannot be accomplished. Second, whenever the algorithm for the mission is shown by the circumstances on the battlefield to be outdated, a human officer can decide *to deactivate* the system (by means of a kill-switch).[391]

Considering the aforementioned discussion, it is legitimate to ask if the terminology *in/on/out-of-the-loop* is indeed helpful. The term *out-of-the-loop* can convey the idea that not only can the human operator not intervene, but also that he/she has no form of control. However, it is important to always bear in mind the structure of machine learning algorithms. A *learner* will deduce a theory from the data collected or, as roboticists prefer to put it, these

387 Gubrud (n 327).

388 Ariel Conn, 'The Problem of Defining Autonomous Weapons' (*Future of Life*, 30 November 2016) <https://futureoflife.org/2016/11/30/problem-defining-autonomous-weapons/?cn-reloaded=1>.

389 The Netherlands (n 278).

390 Peter Margulies, 'The Other Side of Autonomous Weapons: Using Artificial Intelligence to Enhance IHL Compliance' in Eric Talbot Jensen (ed), *The Impact of Emerging Technologies on the Law of Armed Conflict* (Oxford University Press 2018) 406–407 <https://papers.ssrn.com/sol3/papers.cfm?abstract_id=3194713>.

391 Take as an example the DARPA Robotics Challenge Final in 2015 when the competitors were not allowed to intervene with the trial robots when they fell or got stuck. However, the robots could always be deactivated. cf Williams (n 134). This possibility was discussed by many delegations at the 2019 GGE Meeting. cf 'Report of the 2018 Session of the Group of Governmental Experts on Emerging Technologies in the Area of Lethal Autonomous Weapons Systems' (n 193) Annex 4, para 4.

algorithms will follow an *inverse deduction approach*. However, Domingos argues that 'just because a computer can learn doesn't mean they magically acquire a will of their own. Learners learn to achieve the goals we set them; they don't get to change the goals.'[392] It can, therefore, be concluded that the use of machine learning algorithms does not exclude human control. Goals and constraints will be set by human operators and a commander should be able to deactivate the system if, due to supervenient reasons, it can no longer satisfy the preset goal.

2.6 AWS AND CYBER-WEAPONS

Once AWS have been defined, it is important to distinguish those systems from cyber-weapons that also can be considered as autonomous weapons.

The starting point of any comparison between AWS and cyber-weapons is their present status. While cyber-weapons exist and are an actual reality, AWS have not yet been deployed.[393] However, AWS share some common features with cyber-weapons. First, there is the sheer multiplicity of terms used to describe them, for example 'cyber-attack', 'cyberwarfare', 'computer network attack' and 'cybercrime', to quote but a few. Second, there is the heavy dependence on modern systems of data collection and on the internet, both now key elements in any decision whether/when to start an operation or proceed to an attack.[394] Third, there is the same high level of debate regarding the understanding and future regulation of cyber-weapons, although states have perhaps shown more diligence in policing cyber activities than AWS.[395]

392 Domingos (n 94) 45.

393 Mariarosaria Taddeo and Luciano Floridi, 'Regulate Artificial Intelligence to Avert Cyber Arms Race' (2018) 556 *Nature. International Journal of Science* 296; Center for Strategic & International Studies, 'Significant Cyber Incidents' <www.csis.org/programs/cybersecurity-and-governance/technology-policy-program/other-projects-cybersecurity>.

394 In *Reno v American Civil Liberties Union* (1997), the US Supreme Court defined internet as 'an international network of interconnected computers' and the protocols that comprise the Internet constitute, according to the Supreme Court, 'a unique medium-known to its users by cyberspace- located in no particular geographical location but available to anyone, anywhere in the world'. cf Calo (n 60) 517. For the concept of cyber-space and cyber-operations, see Dinstein and Dahl (n 80) Rules 20 and 24.

395 At an informal meeting on 30 May 2017, chaired by the Chairperson-elect of the 2017 CCW Meeting of the High Contracting Parties, Ambassador Matthew Rowland of the United Kingdom of Great Britain and Northern Ireland, on behalf of the President-designate of the Nineteenth Conference of Amended Protocol II, Ambassador Beatriz Londoño Soto of Colombia; the President-designate of the Eleventh Conference of Protocol V, Ambassador Andre Pung of Estonia; and the Chairperson of the Group of Governmental Experts on Lethal Autonomous Weapons Systems (GGE on LAWS), Ambassador Amandeep Singh Gill

The dependence of both cyber-weapons and AWS on complex and inherently non-transparent software will make the attribution of an attack more difficult, calling into question (a) whether the international mechanisms available today are sufficiently robust to cover these new technologies, and (b) how accountability for violations of International Laws caused by both cyber-attacks and AWS are to be attributed.[396] Following this line of reasoning, the *United Nations Institute for Disarmament Research* (UNIDIR) published, in 2017, a report on the problem of the overlapping of these two technologies.[397]

It is not the intention of this work to provide a full account of the problems inherent in cyberwarfare, but to offer some guidelines to understanding the specificities of AWS and cybercrime. 'Cyber reality' has been described as a series of operations intended 'to manipulate, disrupt, deny, degrade, or destroy information resident in computers and computer networks, or the computer network itself, or to gain control over the computer or computer network'.[398] As Schmitt notes, all modern conflicts involve cyber activity in some form, whether it be 'as simple as passing intelligence information or as complicated as bringing down the enemy's integrated air defence system'.[399]

As was discussed at the UNIDIR's 2018 Cyber Stability Conference, there has been, since the early 2000s, a strong digitalisation of the international community and a concomitant towards developing mechanisms of trust and responsibility. The 2013 UNIDIR report *Cyber Security Index: International Security Trends and Realities* notes that, by the end of 2012, the number of national cybersecurity programmes had grown from 69 in 2011 to a 114 in August 2012. Forty-seven states have cybersecurity programmes that allot some role to the armed forces and sixty-seven states have solely civilian programmes.[400] This can

of India, it was announced that due to insufficient funding available, the Group of Governmental Experts on Lethal Autonomous Weapons Systems (LAWS), among other meetings, were cancelled. cf United Nations Office at Geneva, 'CCW – Latest Information' (30 May 2017) <www.unog.ch/80256EE600585943/(httpPages)/3CFCEEEF52D553D5C1257B0300473B77?OpenDocument>; Eric Talbot Jensen, 'The Tallinn Manual 2.0: Highlights and Insights' (2017) 48 *Georgetown Journal of International Law* 735.

396 Kenneth Anderson, 'Why the Hurry to Regulate Autonomous Weapon Systems – But Not Cyber-Weapons' (2016) 30 *Temple International & Comparative Law Journal* 17, 27–32.

397 UNIDIR, 'The Weaponization of Increasingly Autonomous Technologies: Autonomous Weapon Systems and Cyber Operations' (UNIDIR 2017) Nr 7 <www.unidir.org/files/publications/pdfs/autonomous-weapon-systems-and-cyber-operations-en-690.pdf>.

398 HPCR (n 338) 20, Rule M. For a notion of a cyber-attack, cf Oona A Hathaway and Rebecca Crootof, 'The Law of Cyber-Attack' (2012) 100 *California Law Review* 817, 827.

399 Michael N Schmitt, 'The Law of Cyber Targeting. Tallin Paper 7' (2015) NATO Cooperative Cyber Defence Centre of Excellence 1, 2.

400 UNIDIR, 'The Cyber Index: International Security Trends and Realities' (United Nations 2013) UNIDIR/2013/3, 1–5 <www.unidir.org/files/publications/pdfs/cyber-index-2013-en-463.pdf>.

be justified by the importance of the incredibly intricate systems of information available, as seen in Chapter 1, that make states ever more dependent on technology, whilst at the same time countries with low cyber capabilities are more likely to be targeted by cyber-attacks in times of both war and peace.[401]

Until today, regarding cyber-weapons, there have been three particular government efforts to understand the scope of the threat of cyberwarfare. The first attempt, in 2009, was by the Shanghai Cooperation Organization (SCO) – a security cooperation group composed by China, Russia and most of the Soviet Central Asian republics as well as observer states such as Iran, India and Pakistan. This initiative evidenced a wider vision and understanding of the concepts of 'war' and 'weapon', going beyond the traditional interpretations articulated in the IHL framework.[402]

The second effort was developed by a counterpart of SCO, the NATO Cooperative Cyber Defence Centre of Excellence, based in Tallinn in Estonia. This has taken the lead, internationally, in addressing the problem of cyberwarfare and its regulation in accordance with the IHL framework. In that connection it launched, in 2009, a three-year project detailed with surveying cyberwarfare-related questions. More than twenty scholars and government legal advisers congregated in a joint effort to produce the *Tallinn Manual on International Law Applicable to Cyber Warfare* (the *Tallinn Manual*). According to Rule 30 of this work: 'a cyber-attack is a cyber operation, whether offensive or defensive, that is reasonably expected to cause injury or death to persons or damage or destruction to objects'.[403] Discussing the details and nuances of this definition goes beyond the aim of this work, but it is important to mention that IHL can be called upon in the context of a cyber-attack – as Schmitt observes – because there is no normative or practical logic for distinguishing between a cyber-attack that damages objects and injures people and a kinetic operation with precisely the same effects.[404]

401 Baris Celiktas and Nafiz Unlu, 'Cyber Security Power Ranking by Country and Its Importance on World Politics' (2018) 67 *International Journal of Social Science* 469, 473; Liivoja, Leins and McCormack (n 22) 605–606.

402 Cordula Droege, 'Get off My Cloud: Cyber Warfare, International Humanitarian Law, and the Protection of Civilians' (2012) 94 *International Review of the Red Cross* 533, 538–540; Stephen Aris, 'Shanghai Cooperation Organization. Mapping Multilateralism in Transition No. 2' (*International Peace Institute*, 2013) 14 <www.ipinst.org/wp-content/uploads/publications/ipi_e_pub_shanghai_cooperation.pdf>.

403 Michael N Schmitt, *Tallinn Manual 2.0 on the International Law Applicable to Cyber Operations* (NATO Cooperative Cyber Defence Centre of Excellence 2017) 92.

404 Schmitt, 'The Law of Cyber Targeting. Tallin Paper 7' (n 399) 4.

This endeavour resulted in what is known as the *Tallinn Manual 2.0 on the International Law Applicable to Cyber Operations*, released in February 2017.[405] As of 2018, there is no international agreement on how cyber-weapons should be regulated but, as the new manual explains, it 'is meant to be a reflection of the law as it existed at the point of the Manual's adoption by the two International Groups of Experts in June 2016'.[406] As Eric Talbot Jensen explains, the experts have disagreed, as have many others, on vitally important matters such as practice of due diligence, jurisdiction and international responsibility regarding cyber-attacks.[407] However, as the author argues, *Tallinn Manual 2.0* is an important starting point for discussion, in the next few decades, in an area of law in which there is a great need for understanding to create an approach to a new reality.

Tallinn Manual 2.0 is, therefore, a notable example of what can be achieved by experts and states when they cooperate in order to develop responses to new means and methods of warfare. But, although cyber-weapons and AWS represent new technologies of war, they should not be confused.

In order to avoid confusion, the *Summer Study on Autonomy*, published by the US Defence Science Board in June 2016, makes a distinction between two types of system: those employing *autonomy at rest* and those employing *autonomy in motion*. In short, systems incorporating *autonomy at rest* operate virtually, as software, and include planning and expert advisory systems, whereas systems incorporating *autonomy in motion* have a presence in the physical world and, therefore, give rise to a need for terminology that describes *robots* that detect, select and act *alone* or as a *team* (having a human–machine interface).[408]

2.7 CONCLUSION AND THREE FUNDAMENTAL CONSIDERATIONS

In Chapter 2, the current state of the debate concerning the legitimacy of AWS was analysed. One conclusion becomes clear from this chapter: it is almost impossible to find a coherent and well-structured contour of what,

405 Schmitt, *Tallinn Manual 2.0 on the International Law Applicable to Cyber Operations* (n 403).

406 Jensen, 'The Tallinn Manual 2.0: Highlights and Insights' (n 395) 738.

407 ibid 740, 744, 750.

408 The term *robot* is used here as having a physical and material presence on the battlefield. Defense Science Board – Department of Defense, 'Summer Study on Autonomy. June 2016' (June 2016) 5 <www.hsdl.org/?view&did=794641>; Christopher Meissner and Linton Wells, *AI, Autonomy, and the Future Battlefield* (Defense One E-book 2017) 9. For the complexity of an accurate definition of 'robot' cf Lemley and Casey (n 2) 28–29

exactly, is meant by 'AWS', 'LAWS' and 'fully autonomous systems'. States use, indiscriminately, terms that can refer to opposing realities. This can, and certainly does, result in a demotivating confusion that casts legal process into obscurity. In order to provide clarity, this chapter has divided the positions taken by states and NGOs into three different groups. In the first group, an increasing number of states are calling for a pre-emptive ban on AWS. These states are aligned with the arguments presented by NGOs (such as HRW) that AWS cannot be allowed to operate without human oversight. Without addressing the legal aspects of their argument, these states simply reject the whole proposal. The second group, characterised by its abstention from comment on the subject, risks losing their chance to express their views because there remain very few without an opinion one way or another. The third group comprises those states that find the idea of a pre-emptive ban on AWS premature and strategically suspect. Although aware of several critical legal and ethical problems that might arise from the introduction of AWS, these states prefer to pursue clear definitions and further understanding of how, exactly, these systems will operate on the battlefield.

The aforementioned division does not allow, however, for a clear understanding of what is expected of an AWS. The diversity of definitions, added to the absence of a clear distinction between AWS and previous weapon systems, and the lack of distinction between AI's current capacities and those of (as yet hypothetical) future systems do not give any clear indication of a positive way forward. There needs to be a very clear understanding of what an AWS is, taking into account current AI achievements. For this reason, a definition has been proposed to clarify exactly what the deployment of AWS entails.

Note the definition given. A different direction was taken to examine the definitions of AWS that states have most recently put forward, right up until the moment of writing. Three interrelated dimensions deserve special attention: first, the mission entrusted to an AWS, second, the AWS' capability to adapt to the battlefield, and finally, the distinction between control and intervention.

Starting with the first point, when the terms *in/on/out of-the-loop* are used, states and scholars tend to look exclusively at the capabilities of the system. Questions emerge such as 'will AWS have the capability to apply the Rules of Distinction and/or Proportionality, or not? If not, who is to be held accountable?' As important as these questions may be, the *mission* entrusted to the system cannot be overlooked. It is the features of the military operation that will dictate which weapon system is to be deployed. It will be the commander's responsibility to discern the optimal course of action, decide on whether to deploy an AWS and assess the risk of the weapon system's causing any violation of IHL (Articles 49 and 57(2)(a)(i)(ii) API). The second point relates to the concerns raised over the absence of human intervention. Constant human supervision and/or intervention will not be required because the system itself will be able to adapt to the variable and fast-moving events on the battlefield. That is one of several advantages of machine learning algorithms. When that level of 'autonomy' is not possible, due to the prevailing circumstances, the mission will certainly require the deployment of a supervised system. Thus, the adaptiveness and assertiveness of a system are the technical mechanisms which allow human operators to be out-of-the-loop. This is not a novelty pertaining to AWS but a feature of many of the weapons systems currently in deployment.

A different question is whether systems capable of being opened to human intervention should be called 'autonomous', given that such systems work more or less as extensions of the human arm. This opens the stage for the final point to be made. There are no doubts that the openness of a system to human supervision or intervention in its decision-making processes allow for forms for direct human control. However, the relevant question is whether they are the *only* forms of human control. Certainly not. When a system is activated, no scholar disagrees that activation is an instance of human control for which a commander can be held accountable.[409] Nonetheless, very few scholars have raised the possibility of *deactivating* an AWS. As was explained in Section 2.3, 'human supervision' assumes the supervisor's ability to intervene in the operation of a weapon system before it engages the target. Accordingly, it was concluded that human intervention is not possible with an AWS, not only because of the nature of the algorithms involved, as it is the ratio of the design and programming of the algorithm for situation management, that is, to safeguard the adaptability of the system to the circumstances of the battlefield and its assertiveness towards the mission entrusted to the system (*algorithm for the mission*). However, the fact that human operators cannot intervene directly in the decision-making process does not exclude two other possible mechanisms of a more indirect form of human control. First, intense research has been devoted recently to developing self-destructing mechanisms. A technology of self-deactivation would not only prevent the *algorithm for the mission* from being an object of disruption but would also ensure that

409 McFarland, *Autonomous Weapon Systems and the Law of Armed Conflict: Compatibility with International Humanitarian Law* (n 46) 129.

a working AWS does not fall into the hands of the enemy.[410] Second, commanders are obliged to comply with the Rule of Precaution before, during and after an attack and if, in the course of the military operation, the mission entrusted to the system should be cancelled, the commander should always be able to deactivate the weapon system.

410 Mike Elgan, 'Welcome to the Era of Self-Destructing Gadgets, From Phones to Drones' (*Fast Company*, 23 February 2018) <www.fastcompany.com/40532294/invasion-of-the-self-destructing-gadgets>; Craig Smith, 'DARPA Looking at Self-Destructive Drone Technology' (*U.S Patriot*, 21 October 2015) <https://blog.uspatriottactical.com/darpa-looking-at-self-destructive-drone-technology/>.

3

Autonomous Weapon Systems and 'Autonomy'

Weapons or Killer Robots?

3.1 INTRODUCTION

In spite of all attempts to define AWS, there is a true *legal gap* surrounding the concept of 'autonomy' when applied to AWS. The many and diverse anthropomorphic associations that have sprung up have contributed, unhelpfully, to a *misappropriation of language*.[411] The purpose of this chapter is, therefore, to examine and seek a definition of 'autonomy' for the context of technology of warfare. The right understanding of terms will ensure the distinction among different uses of technical autonomy, namely between AWS and cyber technology.

Only an accurate definition of terms will make it possible to understand the human–AWS interface and, first and foremost, what it means to say that an AWS is capable of an 'autonomous' decision-making process. To this end it is proposed that an analysis of John Boyd's OODA Loop model be undertaken to ascertain whether it is possible to establish an analogical match between the way in which an AWS selects an outcome and a human decision-making process. This analysis will facilitate further discussion of one of the most contentious issues besetting the legal status of AWS.

Looking at the intense international debate, as Armin Krishnan points out, it can be seen that there are two possible outcomes. On the one hand, there are those who view military weapon systems as 'human extensions' in the battlespace or as force multipliers. On the other hand, there are those who propose that robots be regarded as 'autonomous agents', possessed of a stand-alone, independent capability with no human decision maker in the loop. The second position holds the opinion that new technologies call for a strict division of tasks into those that may be carried out by humans and those that

[411] Lemley and Casey (n 2) 20.

should be undertaken by robots or other types of systems – in a nutshell, those 'weapons that augment our soldiers and those that can become soldiers'.[412] The proposition that weapons could become soldiers can call for a radical shift in the understanding of international law in general and IHL in particular.

3.2 AUTONOMOUS TECHNOLOGIES OF WAR AND THE PROBLEM OF MISAPPROPRIATION OF LANGUAGE

The expression 'misappropriation of language' is used here to highlight the lack of common ground and semantic clarity among the parties involved in debate about the future of AWS.[413] A diversity of terms and concepts has been used, but these have yet to provide clarity regarding the problems that need to be discussed.[414] The misappropriation of language in which AWS and their regulation are submerged can be looked at from three different angles.[415]

Chapter 1 glanced at the first angle: AWS have been given different labels, for example, 'killer robots', 'fully autonomous weapons', etc., and different categories – some authors regard these systems as already in deployment, but others hold the view that autonomous systems do not yet exist and that, if they are brought into existence, they will force a shift in the current anthropomorphic paradigm. This last hypothesis gives authors like Hin-Yan Liu the grounds to prioritise the ontological question, noting that 'what has been surprisingly absent from the legal consideration [...] are the logically anterior questions as to whether both autonomous and remote weapons can remain meaningfully categorized as "weapons", whether the current legal categorization is adequate to regulate their use, and how their use may challenge the existing legal system'.[416] The same concern was pointed out by Special Rapporteur C. Heyns, who stated that in 'the contemplation of LARS, the distinction between weapons and warriors risks becoming blurred, as the former would take decisions about their own

412 Krishnan, *Killer Robots: Legality and Ethicality of Autonomous Weapons* (n 26) 118.

413 House of Lords Select Committee on Artificial Intelligence (n 51) 22. The term 'misappropriation of language', although related, should not be confused with 'linguistic trick', which expresses that all the problems of AWS' conceptualisation can be solved by a 'linguistic trick'. cf Noll (n 105) 77.

414 Surber (n 311) 1. Chapter 1, Section 1.1.

415 It is important to be aware that *indeterminacy* is already known in international law. However, in the case of AWS, the problem would be more acute. The concept, the nature and the capabilities of such systems are discussed and are also the source of disagreement. Thus, an accurate conceptualisation of the term 'AWS' is previous to the discussion of the norms applicable to their employment. cf Adil Ahmad Haque, 'Indeterminacy in the Law of Armed Conflict' (2019) 95 *International Law Studies* 118.

416 Liu, 'Categorization and Legality of Autonomous and Remote Weapons Systems' (n 23) 628.

use'.[417] The prospect of AWS, therefore, for many authors, constitutes a threat to humankind. The problem with that kind of approach is that it assumes capabilities to be certain that are for the moment hypothetical, without giving a detailed explanation or spelling out the implications in terms of robotics research. States and scholars use a variety of terms and multiple ways of describing the same actuality, which is not helpful in terms of coherence and clear understanding because they give no clear definitions of the concepts discussed.

The second angle from which to look at misappropriation of language is the absence of an agreed definition of 'autonomy' when applied to technology of war. As Crootof notes, 'no one has yet put forward a coherent definition of *autonomy* in weapon systems from a law of armed conflict perspective, which often results in the conflation of legal, ethical, policy and political arguments'.[418]

It is elementary that no question of legality can be answered without a clear understanding of what is meant by 'autonomy' in the context of weaponry;[419] it is at this level that there is truly a *legal gap*. Only an accepted definition of the concept can counteract the obscurity of propositions such as that 'firstly autonomous robots with full lethal force have not yet been deployed and, secondly, autonomous robots are nonetheless already used with varying degrees of autonomy and lethal force',[420] definitions such as 'weapons with the capacity to utilise artificial intelligence to replicate human cognitive reasoning', or arguments such as that human soldiers should always be regarded as 'autonomous weapons systems' or that 'the IHL rules of targeting cannot be applied to AWS without giving them some combatant status'.[421] It is this sort of language that causes sheer chaos in terms of conceptualisation.

The third angle involves the *conceptual migration* of the term 'autonomy'. The word has a semantic value across different fields of knowledge, and in each it signifies a different conceptual reality. The word is used, and referred to by scholars, as if it conveyed the same idea to philosophers, roboticists and lawyers.[422] In fact, what ethicists, lawyers and roboticists understand by the

417 Heyns, 'Report of the Special Rapporteur on Extrajudicial, Summary or Arbitrary Executions, Christof Heyns' (n 10) 28.

418 Crootof, 'The Killer Robots are Here: Legal and Policy Implications' (n 315) 1837–1838, 1841.

419 McFarland, *Autonomous Weapon Systems and the Law of Armed Conflict: Compatibility with International Humanitarian Law* (n 46) 29.

420 Espada and Hortal (n 46) 6.

421 Corn, 'Autonomous Weapons Systems: Managing the Inevitably of "Taking the Man out of the Loop"' (n 372) 212; Chengeta, 'Are Autonomous Weapon Systems the Subject of Article 36 of Additional Protocol I to the Geneva Conventions?' (n 26) 97.

422 Crootof, 'The Killer Robots are Here: Legal and Policy Implications' (n 315) 1844; McFarland, *Autonomous Weapon Systems and the Law of Armed Conflict: Compatibility with International Humanitarian Law* (n 46) 29; Letendre (n 66) 274, 275.

term 'autonomy' is different in each case. For example, to call human soldiers 'autonomous weapons systems' is not only inaccurate but dangerous. The term 'conceptual migration' does have the advantage of making us aware that the word 'autonomy' has a multidisciplinary dimension. Thus, it could be said that in the fields of autonomous systems such as philosophy, law and ethics each constitutes a certain 'form of life' with its independent world representation and its own distinctive language and terminology.[423]

George Bekey suggests, in defining robotic autonomy, that it comprises 'the capacity to operate in the real-world environment without any form of external control, once the machine is activated and at least in some areas of operation, for extended periods of time'.[424] For Scharre 'autonomy is the cognitive engine that powers robots. Without autonomy, robots are only empty vessels, brainless husks that depend on human control.'[425] For Sparrow, on the other hand, an AWS 'is capable of making its own decisions on the basis of reasons that are internal to it and in light of its own experience'.[426]

It is evident that the concept of autonomy is used in different ways. For Sparrow 'autonomy' has an ontological dimension, while for Bekey it does not say anything about the systems' abilities to 'understand' the context of the battlefield. Does this mean that these new autonomous systems will operate only in compliance with strictly determined rules or rather that they will be able to take independent decisions and act on the battlefield without human interference?

3.3 THE WAY FORWARD – ADDRESSING THE LEGAL GAP: THE NEED TO UNDERSTAND THE TERM 'AUTONOMY'

A great deal of effort on the part of international participants has gone into attempting to define 'fully autonomous systems', making use, along the way, of terms such as 'meaningful human control' and 'critical functions', but failing to come up with a clear indication of what they mean. As the Czech Republic stated at the CCW Meeting of Experts in 2015, 'the ultimate decision to end somebody's life must remain under meaningful human control. This principle should be a common understanding in the international community', but 'the challenging part *is to establish what precisely*

423 McFarland, 'Factors Shaping the Legal Implications of Increasingly Autonomous Military Systems' (n 32) 1313–1314.

424 Bekey (n 177) 18.

425 Paul Scharre, *Army of None: Autonomous Weapons and the Future of War* (1st edn, WW Norton 2018) 15.

426 Sparrow, 'Killer Robots' (n 55) 66.

"meaningful human control" would entail'.[427] It is true that some countries – for example, Australia, the Netherlands, Poland and South Africa – have endorsed the importance of this principle, but still none of these countries' delegations were able to offer a clear definition.[428] As the Pakistani delegation observed, the concept of 'meaningful human control [. . .] does not provide *a solution* to the technical, legal, moral and regulatory questions' that arise.[429] In the same vein, at the 2016 CCW Meeting of Experts, the US delegation questioned whether MHC was in fact 'a helpful way to advance our discussion'.[430] In the more recent GGE Meeting, the concept of MHC was not mentioned by states who were concerned, rather, with the issue of how to establish an appropriate level of human–machine interaction.

Another concept notable for its vagueness is that of 'critical functions'. If the concept of MHC is associated with the level of human interference that will be possible in an AWS's decision-making process, 'critical functions' represents the other side of the coin. As a term intended to signify those *functions* of a system that are not autonomous, and that therefore require so-called meaningful human control, it nonetheless lacks precision. Indeed, during the recent international experts' meeting on autonomous weapons systems, a number of states noted the need for clarification of what could be internationally accepted as constituting an AWS, while others considered the term to be simply 'a misnomer'.[431]

427 '2015 Czech Republic CCW Meeting of Experts on LAWS' (*Reaching Critical Will*, 13 April 2015) <www.reachingcriticalwill.org/images/documents/Disarmament-fora/ccw/2015/meeting-experts-laws/statements/13April_CzechRepublic.pdf>.

428 '2016 Australian Statement: General Debate Exchange of Views' (*Reaching Critical Will*, 11 April 2016) <www.reachingcriticalwill.org/images/documents/Disarmament-fora/ccw/2016/meeting-experts-laws/statements/11April_Australia.pdf>; '2016 Netherlands Opening Statement at the General Debate, 3rd Informal Meeting of Experts on LAWS' (*Reaching Critical Will*, April 2016) <www.reachingcriticalwill.org/images/documents/Disarmament-fora/ccw/2016/meeting-experts-laws/statements/12April_Netherlands.pdf>; '2016 Poland Statement CCW Meeting of Experts on LAWS' (*Reaching Critical Will*, 11 April 2016) <www.reachingcriticalwill.org/images/documents/Disarmament-fora/ccw/2016/meeting-experts-laws/statements/12April_Poland.pdf>; '2016 South Africa Statement CCW Meeting of Experts on LAWS' (*Reaching Critical Will*, April 2016) <www.reachingcriticalwill.org/images/documents/Disarmament-fora/ccw/2016/meeting-experts-laws/statements/11April_SouthAfrica.pdf>.

429 '2016 Pakistan Statement on CCW Meetings of Experts on LAWS' (*Reaching Critical Will*, 11 April 2016) <www.reachingcriticalwill.org/images/documents/Disarmament-fora/ccw/2016/meeting-experts-laws/statements/11April_Pakistan.pdf>.

430 Meier, '2016 CCW Informal Meeting of Experts on Lethal Autonomous Weapon Systems. U.S.A. Delegation Opening Statement' (n 197).

431 '2016 UNIDIR Statement at CCW Meeting of Experts on LAWS' (*Reaching Critical Will*, 12 April 2016) <www.reachingcriticalwill.org/images/documents/Disarmament-fora/ccw/2016/meeting-experts-laws/statements/12April_UNIDIR.pdf>.

Since the word 'autonomy', when applied to weapons systems, means different things to different state representatives, developers, manufacturers, military lawyers, human rights activists and scholars, it is crucial to reach an agreed understanding of the concept. Only by addressing the lacuna that exists in the legal literature, when it comes to which systems should be considered autonomous and which not, will it be possible to engage in any meaningful discussions going forward and arrive at a considered position regarding the legitimacy of future systems.[432] As Sparrow rightly points out, it is because the question of the nature and extent of 'autonomy' in AWS has been neglected that the lack of clarity in all discourse surrounding these systems persists.[433] Therefore, to turn the argument on its head, it is pointless to try to gain a comprehensive understanding of all the systems of war available, with their myriad of specific features, without a clear understanding of 'autonomy'.

The aforementioned argument explains, to some extent, why at the 2016, 2017 and 2018 CCW Meetings of Experts the European Union, the United Kingdom and the United States strongly reiterated that existing AWS (e.g. the Patriot/Aegis systems) should not be confused with 'lethal autonomous weapons'.[434] In spite of the fact that no state provides clarification of what, exactly, constitutes a lethal autonomous system, it is evident that the weapons systems deployed by states up to now do not afford the option of considering and balancing different courses of action, let alone that of complying with the principles of distinction and proportionality. It is, therefore, imperative to examine the matter from the point of view of the battlefield, and the types of mission that systems will be required to carry out, and try to come to a reasoned consideration of what it would mean were a system to be truly 'autonomous'.

432 Chris Jenks and Rain Liivoja, 'Machine Autonomy and the Constant Care Obligation' (*ICRC Law and Policy*, 11 December 2018) <http://blogs.icrc.org/law-and-policy/2018/12/11/machine-autonomy-constant-careobligation/?utm_source=ICRC+Law+%26+Policy+Forum+Contacts&utm_campaign=e9de618589-LP_EMAIL_BLOG_POST_2018_12_11_03_37&utm_medium=email&utm_term=0_8eeeebc66b-e9de618589-79024717&mc_cid=e9de618589&mc_eid=b8997e9f4e>; Crootof, 'The Killer Robots are Here: Legal and Policy Implications' (n 315) 1840–1841.

433 Sparrow, 'Killer Robots' (n 55) 65.

434 Meier, '2016 CCW Informal Meeting of Experts on Lethal Autonomous Weapon Systems. U.S.A. Delegation Opening Statement' (n 197); '2017 EU Statement on Lethal Autonomous Weapons Systems (LAWS) Group of Governmental Experts Convention on Certain Conventional Weapons' (*Reaching Critical Will*, 13 November 2017) <www.reachingcriticalwill.org/images/documents/Disarmament-fora/ccw/2017/gge/statements/13Nov_EU.pdf>; '2018 United Kingdom of Great Britain and Northern Ireland. Statement for the General Exchange of Views at the Meeting of the Group of Government Experts on Lethal Autonomous Weapons Systems' (n 284).

3.4 APPROACHING AUTONOMY AND ITS MEANING FOR AWS

Autonomy is invading every single area of human life, and the military and its weapons systems are no exception.[435] As Riza rightly points out, in warfare, consecutive 'technological miracles are now the norm'.[436] The deployment on the battlefield of AWS with increased levels of autonomy will, if indeed they prove to be the next technological miracle, have a fundamental effect on the way in which armies have been structured until today.

In the discussion on AWS, different notions of 'autonomy' are offered by authors when alluding to the *independence* of future systems of war from human operators.[437] On the one hand, 'independence' may be used to indicate the extent to which a system is able to accomplish a certain task without external input. On the other hand, 'independence' may signal that a system's cognitive skills – data collection and the mechanisms for processing that data – are such as to allow it to *take decisions and actions* on the battlefield. Thus, language that until today was used to describe human actions is now used by roboticists as though there were no ontological gap between soldiers and 'autonomous' systems of warfare. It is understandable that there should be a certain need for anthropomorphic metaphors when talking about systems able to perform with a hitherto unknown independence. A problem emerges, however, when the use of the term 'autonomy' leads us into a misleading 'trap of anthropomorphising autonomous systems'.[438]

R. Arkin states that 'autonomy', when applied to AWS, is not used 'in the strictly philosophical sense', but the author does not offer any help as to how the concept should be understood when qualifying weapon systems.[439] It is therefore crucial to scrutinise the meaning of 'autonomy', in the context of AWS, to see whether it is meant at the technical or at the philosophical level. A great majority of legal scholars, unfortunately, prefer not to go into detail about what 'autonomy' really means and opt for one of the definitions already supplied by DoD 3000.09 or the UK Approach.[440] But the term begs clarification. Accordingly, this present section will be divided in two parts. Part I will address

435 'Artificial Intelligence Summit Focuses on Fighting Hunger, Climate Crisis and Transition to "Smart Sustainable Cities"' (n 25).

436 Riza (n 178) 4. cf Chapter 1, Section 1.1.

437 Wagner, 'Autonomy in the Battlespace: Independently Operating Weapon Systems and the Law of Armed Conflict' (n 362) 103.

438 McFarland, 'Factors Shaping the Legal Implications of Increasingly Autonomous Military Systems' (n 32) 1316; McFarland, *Autonomous Weapon Systems and the Law of Armed Conflict: Compatibility with International Humanitarian Law* (n 46) 75–78.

439 Arkin, *Governing Lethal Behavior in Autonomous Robots* (n 34) 37.

440 Cf. Chapter 2, Section 2.5, n 323.

the problems that have arisen around the concept of 'autonomy' as it has been progressively adopted by engineers and roboticists. Part II will look at how the term 'autonomy' is used and, especially, how the major influential policy documents have addressed the concept in relation to weapon systems.[441]

3.4.1 *Part I – The Adoption of the Term 'Autonomy' by Modern Technology*

Some authors consider it impossible to define 'autonomy' since the word carries different meanings in different fields of study. It is true that 'autonomy' is an extraordinary rich concept that can run into complexity and ambiguity due to its long philosophical history.[442] A historical perspective will be helpful to understand how 'autonomy' became a necessary concept for technology and began to be used by roboticists and programmers in order to explain a new genre of system capability.

Looking to the etymology of the word, it can be observed that 'autonomy' comes from the Greek words '*auto*' ('self') and '*nomos*' ('law') so conveys a sense of self-rule and self-governance.[443] Until today, and in spite of different schools of thought, 'autonomy' – understood as the capacity to justify and give reasons for choices and behaviours in life – is still a concept normally applied only to humans. In the words of John Christman, the concept of autonomy denotes the human and individual capacity for critical reflection which enables someone 'to respond adequately to reasons'.[444]

Problems with establishing an adequate vocabulary to describe new technologies began to emerge as engineers and roboticists sought to establish parallels between human decision-making processes and the way in which certain systems are able to process data and arrive at conclusions without direct human involvement. Three moments deserve special attention.

The first step was taken in the mid-1940s. A new branch of applied science named 'cybernetics' was founded by Norbert Wiener and his colleagues.[445] Cybernetics was to be responsible for the first attempt to understand

441 A first attempt to systematise all the different perspectives regarding the term 'autonomy' shared by states; Dustin A Lewis, Gabriella Blum and Naz K Modirzadeh, 'War-Algorithm Accountability' (Harvard Law School PILAC 2016) Research Briefing 21–32 <https://papers.ssrn.com/sol3/papers.cfm?abstract_id=2832734>.

442 Krishnan, *Killer Robots: Legality and Ethicality of Autonomous Weapons* (n 26) 43; Leveringhaus (n 1).

443 Suchman and Weber (n 353) 76; McFarland, *Autonomous Weapon Systems and the Law of Armed Conflict: Compatibility with International Humanitarian Law* (n 46) 30.

444 Christman (n 104); Chesterman (n 4) 249.

445 Norbert Wiener, a professor of mathematics and engineering at MIT, is responsible for the innovative development in science and philosophy that led to a creation of a new branch of

'autonomy' as intrinsic to both machines and humans.[446] As Wiener explains 'the computing machine, and consequently the brain, as a logical machine' is the starting point for understanding two very similar feedback systems.[447] They are created to perform towards an end, a *specified goal*. Moreover, as 'any computing machine is used because machine methods are faster than hand methods' it turns out to be an advantage 'to remove the human element from any elaborate chain of computation and to introduce it only where it is absolutely unavoidable, at the very beginning and the very end'.[448]

Accordingly, the next step was taken with the introduction of 'symbolic artificial intelligence'. 'Intelligence' is understood as the capacity to process symbols, and both intelligence and the human brain are regarded as computational in structure and function. There is nothing special about the human brain, according to this school of thought, that cannot be reproduced in logical and computational language: simply, an input is given, it is processed and finally an output is produced. This assumption led the 'sense-think-act' paradigm to be applied equally to machines and humans. Of course, those who espoused this approach did not claim that it amounted to 'autonomy' as such but rather that it was a technical method of selecting and processing information, an effort to replicate the deductive rational-cognitive method proper to human intelligence, rendering unnecessary the continuous presence of humans during a decision-making process.

It is important to bear in mind that any artificial system will always be a 'hybrid social-technical entity' in the sense that the capacity to perform certain functions is designed and installed by humans. However, the system is said to be 'independent' or 'intelligent' to the extent that it can perform systemic functions without human intervention.[449] Human operators have to intervene only in exceptional circumstances, when for some unexpected reason

ethics, later called 'computer ethics'. In his two more famous books – *Cybernetics* (1948) and *The Human Use of Human beings* (1950) – he included topics that are still important today: computers and security, computers and unemployment, responsibilities of computer professionals, computers for persons with disabilities, information networks and globalisation, virtual communities, teleworking, merging of human bodies with machines, robot ethics, artificial intelligence, and computers and religion, among others. See *Stanford Encyclopedia of Philosophy* (2015), 'Computer and Information Ethics' <https://plato.stanford.edu/entries/ethics-computer/>, Russell and Norvig (n 116).

446 Noll (n 105) 80–81.

447 Norbert Wiener, *Cybernetics: Or Control and Communication in the Animal and the Machine* (2nd edn, MIT Press 1965).

448 Osinga (n 307) 103–104.

449 Sartor and Omicini (n 322) 44–48.

the system cannot complete a certain function. In reality such systems, which are characterised by their *reactive capacity*, can be described only as *automatic* and are not regarded as being capable of fully fledged, autonomous decision-making.[450] An automatic system is not independent when it comes to deciding what specific action should be taken – it reacts automatically to its sensors – but the system does autonomously *sense* the environment and process incoming information by matching sensory clues with its in-built design features (*think*) in order to produce a specified outcome (*act*). An example of this would be a landmine that activates without the need for a human to 'press the button'.[451]

The third step in the development of 'autonomous systems' is a very ambitious one: introducing computers with so-called *cognitive skills*. In this sense the computer's 'knowledge' will, to a large extent, be the outcome of internal activities carried out by the system itself, rather than the result of data given to it through external inputs. According to Daniel Dennett's terminology, systems have an 'intentional stance'.[452] They are programmed with certain pre-given goals and equipped with software that enables them to make the choices best suited to achieving those goals, depending on the data given to and/or collected by the system. These systems combine a capacity to adapt to the circumstances of the battlefield in accordance with the specified goal or *mission*.

While taking into perspective the various modern systems of defence deployed by different states (e.g. Phalanx, Samsung Sentris or fire-and-forget weapons such as the Brimstone), all can be seen to present different levels of complexity and a range of options for human intervention. Take, for example, the Samsung Sentris system of defence. This system is designed to be able to detect and identify targets in daylight within a 4-kilometre radius or at night, using infrared sensors, a radius of 2 kilometres, with provision for either a lethal or a non-lethal response. The significant point about this technology is that there is no necessity for a human decision to confirm the outcome. The system itself is able to adapt to a day or night environment and, depending on the circumstances, can 'decide' on one of the two different outcomes: the use or not of lethal force. The rules built into its algorithms allow it to distinguish different situations and choose the appropriate course of action.

Within the capability to adapt but beyond automated systems that obey a set of rules, there is another type of system that is known as *auto-teleonomic*, owing

450 ibid 54–58.

451 McFarland, *Autonomous Weapon Systems and the Law of Armed Conflict: Compatibility with International Humanitarian Law* (n 46) 30.

452 Daniel C Dennett, *The Intentional Stance* (MIT Press 1989) 237; Sartor and Omicini (n 322) 45–47.

to its capacity to change its patterns of behaviour in order to carry out its purpose and achieve its goals in the particular environment in which it operates.[453] This is the group that promises to open the door to the prospect of AWS. The AI paradigm at stake is no longer the symbolic, but a *behaviour-based artificial intelligence*.[454] In order to support this level of autonomy the system architecture has to be provided with three main features: *adaptiveness*, *teleology* and *multi-level autonomy*.[455] An *adaptive system* aims to become 'independent' by supervised learning or through self-exploration.[456] In the latter, the system deduces the general rules governing a specific experience and adapts its inner states as the environment changes while continuing to focus on its objective and does not depend on the operators' knowledge.[457] If the system's response depends only on the previous knowledge of its designer or operator, it cannot be said to be 'autonomous' according to the behaviour-based paradigm.[458]

Teleological systems are a subset of adaptive systems. These systems are characterised by the fact that they have pre-programmed an explicit representation of their basic cognitive states such as *goals* (representational structures that specify the objective to be achieved by the system), *beliefs* (representational structures that track aspects of the environment) and, finally, *plans* (representational structures that specify how to reach the goals, given the beliefs). These systems are considered by roboticists to be *deliberative*.[459] Teleological systems can, however, be guided by 'norms', elements that play a specific role in the deliberative process. An example of a teleological system would be a norm-guided weapon system able to not only recognise a civilian facility but also to realise that it should not be targeted, thus applying accurately the Principles of Distinction and/or even Proportionality.[460]

Finally, *multi-level autonomy* or *fully autonomous systems* – currently a very limited subset of teleological systems – would entail a system's being *reflective*, demanding an articulation of multi-autonomous agents, each with its individual goals. A fully reflective system should be able to ask itself whether it should

453 Sartor and Omicini (n 322) 49; Suchman and Weber (n 353) 85.

454 Suchman and Weber (n 353) 87.

455 Carlos Fernando Alvarez Gonzalez, 'Análisis de La Estructura y Organización de Los Sistemas Autónomos de Armas Letales (LAWS) a Partir de La Lectura de Arnold Pacey' (2017) 74 *Eikasia revista de Filosofia* 11, 23–24.

456 For an introduction to the complexity of the matter, cf Rodney A Brooks, *Robot. The Future of Flesh and Machines* (Allen Lane 2002) 164–171.

457 Suchman and Weber (n 353) 87.

458 Sartor and Omicini (n 322) 43–44.

459 ibid 52.

460 ibid 65–68.

have a certain *belief*, given the data it has gathered from the environment, whether it should have a certain *intention* and whether it should endorse certain *norms*. In terms of AI, such systems would depend on what is known as a *Human-Based Intelligence* (HBI), a stage of development still a long way from realisation.[461] These systems would operate autonomously, and it would be up to the system to choose the best outcome possible based in its own probability calculus (Bayesian Rule).

As it was seen in Chapter 1, HBI is required for 'fully autonomous weapons' but is still not technically achievable. However, it is already possible to find some adaptive systems – although they follow a pre-given set of rules – so it is evident that AI is evolving towards 'deliberative systems' which would be given a set of representational structures in order to accomplish pre-defined goals. For the purposes of this work, automatic and semi-autonomous systems will not be taken into consideration, since they operate according to pre-given rules and the process is subject to human intervention. At the other extreme, it will also be excluded from 'fully autonomous systems' since such systems remain, at the time of writing, hypothetical. The focus of this work will be AWS supported by machine learning algorithms, capable of adapting to the circumstances and able to select, among pre-established set of possibilities, the best course of action to optimise the mission.

Considering the aforementioned discussion, it is important to recognise and accept 'autonomy' as a *continuum*.[462] It is a term in continuous evolution, a concept in progress, as AI technology develops. Following this line of reasoning, it is crucial to understand the importance of distinguishing hypothetical, future, 'fully autonomous weapons' – multi-level-autonomy systems that are still a long way from realisation – from achievable AWS, which do not at present raise an ontological question regarding their status as weapon systems.

Self-learning algorithms indeed represent a new step in war technology, distinguished by their capability to select the optimal course of action in accordance with the mutable circumstances of the battlefield. These capabilities are already a challenge, but IHL is equipped to address the challenges that AWS entail. What seems to be more difficult is to attempt to regulate

461 'The Return of the Machinery Question' (n 115).

462 'Report of the 2018 Session of the Group of Governmental Experts on Emerging Technologies in the Area of Lethal Autonomous Weapons Systems' (n 193) pt III, s B, para 22 C; '2019 Statement by Ireland. Agenda Item 5(b): Characterization of the Systems under Consideration in Order to Promote a Common Understanding on Concepts and Characteristics Relevant to the Objectives and Purposes of the Convention' (n 282).

autonomous systems that at this time do not exist, such as fully AWS. Thus, the term 'weapon' is still the accurate one to describe the reality of AWS.

Some authors, such as Neha Jain, suggest that the term '*emergent*' should be preferred to 'autonomous' to avoid confusion of terms and the anticipation of ontological questions.[463] It is, indeed, an interesting recommendation to address AWS as emergent AWS but it does not preclude a very clear understanding of what 'autonomy' means. Thus, in light of all considerations made earlier, 'autonomy' is a concept in progress that, traditionally, was taken to mean that a system was capable of operating without human intervention but not of making decisions.[464] AI is taking autonomy to the next level, to cover the new capability of a system to choose and to adapt to different courses of action with a decreased level of human intervention but far from being new artificial agents on the battlefield.[465] It is, therefore, fair to conclude that 'autonomy', as far as AWS are concerned, should be understood as *the capability of a system to perform a set of tasks without human intervention, being able to adapt its own system to obtain the goal with which it was programmed*. In short, AWS are *functionally* autonomous systems.

3.4.2 *Part II – Autonomy: Between Scholars and Policy Documents*

Markus Wagner, among many other scholars and organisations, offers a definition of 'autonomy'. The author notes that it 'is important to distinguish between different levels of autonomy, at least for conceptual purposes'. For this reason he makes a distinction between remotely operated systems, automated systems and 'systems which actually function autonomously'.[466] Regarding the latter, Wagner asserts that AWS

> unlike remotely-operated and automated systems, do not depend on human input either during or immediately prior to their deployment. What distinguishes their functioning is the ability *to independently operate, identify and engage targets without being programmed to target a specific object*. While there is some human involvement prior to sending an AWS on a mission (refuelling and arming), an AWS can carry out a mission with a much higher

463 Neha Jain, 'Autonomous Weapon Systems: New Frameworks for Individual Responsibility' in Nehal Bhuta and others (eds), *Autonomous Weapons Systems: Law, Ethics, Policy* (Cambridge University Press 2016) 306–307.

464 Jenks and Liivoja (n 432).

465 Gonzalez (n 455) 42–44; House of Lords Select Committee on Artificial Intelligence (n 51) 156.

466 Wagner, 'Autonomy in the Battlespace: Independently Operating Weapon Systems and the Law of Armed Conflict' (n 362) 103.

> degree of independence and indeed autonomy. Decisions about which targets to engage and how and when to conduct an attack would be left to the software which, ideally, has been programmed in such a manner as to address a myriad of situations and a changing set of circumstances.[467]

This apparently exhaustive definition of AWS is rather problematic. Although it makes reference to a system's mission, it fails to explain what the relationship would be between the human operators and the mission assigned to the system. Human involvement prior to deployment would be minimal and the system would have an independent capacity to identify, select and engage military targets without human involvement. The question is, what exactly would the system's design and programming be? Will the system choose its own missions? Following the same line of thought, Scharre and Horowitz defined autonomy as the 'ability of a machine, whether hardware or software, that, once activated, performs some task or function on its own'[468] and that, essentially, using such a machine is '*delegating* a task previously done by a person to a machine'.[469]

The term 'delegation' is a term of art among roboticists but its use as a legal term, without further consideration, can hardly be considered appropriate suggesting, as it does, that functionally autonomy implies no human responsibility.[470] Accountability for IHL violations caused by the deployment of AWS will be thoroughly explored in Chapter 5, but it is important for now to point out that there is a common concern, shared by the majority of states party to the CCW and scholars, about how to address the problems of accountability in order to avoid a responsibility vacuum.[471] Thus, the accuracy of terms chosen to describe the new weapon system is highly important.

467 ibid.

468 Scharre and Horowitz, 'An Introduction to Autonomy in Weapon Systems' (n 364) 5.

469 Scharre, 'Autonomous Weapons and Operational Risk: Ethical Autonomy Project' (n 230) preface (our emphasis); 'Final Report. National Security Commission on Artificial Intelligence' (n 15) 21.

470 Sartor and Omicini (n 322) 47–48.

471 Some examples among states at GGE Meetings '2016 Pakistan Statement on CCW Meetings of Experts on LAWS' (n 429); '2018 European Union Statement Group of Governmental Experts Lethal Autonomous Weapons Systems Convention on Certain Conventional Weapons' (*Reaching Critical Will*, 27 August 2018) <https://reachingcriticalwill.org/images/documents/Disarmament-fora/ccw/2018/gge/statements/28August_EU.pdf>; Brazil, '2019 GGE on Laws. Challenges to IHL Item 5(a)' (n 267); Sartor and Omicini (n 322) 68–72; Wagner, 'The Dehumanization of International Humanitarian Law: Legal, Ethical, and Political Implications of Autonomous Weapon Systems' (n 64) 29–39; Crootof, 'War Torts: Accountability for Autonomous Weapons' (n 316); Laura A Dickinson, 'Lethal Autonomous Weapons Systems: The Overlooked Importance of Administrative Accountability' in Eric Talbot and Ronald Alcala (eds), *The Impact of Emerging Technologies on the Law of Armed Conflict*, vol 2 (Oxford University Press 2019) <https://ssrn.com/abstract=3249497>.

The policy documents published by the US Department of Defence are particularly relevant in this connection, not only because the United States is one of the few countries that has a record of continuously developing research into AWS, but also because they highlight the capabilities that an AWS will be expected to feature.

A very important document is the 2012 Task Force Report *The Role of Autonomy in DoD Systems* (hereinafter the *Task Force Report*) to support the arguments developed throughout this work. First, the report points out that 'unfortunately the word "autonomy" often conjures images in the press and the minds of some military leaders of computers making independent decisions and taking uncontrolled action'.[472] Second, the *Task Force Report* notes that 'the value of these systems is not to provide a direct human replacement, but rather to extend and complement human capability in a number of ways'.[473] The report is very clear when explaining that 'autonomy is a capability (or a set of capabilities) that enables a particular action of a system to be automatic or, within programmed boundaries, "self-governing"'.[474] Third, it should be clear that autonomy is a technical capability that can only be explained as a continuum – a continuum of human self-determination, ranging from complete human control to a situation in which 'functions *are delegated* to the computer with only high-level supervision and/or oversight from its operator'.[475] Fourth, all AWS 'are *supervised* by human operators at some level, and autonomous systems are no exception, and the best capabilities result from the coordination and collaboration of humans and machines'.[476]

Considering the aforementioned discussion, AWS are not intended to replace human operators and, consequently, 'autonomy' is a continuum from total human control to supervised/oversight task delegation. Indeed, supervised systems apparently complement human capabilities. Notwithstanding this, as Lucas Kello argues, the way to measure the dimension of a new technology's impact is to ascertain how it limits or expands the scope of human action.[477] In the specific case of AWS, not only will human action expand, but also machines will replace human operators. This is precisely the argument expressed by the United Kingdom when mentioning

472 US Department of Defense, 'Task Force Report: The Role of Autonomy in DoD Systems' (US Department of Defense 2012) 1.
473 ibid Memorandum Dr Paul Kaminski.
474 ibid 21.
475 ibid 4.
476 ibid 24.
477 Kello (n 321) 96.

that one of the advantages of autonomous systems is that they will be able to replace humans to carry out 'dull, dirty [and] dangerous tasks'.[478] However, as seen in Chapter 1, the opportunity of 'safe clauses' contemplating human intervention can be object of discussion and, unfortunately, this problem is not addressed by the *Task Force Report*.[479]

Another important consideration is that the *Task Force Report* reinforces the impossibility of understanding 'autonomy' in isolation from a specific *mission delegated by humans to the system*. Thus, the separation of an AWS from its pre-given mission does not seem to make sense. First, because testing and evaluation can be made only with reference to the success or otherwise of the mission, and second, assessment of the potentialities of autonomous software depends on the specificities of the mission.[480]

In 2013, the US DoD in *Roadmap FY 2013–2038*, as it was seen, reinforced the understanding that 'autonomy' relates to the *mission* entrusted to an unmanned system deploying weapons by distinguishing *autonomous mission execution* from *autonomous mission performance*, clarifying that

> [a]utonomous mission performance may demand the ability to integrate sensing, perceiving, analyzing, communicating, planning, decision making, and executing to achieve mission goals versus system functions. Preprogramming is still a key part and enabler of this kind of operation, but the preprogramming goes beyond system operation and into laws and strategies that allow the system to self-decide how to operate itself. [...] However, if machine learning is employed, autonomous systems can develop modified strategies for themselves by which they select their behavior. *An autonomous system is self-directed by choosing the behavior it follows to reach a human-directed goal*.[481]

This passage confirms the problems that result from 'misappropriation of language'. To refer to an autonomous system as being capable of and 'self-decid[ing]' is to compare humans with machines, leading the discussion down an impenetrable path. Nonetheless, the document confirms that the modern understanding of autonomy centres on the capacity of algorithms to adapt to

478 UK Ministry of Defence, 'Joint Doctrine Publication 0–30.2 Unmanned Aircraft Systems' (n 7) 43, 67; Klein (n 35) 246.

479 Regarding the issue of human intervention and human control during AWS operationality, cf Chapter 1, Section 1.3.2; Chapter 2, Section 2.2.2, 2.5.3.3; Chapter 5, Section 5.1.

480 US Department of Defense, 'Task Force Report: The Role of Autonomy in DoD Systems' (n 472) 11, para 1.4.2.

481 US Department of Defense, 'Unmanned Systems Integrated Roadmap: FY2013–2038' (n 80) 67 (our emphasis).

the variable circumstances encountered on the battlefield in order to reach the human-directed goal.

This last sentence, however, can also be cause of confusion. The *Roadmap FY 2013–2038* points out that autonomous systems' level of autonomy does not go without challenges if machine learning algorithms are applied: it states that 'an autonomous system is self-directed by choosing the behavior it follows to reach a human-directed goal'.[482] What does it mean to say that a system is self-directed and able to choose its own behaviour? The question is not irrelevant as far as questions about liability are concerned.[483]

Lastly, in October 2014, another document, *Role of Autonomous Systems in Gaining Operational Access*, commented: 'autonomy [. . .] should be considered as an intrinsic property of sentient and intelligent creatures. Machines, therefore, *are not autonomous in a literal sense*, but may exhibit "autonomous-like" functions relative to a particular level of human control and situational context.' In conclusion, it adds that 'in the military context it is important that autonomy occurs with oversight – "*autonomy under human control*"'.[484]

To perceive autonomy as 'autonomy under control' is precisely the approach that the *UK Joint Doctrine Publication 0-30.2* (*JDP 0-30.2*) has taken. According to the United Kingdom, as far as autonomous or robotic systems able to set their own rules are concerned, the 'UK policy is that the operation of our weapons will always be under human control as an absolute guarantee of human oversight and authority and of accountability for weapon usage'.[485]

The problem of how to retain effective human control over a machine's behaviour was addressed by 2016 US Defence Science Board Report entitled '*Autonomy*'. This report takes the view that 'autonomy results from delegation of a decision to an authorised entity to take action within specific boundaries' and that the 'system must have the capability to independently compose and select among different courses of action to accomplish goals based on its knowledge and understanding of the world, itself and the situation'.[486]

This report, too, uses the term 'delegation'. While that may in itself be subject to debate, it offers the considerable advantage of presenting autonomy as

482 ibid 67.

483 ibid 115; Suchman and Weber (n 353).

484 Multinational Capability Development Campaign (MCDC) 2013–2014, 'Focus Area "Role of Autonomous Systems in Gaining Operational Access"' (2014); Joint Air Competence Centre, 'Future Unmanned System Technologies: Legal and Ethical Implications of Increasing Automation' (2016) 35 <www.japcc.org/wp-content/uploads/Future_Unmanned_System_Technologies_Web.pdf>.

485 UK Ministry of Defence, 'Joint Doctrine Publication 0–30.2 Unmanned Aircraft Systems' (n 7) paras 2.7, 4.18.

486 Defense Science Board – Department of Defense (n 408) 4.

a functional and limited concept, suggesting that an AWS will operate within pre-established boundaries. However, the way autonomy is presented by the 2016 Report '*Autonomy*' can be seen as a setback in comparison with previous documents. To conceive of 'autonomy' as a delegated capability employed to accomplish goals based on the system's 'understanding of the world, itself and the situation' is a perfect example of 'misappropriation of language'. Moreover, a system that can only operate within *specific boundaries* does not appear to be compatible with a capability to *independently* compose possible courses of action.

The problem that emerges is that the terminology used in connection with 'autonomy' seems to double up. First, a number of publications attempt to distinguish between different levels of 'autonomy' but, as this results in as many classifications as there are authors, it is imperative to understand what 'autonomy' means when applied to technology of warfare.[487] Second, there is a problem in looking at 'autonomy' in dissociation from the mission entrusted to the system. However adaptive, AWS are called upon to be 'assertive' as regards the mission. Third, some authors and reports refer to 'autonomy' as an inevitable condition of future weapon systems, whereas it is clear, for example, that there is no intention on the part of the United States, or the United Kingdom at least, for the foreseeable future, to further develop autonomous systems that could be regarded as 'new agents on the battlefield'.[488] Lastly, it becomes rather difficult to argue that 'autonomy' can be subject to a set of rules while simultaneously suggesting that 'autonomy' is a kind of space in which a system can exercise 'free will'.

In light of the aforementioned discussion, and in view of the definition of AWS proposed in this study, a weapon system that is considered 'autonomous' is a system in which both hardware and software are capable of performing tasks – progressively more complex – that would previously have required

[487] Raja Parasuraman, Thomas B Sheridan and Christopher D Wickens, 'A Model for Types and Levels of Human Interaction with Automation' (2000) 30 *IEEE Transactions on Systems, Man, and Cybernetics – Part A: Systems and Humans* 286, 287; Noel Sharkey, 'Staying in the Loop: Human Supervisory Control of Weapons' in Nehal Bhuta and others (eds), *Autonomous Weapons Systems: Law, Ethics, Policy* (Cambridge University Press 2016) 28; McFarland, 'Factors Shaping the Legal Implications of Increasingly Autonomous Military Systems' (n 32) 1320.

[488] Liu, 'Refining Responsibility: Differentiating Two Types of Responsibility Issues Raised by Autonomous Weapons Systems' (n 18) 327; Heyns, 'Report of the Special Rapporteur on Extrajudicial, Summary or Arbitrary Executions, Christof Heyns' (n 10) para 38; Crootof, 'The Killer Robots are Here: Legal and Policy Implications' (n 315) 1837–1838; US Department of Defense, 'DoD 3000.09. Autonomy in Weapon Systems' (n 7); UK Ministry of Defence, 'Joint Doctrine Publication 0–30.2 Unmanned Aircraft Systems' (n 7).

human intervention. The introduction of machine learning makes it feasible to have systems that, embedded with algorithms designed and programmed for a preset mission, are able to operate without human intervention. The fact that the systems are designed and programmed and that there is, as will be explained in Chapter 4, a stringent requirement that all new weapons are rigorously tested and evaluated before being deployed, there is no reason to argue that functional autonomy excludes human control.[489]

These distinctions will become clearer as the 'autonomous decision-making process' is further explained.

3.5 AN AUTONOMOUS DECISION-MAKING PROCESS: OODA LOOP AND OOSA LOOP

The idea of adaptable and assertive systems can be seductive, surrounded by military and humanitarian advantages,[490] but what does it mean to say that a weapon system can have an autonomous decision-making process with which human operators cannot intervene?

Engineers and roboticists have begun to apply the OODA Loop model in the context of machines and their decision-making processes, as it provides a succinct representation of the natural decision cycle in any imaginable context.[491] The source of the OODA Loop is in Boyd's work, *A Discourse on Winning and Losing*, also known as *The Green Book*.[492] The concept arose from a study of how to win at war and how to gain a competitive advantage in the context of hostilities and the acronym stands for *Observation, Orientation, Decision* and *Action*.[493]

This becomes rather more complex when applied to AWS. Calling to mind the algorithm structures explained in Section 1.3.3, the *algorithm for situation assessment* would include the phases of 'observation' and 'orientation'. The *selection algorithm* would make 'decision' possible and, finally, the *algorithm for situation management* would guide the phase of 'action'.

489 McFarland, *Autonomous Weapon Systems and the Law of Armed Conflict: Compatibility with International Humanitarian Law* (n 46) 30–31.

490 For the numerous advantages that AWS might introduce, cf '2019 UK Statement. Agenda Item 5(a): An Exploration of the Potential Challenges Posed by Emerging Technologies in the Area of Lethal Autonomous Weapons Systems to International Humanitarian Law' (2019) <www.unog.ch/80256EDD006B8954/(httpAssets)/1ED3972D40AE53B5C12583D3003F8E5E/$file/20190318-5(a)_IHL_Statement.pdf>.

491 McFarland, *Autonomous Weapon Systems and the Law of Armed Conflict: Compatibility with International Humanitarian Law* (n 46) 35.

492 Osinga (n 307) 1.

493 ibid 2–5; David G Ullman, '"OO-OO-OO!" The Sound of a Broken OODA Loop' [2007] *The Journal of Defense Software Engineering* 22.

The implementation of the specific algorithms presents challenges and deserves further attention. The first challenges in the situation assessment are the inherent risks associated with the dissociation of communication, namely *the control of data*.[494] There is no reason to doubt that machine learning technology will improve data analysis in *volume, variety and velocity*; however, it is precisely this change that some fear may give rise to numerous problems.[495] As the Chair of the GGE Meetings stated, the possibility that incomplete, biased and inaccurate data sets may occur has caused several states to raise concerns at the GGE Meetings.[496] Clearly, *observation* data need to be processed, according to particular criteria (filters; constraints), to ensure that the observed facts cease being simply a disconnected jumble of detail, and the relevant information emerges to indicate the best course of action.[497] However, the stage of *orientating* data can be more complex. Boyd later developed his work further in order to illustrate the reality of a decision-making cycle.

Many crucial factors contribute to the collected data in order for it to make sense (*orient* also known as *data mining*). A number of implicit variables (e.g. personal experience, tradition, culture of war) and necessary feedback raise questions that lend themselves to an immediate answer, while others may require considerable experience and deliberation.[498]

As David G Ullman explains, *orientation* is a crucial factor to the management of uncertainty (who is who and what is what?) and to the development of alternative courses of action (when and how?), totally dependent, until the emergence of AWS, upon a certain subjective view of the world.[499] Thus, the commanding officer at the time of the design and programming of the

494 Charles Garraway, 'The Application of Superior Responsibility in an Era of Unlimited Information' (2013) 41 *International Humanitarian Law and the Changing Technology* 201–202. Concerning the complex problem of data protection, Eric Schmidt, who chairs the Pentagon's Defence Innovation Advisory Board, considers that the US military needs an entirely new system for storing and managing data if front-lines troops are to be able to find information as easily as any common citizen searches on Google but evidently that new systems cannot be the open Web. cf Patrick Tucker, 'The Pentagon Needs Its Own Google for All Its Data, Says Eric Schmidt' (*Defense One*, 2017) <www.defenseone.com/technology/2017/01/pentagon-needs-its-own-google-all-its-data-says-eric-schmidt/134456/?oref=defenseone_today_nl>.

495 Billy Wheeler, 'How to Find Productive Causes in Big Data: An Information Transmission Account' (2018) 26 *Filozofia Nauki* 5.

496 Gjorgjinski (n 158) s G, para ii.

497 Ullman (n 493) 23; Andrew Hill and Stephen Gerras, 'Systems of Denial: Strategic Resistance to Military Innovation' (2016) 69 *Naval War College Review* 109, 112.

498 Berndt Brehmer, 'The Dynamic OODA Loop: Amalgamating Boyd's OODA Loop and the Cybernetic Approach to Command and Control' (2013) <www.dodccrp.org/events/10th_ICCRTS/CD/papers/365.pdf>.

499 Ullman (n 493) 23–24.

algorithms has to be able to encode all the subjective values thought necessary for a lawful course of action.[500] The question to ask is will it be possible to encode those values within the rules of the *algorithm for situation assessment*?

The second stage refers to the *selection algorithm*. 'D', stands for *decide/decision*. It has become common in the language of engineers, roboticists and, more recently, lawyers to talk about the outcomes produced by computers as though they resulted from the computers' own 'decisions'. The use of descriptive expressions such as 'automation of decision and action selection'[501] and 'autonomous targeting decision'[502] faces obstacles *from the legal point of view*. Looking at the definition of an algorithm as a set of rules that encodes a human goal, it is inaccurate to say that an AWS can arrive at an independent 'decision', as seems to be suggested by Crootof.[503] Autonomous systems do not decide but *select*, according to the embedded rules and oriented data, *the best possible course of action in order to optimise the goal defined by humans*.[504]

The transition is from the previous phase, in which an AWS selects a course of action, to the phase in which the system is called 'to act', or in other words, to engage a target. The last letter 'A', standing for *action*, is nonetheless acceptable if it is understood as the final outcome produced by the system.

Considering the aforementioned discussion, it is possible to argue that the entire structure of algorithms for the mission is better represented by the *OOSA Loop* than the OODA Loop, which is more applicable to a human

500 Gjorgjinski (n 158) s b, para V.

501 Parasuraman, Sheridan and Wickens (n 487) 286; Linell Letendre, for example, although the author recognises that robot's 'decisions' are governed by the rules and constraints of the system's control architecture, and that the system optimises a possible solution, prefers to terminology of robots making decision. Furthermore, as the author states, 'a fully autonomous weapons system is not technically feasible, and human interface is not just a good idea, it is necessary to the control process'. This is a perfect example of misappropriation of language (see Chapter 3, Sections 3.1 and 3.2). See Letendre (n 66) 287–288.

502 Ronald C Arkin, Patrick Ulam and Brittany Duncan, 'An Ethical Governor for Constraining Lethal Action in an Autonomous System' (2009) Technical Report GIT-GVU-09–02 1–2.

503 Crootof, 'War Torts: Accountability for Autonomous Weapons' (n 316) 1349, 1362; Crootof, 'The Killer Robots are Here: Legal and Policy Implications' (n 315) 1856–1857. Sharing the same understanding, the statement by Germany at the 2019 GGE Meeting notes that *autonomy* can be understood as the capacity to 'reason and decide on the most suited approach towards their [pre-defined goals] realization'. '2019 Germany Statement. Statement by Germany – On Agenda Item 5(d) Characterization of the Systems under Consideration in Order to Promote a Common Understanding on Concepts and Characteristics Relevant to the Objective and Purpose of the Convention' (n 313).

504 Muller (n 164) 67; McFarland, *Autonomous Weapon Systems and the Law of Armed Conflict: Compatibility with International Humanitarian Law* (n 46) 35.

decision-making process. The OOSA Loop reflects more accurately the understanding that 'emerging technologies in the area of lethal autonomous weapons systems should not be anthropomorphized'[505] and, also, that AWS will always operate according to the underpinning human–machine interaction and not as 'independent' (teleological) weapon systems.[506]

3.5.1 *Applying the OOSA Loop to AWS: The Problem of the DOODA Loop*

Berndt Brehmer developed Boyd's work, and the author makes some important observations which might raise more difficulties when applying the OOSA Loop to an AWS's decision-making process.[507] First, Boyd's model is *reactive* but also *deliberative* in response to identified threats. Second, the model also ignores modern forms of human decision-making process on the battlefield. Human decisions can no longer be regarded as simply 'feedback-driven', but rather as a complex process of 'feed-forward' and feedback control to update the decision-making process. Thus, according to Brehmer, it is impossible to build a general theory capable of explaining command and control in a logical and deterministic manner, let alone translate it into computer language. Therefore, the author suggests a new model capable of representing the reality of a digital decision-making process: a Dynamic OODA Loop (***DOODA Loop***).

It is at this point that AWS may represent an insurmountable challenge for the conventional International Law paradigm. The *selection algorithm and the algorithm for situation management* will make the *algorithm for the mission* operational, but by that time it will have included new data that might have emerged from the battlefield. It is at this stage that human feedback/intervention is excluded, an AWS will be required to adapt, in a certain way, to re-adapt the *algorithm for the mission* to the unforeseen data from the battlefield. Since human operators cannot intervene at this stage, it is fair to question whether the *algorithm for situation management* will be able to reproduce such a level of complexity, that is, to master the DOOSA Loop.

505 'Report of the 2018 Session of the Group of Governmental Experts on Emerging Technologies in the Area of Lethal Autonomous Weapons Systems' (n 193) Guiding Principles, s A, para H.

506 Gjorgjinski (n 158) s B, paras VII, VIII, IX. This understanding was also adopted by the GGE 2019 report stating that 'the role and impacts of autonomous functions in the *identification, selection or engagement* of a target are among the essential characteristics of weapons systems based on emerging technologies in the area of lethal autonomous weapons systems, which is of core interest to the Group', Group of Governmental Experts on Emerging Technologies in the Area of Lethal Autonomous Weapons System (n 12) para 19 (A).

507 Brehmer (n 498).

Looking at the trilogy of algorithms underpinning the structure of the OOSA Loop, all algorithms will obviously depend upon data. Data are filtered by the sequence of algorithms until the algorithm for situation management takes over. As Major-General Christopher Elliot explains, 'in combat nothing stands still and *circumstances constantly change and evolve requiring a guiding hand at the top*'; therefore, the algorithm for situation management will not only have to orient new data, but will also have to be able to adapt the system to unknown data.[508] As Sartor and Omici point out, in the case of AWS 'additional skills are required to combine norm- and value-based thinking in order to address the conflicts of norms and underlying goals' on the battlefield. A perfect example would be dual-use objects, that is, objects which can be used either for civilian or military purposes.[509] Take as an example one of the most discussed cases of dual-use objects: the NATO attack on the headquarters and studios of Serbian State Television and Radio (RTS) in Belgrade in April 1999, which killed at least sixteen civilians and injured a further sixteen, because it was thought to be used as part of a military command, control and communications network and believed, therefore, to be a legitimate military objective. One of the questions asked was whether RTS was a legitimate military target. The problem of the Principle of Distinction will be further discussed, but for now it is important to ask who could be held accountable if the AWS made an error in classifying RTS as a military target or if the collateral damage clearly excessive? The same question could be raised with other civilian objects such as civilian cars used to transport weapons; a school used as a military haven, but it can also be applied to time sensitive targets, for example, a civilian who participated directly in the hostilities who is targeted after his/her involvement with the armed conflict. The classification of dual-use objects as military targets is situation-dependent, and AWS should be able to master the complexity of the OOSA Loop.

These and other questions are object of debate among international lawyers. However, it is necessary to make an important consideration: if the solution for AWS is that no one can be held accountable, the legal consequences would be not limited to a problem of a 'responsibility gap', but it would include a dangerous process of decriminalisation of IHL well-established international values. These are certainly two outcomes that cannot be accepted by International Law.

508 Christopher L Elliott, *High Command: British Military Leadership in the Iraq and Afghanistan Wars* (C Hurst 2015) 45 (our emphasis).

509 Sartor and Omicini (n 322) 53.

3.5.2 *Concluding Remarks: The Restrictive Nature of the Algorithm for the Mission*

It is impossible to find an author who does not recognise at least some advantages in the capabilities – to be precise the *autonomous* capabilities – of modern systems of warfare. Military targets would be easier to locate, identify, select and engage. However, concerns emerge regarding the potentialities of learning algorithms applied to weapon systems.

In 2017, a group of 116 AI specialists, led by Elon Musk and Alphabet's Mustafa Suleyman, addressed a letter to the UN General Assembly calling again for the ban on autonomous weapons or 'weapons of terror',[510] and, more recently, in 2018 at the CCW GGE Meeting, the numbers of states supporting a ban increased, supporting the argument that there is a precedent in International and Disarmament Law for banning any weapon system which is not under human control.[511]

It is a clear argument that weapons that are not under 'human control' should be banned. What needs clarification, as has been explained, is whether AWS are systems that *will be under human control* but will *operate without human intervention*.[512] Moreover, control over a system should not also be confused with control over the effects of weapons that are considerate indiscriminate per se.

The concept of human intervention has been confused with human control and has led some authors to design tables of different levels of human intervention, and identify which phases and tasks really require intervention from a human operator.

One of the best-known is that offered by Thomas B. Sheridan and William L. Verplank, which recognises ten levels of automation, *Level 1* being 'human does the whole job up to the point of turning it over to the computer to

510 The letter was released at the opening of the International Joint Conference on Artificial Intelligence (IJCAI 2017) in Melbourne, the world's pre-eminent gathering of experts in AI and robotics. The open letter is the first time that AI and robotics companies have taken a joint stance on the issue. cf Samuel Gibbs, 'Elon Musk Leads 116 Experts Calling for Outright Ban of Killer Robots' *The Guardian* (Brussels, 20 August 2017).

511 Ban Lethal Autonomous Weapons, 'Recaps of the UNO CCW Meetings April 9–13' (April 2018) <http://autonomousweapons.org/recaps-of-the-un-ccw-meetings-april-9-13>.

512 This distinction was at the centre of the discussions held by the same state's delegation at the 2018 GGE Meetings. While some delegations insisted on the importance of maintaining 'human control' over every single AWS operation, other delegations focussed more on the importance of a 'human element in the different phases of the lifecycle of a weapon system and the level of control that can be applied at each stage'. 'Report of the 2018 Session of the Group of Governmental Experts on Emerging Technologies in the Area of Lethal Autonomous Weapons Systems' (n 193) Agenda item 6 (b), para 11.

implement' and *Level 10*: 'The computer does the whole job if it decides it should be done, and if so tells human only if it decides he should be told.'[513] This model aptly demonstrates the status of human–machine interaction at any given moment during a military mission. The classification departs from the concept of total 'automation', which allows human operators to 'delegate' some level of control to an automated system, until autonomy is achieved, and human interaction/control is no longer required.[514]

A more recent suggestion was offered by Noel Sharkey and ICRAC in 2018; they propose a list of different levels of 'human control':

1. Human engages and selects target and initiates any attack;
2. Program suggests alternative targets and human chooses which to attack;
3. Program selects target and human must approve before attack;
4. Program selects target and human has restricted time to veto;
5. Program selects target and initiates attack without human involvement.[515]

Going by this analysis, while Levels 1 and possibly 2 provide for what he identifies as the 'minimum necessary conditions for the notion of meaningful control', the rest would not secure a sufficient level of human control. Levels 3 and 4 would give place to 'automation bias', and Level 5 prompts the comment: 'such weapon systems would not comply with international law except in very narrowly bounded circumstances'.[516] The interesting point to note is that both authors and the document seem to identify 'human intervention or involvement' and 'human control' indiscriminately when each term should in fact be understood to refer to a unique concept. No consideration is given to the phase of designing and programming the *algorithm for the mission* as to the possibility of human operators deactivating an AWS or to the possibility of AWS having self-destruct mechanisms.[517]

513 To full understanding of the model presented, cf Parasuraman, Sheridan and Wickens (n 487) 287. McFarland, 'Factors Shaping the Legal Implications of Increasingly Autonomous Military Systems' (n 32) 1320.

514 Titiriga (n 349) 60; Christopher Toscano, '"Friend of Humans": An Argument for Developing Autonomous Weapons Systems' (2015) 8 *Journal of National Security Law & Policy* 189, 193–194.

515 Sharkey, 'Staying in the Loop: Human Supervisory Control of Weapons' (n 487) 34–37; ICRAC – International Committee for Robot Arms Control, 'Guidelines for the Human Control of Weapons Systems' (2018) 3 <https://www.icrac.net/wp-content/uploads/2018/04/Sharkey_Guideline-for-the-human-control-of-weapons-systems_ICRAC-WP3_GGE-April-2018.pdf>.

516 Sharkey, 'Staying in the Loop: Human Supervisory Control of Weapons' (n 487) 34–37.

517 McFarland, *Autonomous Weapon Systems and the Law of Armed Conflict: Compatibility with International Humanitarian Law* (n 46) 49.

Another important consideration to note is that 'autonomy' should not be considered an *inherent* condition of any artificial system, but is, rather, a capability that is designed for a specific mission encoded in the *algorithm for the mission*. It is, therefore, 'incorrect to describe autonomous systems as being "independent" machines that operate "without human control"'.[518] As McFarland sums up, 'a highly autonomous system is one that can execute most or all of the OODA Loops required to achieve some goal, using only the operator's high-level instruction as guidance in the decision stage of a loop, such that the "nearest" human (operator) functions similarly to a commander'.[519]

In light of the aforementioned discussion, understanding 'autonomy' as a spectrum, the complexity of DOOSA Loop will be entrusted to a weapon system whenever those systems demonstrate the capacity to perform according to long-established IHL requirements. Thus, it is fair to argue that the *algorithm for the mission* has, in itself, a restrictive nature that excludes uncontrollable weapons.

The centrality of the mission is also the best method of identifying liability. The programming and maintenance of a system will be always fall within the sphere of human responsibility. What will require serious reflection is the stage at which the *algorithm for situation assessment* may not be able to accurately identify what is happening on the battlefield, and as a result commits semantic or syntax errors, causing violations of IHL.

3.6 THE LEGAL AGENCY OF AUTONOMOUS WEAPON SYSTEMS: QUESTIONING THE INSTRUMENTALIST PARADIGM

From the previous chapters and sections it is clear that the understanding of a weapon system as a tool and its correlative instrumentalist paradigm are being challenged by new AI capabilities.[520] But this challenge is not new; it has occurred throughout the history of military technology that has always considered new weapons 'to be something good' if they proved to be a more effective means of accomplishing a desired end.[521]

518 McFarland, 'Factors Shaping the Legal Implications of Increasingly Autonomous Military Systems' (n 32) 1316.

519 ibid 1325; McFarland, *Autonomous Weapon Systems and the Law of Armed Conflict: Compatibility with International Humanitarian Law* (n 46) 49–52.

520 David J Gunkel, *The Machine Question- Critical Perspective on AI, Robots and Ethics* (MIT Press 2012) 27–36.

521 ibid 25.

In Chapter 2, it was argued that AWS should be understood as 'weapon systems' and not as 'new agents' on the battlefield. However, among some philosophers and lawyers, the perception that autonomous systems are at the end of the scale and should no longer be seen as 'tools' but rather as some sort of 'deliberating entity' is quite evident in the Sheridan and Verplank classification.[522] It is claimed by many authors that AWS will be able to 'understand', 'decide', 'plan', 'adapt' and 'optimise' their behaviour in the dynamic arena that is the battlefield.[523] More recently, in March 2019, Lord Hodge, delivering the Edinburgh Fintech Law Lecture, argued that 'it would be possible for a machine as a separate legal person to own intellectual property and in turn to be owned by a financial institution'.[524] Considerations such as those mentioned earlier cannot be ignored by legal theory.

A full discussion regarding the future of AI goes well beyond the aim of this work. However, it is important to consider the arguments presented by scholars regarding *possible legal agency* for autonomous systems or artificial agents. Little consideration is given to what it really means to say that an artificial system will be a *legal agent*, or to what the legal implications of the introduction of these so-called third existence entities would be.[525] To suggest the possibility of a wholly new genre of legal agents is also to suggest that the same will be entitled to rights and will be bound by concomitant obligations. Altogether, this would amount to positing the emergence of a new paradigm, one in which the term 'autonomous system' would suffer an etymological conversion: *from instrument to sentient collaborator*.[526] Duncan Hollis has raised an interesting question in this connection, reminding us that it is imperative to answer the question of '*who*, exactly, is subject to IHL?'[527]

Samir Chopra and Laurence White have made an important contribution towards answering the questions raised earlier. In 2011, they published *A Legal Theory for Autonomous Artificial Agents*, outlining a possible new legal framework for independent *autonomous artificial agents*, addressed from a philosophical perspective.[528]

522 Parasuraman, Sheridan and Wickens (n 487) 289–290.

523 Gunkel (n 520) 51.

524 Nick Hilborne, 'Let Robots Own Property, Supreme Court Justice Suggests' (*LegalFutures*, 19 March 2019) <www.legalfutures.co.uk/latest news/let-robots-own-property-supreme-court-justice-suggests>.

525 Weng, Chen and Sun (n 55) 66; Lemley and Casey (n 2) 3.

526 Russell and Norvig (n 116) 810–811.

527 Duncan B Hollis, 'Setting the Stage: Autonomous Legal Reasoning in International Humanitarian Law' (2016) 30 *Temple International & Comparative Law Journal* 1, 3–6.

528 Samir Chopra and F Laurence White, *A Legal Theory for Autonomous Artificial Agents* (University of Michigan Press 2011).

Chopra and White suggest a break with the way in which concepts such as 'human autonomy' and 'consciousness' are traditionally understood. A more pragmatic perspective should be adopted because, as the authors emphasise, the history of the philosophy of mind has been characterised by endless and futile discussions about the internal processes of decision-making, and this has created a 'deeply rooted scepticism whether such seemingly inanimate objects could ever meet the conditions for personhood in the broader, philosophical sense'.[529] Is it so important to know why and how a certain action is produced? It does not matter if the agent is acting according to designed and programmed instructions or to a set of personal beliefs, when the coherence of such a descriptive and interpretative framework is at stake.[530] The priority is the quality of the outcomes produced. The outcome is the best indicator of the reasons that underpin decisions and therefore 'the internal composition or architecture of the agent becomes irrelevant'.[531] In short, *what happens in the black box stays in the black box.*

3.6.1 *Autonomous Weapon Systems and Their Legal Status*

The possibility of weapon systems operating and interacting with the environment without human input, with the intention of initiating goal-directed behaviours, has caused some scholars to question whether AWS do not 'appear to subsist between the legal categories of "weapons" and "combatants"'.[532] Crootof and Hin-Yan Liu are among the legal scholars who raise questions about the potential new ontological status of AWS.

According to both authors, it is clear that, until today, 'weapons' and 'combatants' have been completely separate entities; that they are, in fact, regulated differently under IHL accentuates at this point: weapons *are* lawful or unlawful, and combatants *act* lawfully or unlawfully.[533] The entire legal framework of IHL is based on the assumption that a capacity for decision-making pertains only to human beings. The capacity of algorithms to guide autonomous actions on the battlefield, even to the point of deploying armed force, could elevate an AWS to the status of 'active combatant'.[534]

529 ibid 171.
530 ibid 12.
531 ibid 14.
532 Liu, 'Categorization and Legality of Autonomous and Remote Weapons Systems' (n 23) 629.
533 Crootof, 'Weapon, Combatant, Child, Animal: They're All Insufficient Analogies for Autonomous Weapon Systems' (n 182).
534 Liu, 'Categorization and Legality of Autonomous and Remote Weapons Systems' (n 23) 629, 632.

According to Liu, to classify an AWS as a 'weapon' fails 'to acknowledge that these *systems do not inflict violence* in a direct manner but rather serve as intermediary platforms from which they are deployed and fails to capture their varying levels of autonomy over the use of force'. However, neither can they be regarded as 'soldiers'; the legal status of a combatant excludes any kind of machine or artificial agent.[535] Observing that 'the capacity for autonomous decision-making pushes these technologically advanced systems to the boundary of the notion of "combatant"', the author does not seek 'to consider autonomous systems as "combatants" because of the profound implications this would entail for IHL'.[536]

Liu's argument got him into a tangle. First, looking at weapons deployed today, it is difficult to distinguish the weapon from its platform. The two items form a unity, a 'weapons system'. In some systems – such as drones – it is possible to distinguish the platform from the weapon, and would be difficult to argue that the platform was not also specifically designed to inflict harm. As far as the second part of the argument goes, the author recognises a dead end, but it cannot be the answer to abandon a question in a kind of limbo.

A different approach is taken by Crootof. The author opts to look at three possible analogies (children, animals and weapons) and concludes that 'these three types of entities all share two traits: they are *autonomous* and, by extension, may sometimes act in unpredictable ways resulting in serious violations of international humanitarian law; and, if they do so, *they cannot be held criminally* liable under existing international criminal law'.[537]

The author recognises that, despite 'the terminological confusion that plagues this topic', the question of what should be understood by 'autonomy' is never addressed.[538] It would be important to understand why children, animals and weapons can be included in the same analytic category. It is believed that AWS will have the capacity to be 'independent actors', but without further explanation the same questions will continue to return our minds over and over again.[539] The author concludes that 'there are these fringe aspects to autonomous weapons that suggest a need for a third category of law'. The solution, according to the author, is to promote a 'Convention on Certain Unconventional War Fighters', totally inspired by Tort Law.[540] At the same

535 ibid 629.

536 ibid 636.

537 Crootof, 'Autonomous Weapon Systems and the Limits of Analogy' (n 182) 4.

538 Liu, 'Categorization and Legality of Autonomous and Remote Weapons Systems' (n 23) 632.

539 Crootof, 'Autonomous Weapon Systems and the Limits of Analogy' (n 182) 57.

540 Crootof, 'War Torts: Accountability for Autonomous Weapons' (n 316) 1386–1389; Lewis, Blum and Modirzadeh (n 441) 87.

time, the author acknowledges that 'artificial intelligence has not advanced to a point where an autonomous weapon system could be said to have acted intentionally or recklessly'.[541] Without a clear definition of what an AWS is and how it is to be used, there is no escaping a plethora of questions about some phantom possibility.

Considering the aforementioned discussion, it can be concluded that there seems to have been a lack of reflection upon what underpins legal agency, and what we expect AWS to be in reality. Chopra and White propose a new approach, suggesting the application of the legal theory of delegation to the realm of autonomous systems.

3.6.2 *Suggested Legal Agency for AWS: 'Qui facit per alium, facit per se'*

Some reflection on robotics and autonomous systems has been offered but, as Neil Richards and William Smart point out, there is still very little scholarship exploring the intersection between law and robotics. More specifically, research is needed into the meeting place between law and the development and deployment of AWS.[542] The way in which AWS are perceived will have important legal consequences. Thus, whether AWS are considered to be 'artificial legal agents'[543] or, alternatively, as new and more sophisticated human tools of war, both situations contemplate two very different legal paths.[544]

Crootof does not draw any conclusion as regards the problem of simultaneously categorising AWS as '*weapons*' and as '*independent actors*'.[545] Some authors take it further, suggesting that 'granting legal recognition to non-human entities should not pose insurmountable problems since it has already been done for corporations'.[546] This line of reasoning seems to be adopted by the European Parliament, according to which 'the most sophisticated autonomous robots could be established as having *the status of electronic persons with*

541 Crootof, 'Autonomous Weapon Systems and the Limits of Analogy' (n 182) 15.

542 Richards and Smart (n 2) 11.

543 Weng, Chen and Sun (n 55) 275.

544 'Report of the 2018 Session of the Group of Governmental Experts on Emerging Technologies in the Area of Lethal Autonomous Weapons Systems' (n 193) Guiding Principles, s A, para H.

545 Crootof, 'Autonomous Weapon Systems and the Limits of Analogy' (n 182) 57.

546 Frank Wells Sudia, 'A Jurisprudence of Artilects: Blueprint for a Synthetic Citizen' (2001) 6 *Journal of Future Studies* 65, 70; Duncan MacIntosh, 'Autonomous Weapons and the Nature of the Law and Morality: How the Rule-of-the-Law-Values Requires Automation of the Rule of Law' (2016) 30 *Temple International & Comparative Law Journal* 99, 124; Hilborne (n 524).

specific rights and obligations, including that of making good any damage they may cause', as per the report prepared by Mady Delvaux.[547]

It becomes clear from the report that a weapon is excluded from having a 'legal personality', at least for the time being. This position is consistent with the resolution adopted by the European Parliament on 25 February 2014 (2014/2567 (RSP)).[548] The resolution called all Member States and the Council to 'ban the development, production and use of fully autonomous weapons which enable strikes to be carried out without human intervention'.[549] Although this resolution passed by a vote 534/49, it would be necessary to have access to the Council's declarations to know exactly what was being banned by the European Parliament, since most of the European states deploy only supervised autonomous systems.[550] At the 2018 CCW GGE Meetings, the European Union (hereinafter EU) admitted the feasibility of AWS and suggested 'a set of common principles' to reaffirm 'that international law, including IHL and Human Rights Law, applies to the development and use of all present and future weapons systems, and sets out some key elements of human control'.[551] In no place, however, can a suggestion for a pre-emptive ban on AWS be found. At the same time, a statement by the EU Observer was made to the effect that 'an amendment to the bill, which said [. . .] fully autonomous weapons should not be eligible for funding, was scrapped at the request of the Council'.[552] Instead, the

547 European Parliament Committee on Legal Affairs, 'Draft Report with Recommendations to the Commission on Civil Law Rules on Robotics' (2016) 2015/2103 (INL), para 59 (g) <www.europarl.europa.eu/sides/getDoc.do?pubRef=-//EP//NONSGML%2BCOMPARL%2BPE-582.443%2B01%2BDOC%2BPDF%2BV0//EN>; 'Robots Could Be Given Legal Status as "Electronic Persons" in Europe' *Daily Times* (Pakistan, 15 January 2017) <http://dailytimes.com.pk/infotainment/15-Jan-17/robots-could-be-given-legal-status-as-electronic-persons-in-europe>; 'Open Letter to the European Commission Artificial Intelligence and Robotics' (April 2018) <www.robotics-openletter.eu/>.

548 European Parliament, 'European Parliament Resolution of 27 February 2014 on the Use of Armed Drones' (n 187).

549 ibid.

550 Campaign to Stop KILLER ROBOTS, 'European Parliament Resolution a First' (27 February 2014) <www.stopkillerrobots.org/2014/02/europeanparliament/>.

551 European Union, 'EU Statement at CCW. Agenda Item 6d: "Possible Options for Addressing the Humanitarian and International Security Challenges Posed by Emerging Technologies in the Area of Lethal Autonomous Weapons Systems in the Context of the Objectives and Purposes of the Convention without Prejudging Policy Outcomes and Taking into Account Past, Present and Future Proposals"' (*Reaching Critical Will*, 2018) <https://reachingcriticalwill.org/images/documents/Disarmament-fora/ccw/2018/gge/statements/29August_EU.pdf>. The position of the EU remained the same at the 2019 GGE Meeting. cf '2019 EU Statement. 5(a) An Exploration of the Potential Challenges Posed by Emerging Technologies in the Area of Lethal Autonomous Weapons Systems to International Humanitarian Law' (n 15).

552 Peter Teffer, '"Killer Robot" Projects Eligible for EU Defence Fund' (*EU Observer*, 23 May 2018) <https://euobserver.com/science/141885>.

proposed regulation setting up the €500 million fund would merely say that projects would not be eligible if their end product was 'prohibited by international law'.[553]

It would be interesting to know what the EU understanding is of 'fully autonomous weapons' since, at the time of writing, no definition has been given. What has been requested by the EU is that 'humans need to remain in control of the development, deployment and use with regard to possible military applications of emerging technologies in the area of LAWS, including AI, and prevent the use of such technologies in a way that would violate international law.'[554] Thus, the EU does not give any guidelines as to why 'autonomous systems' (which apparently excludes weapon systems) should be granted legal personhood, or what we are to understand by 'fully autonomous systems' and why they should be excluded from legal personhood.

Chopra and White, among other scholars, advance the possibility that artificial agents could be 'coherently considered as agents for the purpose of a legal system if their *intentional actions can be shown to be causes of events that comprise the domain of interest for the legal system in question*'.[555] Although the authors do not focus their analysis on future autonomous systems of war, they develop a legal theory applicable to all types of autonomous systems.

The point of departure is necessarily the fact that legal practice distinguishes between two types of legal personalities: *dependent agents* and *independent agents*. A *dependent legal person* can only act through the agency of another legal person in exercising some or all of its legal rights (i.e. children, adults who are 'of unsound mind', inanimate objects, such as ships and temples, and abstract legal entities, such as corporations) and an *independent legal person* is *sui juris*, that is, truly autonomous from the legal point of view.[556] Thus, *only the first type* is likely to be accorded to 'artificial agents unless or until they attain a very high degree of autonomy', though no insight is given as to what a 'very high degree' might be.[557]

553 Kelsey Atherton, 'European Union Negotiations Could Allow the Funding of Armed Autonomous Robots' (*C4SRNET*, 24 May 2018) <www.c4isrnet.com/unmanned/2018/05/24/negotiations-pave-way-for-eu-funding-of-armed-autonomous-robots/>.

554 European Union, '2019 EU Statement Agenda Item 5(d): "Review of the Potential Military Applications of Related Technologies in the Context of the Group's Work"' (*Reaching Critical Will*, 2019) <https://reachingcriticalwill.org/disarmament-fora/ccw/2019/laws/statements>.

555 Chopra and White (n 528) 17 (our emphasis); Lokhorst and Hoven (n 273) 150.

556 Chopra and White (n 528) 159.

557 ibid.

Roboticists and philosophers, in order to describe this capability, have developed a *theory of delegation*. Chopra and White argue the need to review the rigidity of the anthropocentric and instrumentalist paradigms to make way for a more pragmatic approach, capable of including artificial agents under the category of legal agents.[558] According to the authors, it would be possible to regard artificial agents as delegated 'legal agents' under the Latin maxim *qui facit per alium, facit per se* (he who acts through another is deemed in law to do it himself).[559] This suggestion would allow artificial agents to be legitimately seen as 'legal persons'. The authors are clear when they emphasise that artificial agents would no longer be regarded as 'extensions of humans', but rather, 'they may be understood as persons for a particular purpose or set of legal transactions'.[560]

On the one hand is found the *delegator agent* (who does or does not intentionally pre-select what the system will choose to do on the battlefield), while on the other is found the *delegated system* or *agent*.[561] The act of delegating is a well-established principle of law but a lack of attention to the specificities of the term, in different fields of knowledge, can easily lead to a *misappropriation of language*.[562]

The word 'agent' has an intuitive meaning in everyday life of something/someone able to take actions. To be an agent is to be the originator of an action, to be driven by motivations, purposes, desires and freely chosen decisions. Thus, 'agent' is the shorthand for 'intentional agent', since actions are not genuine actions unless they are '*intentional under some description*'. As David Gunkel explains, 'actions are doings, but not every doing is an action'; for example, breathing versus intentional killing. In order to accept 'intentional agents', it is necessary to identify a mental state, an intentionality animating the observed action.[563] Thus, an act of delegation is characterised 'in terms of the particular set of mental states (cognitive ingredients) of the agents involved in the interaction', which could not apply to an AWS.[564]

According to Cristiano Castelfranchi and Rino Falcone, it would be possible to envisage a new meaning of 'delegation' in which, externally, there is *no*

558 This understanding is expressly rejected by the 'Report of the 2018 Session of the Group of Governmental Experts on Emerging Technologies in the Area of Lethal Autonomous Weapons Systems' (n 193).

559 Chopra and White (n 528) 18.

560 ibid.

561 Sartor and Omicini (n 322) 48.

562 Chapter 3, Section 3.2.

563 Gunkel (n 520) 19.

564 Cristiano Castelfranchi and Rino Falcone, 'Towards a Theory of Delegation for Agent-Based Systems' (1998) 24 *Robotics and Autonomous Systems* 141.

interaction between the agents, the delegation being only in the mind of one, the delegator (*unilateral delegation*): in this case, delegation could be established between a cognitive and a non-cognitive agent.[565] In a situation involving *unilateral delegation*, the delegated is a mere tool and instrument of the delegator and the delegation is closed, every operation being defined and specified.

The term *unilateral delegation* does not excite any questions. In terms of liability, the delegator would be responsible for the *mission entrusted* to the system, because the 'rationality of delegation is reduced to the level of trust the agent requires for delegating'.[566] This, indeed, describes the situation of an automated system. The outcome, if the system performs according to the design and program, is the one pre-established by a human operator.

There are two other situations envisaged by the authors, however, that are more complex: *open delegation* and *over-* or *critical-help*, where the systems are required to use some discretion or, in the second type, even to take their own initiative.[567] Could AWS be included in the category of *open delegation*?

The institute of legal agency is based on a very close relationship between a principal and an agent. In fact, legal agency could be defined as follows:

> The fiduciary relationship that arises when a person (a principal) manifests assent to another person (an agent) that the agent shall act on the principal's behalf and subject to the principal's control, and the agent manifests assent or otherwise consents so to act.[568]

From this definition three structural elements become clear: first, legal agency requires a *consensual relationship* in which the agent agrees to act on behalf of another person. Second, the principal has a right to *control the actions of the agent*. Third, legal agency also has an *external dimension*. The agent will be responsible for establishing new legal relationships between the principal and third parties, both agent and third party having their specific spheres of rights and obligations.[569]

Regarding the consensual relationship, Chopra and White, in the absence of any real consent or agreement, contract or any other legal form of commitment, would not exclude the possibility of an agent being placed under legal obligations to its principal. This capability could be installed by the programmer, by means of an algorithm that '*translates*' their fiduciary duties into terms applicable to artificial agents. The fulfilment of their duties would just be

565 ibid 141.
566 ibid 141–144; Meissner and Wells (n 408).
567 Castelfranchi and Falcone (n 564) 3.
568 Chopra and White (n 528) 18.
569 ibid.

a question of empirical assessment, and whatever internal procedure was followed would be irrelevant.[570]

An act of 'consent', however, is not a mere detail, it is highly significant. It is consent that distinguishes between self-defence and murder, for instance, between accident and crime and between theft and donation. The requirement for 'consent' does not mean that 'consented acts' are necessarily justified or right, but it does show that individual acts such as personal consent and human reflection are valued.[571] Consequently, the impossibility of its giving 'real consent' makes possible to recognise an 'instrument', an 'armchair', but not an *autonomous legal agent*.

The relationship of 'control' could be, nonetheless, interesting to explore. Normally, the 'principal' does not intervene in the way the delegated task is performed by the agent but controls his/her results. However, intentionality is understood, by Chopra and White, as 'the capacity to act in accordance with specific reasons and purposes'. At the same time, the authors recognise that autonomous systems will depend on algorithms so complex that it will be almost impossible to know the reasoning that underpins their actions. However, the program will be the *final authority* and will simply be dependent on a third-person verification.[572]

Although seductive, to argue that the program will work without human intervention, according to 'its own reasons', is at odds with AI at its present stage of development, and with what teleological system is. If the system operates, as the authors propose, as a dependent agent, and the program is their 'final authority', it seems to be a *non sequitur* to argue that autonomous systems can 'have their own reasons'. As will be seen in Chapter 5, this question is highly relevant. The authors argue that algorithm complexity is most probably unintelligible for humans, referring to the system's 'black box' mode of operation and to the 'intentional stance' of artificial agents, that is, the system's capability to act in accordance 'with a coherent set of generalizations pertaining to intentional agents'.[573] This is not the place to develop the analogy established by Chopra and White between artificial agents' and corporations' intentionality. However, the authors make the important point that in order to cut through the complexity of the system, it should be possible 'to query the program to determine the reasons for its actions, perhaps by

570 ibid 21.

571 Raphael Bitton, 'Intelligence Agents, Autonomous Slaves and the U.S. Supreme Court's Wrong (and Right) Concept of Personal Autonomy' (2014) 7 *European Journal of Legal Studies* 5, 8, 14.

572 Chopra and White (n 528) 15.

573 ibid 17.

writing a trace program, running a test routine, or simply by asking it'.[574] A possible legal mechanism to 'query the program' will be examined in detail in Chapter 5, but it is important to highlight here that such a mechanism might have the potential to guarantee the transparency of autonomous systems and be a remarkably valuable way of establishing liability for unlawful outcomes caused by AWS.

Applying the legal theory of delegation to AWS is to fall into the trap of 'misappropriation of language', implying, as it does, an acceptance that autonomous systems would be legal agents on the battlefield.[575] The incoherence of the argument becomes evident when the problems of accountability emerge and it becomes necessary to deal with 'things' dependent on human responsibility or Tort Law. Having said this, it is possible to make use of the term 'open delegation' but only if 'discretion' is understood as 'the capability of the system to adapt to the mutable circumstances of the environment', and not as any implying any sort of capacity for self-critical analysis.[576] In this situation, the program, designed and programmed by human operators, can indeed be the 'final authority' for systems that do not require human intervention while performing the tasks entrusted to them.

3.7 CONCLUSION

The debate on weaponised autonomous systems will surely intensify in the near future, depending on the possibilities opened up by future technology. This chapter has sought to clarify what we should understand by 'autonomy' when applied to technology of war, and to explain why autonomous systems should be regarded as new 'weapons' and not as new agents on the battlefield.

Once 'autonomy' is understood as the 'capability to operate without human intervention', it becomes clear that 'autonomy' does not exclude the possibility of human control. Not only is human control possible at the stage of designing and programming an AWS, but also after the system is deployed, by using the self-destruct or deactivating mechanisms. In the situation in which violations of IHL caused by AWS occurred, another mechanism of human control is querying the *algorithm for the mission* regarding the data and logic followed by the system in the course of the OOSA Loop.

It was argued that the acronym should be OOSA Loop in order better to describe the three types of algorithms involved and to make it clear that these

574 ibid 15.

575 Chapter 3, Section 3.2.

576 Christman (n 104).

systems are unable to make decisions, but they can *select*, according to the algorithm for the mission, the optimal course of action, in order to optimise the mission entrusted to the system.

Lastly, suggestions that some authors have put forward in the debate about the legal status of AWS were the object of analysis. To the idea that AWS blur the distinction between 'weapon' and 'combatant' we responded that it is crucial to remember that, although an AWS is capable of selecting *the* course of action, it does not mean that it has any form of mens rea or capacity for self-critical analysis. The analogies between children, animals and AWS do not provide very much help and there are no reasonable arguments in support of the notion that AWS will be independent agents on the battlefield. The proposition that the legal institute of delegation might be a solution to the problem of accountability fails because of the impossibility of a consensual relationship between a human operator and an AWS. The term 'delegation' can only apply if we agree to take the engineering term '*open-delegation*' to refer to a form of unilateral delegation in which the human principal directs the AWS to adapt to changing circumstances on the battlefield in accordance with a plan designed by human operators.

4

AWS and the IHL Requirements

4.1 INTRODUCTION: THE NECESSITY FOR AN INDEPENDENT LEGAL DISCOURSE

Furthermore, the character of conflict is changing because of advances in technology, new strategies, and the evolving global geopolitical context – all of which challenge previous conceptions of warfare.

USA National Intelligence Council, Global Trends: Paradox of Progress (2017).

A legal discourse is necessary to regulate new technology of warfare but is not always welcome. AWS are highly complex *technical* systems, and it has been suggested that 'there is little lawyers can meaningfully comment on'.[577] Engineers and roboticists are the originators of a third revolution in lethal weaponry, the promoters of a paradigm shift in the way war is conducted.[578] Notwithstanding this, legal doctrine has always played an important role in the implementation of new technology in previous military revolutions, not with the aim of preventing development but of protecting those humanitarian values, common to the international community, that are enshrined in International Law in general, and IHL in particular.

Technology of warfare depends on human design and programming and thus it cannot be 'neutral', but it should be entirely committed to promoting long-established international values. Above all, the concern is about the protection of those normative values that question emergent technologies, prompting careful deliberation about their implementation, the need for

[577] Henderson, Keane and Liddy (n 19) 342.

[578] Coker, *Future Wars* (n 68) 68–74; Christopher Coker, *Warrior Geeks – How 21st Century Is Changing the Way We Fight and Think About War* (Hurts 2013) 30; Steven Grove, 'A Manual Adapting the Law of Armed Conflict to Lethal Autonomous Weapon Systems' [2016] *Margaret Thatcher Centre for Freedom* 1, 9.

protective measures, the extent to which a machine–human interface is required and, crucially, about accountability for the inevitable errors and violations that occur in battle.

This chapter aims to address the legal questions arising from a scrutiny of Weapons Law and the Law of Targeting. Only then will it be possible to determine if AWS, intrinsically, present a legal problem hitherto unencountered.

Looking at the corpus of IHL, the possibility of using AWS on the battlefield raises important considerations. For now, two are particularly relevant: first, what freedoms, exactly, do states have to introduce new technology of war into the battlefield? Second, Article 36 API stipulates that the study, development and acquisition of new technologies of war be determined by IHL rules – how is this to be monitored? US Policy Directive *DoD 3000.09* stipulates that before any decision is taken to enter into formal development of new weaponry, it is imperative to ensure that 'plans are in place for V&V [Verification and Validation] and T&E [Test and Evaluation] to establish system reliability, effectiveness and suitability under realistic conditions, including possible adversary actions'.[579] These tests and validations, as the document also states, must be carried out in accordance with international humanitarian standards. However, the question that emerges is whether it will be possible or not to verify, test and evaluate all possible combinations of variables which the AWS would encounter before the system is deployed on the battlefield?[580]

4.2 IHL AND THE LAW OF WEAPONRY

IHL enshrines in its corpus an equitable balance between *military necessity* – the principle that justifies the use of all measures that are not prohibited by the Law of War to defeat the enemy as quickly and efficiently as possible that are not prohibited by the Law of War[581] – and the *Principle of Humanity* – a set of rules protecting those who are not involved in a conflict and protecting those who are involved from unnecessary harm.[582] Each rule of IHL constitutes

579 US Department of Defense, 'DoD 3000.09. Autonomy in Weapon Systems' (n 7) 7.

580 McFarland, *Autonomous Weapon Systems and the Law of Armed Conflict: Compatibility with International Humanitarian Law* (n 46) 171.

581 US Department of Defense, *Department of Defense Law of War Manual* (General Council of the Department of Defense 2015) 52, para 2.2; Nobuo Hayashi, 'Contextualizing Military Necessity' (2013) 27 *Emory International Law Review* 189, 223.

582 Michael N Schmitt and Eric W Widmar, '"On Target": Precision and Balance in the Contemporary Law of Targeting' (2014) 7 *Journal of National Security Law & Policy* 379, 380; Nils Melzer, *Interpretative Guidance on the Notion of Direct Participation in Hostilities* (ICRC 2009) 78–79 <www.icrc.org/en/doc/assets/files/other/icrc-002-0990.pdf>; Lubell (n 217) 140–155; Michael N Schmitt, 'Military Necessity and Humanity in International

a dialectical compromise between 'these two opposing forces', as Schmitt points out.[583] Any legal assessment of AWS' legality will necessarily involve an analysis of whether they comply with the legal norms that states have designed throughout the centuries to maintain the balance of IHL, in particular the customary and conventional international rules concerning means and methods of warfare.[584]

The history of warfare and the centrality of the state show that 'military necessity' has always been a priority on the battlefield – as the doctrine of *Kriegsraison* (necessity of war overrules the manner of warfare, known as well as *total* or *absolute war*) demonstrates – but throughout the ages there has been an increasing sensitivity towards protecting humanitarian values on the battlefield.[585] As Judge Weeramantry argued in the 1996 *Advisory Opinion*, the strength and principles of the humanitarian laws of war can be traced back many centuries in many cultures – Hindu, Buddhist, Chinese, Christian, Islamic and traditional African – and 'these cultures have all given expression to a variety of limitations on the extent to which *means can be used for the purposes of fighting one's enemy*'.[586] IHL has evolved not only to include the Law of Weaponry but also subjects such as the protection of civilians and combatants in *hors de combat*, the classification of military targets, the protection of cultural property and even the establishment of an international court for the prosecution of those who violate substantially the norms of IHL.

Humanitarian Law: Preserving the Delicate Balance' (2010) 50 *Virginia Journal of International Law* 796–798; Knut Dormann and Jose Serralvo, 'Common Article 1 to the Geneva Conventions and the Obligation to Prevent International Humanitarian Law Violations' (2014) 96 *International Review of the Red Cross* 707, 708; International Committee of the Red Cross, *Commentary on the Additional Protocols of 8 June 1977 to the Geneva Conventions of 12 August 1949* (n 347) 683, para 2206.

583 Schmitt, 'Military Necessity and Humanity in International Humanitarian Law: Preserving the Delicate Balance' (n 582) 798.

584 Schmitt and Thurnher (n 328) 232.

585 The concept of 'total war' was first written about in France during World War I by Alphonse Séché and Georges Blanchou. Total war is distinguished by its unprecedented intensity and extent. Total War is fought heedless of the restraints of morality, custom or international law, requiring the mobilisation not only of armed forces but also of whole populations with no distinction whatsoever between combatants and civilians. A slightly different concept is that of 'absolute war' as presented by Clausewitz in *On War* (Book VIII). Although it is impossible to look at Clausewitz as wholly innocent and free of any genocidal intentions, the fact is that 'absolute war' means a war between armies and not between societies. Beatrice Heuser, *Reading Clausewitz* (Pimlico 2002) 116–123; cf Stefan Oeter, 'Methods and Means of Combat' in Dieter Fleck (ed), *The Handbook of International Humanitarian Law* (2nd edn, Oxford University Press 2009) 127; International Committee of the Red Cross, *Commentary on the Additional Protocols of 8 June 1977 to the Geneva Conventions of 12 August 1949* (n 347) 390.

586 *ICJ, Advisory Opinion on the Legality of the Threat and Use of Nuclear Weapons, Judgment* (n 265) para 478; Roberts and Guelff (n 263) 3.

The Law of Weaponry tries, on its part, to ensure that in the heat of battle the means and methods of war comply with internationally recognisable norms.[587] The 1868 St Petersburg Declaration was the first international effort to moderate conflicting interests on the battlefield in which states 'by common agreement fixed the technical limits at which the necessities of war ought to yield to the requirements of humanity', establishing two important principles: first, the principle that the belligerent parties to a conflict do not enjoy unlimited powers, and, second, the customary principle prohibiting the use of means of warfare that cause unnecessary suffering.[588]

The St Petersburg Declaration led to two further declarations renouncing certain means of warfare. Negotiated in The Hague at the First Hague Peace Conference of 1899 and the Second Hague Peace Conference of 1907, these came to be known as 'Hague Law' and today form part of the corpus of Customary International Law. These declarations have their limitations since they were binding only on contracting parties and would not be applicable to a non-contracting party if it were to join a conflict.

The level of violence that erupted during World War I drew attention to the failure of Hague Law to deal with new means and methods of war. In spite of several efforts made after that war to limit the escalation of such violence, it was in the period after World War II, with the advent of the UN Charter, that a system was created to govern disarmament and the regulation of armaments. According to Article 26 of the UN Charter, 'the Security Council shall be responsible for formulating, with the assistance of the Military Staff Committee [. . .], plans to be submitted to the Members of the United Nations for the establishment of a system of regulation of armaments'. In the same spirit, Article 11 of the UN Charter provides that the General Assembly may make recommendations to its Members, or to the Security Council, with respect to 'the principles governing disarmament and the regulation of armaments'. Although the intention of these provisions was laudable, it was really not until the modern *Jus in Bello* that true restrictions, in terms of means and methods of warfare, were established.[589]

On 12 August 1949, a diplomatic conference held in Geneva approved the text of four conventions to which more states have become party than to any other agreements on the laws of warfare. The four Geneva Conventions (GC) are a result of efforts developed before World War II and from the experience

587 Boothby, *Weapons and the Law of Armed Conflict* (n 210) 1.

588 ibid 19; Roberts and Guelff (n 263) 54–55; Chengeta, 'Are Autonomous Weapon Systems the Subject of Article 36 of Additional Protocol I to the Geneva Conventions?' (n 26) 84–86.

589 Christine Chinkin and Mary Kaldor, *International Law and New Wars* (Cambridge University Press 2017) 301–302.

of war. They deal respectively with (I) the wounded and sick among armed forces in the field, (II) the wounded, sick and shipwrecked in armed forces at sea, (III) prisoners of war and (IV) civilian persons in time of war.

While the Hague Law had concentrated on the rights and duties of combatants and the means of conducting warfare, the Geneva Law emphasised the protection of the civilian population in warfare and defined the categories of protected persons. The reality is that, as the ICJ stated in the 1996 *Advisory Opinion*, 'these two branches of law [...] have become so closely interrelated that they are considered to have gradually formed one single complex system, known today as international humanitarian law'.[590]

The seminal event in the treaty-based shift came with the adoption of the 1977 Additional Protocols to the 1949 Geneva Conventions. Two factors were particularly important: the new style of guerrilla warfare, and the spread of non-international armed conflicts. Both phenomena placed civilians and their property at risk. In response, the API and APII were adopted – the former governing international armed conflicts, and the latter focusing on non-international armed conflicts. API was unique in its joinder of the 'Hague' and 'Geneva' Law. The Diplomatic Conference that drafted the two Protocols amounted to the first comprehensive endeavour to carefully assess where the balance lay between military necessity and humanity, especially in the conduct of 'hostilities'. In particular, it elaborated the customary law Principle of Distinction, including its key components: prohibition of indiscriminate attacks, the Principle of Proportionality and the rules for precautions in attack. The introduction of the Additional Protocol I signalled a new, emerging sensitivity to the importance of recognising a humanitarian element in International Law.[591]

Recent developments pertaining to the Law of Weaponry can more accurately be categorised as arms-control treaties, such as the 1997 Ottawa Convention on Anti-personnel Mines. However, a word needs here to be said also about the 1980 *Convention on the Prohibitions or Restrictions on the Use of Certain Conventional Weapons which may be deemed to be Excessively Injurious or to have Indiscriminate Effects* (CCW). Five Protocols were annexed to the CCW: Protocol I prohibits the use of weapons that cause injury through non-detectable fragments; Protocol II (updated in 1996) prohibits or restricts the use of mines, booby traps and other devices; Protocol III

590 ICJ, *Advisory Opinion on the Legality of the Threat and Use of Nuclear Weapons, Judgment* (n 265) para 75; Gary D Solis, *The Law of Armed Conflict: International Humanitarian Law in War* (Cambridge University Press 2010) 83.

591 Schmitt, 'Military Necessity and Humanity in International Humanitarian Law: Preserving the Delicate Balance' (n 582) 795.

prohibits or restricts the use of incendiary weapons; Protocol IV, adopted in 1996, prohibits the using of blinding lasers – a true landmark in terms of Law of Weaponry as it is the first pre-emptive ban of a specific weapon. Protocol V, adopted in 2003, recognises the serious post-conflict humanitarian problems caused in the aftermath of war, asking from the parties that they assist in the clearing of unexploded devices, together with supplying information as to their use.

The adoption of the CCW has provided for the negotiation of Protocols to address particular weapons that are of concern mainly due to the serious humanitarian consequences attendant upon their deployment. It is in the line of questioning concerned with the humanitarian element of IHL that the discussions surrounding AWS are being developed. Since 2014, therefore, AWS and LARS have been under the scrutiny of the CCW delegations that have met annually, the last meeting held in September 2020.[592] The purpose of these discussions has been to agree upon a new protocol, designed specifically to address the undoubted dangers associated with the proposed new type of war technology.

4.3 INTERNATIONAL HUMANITARIAN LAW AND NEW 'MEANS AND METHODS OF WARFARE'

4.3.1 *The Relevance of Legal Discourse When Debating AWS*

In a recent interview, Mary Wareham, Arms Adviser at Humans Rights Watch (HRW), stated:

> If fully autonomous weapons systems were to commit a crime, it would be virtually impossible to hold anybody responsible for that. The bottom line is the ethical one. It's about if we're comfortable allowing a machine to take a human life on the battlefield, in policing, in law enforcement, in border control. We need to start acting before it gets too late and the window is closing.[593]

The first part of the statement would be reason enough for a debate. If a fully autonomous system were to commit a 'crime', nobody could be held accountable, because the system would be the responsible agent – but a 'war crime' always demands mens rea. Thus, the term 'crime' is probably not the most helpful one to choose but, as explained in previous chapters, it always depends

592 United Nations Office at Geneva (n 395).
593 Israel Homeland Security (iHLS), 'Conflict Over Killer Robots Continues. Interview with Mary Wareham' (2017) <https://i-hls.com/archives/78547>.

upon what is considered a 'fully' autonomous system. These issues will be further developed, so the focus of our attention will for now be on the second part of the statement.

The second part of the statement claims that the 'bottom line is the ethical one'. This, however, merits attention. The quotation implies, first, a 'responsibility gap', but at the same time considers the AWS question to be all about an ethical choice. There is no doubt that the development of AI, and especially its application in technology of war, raises several crucial ethical questions; these were addressed in Chapter 2. However, the proposal here is that before basing decisions about the future of AWS on ethical grounds, a legal survey should be carried out to analyse the ways in which their detractors allege that IHL, in legitimising such systems, fails to protect its humanitarian values. For example, in the course of this study, it will be seen that the argument against AWS based on fear of a 'responsibility gap' is without foundation.[594] This recognition will certainly have a bearing on any moral argument against AWS. Equally important will be to give due consideration to the reasons that might be offered in support of the development of AWS.

Considering the aforementioned discussion, two other considerations regarding the future acceptance of AWS are particularly important. The first consideration is that the study and development of AWS are not the result self-centred engineering research but emerge in response to the new realities and challenges of the battlefield; the two realities are intertwined.

A number of authors have explored the concept of *hybrid warfare*, to aid reflection upon the nature of modern armed conflicts, which are no longer restricted by the comparative symmetry of inter-state conflicts or circumscribed by clearly defined physical battlefields.[595] The presence of new, organised and armed non-state actors, and the technological progress (chiefly this applies to information systems), has completely changed the way a conflict is fought. As the American National Intelligence Council Report – *Global*

594 Chapter 5, Section 5.3.

595 Yuriy Danyk, Tamara Maliarchuk and Chad Briggs, 'Hybrid War: High-Tech, Information and Cyber Conflicts' (2017) 16 *Connections: The Quarterly Journal* 5, 5–7; Yulia Razmetaeva, 'Hybrid War, Information Technologies and the Legal Vacuum in the Digital World' (2017) 355; Aurel Sari, 'Hybrid Warfare, Law and the Fulda Gap' in Winston S Williams and Christopher Ford (eds), *Complex Battle Spaces* (Oxford University Press 2017) <https://papers.ssrn.com/sol3/papers.cfm?abstract_id=2927773>; Battina Renz, 'Russia and "Hybrid Warfare"' (2016) 22 *Contemporary Politics* 283, 283–284; Damien Van Puyelde, 'Hybrid War – Does It Even Exist?' (*NATO Review Magazine*, 2015) <www.nato.int/DOCU/review/2015/Also-in-2015/hybrid-modern-future-warfare-russia-ukraine/EN/index.htm>; 'Hybrid Threats' (*Hybrid CoE: The European Centre of Excellence for Countering Hybrid Threats*, 17 August 2017) <www.hybridcoe.fi/hybrid-threats/>.

Trends 2030: Alternative Trends – argues: 'this competition is not new, but the evolution of "hybrid adversaries" who combine irregular tactics with advanced standoff weaponry, add new dimensions to it'.[596] This new trend justifies the continuing interest of states in the development of technology, which 'involves precision, indeed surgical, strikes on particular houses, vehicles, and buildings often located in heavily populated areas'.[597]

The second consideration concerns the nature of IHL. In the *Tadić Case*, the court argued that 'a State-sovereignty-oriented approach has been gradually supplanted by a human-being-oriented approach. Gradually the maxim of Roman Law *hominum causa omne jus constitutum est* (all law is created for the benefit of human beings) has gained a firm foothold in the international community as well.'[598] This quotation should not be interpreted as a recommendation to discard the long-established customary and treaty international rules that legitimise states' recourse to military operations whenever they become involved in conflict. The humanitarian priorities of IHL prohibit any attempt to wage *total war* (the *Kriegsraison* doctrine) and set limits on means and methods that states can use.[599] Nonetheless, IHL does not seek to reject the rights of states to develop new technologies of warfare and act according to the 'necessity' dictated by the battlefield. In light of the aforementioned discussion, as the ICJ emphasised, recalling the *Corfu Channel Case*, 'elementary considerations of humanity' nourish the laws of armed conflict in order to promote the threshold of protection of the human person, which cannot be overturned, even by legitimate military purposes.[600] But these limits should be understood only as limits to states' rights to pursue their military objectives on the battlefield.[601]

It is in the light of the aforementioned considerations that the legitimacy of AWS ought to be determined, the question being: 'to what degree should AWS

596 United States of America, National Intelligence Council, 'Global Trends 2030: Alternative Worlds' (*Atlantic Council*, 2012) 72 <www.atlanticcouncil.org/wp-content/uploads/2019/09/global-trends-2030-nic-lo.pdf>.

597 Boothby, *Weapons and the Law of Armed Conflict* (n 210) 255.

598 *Prosecutor v Duko Tadic, Decision on the Defence Motion for Interlocutory Appeal on Jurisdiction* [1995] ICTY – Appeals Chamber IT 94 1 AR72 para 97; Gerhard Hafner, 'Some Thoughts on the State-Oriented and Individual-Oriented Approaches in International Law' (2013) 14 *Austrian Review of International and European Law Online* 27, 28–30.

599 Hayashi (n 581) 193.

600 *ICJ, Advisory Opinion on the Legality of the Threat and Use of Nuclear Weapons, Judgment* (n 265) 79.

601 Hayashi (n 581) 194.

be considered incompatible with IHL standards?' In order to define the contours of the problem, it is now necessary to look at the rules that impose limits on the study, development and acquisition of new warfare technologies.

4.4 THE LIMITED FREEDOM OF STATES TO DEVELOP NEW WEAPONS: THE AUTHORITY OF ARTICLES 35 AND 36 API

This section addresses the IHL rules that govern the (1) nature of weapons, (2) study, development and adoption of new weapons and (3) use of technology on the battlefield. These rules can be organised into two groups that are different, although complementary. The first group includes the norms that seek, a priori, to guarantee the legality of means and methods of warfare (Article 35 API) and ensure that all research into, and development of new weapons, means and methods of warfare respect International Law (Article 36 API). The second group includes norms that work a posteriori. These look not so much at the *legality* per se, but at the rules regarding *the use* of such means and methods of warfare as are deployed by a party to the conflict – the fundamental norms concerning the legality of any attack: *Precaution* (Article 57 API), *Distinction* (Articles 48 and 51(4) API) and *Proportionality* (Articles 51 (5) and 57(2)(b) (iii) API).

4.4.1 *The Requirements of the Law of Weaponry: Article 35 API*

As a starting point, it is important to bear in mind that those responsible for the development, acquisition and adoption of new weapon systems will be concerned in the first place with the legal constraints that might render the equipment *unlawful* per se.[602]

Article 35 API essentially reaffirms well-established customary principles concerning the nature of weaponry. It provides that:

1. In any armed conflict, the right of the parties to the conflict to choose methods or means of warfare is not unlimited.
2. It is prohibited to employ weapons, projectiles and material, and methods of warfare of a nature to cause superfluous injury or unnecessary suffering.
3. It is prohibited to employ methods or means of warfare which are intended, or may be expected, to cause widespread, long-term and severe damage to the natural environment.

[602] Schmitt, 'Autonomous Weapon Systems and International Humanitarian Law: A Reply to the Critics' (n 328) 8; Schmitt and Thurnher (n 328) 244–250.

Some authors, when analysing the legality of AWS, focus immediately on the obligations deriving from the law of targeting, but such an analysis is legitimate only after a weapon system has been declared *lawful* per se.[603] The ICJ, in the 1996 *Advisory Opinion*, explains that evaluation of the lawfulness of a weapon is prior to, and independent of the legitimate use of force under the UN Charter (*Jus ad Bellum*), and independent of the way it is used during the hostilities (*Jus in Bello*).[604]

Paragraphs (1) and (2) of Article 35 API illustrate the prohibition of means of warfare which would cause excessive suffering, that is *maux superflus*, as enshrined in the antecedent St Petersburg Declaration of 1868, and later codified by a formula nearly identical to that outlined in Article 23 of the Hague Regulations. The content of these prescriptions and 'the texts constituting the fabric of humanitarian law' were summarised by the ICJ in the 1996 *Advisory Opinion* by 'two cardinal principles'. The first principle enshrines '*the protection of the civilian population and civilian objects and establishes the distinction between combatants and non-combatants; States must never make civilians the object of an attack and must consequently never use weapons that are incapable of distinguishing between civilian and military targets*', and according to the second, '*it is prohibited to cause unnecessary suffering to combatants: it is accordingly prohibited to use weapons causing them such harm or uselessly aggravating their suffering. In application of that second principle, States do not have unlimited freedom of choice of means in the weapons they use.*'[605]

Considering the aforementioned principles, the ICJ concluded that both principles are part of '*Jus Cogens*' as defined in Article 53 of the Vienna Convention on the Law of Treaties of 23 May 1969, adding that '*all States are bound by those rules in Additional Protocol I, which, when adopted, were merely the expression of the pre-existing customary law*'.[606]

603 Chantal Grut, 'The Challenge of Autonomous Lethal Robotics to International Humanitarian Law' (2013) 18 *Journal of Conflict & Security Law* 5, 11–14; Wagner, 'Taking Humans Out of the Loop: Implications for International Humanitarian Law' (n 85) 5–10; Wagner, 'The Dehumanization of International Humanitarian Law: Legal, Ethical, and Political Implications of Autonomous Weapon Systems' (n 64) 1384–1399; Kastan (n 358) 59–62.

604 *ICJ, Advisory Opinion on the Legality of the Threat and Use of Nuclear Weapons, Judgment* (n 265) 39, 74.

605 ibid 78.

606 Article 53 provides 'A treaty is void if, at the time of its conclusion, it conflicts with a peremptory norm of general international law. For the purposes of the present Convention, a peremptory norm of general international law is a norm accepted and recognized by the international community of States as a whole as a norm from which no derogation is permitted and which can be modified only by a subsequent norm of general international law having the same character', ibid 83, 84.

It is not surprising that these two cardinal principles have also been endorsed by Article 8(b)(xx) ICC Statute, regarding the employment of 'weapons, projectiles and material and methods of warfare' which are of a nature to cause violations of those principles. The International Committee of the Red Cross Customary Law Study (hereinafter ICRC Study) also endorses the two cardinal principles, stating that 'state practice establishes this rule as a norm of customary International Law applicable in both international and non-international armed conflicts'.[607] The implementation of these two principles is further exemplified by the five protocols to the CCW and by the GGE 2019 report.[608]

These considerations point to the necessary conclusion that, as regards the nature of new weapon systems, there is no question about the applicability of the two cardinal principles to the process of study, development and acquisition of AWS. As the ICJ explicitly states, the '*intrinsic character of the legal principles in question which permeate the entire body of law of armed conflict [...] apply to all kinds of weapons, those of the past, those of the present and those of the future*'.[609] Thus, the first test must be to ascertain whether or not AWS can be considered *indiscriminate* per se.

The first cardinal principle, as enunciated by the ICJ, stipulates that weapons must be capable of direction at specific military targets (individuals and objects). The imperative rule appears in API under the headings 'protection of the civilian population' (Article 51 (1) API) and 'general protection of civilian objects' (Article 52 (1) API), with the natural corollary that 'means and methods of warfare which cannot be directed at a specific objective' will render the attack *indiscriminate* (Article 51 (4)(b) API).[610]

In view of the long customary tradition behind the second principle enunciated by the ICJ, Judge Rosalyn Higgins adds that 'unnecessary suffering' does not operate as a general prohibition but is, rather, directed at the *protection of*

607 Jean-Marie Henckaerts and Louise Doswald-Beck, *Customary International Humanitarian Law. Volume I: Rules* (ICRC – Cambridge University Press 2009) Rule 70; Jean-Marie Henckaerts, 'Study on Customary International Humanitarian Law: A Contribution to the Understanding and Respect for the Rule of Law in Armed Conflict' (2005) 87 *International Review of the Red Cross* 175.

608 Group of Governmental Experts on Emerging Technologies in the Area of Lethal Autonomous Weapons System (n 12) para 17 (H).

609 *ICJ, Advisory Opinion on the Legality of the Threat and Use of Nuclear Weapons, Judgment* (n 265) para 86.

610 Boothby, *Weapons and the Law of Armed Conflict* (n 210) 66–68; Chengeta, 'Are Autonomous Weapon Systems the Subject of Article 36 of Additional Protocol I to the Geneva Conventions?' (n 26) 84–85.

combatants – since other provisions serve the purpose of protecting civilians. Higgins explains that certain weapons that cause vastly greater suffering have never been subjected to specific prohibitions, nor, in general, used by states in practice, because they have always been regarded as 'clearly prohibited by application of the "unnecessary suffering" principle'.[611]

When applying this principle to AWS, as Schmitt remarks, it is unlikely that AWS will violate the 'unnecessary suffering' threshold, since the novelty of AWS lies not so much in the munition itself but in the system's capacity for autonomous selection-making; this, in fact, might well prove to enhance the reliability of a targeting process.[612] If it is bore in mind that the selection-making process will execute a human-designed and pre-given mission, there is no reason why those systems should be objects of concern.[613]

At this stage, it is important to envisage two very different scenarios. The first is that in which the weapon is considered *indiscriminate* per se, because it is incapable of being aimed at a specific military target and/or its effects cannot be controlled. The second, in contrast, is when a weapon system is *used intentionally* for an indiscriminate attack (e.g. fired at civilians) or when the legitimate use of the weapon *causes unlawful outcomes due to malfunctions* or *errors* (e.g. the Brimstone missile that hits a civilian object).[614] API Article 51 (4) (5) aptly illustrates the distinction: it establishes the conditions that render an attack *indiscriminate*, and goes on to give two examples that deserve further attention. As it is easily recognised, these examples involve the lawfulness of human decisions and not of the weapons per se; it is the intention behind the attack that violates the rules of Distinction and Proportionality. As Boothby rightly points out, proportionality has no direct applicability to the process of legitimising a weapon. As the author explains, '*what is proportionate can only be meaningfully determined in relation to an attack on a particular occasion*, perhaps a specific time, using particular weapons and specified attack

611 Rosalyn Higgins, 'Dissenting Opinion of Judge Higgins, ICJ Nuclear Weapons Advisory Opinion' (1996) 12–13, 16 <www.icj-cij.org/public/files/case-related/95/095-19960708-ADV-01-14-EN.pdf>.

612 Schmitt, 'Autonomous Weapon Systems and International Humanitarian Law: A Reply to the Critics' (n 328) 9; Schmitt and Thurnher (n 328) 244–248.

613 Some scholars, however, understand AWS not as 'means of warfare' but rather as a new method of warfare, for example, because the expected outcome is encoded on the AWS. For that reason, Chengeta, among others, argues that AWS would be unlawful per se if such systems will not be able to comply with the 'cardinal principles' of IHL. See Chengeta, 'Are Autonomous Weapon Systems the Subject of Article 36 of Additional Protocol I to the Geneva Conventions?' (n 26) 83–84; Jenks and Liivoja (n 432).

614 Schmitt, 'Autonomous Weapon Systems and International Humanitarian Law: A Reply to the Critics' (n 328) 8–10; Schmitt and Thurnher (n 328) 244.

profiles'.[615] In light of these considerations, the arguments presented by HRW and others that AWS 'would face great, if not insurmountable, difficulties in reliably distinguishing lawful and unlawful targets as required by international humanitarian law' can result difficult to accept.[616]

The rules of Distinction and Proportionality are by no means easy to apply and their application is still a source of debate among scholars.[617] However, AWS have not yet been deployed; they are still being tested and evaluated and, therefore, it remains to be proven that they might present 'insurmountable' obstacles in terms of the rules of Distinction and Proportionality. Another aspect in which HRW's report can be misleading is the fact that assumptions about future warfare technology achievements can be easily proven wrong.

Completely different is the position of 252 leading roboticists arguing that 'once developed, lethal autonomous weapons will permit an armed conflict to be fought at a scale greater than ever, and at timescales faster than humans can comprehend. These can be weapons of terror, weapons that despots and terrorists use against innocent populations, and weapons hacked to *behave in undesirable ways*.'[618] In this case, the concern is not about AWS' legal compliance, but about the risks inherent in AI, the unpredictability and vulnerability and, finally, the use made of AWS.

A final question that deserves attention is whether unpredictable systems, such as AWS, should be considered *indiscriminate* per se and therefore be pre-emptively banned. In Chapter 1, it was seen that AWS could be labelled 'unpredictable' because they will have non-deterministic algorithms embedded in their operating systems. Machine learning algorithms operate based on probabilities (statistics) with the result that the outcomes can only be 'expected'. Thus, AWS could represent a higher level of uncertainty regarding the outcome, especially given that they are to operate without the intervention of human operators in the selection-making process.

The possibility of AWS producing unpredictable unlawful outcomes is a matter of utmost importance. However, it is not accurate to directly associate 'system unpredictability' with unlawful outcomes parallel to war crimes. In

615 Boothby, *Weapons and the Law of Armed Conflict* (n 210) 256 (our emphasis).

616 Human Rights Watch, 'Making the Case: The Dangers of Killer Robots and the Need for a Preemptive Ban' (n 216) 5–7; Human Rights Watch and International Human Rights Clinic, 'Losing Humanity: The Case against Killer Robots' (n 30) 30–32; Heyns, 'Report of the Special Rapporteur on Extrajudicial, Summary or Arbitrary Executions, Christof Heyns' (n 10) paras 69–70; Thompson Chengeta, 'Measuring Autonomous Weapon Systems against International Humanitarian Law Rules' (2016) 5 *Journal of Law and Cyber Warfare* 66.

617 Dinstein (n 210) 255–257; Henckaerts and Doswald-Beck (n 607) ch 4, Rule 14.

618 Gibbs, 'Elon Musk Leads 116 Experts Calling for Outright Ban of Killer Robots' (n 510) (our emphasis).

one way or another every weapon system, manual, automated or autonomous, is unpredictable. Malfunctions unfortunately happen in the battlefield, sometimes causing damage to the civilian population. In this regard, AWS could be said to be 'vulnerable', as could any other system. The problems emerge with 'syntactic errors', that is when the system fails to accurately 'read' the properties of the physical world, and that can happen at any or all stages of the OOSA Loop. One such 'error' could create a chain of errors leading to a disruption of the mission and causing unpredictable outcomes. These unpredictable results, if unlawful, could give rise to two different types of IHL violation: breaches of IHL, resulting in 'administrative accountability', and 'war crimes' that result in international criminal responsibility.[619]

The concept of 'war crimes' depends in itself on the seriousness of the violation committed. These elements will be explored in Chapter 5, but for now it is important to establish the possibility that *unpredictable outcomes* may be caused by an AWS' errors. However, we should not confuse 'unpredictable outcomes' with the 'uncontrollable effects' of a specific weapon. The latter relate to 'indiscriminate weapons', especially if the five CCW protocols designed to prevent 'unnecessary suffering' are taken into account.

Science fiction paints fanciful scenarios and creates unrealistic expectations about what an AWS can do or how it will perform, but it should not be forgotten that AWS may well employ weapons already in use today. It will be the task of the autonomous platform, as a component of an autonomous system, not only to select the optimal course of action but also to deploy the most appropriate weapon or munition to engage the military target in sight. Thus, if the weapon selected by the AWS is the only possible weapon to achieve the mission, there is no reason to suppose that the system will be indiscriminate per se.

It is a state's prerogative to develop new war technology, but not without limits (Article 35 (1) API).[620] It is possible to identify three sets of limits. The

619 'Administrative accountability' refers to the disciplinary and administrative liability of individuals that can be pursued beyond individual criminal responsibility. Robert Cryer and others, *An Introduction to International Criminal Law and Procedure* (2nd edn, Cambridge University Press 2010) 387.

620 At 2019 GEE, the statement presented by Brazil provided that 'the Convention (CCW) is predicated on the principle that the "right of parties to an armed conflict to choose methods and means of warfare is not unlimited". The decision to negotiate and adopt a humanitarian convention with a flexible framework to deal with specific weapons systems was taken under the premise that the cardinal principles of IHL – such as precaution, distinction, proportionality, military necessity and humanity – always apply, but may need to be further articulated and specified, in a legal manner, to ensure compliance. As technological development quickly accelerates and is weaponized, this need becomes ever more patent.' cf Brazil, '2019 GGE on Laws. Challenges to IHL Item 5(a)' (n 267).

first limit comprises the values that IHL enshrines in the customary and conventional norms against which new technologies are tested and evaluated. The tests should cover the study, development, acquisition and deployment of autonomous systems in order to evaluate whether AWS might violate IHL rules (Article 36 API). The second limit is more in the nature of a political argument. New technologies develop not only because of the cultural nature of the enemy but also because of its ability to influence the balance of power among states. Looking at the nature of modern conflicts, it is hard to envisage a situation in which a state would have any interest in losing control of its weaponry. The third and final limit comprises an argument of 'humanitarian hope'. One advantage of developing AWS is related to the fact that AWS 'would not act out of revenge, panic, anger [...] unless specifically programmed to do so, robots would not cause intentional suffering on civilian populations'. They will be unable to disobey orders, and will be faster and more precise than other means of combat.[621] Thus, AWS promise to be more accurate than human soldiers, and this also goes against the possibility of their being classed as indiscriminate weapons.

In conclusion, it is difficult to accept that AWS can be described as indiscriminate per se. The novelty of AWS is not so much related to the 'weapon' that can be released but to the incorporated system. It is the latter that will facilitate the autonomous selection-making process. However, a system will always be constrained by the rules inherent in its design and programming. It is fair to assume that those rules must encode the IHL and ROE standards. Taking into account the enhancement of humanitarian values that AWS have the potential to introduce on the battlefield, it may legitimately be concluded that AWS present themselves as *discriminate* weapon systems.

4.4.2 *Article 36 API: The Importance of AWS Legal Reviews*

The process of reviewing the legality of new weapons is not new.[622] The reference in modern international treaties to the need to carry out legal reviews of new weapons, means and methods of warfare is found in Article 36 of Additional Protocol I of 1977:

> In the study, development, acquisition or adoption of a new weapon, means or method of warfare, a High Contracting Party is under an obligation to

621 Heyns, 'Report of the Special Rapporteur on Extrajudicial, Summary or Arbitrary Executions, Christof Heyns' (n 10) paras 53–54; Coker, *Future Wars* (n 68) 86; Scharre, *Army of None: Autonomous Weapons and the Future of War* (n 425) 13.

622 kellenberger (n 74) 809–810.

determine whether its employment would, in some or all circumstances, be prohibited by this protocol or by any other rule of International Law applicable to the High Contracting Party.

Article 36 functions as a link between IHL rules and the proposed introduction of new weapons in the battlespace and is the trigger for states, signatories of Additional Protocol I, to proceed with the necessary reviews.[623] However, in order for a legal review to be effective, the legal requirements have to be testable, quantifiable and measurable and, therefore, fulfil the difficult task of 'bridging the disconnect that often exists between the definitions of technical requirements and the desired operational performance'.[624] This section aims to examine the operationality of Article 36 API when applied to AWS to prevent systems performing unlawfully or in an unpredictable manner. Could it be considered that Article 36 and the mechanisms of legal review of these weapons are sufficient to prevent AWS causing unpredictable outcomes?

There can be no doubt that IHL applies to new weapon systems, and indeed all technology deployed on the battlefield; this is explicitly recognised in Article 36 API but, as Jakob Kellenberger points out, applying pre-existing rules to new technology of warfare always raises the question of whether those rules will be found sufficient to meet the challenge of AWS.[625] First and foremost, the complexity of these systems certainly requires a multidisciplinary legal review in which roboticists, engineers, commanders and lawyers have to participate together.[626] This participation process is crucial in order to guarantee the systems' predictability and to create that level of trust in the commander that decides to deploy an AWS.[627]

In order to address the challenges presented by the requirement for legal review of AWS, first, it is important to look at the nature of Article 36, and, second, to look at the actual problems surrounding the specificities of AWS. Starting with the first, it is debatable, indeed, whether Article 36 has the status of customary law, and unclear how, exactly, states are supposed to review

623 Dinstein (n 210) 80–81; International Committee of the Red Cross, *Commentary on the Additional Protocols of 8 June 1977 to the Geneva Conventions of 12 August 1949* (n 347) 421, para 1463; Liivoja, Leins and McCormack (n 22) 620.

624 Alan Backstrom and Ian Henderson, 'New Capabilities in Warfare: An Overview of Contemporary Technological Developments and the Associated Legal and Engineering Issues in Article 36 Weapons Reviews' (2012) 94 *International Review of the Red Cross* 483, 508–509.

625 kellenberger (n 74) 810.

626 Backstrom and Henderson (n 624) 483–484.

627 ibid 508; Heather M Roff and David Danks, '"Trust but Verify": The Difficulty of Trusting Autonomous Weapons Systems' (2018) 17 *Journal of Military Ethics* 1, 3–4; Noll (n 105) 89.

the legality of these new weapons.[628] The ICRC study does not mention the obligations enshrined in Article 36 API as part of customary IHL.[629] Darren Stewart, instead, argues that Article 36 API obligations relate to the customary obligations as codified in Article 35 API.[630] At the same time, the 2014 Arms Trade Treaty, although 'reaffirming the sovereign right of any State to regulate and control conventional arms exclusively within its territory, pursuant to its own legal or constitutional system', establishes as one of its principles 'the primary responsibility of all States in *establishing and implementing their respective national control systems*'.[631]

In spite of the aforementioned discussion, the body of Article 36 API states that there is the obligation to determine if '*in some and all the circumstances*' the weapon system can be considered unlawful according to the API or '*any other rule of International Law applicable to the High Contracting Party*'. Thus, as James Fry argues, the expression 'in some and all the circumstances' should be read as an element of 'contextualism', allowing the precept to be interpreted in light of the contemporary circumstances and challenges.[632] This position could be rather challenging if it meant a politicisation of the rule of law, but it is understood here to mean the *contextual relevance* required for the assessment of the legality of every new weapon system before it is employed by any state.[633]

A context-dependent analysis illustrates, first, the fact that IHL is open to the challenges of changing times and new technologies of war. If AWS are an answer to the hybrid nature of modern conflicts, lawyers and roboticists working together can adopt specific guidelines for each system in order to 'predict actual performance'.[634] Second, it reinforces the fact that a new

628 Darren M Stewart, 'New Technology and the Law of Armed Conflict' in Raul A Pedrozo and Daria P Wollschlaeger (eds), *International Law and the Changing Character of War*, vol 87 (US Naval War College 2011); Fry (n 333) 468. The recent *Oslo Manual on Select Topics of the Law of Armed Conflict* states, for example, that 'Article 36 of API has not yet crystallized as customary international law, and therefore non-contracting Parties are not legally bound to abide by the full extent of its strictures'. See Dinstein and Dahl (n 80) Rule 7; Seixas-Nunes (n 240).

629 Henckaerts and Doswald-Beck (n 607).

630 Stewart, 'New Technology and the Law of Armed Conflict' (n 628) 283.

631 'Arms Trade Treaty' (2014) preamble, principles <https://thearmstradetreaty.org/treaty-text.html> (our emphasis).

632 Fry (n 333) 459.

633 International Committee of the Red Cross, *A Guide to the Legal Review of New Weapons, Means and Methods of Warfare. Measures to Implement Article 36 of the Additional Protocol I of 1977* (2006); Vincent Boulanin and Maaike Verbruggen, 'Article 36 Reviews Dealing with the Challenges Posed by Emerging Technologies' (Sipri – Stockholm International Peace Research Institute 2017) 4 <www.sipri.org/sites/default/files/2017-12/article_36_report_1712.pdf>.

634 Backstrom and Henderson (n 624) 510; Letendre (n 66) 294.

weapon must be tested according *to the circumstances for which it was designed* (the mission) at any stage when a new weapon is incorporated in a state's arsenal.[635] Third, legal reviews are not limited only by API obligations but also by the consuetudinary norms of IHL applicable to all states, be they party or non-party to the API. This seems to be interpretation of the ICRC when it states that the obligation to proceed to legal reviews not only applies to 'weapons in the widest sense'[636] but it also 'applies to *all* States, regardless of whether or not they are party to Additional Protocol I'.[637]

Following on from the aforementioned discussion, states are under an obligation to determine whether a new weapon may prove to be unlawful.[638] Originally an internationalised control procedure was attempted, but this proved impracticable owing to the legitimate requirement for secrecy surrounding weapons development;[639] responsibility for new weaponry devolved upon internal and domestic mechanisms.[640] Despite strenuous efforts on the part of the international community, states hold fast to the conviction that questions concerning new weaponry should remain internal, and strict control should be maintained over the content of any published reviews.[641] For this matter, the

635 Fry (n 333) 468–469.

636 International Committee of the Red Cross, A *Guide to the Legal Review of New Weapons, Means and Methods of Warfare. Measures to Implement Article 36 of the Additional Protocol I of* 1977 (n 633).

637 ibid.

638 ibid 4. Brazil at the 2019 GGE Meeting recognised, however, Article 36 as 'a corollary of customary international law'. cf Brazil, '2019 GGE on Laws. Challenges to IHL Item 5(a)' (n 267).

639 In 2019, the Russian Federation stated that 'Russia adheres to its relevant obligations and deems it unnecessary to elaborate a universal mandatory mechanism for "legal reviews," especially just for LAWS'. The Russian Federation, '2019 Group of Governmental Experts: Potential Opportunities and Limitations of Military Uses of Lethal Autonomous Weapons Systems' (n 5) para 8.

640 International Committee of the Red Cross, *Commentary on the Additional Protocols of 8 June 1977 to the Geneva Conventions of 12 August 1949* (n 347) para 1470; Oeter (n 585) 137. According to the ICRC, some states (Australia, Belgium, the Netherlands, Norway, Sweden, the United States) have made available the instruments of setting up these mechanisms available to the ICRC. Some other states (the United Kingdom, France and Germany) have communicated to the ICRC that they carried out these reviews, but the internal procedures were not made available. cf International Committee of the Red Cross, *A Guide to the Legal Review of New Weapons, Means and Methods of Warfare. Measures to Implement Article 36 of the Additional Protocol I of 1977* (n 633) 5–6.

641 In this sense, it is difficult to understand the ICRC Guide to the Legal review of new weapons, which suggests that, according to Article 84 API, the states 'shall communicate to one another as soon as possible [...] the laws and regulations which they may adopt to ensure its application' and the other states parties to the protocol may ask to be informed about this procedure. The secrecy inherent to the study and development of AWS will not ever allow this communication. cf International Committee of the Red Cross, A *Guide to the Legal*

decision of the ICJ in the 1996 *Advisory Opinion* is important when it reaffirmed the doctrine of the *Lotus Case*, stating that 'restriction upon the independence of States cannot [...] be presumed' and that International Law leaves open a 'wide measure of discretion which is only limited in certain cases by prohibitive rules'.[642]

Leaving aside the intended internationalisation of legal reviews, it is vital to emphasise that such reviews would have an important bearing on the future of AWS. The review work would be a preliminary step towards ensuring that AWS comply with International Law, testing and evaluating the situations and scenarios in which the system is designed to operate autonomously. At the same time, legal reviews could help with the procedure of deploying AWS, establishing guidelines for their use and spelling out the levels of acceptable predictable risk and of human intervention or supervision required.[643] Moreover, as established by the *US Department of Defense Law of War Manual* (hereinafter the LWM), legal reviews are important because even if the weapon is not prohibited, 'the review should also consider whether there are legal restrictions on the weapon's use that are specific to that type of weapon'.[644]

The legal reviews, as far as AWS are concerned, are likely to face two main challenges – one technical and one political – that could call into question any possibility of that weapon being judged capable of IHL compliance. This starts with the technical challenge. When discussing the definition of AWS, it was noted that these systems will be designed and programmed for an intended mission. This argument is supported by the LWM, which states that 'the use of weapons in accordance with their design intent and the doctrine that has been promulgated for their use *contributes to compliance with Law of War* obligations *with respect to weapons* because the legality of the weapon would have been reviewed based on its intended use'.[645]

Review of New Weapons, Means and Methods of Warfare. Measures to Implement Article 36 of the Additional Protocol I of 1977 (n 633) 20; Sean Watts, 'Autonomous Weapons: Regulation Tolerant or Regulation Resistant' (2016) 117 *Temple International & Comparative Law Journal* 177–179.

642 ICJ, *Advisory Opinion on the Legality of the Threat and Use of Nuclear Weapons, Judgment* (n 265) para 21. Another example can be offered. The Arms Trade Treaty (2014), in its Preamble, reaffirms 'the sovereign right of any State to regulate and control conventional arms exclusively in its territory, pursuant to its legal and constitutional system'. 'Arms Trade Treaty' (n 631) preamble, para 4.

643 Backstrom and Henderson (n 624) 511; Lt Col Alexander Bolt, 'The Use of Autonomous Weapons and the Role of the Legal Adviser' in Dan Saxon (ed), *International Humanitarian Law and the Changing technology of War*, vol 41 (Martinus Nijhoff 2013) 125.

644 US Department of Defense, *Department of Defense Law of War Manual* (n 581) 339, para 6.2.2.

645 ibid 340, para 6.3.1.

However, it also added that a mission can include several operational systems, introducing a level of complexity unprecedented before the advent of AWS. Calling to mind the triple structure of the *algorithm for the mission*, the way in which the operational dimension of AWS can be decentralised can easily be envisaged. As has been noted by some authors, the amount of data and the diversity of operational systems can be so massive that 'not only is it impossible to test all of them directly, it is not even possible to test more than an insignificantly small fraction of them'.[646] Another factor that deserves attention is how black box systems are to be tested. The selection-decision process will be unintelligible to their operators; if it is possible only to test the efficiency of the outcomes, can the test be considered rigorous? This question becomes even more pertinent when situations are envisaged in which AWS are required to deal with new data from the battlefield. Experts have suggested a number of additional criteria according to which legal reviews of AWS could be organised.[647] However, since machine learning algorithms learn new data from the environment and operate by means of trial and error, it seems unreasonable to imagine that every single situation or scenario of war can be tested.[648]

The second challenge is a political one. In spite of the obligations enshrined in Article 36 API, very few countries have instituted formal review procedures; some states that manufacture weapons are not party to the API; others have not published the results of informal legal reviews.[649] Since the first CCW

646 Backstrom and Henderson (n 624) 512; Noll (n 105) 88–89; McFarland, *Autonomous Weapon Systems and the Law of Armed Conflict: Compatibility with International Humanitarian Law* (n 46) 62, 171.

647 Boothby, *Weapons and the Law of Armed Conflict* (n 210) 347–349; Michael W Meier, 'Lethal Autonomous Weapons Systems (Laws): Conducting a Comprehensive Weapons Review' (2016) 30 *Temple International & Comparative Law Journal* 119, 127–132.

648 A sign of hope for the legal reviews and testing of AWS may be the *digital twin technology*. A digital twin is 'the virtual representation of a physical object or system across its life cycle. It uses real-time data and other sources to enable learning, reasoning and dynamically recalibrating for improved decision making.' Such technology can help understand not only how products *are* performing, but also how they *will* perform in the future. As the UK AI Council argues, 'developing those AI applications and AI models and testing with synthetic data, there comes a point when you must begin to model and rehearse in the real world with messy, unpredictable and diverse environments'. See' AI Roadmap' (UK AI COUNCIL 2021) 25 <https://www.gov.uk/government/publications/ai-roadmap> accessed 3 March 2021; Maggie Mae Armstrong, 'Cheat Sheet: What Is Digital Twin?' (*IBM*, 4 December 2020) <www.ibm.com/blogs/internet-of-things/iot-cheat-sheet-digital-twin/>; Bernard Marr, 'What Is Digital Twin Technology – And Why Is It So Important?' (*Forbes*, 2017) <www.forbes.com/sites/bernardmarr/2017/03/06/what-is-digital-twin-technology-and-why-is-it-so-important/?sh=79b020922e2a>.

649 In the 2006 ICRC Guide for Weapons Review, it is mentioned that only the United States, the United Kingdom, Belgium, the Netherlands, Norway, Sweden, Australia, Canada, France and Germany as states had developed a weapons review system. International

meeting of experts in 2014, the question of examining whether AWS will have the capability to be IHL compliant and the obligation to conduct legal reviews have been matters of debate among the states party to the CCW. However, at the 2016 CCW Meeting of Experts on Lethal Autonomous Weapons, with the exception of China and India, states' representatives (among them Australia, Belgium, Canada, France, Germany, Israel, Japan, the Netherlands, Poland, Russian Federation, Sierra Leone, Sweden, the United Kingdom and the United States) endorsed the proposition that the review process be regarded as crucial in ensuring that AWS are lawful and are used lawfully. At the same time, some states – Australia, Belgium, Germany, Israel, Sweden, the United Kingdom and the United States – provided explanations and/or updates of their weapons review processes.[650] In the GGE 2018 Final report, the governmental experts underlined the importance of AWS legal reviews in two different ways. First, they recognised the insistence on the part of some states' delegations that the best way to address potential risks would be to reinforce the importance of Article 36 API. Second, they noted that 'in accordance with States' obligations under international law, in the study, development, acquisition, or adoption of a new weapon, means or method of warfare, determination must be made whether its employment would, in some or all circumstances, be prohibited by international law'.[651]

Crootof has already drawn attention to the question of what would constitute a sufficient legal review in the case of AWS, focusing mainly on the technical challenges.[652] However, the political challenge seems to be the most urgent one at the time of writing since states have already expressed willingness to establish some future guidelines for legal reviews. In this regard, India's example illustrates the two challenges. India has addressed the technical problem by stating that the way in which the obligations enshrined in Article 36 API would work in practice is an unknown, and, regarding the political argument, Shashank Reddy has suggested that, since Article 36 API has not become part of Customary International Law, and India is not party to

Committee of the Red Cross, *A Guide to the Legal Review of New Weapons, Means and Methods of Warfare. Measures to Implement Article 36 of the Additional Protocol I of 1977* (n 633) 5, footnote 8; cf Fry (n 333) 455; Boothby, *Weapons and the Law of Armed Conflict* (n 210) 342–344.

650 Chris Ford and Chris Jenks, 'The International Discussion Continues: 2016 Experts Meeting on Lethal Autonomous Weapons' (*Just Security*, 20 April 2016) <www.justsecurity.org/30682/2016-ccw-experts-meeting-laws/>.

651 'Report of the 2018 Session of the Group of Governmental Experts on Emerging Technologies in the Area of Lethal Autonomous Weapons Systems' (n 193) pt III, s A d, s E, para 28.

652 Crootof, 'Autonomous Weapon Systems and the Limits of Analogy' (n 182) 9–10.

the API, it is legitimate for India 'to develop a domestic regime that fixes liability for the actions of these weapons and lays down rules of engagement and conditions for export', adding that 'while the international debate is still raging, there is no reason why India cannot move forward with establishing a domestic regime'.[653]

A different position is taken by the United States. The 2012 *DoD 3000.09* stipulates that 'systems will go through rigorous hardware and software verification and validation (V&V) and realistic system developmental and operational test and evaluation (T&E)' and these measures, among others, will 'certify that operators of autonomous and semi/autonomous weapon systems have been trained in systems capabilities in order to exercise appropriate levels of human judgement in the use of force and employ systems with appropriate care in accordance with the Law of War, applicable treaties, weapon system safety rules, and applicable ROE'.[654] Although no reference is made to Article 36 API, the LWM establishes a parallel between the obligations enshrined in that provision and US practice, stating that 'the DoD policy and practice of conducting legal reviews of weapons preceded this API provision'.[655] On this issue, the US 2021 Final Report addresses severe criticisms to the Chinese and Russian Governments for their policies regarding autonomous technology of warfare.[656] However, the fact that some states are not party to the API does not mean that states develop their own criteria as the statement from India seems to suggest.[657] As Boothby notes, for states non-party to the

653 Reddy (n 52) 12.

654 US Department of Defense, 'DoD 3000.09. Autonomy in Weapon Systems' (n 7) 3, 9, 12 (our emphasis). More recently, however, in the US *Executive Order on Maintaining American Leadership in Artificial Intelligence* it is stated that 'continued American Leadership in AI is of paramount importance to maintaining the economic and national security of the United States' and, therefore, 'the United States must drive development of appropriate technical standards and *reduce barriers to the safe testing and deployment of AI technologies* in order to enable the creation of new AI-related industries and the adoption of AI by today's industries'. cf Donald Trump, 'US Executive Order on Maintaining American Leadership in Artificial Intelligence' (*Federal Register*, 14 February 2019) s 1, B <www.federalregister.gov/documents/2019/02/14/2019-02544/maintaining-american-leadership-in-artificial-intelligence>.

655 US Department of Defense, *Department of Defense Law of War Manual* (n 581) 315.

656 'Final Report. National Security Commission on Artificial Intelligence' (n 15) 95.

657 In 2019, however, India seems to have changed its initial position, stating that 'the lawfulness of weapon and weapon systems itself and whether it is qualified for use in an armed conflict is determined under the principles of Law of Armed Conflict (LOAC). To be lawful, a weapon must satisfy all the requirements, i.e. the weapon must be able to discriminate between military and non-military targets, it must not cause unnecessary suffering and it must not be uncontrollable.' '2019 Statement by India: An Exploration of the Potential Challenges Posed by Emerging Technologies in the Area of Lethal Autonomous Weapons Systems to International Humanitarian Law' (2019) <www

API, there is '*an implicit obligation*, attested to by the practice of certain States before the adoption of API, [that] *applies specifically to the acquisition or use of new means of warfare*'.[658]

Considering the aforementioned discussion, it is important to always bear in mind that the fundamental rules underpinning the legitimacy and use of weapons have become part of international customary law and, therefore, they are part of the body of International Law that states must comply with. Regarding the national legal reviews, and how exactly they are done, is a matter for the discretionary power of states. Notwithstanding this point, whatever the concrete position of a state regarding the obligation enshrined in Article 36 API – to establish its own unpublicised national review or to adopt the legal review made by another state – no state can obliterate the obligations of the consuetudinary values enshrined in IHL, let alone the *Jus Cogens*, depending upon the conduct of the parties to an armed conflict.

To conclude, the understanding underpinning this work is that it needs to be possible to encode all IHL values and constraints at the moment of designing and programming the *algorithm for the mission*. The commander shall take all feasible precautions to authorise the deployment of an AWS only when the dictates of military necessity require its capabilities; when the exceptional case arises of unforeseeable malfunctions and errors causing violations of IHL, the international legal framework shall be able to provide responsibility mechanisms. Apart from this, the results obtained from tests and evaluations collected during legal reviews are useful in helping engineers and roboticists to understand what can be codified and how far it is possible to measure the risk of a mission without human intervention.

4.4.3 *AWS and the Role of the Legal Adviser*

The ICRC recommends that Article 36 API should be complemented by Article 82API, which requires that legal experts be present to advise military commanders on the application of IHL at every stage of a new weapon review.[659] Article 82 API provides:

.unog.ch/80256EDD006B8954/(httpAssets)/4C330E6B0BDD4C20C12583D2003C36AF/$file/5+a+26+Mar+2019+forenoon.pdf>.

658 Boothby, *Weapons and the Law of Armed Conflict* (n 210) 342–343.

659 International Committee of the Red Cross, A *Guide to the Legal Review of New Weapons, Means and Methods of Warfare. Measures to Implement Article 36 of the Additional Protocol I of 1977* (n 633).

> The High Contracting Parties at all times, and the Parties to the conflict in time of armed conflict, shall ensure that legal advisers are available, when necessary, to advise military commanders at the appropriate level on the application of the Conventions and this Protocol and on the appropriate instruction to be given to the armed forces on this subject.

The interesting and challenging question is 'what role could legal advisors play before and during military operations performed by an AWS?' In the previous section, it was argued that legal reviews cannot be the result solely of lawyers' contributions, but will result, rather, from a partnership between technicians of the different disciplines required, depending on the complexity of a mission. Thus, how might the obligation enshrined in Article 82 API be met in practice?

It is challenging. First, the ICRC Customary IHL identifies 'legal advisors for armed forces' as a rule of Customary International Law but Rule 141 provides that

> [e]ach State must make legal advisers available, when necessary, to advise military commanders at the appropriate level on the application of International Humanitarian Law.[660]

The customary norm has a less stringent formulation, suggesting that legal advisors are required only when military commanders consider it necessary. The challenge, however, is not so much the formulation but state practice regarding the presence of legal advisors in the armed forces. Looking to the few states with Military Manuals that make explicit reference to the presence of legal advisors, it is possible to identify two groups. The first group makes the presence of legal advisers compulsory, and includes Australia, Canada, Germany, Italy, the Netherlands, the United Kingdom and the United States. The second group is formed by states whose Military Manuals refer to the presence of legal advisers only in their armed forces, and comprises Belgium, Burundi, Israel and the Russian Federation.[661] Thus, from the ICRC database it can be concluded that there may not be as much legal guidance available as Article 82 API might suggest.

In this regard, the UK Ministry of Defence, in the course of the UK public inquiry concerning the death of Baha Mousa, argued that the presence of legal advisers should be made more readily available due to 'the increasingly complex, detailed and extensive nature of IHL', and at the same time stated

660 ICRC, 'Rule 141: Legal Advisers for Armed Forces' (*IHL Database Customary IHL*, July 2018) <https://ihl-databases.icrc.org/customary-ihl/eng/docs/v1_rul_rule141>.

661 ibid.

that 'there are not enough of such legal advisers even to the British armed forces, still less those of more than a hundred other States party to [the 1977] Additional Protocol I and, secondly, in the operational theatre a much broader set of skills are required'.[662]

In light of the observations made here, the presence of legal advisers may be compromised as far as the deployment of AWS is concerned. It has to be said that it is also difficult to identify, in the abstract, what the role of a legal adviser might be. There are two key moments in the process of preparing an AWS at which legal advisors may be asked to intervene. First, there is the moment of designing and programming the AWS' *algorithm for the mission*. A lawyer could be of assistance at the stage of testing for IHL compliance and establishing acceptable levels of risk, for example gauging how far an AWS can assess Proportionality, or establishing the constraints attendant upon ensuring observance of the Principle of Distinction.[663] Then there is the moment at which the system is activated; after this stage human intervention will, as matters stand, no longer be possible. The point is this: while commanders could make use of legal advice when dealing with the unpredictability of the battlefield, AWS will remain 'alone', exclusively dependent on their *algorithms for the mission* – which may in fact increase the risk of unpredictability.

4.5 THE RULES OF PRECAUTION PRECEDING AN ATTACK

No battle plan survives contact with the enemy.

Helmuth von Moltke

In preparing for battle, I have found that plans are useless but planning is indispensable.

President D Eisenhower

The opening quotations illustrate that the circumstances of a battlefield and the way the enemy operates are by their very nature unpredictable. In addition to these elements, the battlefield will also be faced with the unknown challenges that an AWS represents. In Chapter 3, when the selection-making process of an AWS was considered, the OOSA Loop was assumed to be an interactive process. A key stage of this process, namely the algorithm for situation management, relies on a multiple chain of feedback (battlefield ↔

662 ibid.

663 This is the position taken by the Australian Government. cf Australia (n 267) paras 4–6; Letendre (n 66).

AWS). The ability of the system to 'update' itself will, at the same time, need to be complemented by 'assertiveness' towards the mission.[664]

The question of whether the future deployment of AWS will require special precautions or, on the other hand, whether it might make the applicability of the rules of Precaution rather difficult is the aim of this chapter. Strangely enough, the objections that have been put forward by scholars who, hostile towards AWS, describe them as 'inherently unpredictable systems'[665] do not take into account the importance of the rules of Precaution enshrined in Article 57 API while at the same time recognise that AWS rely on computer programs.

The *International Law Association Study Group on the Conduct of Hostilities in the 21st Century* (hereinafter the *Study Group*) has also pointed out that compared with those fundamental principles of IHL, the rules of Distinction and Proportionality, 'the issue of precautions has remained under-researched and more problematically under-emphasized'.[666] Given that 'there are no such things as error-free wars or casualty-free wars' it is vitally important, especially in the case of AWS, that precautions are taken to avoid any foreseeable '*semantic and syntactic errors*'.[667] Marco Longobardo is right to support the argument that it is probably Article 57 API that sets out most clearly the challenges that are likely to be posed for autonomous weapon systems when it comes to a legal review.[668] Thus, it is important, before any consideration, to notice also that state practice and the *ICRC Study* acknowledge that precautionary rules, more specially those codified in Article 57 API, are part of international customary law,

664 cf Chapter 3, Section 3.5.1. Geoffrey S Corn, 'War, Law, and the Often Overlooked Value of Process as a Precautionary Measure' (2015) 42 *Pepperdine Law Review* 419, 433. cf Chapter 3, Section 3.5.1.

665 Crootof, 'War Torts: Accountability for Autonomous Weapons' (n 316) 1348. The author also argues that AWS are 'inherently unlawful' and 'inherently indiscriminate'. cf Crootof, 'The Killer Robots are Here: Legal and Policy Implications' (n 315) 1872, 1885.

666 International Law Association Study Group on the Conduct of Hostilities in the 21st Century, 'The Conduct of Hostilities and International Humanitarian Law: Challenges of 21st Century Warfare' (2017) 93 *International Law Studies* 322, 372.

667 WJ Fenrick, 'Targeting and Proportionality during the NATO Bombing Campaign against Yugoslavia' (2001) 12 *European Journal of International Law* 489.

668 Longobardo argues that 'the principle of precaution, albeit strictly related to the principles of distinction and proportionality, is an autonomous source of obligations under international humanitarian law, which has the peculiar capacity to allow a scrutiny of the preparatory conduct that anticipates actual hostilities, even though such conduct has been traditionally considered outside the scrutiny of international law'. See Marco Longobardo, 'Training and Education of Armed Forces in the Age of High-Tech Hostilities' in Elena Carpanelli and Nicole Lazzerini (eds), *Use and Misuse of New Technologies: Contemporary Challenges in International and European Law* (Springer 2019) 80–81; Jenks and Liivoja (n 432).

applicable in both international and non-international armed conflicts.[669] It will be at this stage that 'those who plan and decide upon an attack' will be responsible for drawing up the necessary operation constraints for autonomous systems.[670]

Article 57, entitled 'Precautions in attack', provides that:

1. In the conduct of military operations, constant care shall be taken to spare the civilian population, civilians and civilian objects.
2. With respect to attacks, the following precautions shall be taken:
   (a) Those who plan or decide upon an attack shall:
      (i) do everything feasible to verify that the objectives to be attacked are neither civilians nor civilian objects and are not subject to special protection but are military objectives within the meaning of Paragraph 2 of Article 52 and that it is not prohibited by the provisions of this Protocol to attack them;
      (ii) take all feasible precautions in the choice of means and methods of attack with a view to avoiding, and in any event to minimising, incidental loss of civilian life, injury to civilians and damage to civilian objects;
      (iii) refrain from deciding to launch any attack which may be expected to cause incidental loss of civilian life, injury to civilians, damage to civilian objects or a combination thereof, which would be excessive in relation to the concrete and direct military advantage anticipated;
   (b) An attack shall be cancelled or suspended if it becomes apparent that the objective is not a military one or is subject to special protection or that the attack may be expected to cause incidental loss of civilian life, injury to civilians, damage to civilian objects or a combination thereof, which would be excessive in relation to the concrete and direct military advantage anticipated;
   (c) Effective advance warning shall be given of attacks which may affect the civilian population, unless circumstances do not permit.
3. When a choice is possible between several military objectives for obtaining a similar military advantage, the objective to be selected shall be that the attack on which may be expected to cause the least danger to civilian lives and to civilian objects.

669 *Prosecutor v Krupreskic* [2000] ICTY Case IT-95-16-T para 524; Henckaerts and Doswald-Beck (n 607); International Law Association Study Group on the Conduct of Hostilities in the 21st Century (n 666) 372–373.

670 Boothby, *Weapons and the Law of Armed Conflict* (n 210) 254.

4. In the conduct of military operations at sea or in the air, each party to the conflict shall, in conformity with its rights and duties under the rules of International Law applicable in armed conflict, take all reasonable precautions to avoid losses of civilian lives and damage to civilian objects.
5. No provision of this article may be construed as authorizing any attacks against the civilian population, civilians or civilian objects.

Paragraph 1 of Article 57 API explains the purpose of any precautionary rule in any military operation. This paragraph not only sums up obligations enshrined in previous rules – to be precise, Articles 48 (*Basic rule*) and 51 (*Protection of the civilian population*), which consecrate the general immunity conferred on the civilian population and prohibit indiscriminate attacks, and Articles 52 (*General protection of civilian objects*) and 54 (*Protection of objects indispensable to the survival of the civilian population*), which restrict attacks to military targets and protect civilian objects – but, more importantly, also reveals the tension inherent in IHL, that is, the balance between the necessity to proceed with military operations and the protection of Principle of Humanity.[671] As Geoffrey Corn points out, 'all the rules developed for this purpose *have a precautionary effect* because, through compliance, the risk to the civilian population is mitigated'.[672]

Adding to the value of these norms of Customary International Law, the ICJ has also defined the Principle of Distinction as 'intransgressible principles of international customary law', and there is also no doubt, according to the ICJ, of the importance of Principle of Proportionality for the legitimacy of planned and executed attacks.[673] Thus, whichever specific feature of battle the deployment of an AWS reveals, the rules of Precaution in attack will acquire a revitalised importance. Once an AWS is activated, no human intervention is allowed along the OOSA Loop but, as has been explained, that does not exclude human control *ex ante*, that is, encoding all the precautionary rules when designing and programming the *algorithm for the mission*, or ex post, that is, incorporating a mechanism for *self-destruction* or providing the commander with the means *to deactivate* the system if supervenient changes in the battlespace so require. The importance of the precautionary rules mentioned earlier shall now be the object of further attention.

671 International Committee of the Red Cross, *Commentary on the Additional Protocols of 8 June 1977 to the Geneva Conventions of 12 August 1949* (n 347) para 2189; Corn, 'War, Law, and the Often Overlooked Value of Process as a Precautionary Measure' (n 664) 426.

672 Corn, 'War, Law, and the Often Overlooked Value of Process as a Precautionary Measure' (n 664) 426 (our emphasis).

673 ICJ, *Legality of the Threat or Use of Nuclear Weapons, Advisory Opinion*, paras 42–43, 79.

4.5.1 *Precaution ex ante and ex post the Decision to Attack*

The final redaction of Article 57 API has been the subject of long discussions but it is now a common understanding that this disposition creates obligations only for military commanders.[674] It follows that IHL rules demand that (1) military commanders do *everything feasible* to *verify* all information and ensure that AWS only attack legal targets; (2) AWS be regarded as the weapon system that will cause least civilian harm; (3) the military commander is able to cancel or suspend an attack if information from the battlefield so requires; and (4) the commander gives advance warning of any attack which may cause civilian harm, unless circumstances do not permit.[675]

One strand of the discussion concerns what should be understood by the obligation upon the commander to 'do everything feasible' to prevent violations of IHL. Taking our understanding from the *Study Group*, that 'feasibility is to be determined from an *ex ante* perspective, i.e., prior to (*and if possible during*) the attack and on the basis of the information available at the time; not with hindsight', it is clear that precautionary rules can be applied in the case of AWS.[676] The precautionary rules ex ante will be analysed in the following sections. For now, it is important to focus on the proposition that precautionary measures might be taken *during* the attack.

In the course of Chapter 2, 'weapon system' was defined as 'a system that includes the munition(s) (weapons) as well as the platform from where munitions can be released' and it has, up until today, been possible to distinguish physically between the two components (platform/munition), although for legal purposes they are a single 'weapon system'.[677] Taking just for now the duality of a 'weapon system', the part that should be considered autonomous is the platform as the Russian Federation's definition of AWS stated;[678] once the

674 Check for this purpose Switzerland, Declaration made upon signature and reservation made upon ratification of Additional Protocol I; Austria, Statement at the Diplomatic Conference leading to the adoption of the Additional Protocols; United Kingdom, Reservations and declarations made upon ratification of Additional Protocol I. cf Roberts and Guelff (n 263) 500, 509–510.

675 Ian Henderson, *The Contemporary Law of Targeting: Military Objectives, Proportionality and Precautions in Attack under Additional Protocol I* (Martinus Nijhoff 2009) 159–160; Tim McFarland, 'Autonomous Weapons and Human Control' (*ICRC Law and Policy*, 18 July 2018) <http://blogs.icrc.org/law-and-policy/2018/07/18/autonomous-weapons-and-human-control/?utm_source=ICRC+Law+%26+Policy+Forum+Contacts&utm_campaign=42ad0b02fc-EMAIL_CAMPAIGN_2018_07_18_11_11&utm_medium=email&utm_term=0_8eeeebc66b-42ad0b02fc-79024717&mc_cid=42ad0b02fc&mc_eid=b8997e9f4e>.

676 International Law Association Study Group on the Conduct of Hostilities in the 21st Century (n 666) 375.

677 Chapter 2, Section 2.5.

678 Chapter 2, Section 2.4.

munition is released, there is no reason to distinguish AWS from any other weapon. In light of this it can be difficult to understand what, exactly, precautions taken '*during the attack*' might be.

Lt Colonel Alexander Bolt examines this question, pointing out that if 'the time lag between the release of the weapon and when it will cause its effects is acceptable', human intervention might be possible but that, if that time is considered 'unacceptable', no intervention could take place.[679] The understanding of the term '(un)acceptable time lag' will depend on the commander's judgement, and for that only he/she can be responsible. However, as clear as Bolt's argument might seem, it is actually quite difficult to apply. The complexity of AWS, whether it results from their operating in swarm mode or from the sheer number and sophistication of the inbuilt algorithms, begs the question of whether any human operator could intervene to forestall an outcome before the munition is released.

Theoretically, a commander can only act ex post and deactivate the system. Nonetheless, this would be possible only if the mission delegated to the system were no longer required and the commander had the time to deactivate the system within an acceptable time cancelling or suspending an attack (Article 57(2)(b) API). Whether that possibility can even be considered in the fog of the battlefield remains to be seen. Otherwise, deactivation is only possible, in reality, once the system has caused a violation of IHL, and the commander opts to deactivate or suspend the AWS in order to comply with the 'precautions against the effect of attacks' (Article 58(c) API). Aside from those two possibilities, a 'self-destruction mechanism' was mentioned. For this case the Convention for Cluster Munitions (hereinafter CCM) can be of great help.

Article 2 (9) CCM provides that a 'self-destruction mechanism means an incorporated automatically-functioning mechanism which is in addition to the initiating mechanism of the munition and which secures the destruction of the munition into which it is incorporated'.[680] A self-destruct mechanism in the case of AWS would be a secondary mechanism, not to be activated when a 'submission failed to detonate on impact', but to be designed as part of the *algorithm for the mission* when technically possible.[681] This mechanism would prevent the munition from being released or detonating whenever the system detected that it could not adapt owing to new circumstances facing it.

679 Bolt (n 643) 147–150.

680 ICRC, 'Convention on Cluster Munitions' (8 January 2010) <www.icrc.org/en/doc/assets/files/other/icrc_002_0961.pdf>.

681 Gro Nystuen and Stuart Casey-Maslen (eds), *The Convention on Cluster Munitions: A Commentary* (Oxford University Press 2010) 231–232.

A question that has to be asked is 'what level of trust can be placed in such a mechanism?' That is, if the secondary system fails to act, would it be considered a malfunction or an error of the system?

These questions are not overlooked by roboticists such as R. Arkin, who has envisaged the *Ethical Governor*. When an AWS is deployed, and the system comes to a course of action which would involve lethal force, a confirmation would be required from the Ethical Governor.[682] This mechanism would be tasked with performing an evaluation of the 'ethical appropriateness of any lethal response that has been produced by the robot architecture prior to its being enacted'.[683]

Aside from the (arguably problematic) nature of the author's terminology, this measure is introduced in order to allow another component of the system to give a 'second opinion' before any lethal behavioural response is authorised. If the Ethical Governor were called into action, it would send a notification to the system in order to enable a re-planning of the pre-given mission.[684] Such a proposition could well be inspired by the legal advisor's role, a second opinion on the legality of or opportunity for an attack. However, what is really being described is a system within a system: the 'first layer' operational system, plus a system with the capability *to confirm or override the first course of action chosen by the 'first layer' system*. Arkin's suggestion does not include a self-destruction mechanism but a secondary system able to ponder values already pondered by the first system. A technical question for curious lawyers is whether the Ethical Governor could actually operate efficiently in situations involving time-sensitive targets. Another important question with legal implications arises from Arkin's admission that there is the possibility of a system failing. Thus, what guarantee is there that the 'system within a system' would perform lawfully? If it does not, should it be considered a malfunction or an error of the system?

In light of all these considerations, it is possible to conclude that whereas AWS could potentially introduce numerous advantages to the battlefield, they would be dependent on a set of conditions:

1. Commanders would be able to encode all the constraints that the mission requires ex ante. For this purpose, commanders should have

682 Arkin, *Governing Lethal Behavior in Autonomous Robots* (n 34) 135.

683 ibid 127–128. It needs to be said that in later works, R Arkin extends the action of the Ethical Governor to no lethal actions when the author argues that 'this component is a transformer/suppressor of system-generated lethal action to ensure that it constitutes an ethically permissible action, *either nonlethal or obligated ethical lethal force*'. cf Arkin, Ulam and Duncan (n 502).

684 Arkin, *Governing Lethal Behavior in Autonomous Robots* (n 34) 65–66.

available all the multidisciplinary technical help that the mission demands, legal advisers among them.

2. Once the system is activated, and in the case of new circumstances emerging on the battlefield, two responses are possible. First, the system is able to adapt the pre-established constraints and proceed with the pre-given mission. Second, the system is not able to adapt and has an inbuilt 'self-destruction mechanism', which can operate as a precautionary measure.
3. Precautions during the attack are only possible if munitions were not released, allowing the commander to cancel or suspend the attack. In the event that new circumstances on the battlefield make the mission redundant or introduce the risk of violating IHL, commanders should be able to deactivate the system in 'acceptable time' (Article 57(2)(b) API).

4.5.2 *Precautions and the Principle of Distinction*

Among the primary tenets underlying IHL is the Principle of Distinction, classified by the ICJ as 'cardinal' and 'imperative'.[685] The principle is enshrined in Article 48 API:

> In order to ensure respect for and protection of the civilian population and civilian objects, the Parties to the conflict shall at all times distinguish between the civilian population and combatants and civilian objects and military objectives and accordingly shall direct their operations only against military objectives.

The importance of the Principle of Distinction is also enshrined in the first precautionary rule codified in Article 57, stating that 'commanders shall do everything feasible to verify that the objectives to be attacked are [. . .] military objectives' (Article 57(2)(a)(i) API).[686]

Before addressing the relevant specificities of the rules of Distinction, some considerations should be undertaken. First, it is not the intention of this section to cover all the complexity that the rules of Distinction entail but

685 *ICJ, Advisory Opinion on the Legality of the Threat and Use of Nuclear Weapons, Judgment* (n 265) 78.

686 The ICRC Commentary gives examples of categories subject to special protection, cultural objects and places of worship (Article 53API); works and installations containing dangerous forces such as nuclear generating stations (Article 56 API); medical units (Article 12 API) and Protection of civilian medical and religious personnel (Article 13 API). cf International Committee of the Red Cross, *Commentary on the Additional Protocols of 8 June 1977 to the Geneva Conventions of 12 August 1949* (n 347) para 2194.

only those requirements with which AWS would have to comply. Second, as has been explained in the course of this work, questions about AWS are above all engineering questions. A lawyer's task is simply to organise and make visible the long-established safeguards enshrined in IHL. Thus, to the scholars and NGOs who claim that there is an 'inherent inability of autonomous and even automated weapon systems to distinguish', the answer should be that such types of assertions would be accurate if the object analysis is the capability of current military technology.[687] A lawyer can hardly be expected to anticipate what sort of warfare future technology will be capable of accomplishing.[688]

Considering the considerations made, in order for a targeting process to comply with the Principle of Distinction, it must be planned and decided upon in accordance with the *information available* at the moment of planning. The *ICRC Commentary* underlines the importance of checking the precision and accuracy of the information available, suggesting that in situations of doubt – 'even if there is only slight doubt' – commanders should call for additional information. The *Commentary* goes on to add that 'the evaluation of the information obtained must include a serious check of its accuracy'.[689] This was questioned by Italy, Spain and the United Kingdom, who stated that, speaking realistically, a military commander can only make a decision based on 'all sources which are *reasonably* available to them at the relevant time'.[690] The same understanding is shared by the *Study Group*.[691] In short, a 'good-faith assessment' will be all that is required from a commander when deciding on the deployment of an AWS.[692] The assessment will be based, as well, on the assumption that the AWS will be able to comply with the *distinction*. Whether the commander will encode pre-determined criteria for the identification and selection of military targets (the 'who?' or 'what?' of the targeting process) or will delegate that task to the system shall be a constitutive part of the assessment carried out by the commander.

Distinction encompasses two primary rules: Article 51 API (*General Protection of the Civilian Population*) and Article 52 API (*General Protection*

687 Bradan T Thomas, 'Autonomous Weapons Systems: The Anatomy and the Legality of Lethality' (2015) 37(1) *Houston Journal of International Law* 235, 265.

688 McFarland, *Autonomous Weapon Systems and the Law of Armed Conflict: Compatibility with International Humanitarian Law* (n 46) 28.

689 International Committee of the Red Cross, *Commentary on the Additional Protocols of 8 June 1977 to the Geneva Conventions of 12 August 1949* (n 347) para 2195.

690 Roberts and Guelff (n 263) UK interpretative declaration, 510.

691 International Law Association Study Group on the Conduct of Hostilities in the 21st Century (n 666) footnote 526.

692 Henderson (n 675) 165.

of Civilian Objects). Determining who a civilian is, in modern conflicts, has become a tremendous challenge due to the numerous 'grey areas' in which civilians can be involved. In order to suggest a possible criterion, we will follow those presented by the *ICRC Interpretative Guidance on the Notion of Direct Participation in Hostilities under International Humanitarian Law* (2009) (hereinafter, *Interpretative Guidance*).[693]

For the identification of individuals, the Principle of Distinction requires that 'at all times' combatants must be distinguished from civilians since 'the civilian population as such, as well as individual civilians, shall not be an object of attack' (Article 51 (2) API). Therefore, combatants who 'have the right to participate directly in hostilities' (Article 43 (1)(2) API) are 'obliged to distinguish themselves from the civilian population while they are engaged in an attack or in a military operation preparatory to an attack' (Article 44 (3) API). Notwithstanding this contrast between *combatant and civilian, armed forces and civilian population*, there is no specific definition of 'armed forces'. Instead, a set of requirements is laid out (Article 4 (1)(2)(3)(6) GCIII; Article 43 API). Civilians, in situations of both international and non-international armed conflict, are defined negatively (Article 50 API) and are not expected to participate directly in the hostilities, except in the very specific situation of *levée en masse* (Article 50 API; Article 4 (A) (6) Geneva Convention III).[694]

In the situation of *international armed conflict*, civilians are all those people who are neither members of the armed forces nor party to the conflict nor participants in a *levée en masse*. In the situation of *a non-international armed conflict*, civilians are those individuals who are not members of state's armed forces, or of organised armed groups, or party to the conflict. They are, therefore, entitled to protection against direct attack unless and for such time as they *take a direct part in hostilities* (hereinafter DPH) Article 1 (1) APII; Article 13 APII.[695] According to the Interpretative Guidance, three criteria must be met

693 For further development of the ICRC perspective, Nils Melzer, *Targeted Killing in International Law* (Oxford University Press 2008) 300–362. Presenting a strong critique of the Interpretative Guidance cf Michael N Schmitt, 'The Interpretive Guidance on the Notion of Direct Participation in Hostilities: A Critical Analysis' (2010) 1 *Harvard Law School National Security Journal*.

694 Article 4(A)(6) GC III provides that 'inhabitants of a non-occupied territory, who on the approach of the enemy spontaneously take up arms to resist the invading forces, without having had time to form themselves into regular armed units, provided they carry arms openly and respect the law and customs of war' should be considered prisoners of war. Melzer, *Interpretative Guidance on the Notion of Direct Participation in Hostilities* (n 582) 20, 36.

695 Solis (n 590) 202–216.

for a civilian to be regarded as participating in the hostilities. First, there is *threshold of harm*; second, a *direct causal link* between the act and the harm likely to result, and third, the act must be specifically designed to directly cause the required threshold of harm *in support of a party to the conflict and to the detriment of another* (belligerent nexus).[696] An element that must be taken into consideration is that a civilian is deemed to be DPH if he/she participates sporadically in the hostilities, and as a result loses his/her protection for the duration of his/her participation in the hostilities.

Aside from the traditional category of 'armed forces', it is possible to find other organised armed groups on the battlefield that may or may not satisfy the criterion of *Distinction* as established by IHL; these groups are to be regarded as party to the armed conflict.[697] In *non-international armed conflict*, organised armed groups constitute the armed forces of a non-state party to the conflict, and consist only of civilians whose *continuous function* it is to take a direct part in hostilities ('continuous combat function', hereinafter CCF).[698] As the *Interpretative Guidance* explains, to be categorised as CCF 'requires lasting integration into an organized armed group acting as the armed forces of a non-State party to the conflict'.[699]

As the ICTY took the opportunity of observing in the *Tadić Case*, whenever civilians decide upon 'direct participation in the hostilities', it gives place to '*a grey area between combatants and non-combatants and that notion may not be sufficiently defined to determine in all cases who are those qualified as civilians*'.[700] The *Interpretative Guidance*, for example, considers that an individual who 'has repeatedly directly participated in hostilities in support of an organized armed group in circumstances indicating that such conduct constitutes a continuous combat function rather than a spontaneous, sporadic, or temporary role assumed for the duration of a particular operation' should be considered an individual in CCF. The identification of a person who is *hors de combat*

696 Melzer, *Interpretative Guidance on the Notion of Direct Participation in Hostilities* (n 582) 46.

697 The state party to a conflict, to whom organised armed groups belong to, will be responsible for the acts committed by such groups under the International Law of State Responsibility. More difficult is to determine the level of control (Overall control? Effective Control?) to hold a state responsible under International Law, which will always depend on a case by case analysis. James Crawford, *The International Law Commission's Articles on State Responsibility: Introduction, Text and Commentaries* (Cambridge University Press 2003) 110–112; Melzer, *Interpretative Guidance on the Notion of Direct Participation in Hostilities* (n 582) 23.

698 Melzer, *Interpretative Guidance on the Notion of Direct Participation in Hostilities* (n 582) 36.

699 ibid 34.

700 *Prosecutor v Tadić, Opinion and Judgement* [1997] ICTY IT-94-1-T para 637.

and the distinction between voluntary and non-voluntary 'human shields' constitute further grey areas.[701] These are all situations that require not only the ability to detect but also to make sense of situations, gauging accurately the mental states of the individuals or groups observed in order to proceed to a targeting decision.[702]

The other aspect of the Principle of Distinction, that is distinguishing between civilian objects and military objectives, is also not easy to apply in practice. Articles 23(g) and 25 HR establish prohibitions against attacks on an enemy's property and undefended towns, villages, dwellings and buildings; Article 52 (1) API states that 'civilian objects shall not be the object of attack or reprisals' opting to define negatively 'civilian objects are all objects which are not military objects as defined in Paragraph 2'. Thus, 'attacks shall be limited to military objectives' (Article 52 (2) API).[703] In addition to these requirements, military targets must be individualised and defined by their material and physical structure.[704]

In terms of the law of targeting the information available about the use or potential use of certain objects by attackers is vitally important, more so than the intrinsic nature of the object. In order to provide some clarity about military targets, Article 52(2) API, reflecting Customary International Law, provides a definition of military objectives which sets out two criteria. First, the object must contribute *effectively* (and not simply indirectly or potentially) to *the military action of the enemy*. Second, its destruction, capture or neutralisation must give a '*definite military advantage*'.[705]

Considering the aforementioned discussion, three things should be noted. First, as Ian Henderson points out, if an object is subjectively evaluated as making an effective military contribution to the defending party, the criteria of *nature, location, purpose* or *use*, as defined by API, becomes redundant and the evaluation becomes an automatic process which does not need to be explained.[706] Second, application of the criteria of *nature, location, purpose*

701 Melzer, *Interpretative Guidance on the Notion of Direct Participation in Hostilities* (n 582) 56–58. For further examples, cf Marcello Guarini and Paul Bello, 'Robotic Warfare: Some Challenges in Moving from Noncivilian to Civilian Theatres' in Patrick Lin, Keith Abney and George A Bekey (eds), *Robot Ethics: The Ethical and Social Implications of Robotics* (MIT Press 2012) 130.

702 Thomas (n 687) 263; Guarini and Bello (n 701) 134.

703 Melzer, *Interpretative Guidance on the Notion of Direct Participation in Hostilities* (n 582) 348; Marco Sassoli, 'Legitimate Targets of Attacks under International Humanitarian Law' (Harvard Program on Policy and Conflict Research 2003) 1.

704 International Law Association Study Group on the Conduct of Hostilities in the 21st Century (n 666) 333–334.

705 ibid 328, 344–345.

706 Henderson (n 675) 53–54.

or *use* is crucial when the value of the military object changes due to mutable circumstances on the battlefield, creating situations of doubt. Indeed, as the *Study Group* points out, Article 52(2) API introduces a temporal dimension. An object that is normally used for civilian purposes may turn into a military objective when used temporarily for military purposes and vice versa.[707] For example, a civilian car that is used by soldiers, or abandoned military facilities that are occupied by civilians escaping the hardships of war. Then there are objects of *dual use*, that is, objects that simultaneously serve military and civilian purposes. For example, a factory that produces civilian cars and military vehicles; a building in which some floors are occupied by civilians and others are for military purposes.[708] The examples are endless and can create very complex decision-making processes, especially when the Principle of Proportionality is involved; this will be explained in Section 4.4.4.

Finally, the interpretation of the expression 'definite military advantage' demands attention. The problem emerges mainly when compared with the expression 'concrete and direct military advantage' Article 57(2)(a)(iii) API, as used in the assessment of proportionality. The use of the word 'definitive' helps to understand that the anticipated military advantage must not be hypothetical and speculative but rather concrete and perceptible.[709] However, the second expression adds another element in relation to the Principle of Proportionality. While in selecting a target it is sufficient that the object presents a definite military advantage, in the case of proportionality assessment, military advantage would require a higher level of certainty.

4.5.3 *The Principle of Distinction and the Future of AWS*

From the previous section it can be concluded that the Principle of Distinction creates an 'umbrella' over protected people and objects. At the operational level, the fog of the battlefield can create real obstacles to correctly identify *who is who* and *what is what*. Considering the process of 'decivilianisation of civilians' innate to the hybrid character of modern conflicts, distinction is, first and foremost, difficult even for humans.[710] The questions raised by the Principle of Distinction, in the course of military operations, are not

[707] International Law Association Study Group on the Conduct of Hostilities in the 21st Century (n 666).

[708] ibid; Henderson (n 675) 58–59.

[709] Henderson (n 675) 63.

[710] Chengeta, 'Measuring Autonomous Weapon Systems against International Humanitarian Law Rules' (n 616) 84. For the complexity of situations of distinction, cf Scharre, *Army of None: Autonomous Weapons and the Future of War* (n 425) 254–255.

limited, however, to the distinction between civilians/combatants or civilian objects/military targets. Article 43(2) API, for example, excludes from the category of combatants 'medical personnel and chaplains covered by Article 33 of the Third Geneva Convention'.[711]

IHL has almost exclusively focused on the protection of civilians, combatants and other human beings but other categories include the protection of the environment and, progressively, the protection of animals. The protection of the environment is mentioned in Articles 35(3) and 55 API, and animals can be used as instruments of war but can also be victims. Thus, animals could well require protection, not only because the norms protecting environmental values include the protection of wildlife but also because animals can be categorised as 'civilian objects' since the survival of populations can depend on their protection (Article 52 API). However, to introduce another element of complexity, animals could be legitimately targeted if their 'nature, location, purpose or use make an effective contribution to military action and whose total or partial destruction, capture or neutralization, in the circumstances ruling at the time, offers a definite military advantage'.[712] Evidently, considering animals to be a protected category (a result of the increasing awareness of environmental challenges), they ought to be distinguished and not targeted, and to be taken into account in the proportionality assessment.

The aforementioned facts should not be taken as insurmountable obstacles but as a challenge for roboticists. An example can be given. According to the *Galić Case*, 'the clothing, activity, age, or sex of a person are among the factors which may be considered in deciding whether he or she is a civilian', and that 'a person shall be considered to be a civilian for as long as there is a doubt as to his or her real status'.[713]

Roboticists, such as Noel Sharkey, argue that despite decades of research, current 'automatic target recognition methods' only work in uncluttered environments featuring military objects such as tanks in the desert and ships at sea.[714]

711 Solis (n 590) 188.

712 Jérôme Hemptinne, 'The Protection of Animals during Warfare' (2017) 111 *American Journal of International Law (Unbound)* 272–273; Marco Roscini, 'Animals and the Law of Armed Conflict' (2017) 47 *Israel Yearbook on Human Rights* 35, 45–48.

713 *Galić Case* [2003] ICTY (Trial Judgement) IT-98-29-T 48, 50; Ian Henderson and Bryan Cavanagh, 'Unmanned Aerial Vehicles: Do They Pose Legal Challenges?' in Hitoshi Nasu and Robert McLaughlin (eds), *New Technologies and the Law of Armed Conflict* (Springer 2014) 205.

714 Noel Sharkey, 'Autonomous Weapons and Human Supervisory Control' (*ICRC*, 26 March 2014) 29 <www.icrc.org/eng/resources/documents/reprt/05-13-autonomous-weapons-report.htmo>. For further development of technological progress regarding computer visual recognition and speech recognition, see Ted W Schroeder, *Lethal Autonomous Weapon*

Authors, such as Scharre, argue that 'new machine learning processes are extremely vulnerable to "fooling image attacks"'.[715] This is the present stage of technology; however, what must be noted is that warfare technology, as it stands today, is not able to comply with certain levels of Distinction and that, therefore, deciding in favour of its employment would be a *human* unlawful decision.

The current limitations of war technology should not necessarily lend credence to the campaign for a pre-emptive ban on AWS. It should, rather, encourage legitimate expectation: to wait and see how technology will rise to the challenge of complying with IHL. Following this line of thought David Gunning's speculations sound persuasive when he states that 'the effectiveness of these systems is limited by the machine's current inability to explain their decisions and actions to human users'. A future that includes *Explainable AI (XAI)* depends on the development of machine learning to the point at which it can provide explanatory dialogues with the end user.[716] Thus, it can be said that warfare technology does not develop with its back turned to the long- and well-established values of International Law but more via dialogue between legal requirements and new technological achievements.

Another important question is how to reply to arguments such as those invoked by Sparrow and Sharkey, respectively, that the capability to recognise the behaviour of individuals in DPH or *hors de combat* would have the most serious ethical consequences, because it would require the AWS to understand our actions – *what they mean* – the sort of understanding that is inherent to ethical and reasoning behaviour. Alternatively, it would require that the available technology (cameras, infrareds, sonar, lasers, etc.) was sufficiently sophisticated to make a quantitative analysis accurate enough to identify certain military targets. However, according to those authors, such technology cannot operate *out-of-the-loop* and, in case of doubt, a human operator has always to intervene in the system's selection-making process.[717]

Systems in Future Conflicts (Ted W Schroeder 2017) 16–20; Liivoja, Leins and McCormack (n 22) 615.

715 Scharre, *Army of None: Autonomous Weapons and the Future of War* (n 425) 253.

716 David Gunning, 'Explainable Artificial Intelligence (XAI)' (*DARPA – Defense Advanced Research Projects Agency*) <www.darpa.mil/program/explainable-artificial-intelligence>; Deeks, Lubell and Murray (n 25) 20. A similar position was taken at the CCW GGE' meetings when the Chair summarised that 'a related characteristic of importance is *explainability*, whether a system allows an operator to understand why it performs in a particular way'. cf Gjorgjinski (n 158) s H, para V. cf Noll (n 105) 83.

717 Robert Sparrow, 'Twenty Seconds to Comply: Autonomous Weapon Systems and the Recognition of Surrender' (2015) 91 *International Law Studies* 699, 702–703, 705–709; Robert Sparrow, 'Robots and Respect: Assessing the Case against Autonomous Weapon Systems' (2016) 30 *Ethics and International Affairs* 93, 101; Noel Sharkey, 'Saying "NO!" to Lethal Autonomous Targeting' (2010) 9 *Journal of Military Ethics* 369; Wagner, 'The

The importance and relevance of these situations cannot be ignored, but it has also to be said that some of these problems are not exclusive to AWS but apply to weaponry in general. It is also true that comparisons with human soldiers' capabilities can be misleading since AI uses very different methods. The importance of the *algorithm for the mission* should always be kept in mind, not only because commanders can encode criteria that will enable the machine to discriminate on the battlefield between *who is who* (e.g. a soldier *hors de combat*) and *what is what*, but also because the operative algorithms will be limited by the technology available.[718]

Be that as it may, the current reality is, according to DARPA, that there are three factors that impede the deployment of AWS. First, because there is still a substantial requirement for a human operator. Second, for systems engineering to achieve high levels of autonomy in 'uncertain, unstructured and dynamic environments' is a difficult challenge. Third, the directives of the US Department of Defence require 'predictable behavior and strong assurance', which cannot be ensured by 'inherently unpredictable' machine learning techniques, especially as the 'mathematical framework to provide guarantees on correctness' is lacking.[719] These present deficiencies, however, should not exclude AWS from being deployed in very special circumstances.

As the vast majority of authors argue, for the time being it might be impossible to encode the rules of Distinction to mathematical formulas, or to build technology able to meet all the demands of a situation that requires discrimination between civilian and military objects.[720] However, authors such as Waxman, Anderson, Henderson, Kean and Liddy and Boothby consider that it is possible to deploy AWS when the target is clearly an item of military equipment, or where it is reasonable to suppose that no civilians are

Dehumanization of International Humanitarian Law: Legal, Ethical, and Political Implications of Autonomous Weapon Systems' (n 64) 1392.

718 As the *HPCR Commentary* explains, an intention to surrender has to be clearly signalled in good faith to the enemy, for instance by displaying a white flag or discarding one's weapons. However, the *HPCR Commentary* adds an important point. The group of experts responsible for the *Commentary* 'insisted that an attack need not be aborted merely because someone on the ground is raising his hand or waving a white flag [...] however if a large number of units surrenders collectively and ground forces can be summoned to take care of the surrendering enemies, they cannot be attacked'. HPCR (n 338) 103.

719 Sandeep Neema, 'Assured Autonomy' (*DARPA – Defense Advanced Research Projects Agency*) <www.darpa.mil/program/assured-autonomy>.

720 Robert Sparrow considers that the Principle of Distinction can never be reduced to mathematical formulas. Sparrow, 'Killer Robots' (n 55) 67; Sparrow, 'Robots and Respect: Assessing the Case against Autonomous Weapon Systems' (n 717) s 2.1.1.2.

present.[721] For example, systems that operate on a 'machine versus machine' basis, or perform underwater attacks, would raise fewer concerns.[722]

More interesting is the position taken by Markus Wagner, who, although the author shares the aforementioned understanding, adds a 'safe clause': military targets 'have to be determined in an abstract and a priori fashion' and, in situations of doubt, AWS 'will have to be accordingly programmed to abort missions in such instances'.[723] Taking into account that the author accepts the definition of AWS given by the *DoD 3000.09* and HRW, it is important to note that the solution pointed out by Wagner excludes from AWS the capability to identify targets.[724] This seems to be at odds with the development of machine learning and to more complex types of missions. However, the argument is pertinent since it seems to reinforce the idea that certain types of missions can only be contemplated when the system is encoded with self-destructing mechanisms.

In light of the aforementioned discussion, it is fair to conclude that IHL demands, in terms of distinction, a level of certainty that AWS do not seem capable of in the near future. Thus, military commanders can only deploy AWS when there is a high level of certainty regarding the nature and status of individuals and objects on the battlefield or when the *algorithm for the mission* contemplates the possibility of activating mechanisms of self-destruction.

4.5.4 *The Requirements of the Principle of Proportionality*

The term 'proportionality' does not find explicit mention in Additional Protocol I, but the Principle of Proportionality is reflected in a number of provisions (Articles 51 (5)(b) and 57(2)(a)(iii) API). Nonetheless, it is a norm of Customary International Law applicable in both international and non-international armed conflicts.[725]

721 Anderson and Waxman, 'Law and Ethics for Autonomous Weapon Systems: Why a Ban Won't Work and How the Laws of War Can' (n 324) 11; Henderson, Keane and Liddy (n 19) 7; William Boothby, 'Some Legal Challenges Posed by Remote Attack' (2012) 94 *International Review of the Red Cross* 579, 585; Benjamin Kastan, 'Autonomous Weapons Systems: A Coming Legal "Singularity"?' (2014) 2013 *Journal of Law, Technology & Policy* 45, 60–61.

722 Anderson and Waxman, 'Law and Ethics for Autonomous Weapon Systems: Why a Ban Won't Work and How the Laws of War Can' (n 324) 6.

723 Wagner, 'The Dehumanization of International Humanitarian Law: Legal, Ethical, and Political Implications of Autonomous Weapon Systems' (n 64) 1391.

724 ibid 1383, footnotes 47–48.

725 *Kupreškić et al* (n 271) para 524; Henckaerts (n 607) Rules 14, 46. Markus Wagner that the rule of proportionality goes back to St Thomas Aquinas. cf Wagner, 'The Dehumanization of International Humanitarian Law: Legal, Ethical, and Political Implications of Autonomous Weapon Systems' (n 64) 1394.

Article 51 (5)(b) and sub-paragraph (a)(iii) of Article 57 API lay down the rule of Proportionality that prohibits attacks which 'may be expected to cause incidental loss of civilian life, injury to civilians, damage to civilian objects, or a combination thereof which is likely to be *excessive* to the concrete and direct military advantage anticipated'. As Adil Ahmad Haque points out, the Principle of Proportionality '*seems* to call for a comparison between two incommensurable values – civilian losses and military advantage – irreducible to any more basic value'.[726] Proportionality translates a *dynamic relationship* between 'collateral damage' and the 'concrete and direct military advantage anticipated'. Thus, although individuals and objects may well change status during the hostilities, the term 'anticipated' clarifies that 'proportionality is assessed ex ante, not ex post', according to the information that is available at the time of deciding upon an attack.[727] Following this line of argument, the *ICTY Final Report to the Prosecutor by the Committee Established to Review the NATO Bombing Campaign Against the Federal Republic of Yugoslavia* (hereinafter *NATO Bombing Final Report*) states that 'the main problem with the Principle of Proportionality is not whether or not it exists but what it means and how it is to be applied [...] one cannot easily assess the value of innocent human lives as opposed to capturing a particular military objective'.[728]

Considering the aforementioned, it is important to note that an attack, in order to be considered proportionate, does not exclude the presence of 'collateral damage'.[729] What IHL does not accept is that the damage caused to protect categories of persons or objects is *excessive* in relation to the 'concrete and direct military advantage anticipated' by commanders.

The problems of the definition and application of the Principle of Proportionality have been discussed by almost every IHL lawyer because, as

726 Adil Ahmad Haque, 'A Theory of Jus in Bello Proportionality' in Jens David Ohlin, Larry May and Claire Finkelstein (eds), *Weighing Lives in War* (Oxford University Press 2017) 192 (our emphasis).

727 Gregory S McNeal, 'Targeted Killing and Accountability' (2014) 102 *The Georgetown Law Journal* 681, 750 ; Schmitt and Widmar (n 582) 405.

728 'ICTY Final Report to the Prosecutor by the Committee Established to Review the NATO Bombing Campaign against the Federal Republic of Yugoslavia' (2000) para 48 <www.icty.org/en/press/final-report-prosecutor-committee-established-review-nato-bombing-campaign-against-federal>.

729 The harm to civilians is technically labelled 'incidental injury', while that to civilian objects is 'collateral damage'. As common use fails to distinguish the two, collateral damage here refers to both types of damage. It can be defined as 'unintentional or incidental injury or damage to persons and objects that would not be lawful military targets in the circumstances ruling at the time'. cf Chairman of the Joint Chiefs of Staff Instruction, 'No-Strike and the Collateral Damage Estimation Methodology' (13 February 2009) D-2 <www.aclu.org/sites/default/files/field_document/drone_dod_3160_01.pdf>.

Francoise Hampson explains, 'proportionality could be like an elephant – difficult to define but easy to recognise'.[730] In spite of all the difficulties its application might present, proportionality is a fundamental principle of IHL and, therefore, must be taken into account. As argued by the Trial Chamber in the *Kupreškić Case*, 'even in a situation of full-armed conflict, certain fundamental norms still serve to unambiguously outlaw such conduct, such as the rules pertaining to proportionality'.[731]

As has already been explained, the rules of Precaution requires that those who plan or launch an attack take all feasible precautions to *verify* the nature of the targets and to *choose* means and methods to avoid, or in any event to minimise, 'incidental loss of civilian life, injury to civilians and damage to civilian objects' (Article 57 (2)(a)(ii) API). These requirements lead to the conclusion that commanders are legally and 'morally responsible for activating an AWS only if their knowledge licenses the judgement that the risk of running counter to IHL requirements is acceptably low'.[732] Indeed, the Trial Chamber in the *Galić Case* specified that 'in determining whether an attack was proportionate it is necessary to examine whether a reasonably well-informed person in the circumstances of the actual perpetrator, making use of the information available to him or her, could have expected excessive causalities to result from the attack'.[733] However, sometimes it can be almost impossible to discover how much information the commander had at the time of the attack. The *Blaškić Case* is a perfect example: the Appeals Chamber decided that it was impossible to determine the nature of the attacks on 16 April 1993, since the testimonies revealed completely different numbers of civilians present at the time of the attack.[734]

The observations made about the mandatory rules of Distinction are also applicable to Proportionality. If AWS are not capable of complying with the Principle of Proportionality, they should be considered unlawful and not be deployed. Before pronouncing such a fate, however, it is vital to understand

730 Francoise Hampson, 'The Principle of Proportionality in the Law of Armed Conflict' in Sarah Perrigo and Jim Whitman (eds), *The Geneva Conventions under Assault* (PlutoPress 2010) 54; Chengeta, 'Measuring Autonomous Weapon Systems against International Humanitarian Law Rules' (n 616) 112; Shara Darcy, *Judges, Law and War: The Judicial Development of International Humanitarian Law* (Cambridge University Press 2014) 150–151.

731 *Kupreškić et al* (n 271) para 513.

732 Tamburrini (n 324) 131.

733 *Galić Case* (n 713) para 58. Another example of the fundamental value of the information available at the moment of the attack, 'ICTY Final Report to the Prosecutor by the Committee Established to Review the NATO Bombing Campaign against the Federal Republic of Yugoslavia' (n 728) para 24.

734 *Prosecutor v Tihomir Blaškić* [2004] Appeals Chamber IT-95-14-A para 441.

what Proportionality entails. Looking at the API provisions that establish the rules of Proportionality, it is important to set out (a) the value to be assigned to 'concrete and direct military advantage', (b) the method to be used to ascertain whether 'collateral damage' is *excessive* in relation to that value and, (c) whether mathematical methodologies such as the Collateral Damage Estimate Methodology (hereinafter CDEM) can be regarded as accurate instruments for assessing Proportionality.

Regarding the terms 'concrete and direct', the *Study Group* states that the 'qualifiers "concrete and direct" fulfil different important functions. "Concrete" means that there has to be a *real* (i.e. a tangible or measurable) effect, while "direct" refers to the chain of causation'. The expected military advantage must be sufficiently evident. As such, it cannot be 'based merely on hope or speculation'.[735] These qualifiers are believed to be more restrictive than that used to qualify a legitimate military object, that is that its removal will result in a 'definite military advantage' (Article 52(2) API). It follows, therefore, that a 'concrete and direct' military advantage needs to be more than a remote advantage gained at some unknown time in the future.

Regarding '*excessive*', the term means that what is regarded as 'proportionate' in terms of an attack must be *clearly discernible*, such that the military commander can be held accountable for his/her judgement (Article 8(2)(b)(iv) of the ICC Statute).[736] In the *Galić Case*, the Trial Chamber stated that if casualties are expected to be excessive, 'the attack should not be pursued', adding that 'it is necessary to examine whether a reasonably well-informed person in the circumstances of the actual perpetrator, making reasonable use of the information available to him or her, could have expected excessive civilian casualties to result from the attack'.[737] The Trial Chamber does not establish an objective criterion, 'excessiveness' is simply not defined. Thus, ICTY opted to establish a space of *legitimate discretion*, in which a commander should decide 'wilfully and in knowledge of the circumstances' that collateral damage would not, in his personal judgment, be excessive.[738]

What must be taken into consideration, therefore, is the potential military advantage the attacker (the commander, the military hierarchy) has in mind.[739]

735 International Law Association Study Group on the Conduct of Hostilities in the 21st Century (n 666) 364.
736 Dinstein (n 210) 102–121.
737 *Galić Case* (n 713) para 58.
738 ibid 59; International Law Association Study Group on the Conduct of Hostilities in the 21st Century (n 666) 369.
739 Wagner, 'Autonomy in the Battlespace: Independently Operating Weapon Systems and the Law of Armed Conflict' (n 362) 118.

This becomes complex when the *effects of the attack* are taken into account. It has been hotly debated whether proportionality should take into account only the *direct effects of an attack* (the immediate effects caused, e.g. the number of civilian casualties, the number of civilian buildings affected) or should also include the *foreseeability of the indirect effects of the attack* (e.g. the long-term consequences of targeting a civilian infrastructure such as a bridge, preventing civilians from obtaining living supplies; attacks to the natural environment). The *Study Group* has concluded that to include only the direct effects in the proportionality assessment would be too narrow an interpretation, highlighting the importance of 'reasonable foreseeability in relation to determining indirect effects'.[740]

To sum up, as Hampson rightly points out, the IHL framework 'simply indicates what is lawful and unlawful. It is not a substitute for the exercise of discretion by a commander', because an outcome might be legal but 'not right or wise, morally and militarily'.[741] In other words, the whole assessment of what can be considered *excessive* rests on the personal, subjective perception of those who plan and decide on an attack. There is no serious alternative, because there is no way of objectifying or quantifying all the elements that go into the making of a human decision.[742]

In light of the aforementioned discussion, R. Arkin argues that it is possible for the *algorithm for the mission* to select 'the weapon system that ensures that it will not violate any proportionality prohibitions or LOW'; and he goes on to explain that 'the proportionality optimization algorithm uses [...] statistics as well as incoming perceptual information to determine the battlefield carnage in a *utilitarian manner* by estimating the amount of structural damage and the number of non-combatant/combatant/friendly casualties that result from the use of a weapon system at a particular target location'.[743] Arkin's interpretation leaves many questions without answers; however, one of them is signally relevant.

740 International Law Association Study Group on the Conduct of Hostilities in the 21st Century (n 666) 354. It is possible to include within the category of 'indirect effects' the consequences to the natural environment. The problem is, however, how that assessment can be done or how the value of the environment has been taken into account in the proportionality judgement made by military commanders. Dieter Fleck, 'The Protection of the Environment in Armed Conflict: Legal Obligations in the Absence of Specific Rules' (2013) 82 *Nordic Journal of International Law* 7, 10–11; International Law Association Study Group on the Conduct of Hostilities in the 21st Century (n 666) 362.

741 Hampson (n 730) 52; Michael N Schmitt, 'Targeting and Humanitarian Law: Current Issues' (2006) 80 *International Law Studies* 150, 152. Wagner argues, for example, that proportionality 'is almost entirely a qualitative exercise' requiring human judgement. cf Wagner, 'The Dehumanization of International Humanitarian Law: Legal, Ethical, and Political Implications of Autonomous Weapon Systems' (n 64) 1397.

742 Dinstein (n 210) 22.

743 Arkin, 'Governing Lethal Behavior in Autonomous Robots' (n 34) 186–187 (our emphasis).

The author seems to commend the application of a utilitarian perspective for determining Proportionality but, as can easily be seen, the 'concrete and direct military advantage' does not depend only upon quantifiable criteria. Indeed, the value of a single military target may be so high that a higher level of collateral damage is justified.[744]

Be as it may, the advent of AWS can add extra complexity to the proportionality assessment. The simple fact that AWS will not allow human intervention means one of two things: either the commander establishes a specific parameter for proportionality or the system must be capable of adapting to changed circumstances and reassessing the pre-established proportionality parameters. Following this line of reason two realities, involving proportionality, deserve further consideration. First, could AWS be programmed for *targets of opportunity*? Second, could the necessary exercise of discretion by a commander when assessing proportionality, as argued by Hampson, be replaced by computer programs such as the such as the *Collateral Damage Estimate Methodology*.

4.5.5 *The Situation of Targets of Opportunity*

In theory, it is possible to envisage AWS involved with possible courses of action requiring different proportionality assessments. Bearing in mind the OOSA Loop model and recalling that 'S' stands for *selection*, an AWS should be capable of selecting the best course of action to achieve the necessary outcome, depending upon the prevailing circumstances and respecting the Principle of Proportionality. This can be vitally important if *targets of opportunity* are taken into consideration. As Schmitt writes, the 'effects-based operation' (EBO) is a new targeting doctrine that replaces the 'attrition warfare' model.[745] According to the latter, targeting operations obey a pre-planned target list and targets are engaged gradually and sequentially according to the plan. In opposition, a 'target of opportunity' 'is a target visible to a surface or air sensor or observer, which is within range of available weapons and against which fire has not been scheduled or requested'.[746] Thus, these targets come as unplanned and unanticipated but present a concrete and direct military

744 Classic utilitarianism claims that an act is morally right if and only if that act maximises the good, that is, if and only if the total amount of good for all minus the total amount of bad for all is greater than this net amount for any incompatible act available to the agent on that occasion. In short, 'the greatest happiness for the greatest number'. cf Walter Sinnott-Armstrong, 'Consequentialism', *Stanford Encyclopedia of Philosophy* (2015) <https://plato.stanford.edu/entries/consequentialism/>.

745 Schmitt, 'Targeting and Humanitarian Law: Current Issues' (n 741) 152.

746 'Target of Opportunity' in *The Oxford Essential Dictionary of the U.S. Military* (Oxford University Press 2002).

advantage.[747] An example can be given: an AWS is deployed to destroy a military compound but identifies a military aircraft which aims to destroy the system. The aircraft can be considered a *target of opportunity*. Leaving aside any questions about an eventual right of self-defence, the question is highly relevant because, in the situation presented, an AWS, as an adaptable system, would have to prioritise one of the targets, according to the circumstances prevailing at the time.

A human operator deciding on this strike could simultaneously coordinate several strikes, prioritising targets, respecting the mission, treating the enemy to attack by way of 'an integrated complex system'.[748] In the situation of AWS, because its capability to optimise missions by adapting as it went, selecting targets while attending to different possible courses of action, it would need all possible precautionary measures to be in place, namely proportionality.

Further to the aforementioned discussion, it is possible to envisage some factors that could cause difficulties. As argued by the *Study Group*, an EBO necessarily demands, on the part of the commander, the capacity to design and program an *algorithm for the mission* capable of taking into account not only the direct effect of an attack, but also the possible advantages of an EBO. Another element to add to the mix is the fact that 'targets of opportunity' have themselves an element of surprise, that is, they cannot be fully pre-determined. If new circumstances on the battlefield demand a reassessment of proportionality, an AWS has to be able to readapt fast in order to respond in what is a multi-feedback dynamic structure.[749] These capabilities remain to be designed and tested by roboticists.

4.5.6 *The Purpose and Aim of the Collateral Damage Estimate Methodology (CDEM)*

The CDEM is a methodology designed to assist attackers in assessing proportionality. It can be defined as 'a body of joint standards, methods, techniques and processes to conduct collateral damage analysis and produce collateral damage estimates'.[750] As said, CDEM is designed to *assist* and not to *decide* on

747 An example is given: 'a nuclear target that is observed or detected after an operation begins and that has not been previously considered, analyzed, or planned for a nuclear strike. Generally fleeting in nature, it should be attacked as soon as possible within the time limitations imposed for coordination and warning of friendly troops and aircraft.' ibid.

748 Henderson (n 675) 126–127; Schmitt, 'Targeting and Humanitarian Law: Current Issues' (n 741) 154–155.

749 cf Chapter 3, Section 3.5.1.

750 Chairman of the Joint Chiefs of Staff Instruction (n 729) D-2; Schmitt and Thurnher (n 328) 254; Wagner, 'The Dehumanization of International Humanitarian Law: Legal, Ethical, and Political Implications of Autonomous Weapon Systems' (n 64) 1398.

proportionality and it is, therefore, important to distinguish CDEM from a *Collateral Damage Assessment* (CDA) that is the result of '*an analytical judgement derived by determining the amount and effects of collateral damage post target engagement*'.[751]

Many countries use techniques such as CDEM to ensure, with the highest level of certainty possible, that the effects of an attack will not be excessive.[752] Thus, the operational system of the 'CDEM is built around five mutually dependent CDE Levels (CDE Levels 1 through 5). Each level is based on a progressively refined analysis of available intelligence, weapon type and future effects, physical environment, target characteristics and delivery scenarios with specific risk thresholds established for each of the five CDE levels.'[753]

CDE Levels 1, 2 and 3 mitigate risk to less than 10 per cent of serious wounds from fragmentation or other damage to non-combatants. At Level 4, the mitigating risk may be less than 1 per cent in respect of collateral damage to structures. The main concern is still civilian casualties, and takes as the departing point the assumption that civilian casualties will be caused mainly by structures' warhead blast effects. CDE Level 5 (e.g. the situation involving dual-use objects, when all the individuals are classified as civilians) means that there are no technical options that can prevent harm to civilians. In the specific case of the United States, only the Secretary of Defence or the President can authorise an attack after the proportionality analysis is complete.[754]

In spite of all the advantages that CDEM brings to the proportionality assessment, it is important to bear in mind that even CDEM is not an exact science and cannot replace the human decision when it comes to assessing the excessiveness of an attack.[755] Although CDEM follows a set of rules and can generate estimated values, it is grounded in scientific evidence derived from research, experiments, history and battlefield intelligence, and is designed to adapt to time-critical events; there are also some guarantees that it cannot provide.[756] Indeed, the US army, while recognising the value of CDEM, also argues that it 'should not be construed as state practice with respect to

751 Chairman of the Joint Chiefs of Staff Instruction (n 729) D-2.
752 McNeal (n 727) 745.
753 Chairman of the Joint Chiefs of Staff Instruction (n 729) D-A-1.
754 McNeal (n 727) 746; Chairman of the Joint Chiefs of Staff Instruction (n 729) D-A-8, D-A-11.
755 Wagner, 'The Dehumanization of International Humanitarian Law: Legal, Ethical, and Political Implications of Autonomous Weapon Systems' (n 64) 1398; Schmitt and Thurnher (n 328) 254.
756 Chairman of the Joint Chiefs of Staff Instruction (n 729) D-1. McNeal (n 727) 741.

Customary International Law [. . .] *nothing in the CDEM limits or increases the rights and obligations of any US military commander or Service member under the LOW*'.[757] Aside from the fact that the responsibility of the commander to decide on proportionality is not excluded, CDEM does not constitute an absolutely infallible methodology, and its estimates demand human confirmation.[758] The *Study Group* argues that 'a quasi-mathematical assessment [of proportionality] may sometimes be possible' but does not exclude the absolute necessity of human discernment.[759] Thus, the deployment of AWS in projects such as CODE, launched by DARPA, do not regard human operators as simply 'conscious machines' there to uncritically confirm the system's estimates (automation bias).[760]

Whatever the scenario chosen, the future seems gloomy as regards AI being able to fulfil the legal requirements of proportionality. First, if a weapon system is not to allow human intervention, a proportionality reassessment seems to be unfeasible. Second, if human intervention were to be made possible, there is still the danger of 'automation bias', since it is unlikely that human operators would be able to fully grasp the complexity of the selection-making process operated by the system. It could end by scapegoating those who had never had any control in the design, programming or even the deployment of an AWS but simply operate the system on the battlefield. Third, reliance on methodologies such as the CDEM (or similar) could lead to terrible legal consequences. As there is no system that can be relied upon as infallible, there remains the risk that malfunctions at the level of proportionality could lead to the decriminalisation of IHL violations. This last problem will be addressed in Chapter 5.

4.6 CONCLUSION

The entire body of IHL is characterised by an inherent tension between two fundamental but contrasting values: the protection of the civilian population/

757 Chairman of the Joint Chiefs of Staff Instruction (n 729) D-4 (our emphasis).

758 ibid D-A-5.

759 International Law Association Study Group on the Conduct of Hostilities in the 21st Century (n 666) 369.

760 CODE stands for DARPA's Collaborative Operations in Denied Environment (CODE) program that aims to improve the capabilities of systems to work orchestrated – the capabilities UAV to work together under a single person's supervisory control – in order to answer better to the operational challenges posed by dynamic, remote engagements against highly mobile targets in contested electromagnetic environments. cf Scott Wierzbanowski, 'Collaborative Operations in Denied Environment (CODE)' (*DARPA – Defense Advanced Research Projects Agency*) <www.darpa.mil/program/collaborative-operations-in-denied-environment>. cf Chapter 2, Section 2.3.2. cf Beard (n 59) 669–670.

civilian objects and the necessity for legitimate military operations, particularly those deploying lethal force. New technology of war, new weapon systems and autonomous weapon systems are required to keep that balance.

In order to manage the acceptance of this reality, it is important to distinguish between two different steps. As a first step, it is crucial to determine whether AWS should be considered illegitimate per se. In this connection, Article 35 API establishes that states are not entitled to employ weapons, or any method of war, that prove to be the cause of 'superfluous injury or unnecessary suffering'. Therefore, there are limits on states' sovereignty regarding the nature of the effects that might be caused on the battlefield by means and methods of warfare. AWS, seen in this light, do not represent a danger to IHL values because there is no reason to believe that these weapons can be considered indiscriminate per se. The second step relates to the way new technologies are introduced, and comprises a double-staged legal mechanism. First, there is the legal safeguard that works a priori, namely the mechanism of legal review as laid down by Article 36 API. Although the Article is not considered a norm of Customary International Law, and some states are not signatories to the API, the fact is that all states are bound by the consuetudinary norms of IHL that regulate the use of weapons. In this regard, since 2016 the CCW Meetings of Experts have reiterated the need for a transparent, international, legal review of AWS. The demand for a legal review process to be made obligatory, however, is encountering some difficulties among the world's most influential weapons manufacturers (excepting the United States), which prefer for reasons of security to keep legal review of weapons an exclusively domestic process. But this preference does not excuse any state from complying with the norms of IHL.

Once a weapon is considered to be IHL compliant, the imperatives of the Law of Targeting become the priority. The rules of Precaution (Article 57 API), which include two fundamental customary principles of IHL, Distinction and Proportionality, are applicable to both international and non-international armed conflicts. Thus, military commanders are obliged to take all feasible precautions before an attack in order to respect the requirements of Distinction and Proportionality.

These two principles challenge the legitimacy of AWS. Looking at the triple structure of the algorithms embedded in an AWS' operating system, commanders can design and program algorithms for the mission with precise criteria as to *who is who* and *what is what*. However, what cannot be programmed is information that is not known by the AWS's human operatives before an attack. With regard to Proportionality, the prospect is even less clear. According to IHL, Proportionality is not founded on quantitative but rather on qualitative assessments, depending on the capacity of a commander to discern what is happening and take action accordingly on the battlefield. Although mathematical formulas can be of great help in straightforward situation assessment, it would be taking a 'legal risk' to presume that a system, however sophisticated its algorithms, was capable of determining Proportionality parameters in a complex and fast-changing situation.

In short, all is dependent on the future development of technology and its capacity to prove that the long- and well-established principles of IHL would not be at risk from the deployment of AWS. Until that stage of development is achieved, it remains the responsibility of the military commander to take all the precautionary measures necessary to avoid misinterpretations of situations, and consequent catastrophes on the battlefield.

5

Accountability and Liability for the Deployment of Autonomous Weapon Systems

Nowhere in the near future can I envision an intelligent artefact bearing responsibility for its own actions. Thus, I advocate effective and informed acknowledgement of responsibility at all levels by humans prior to its use.

R Arkin

In Chapter 3, it was proposed that an AWS should be definitively described as a '*weapon system designed and programmed for a mission to be adaptive and identify, select and engage military targets without human intervention*'.[761] This definition is based on the premise that AWS are more sophisticated weapon systems than have been seen before and refutes the argument that such systems might be regarded as 'quasi-agents', let alone 'new agents', on the battlefield.[762] One of the main arguments for such definition is the fact that AWS will be functionally autonomous, able to perform all the stages of the OOSA Loop by virtue of their design and programming. Aside from these a priori elements of human control, after the deployment of an AWS human operators will still be able to retain control of the system by means of its inbuilt mechanisms of self-destruction or by deactivating the weapon system.

In spite of the apparent operationality of AWS, it is impossible to exclude from the horizon situations in which the system might fail to operate properly, resulting in outcomes that breach IHL regulations. The first question to be addressed is the problem of accountability. Indeed, the deployment of AWS begs very serious questions of accountability.[763] According to some authors, previous weapon systems, such as automatic, tele- or remotely operated

[761] cf Chapter 2, Section 2.5.

[762] cf Chapter 3, Section 3.5.

[763] Lewis, Blum and Modirzadeh (n 441) 5–6; McFarland, *Autonomous Weapon Systems and the Law of Armed Conflict: Compatibility with International Humanitarian Law* (n 46) 127.

systems, did not raise new accountability problems simply because the actions taken by those systems could be directly attributed to a human operator or to a military commander.[764] However, because AWS would be dependent on machine learning algorithms, a paradigm shift is required, because when a system is able to adapt, select and engage targets without human intervention, there is no one to be held accountable.[765] Autonomous weapons could cause insuperable 'barriers to accountability' because 'instead of identifying a single individual whose faulty actions caused injuries, we find that we must *unravel a messy web of interrelated causes and decisions*'.[766]

Concern about the problems surrounding the future of accountability is shared, not only by academics, but also by the majority of states party to the CCW. A number of states – at the CCW Meetings of Experts, and more recently the GGE – have called for the question of accountability to receive urgent address.[767] In this regard, the statement presented at the GGE in 2017 by Norway is particularly relevant:

> It is easy to foresee situations in which no one can be held responsible if fully autonomous weapons are used in violation of international law. This potential *accountability gap* can have very serious consequences and erode the substantial progress that has been achieved in this area over the last few years.[768]

[764] This does not exclude the problem of lack of transparency and accountability for drone strikes at global and national level. Stewart, 'New Technology and the Law of Armed Conflict' (n 628); Allen Buchanan and Robert O Keohane, 'Toward a Drone Accountability Regime' (2015) 29 *Ethics & International Affairs* 15; Daniel N Hammond, 'Autonomous Weapons and the Problem of State Accountability' (2015) 15 *Chicago Journal of International Law* 652, 663; Heyns and others (n 257) 793.

[765] Brent J Steele and Eric A Heinze, 'From Smartto Autonomous Systems: Confounding Territoriality and Moral Agency' in Caron E Gentry and Amy E Eckert (eds), *The Future of Just War: New Critical Essays* (University of Georgia Press 2014) 98; Tim McFarland and Tim McCormack, 'Mind the Gap: Can Developers of Autonomous Weapons Systems Be Liable for War Crimes?' (2014) 90 *International Law Studies* 361, 362.

[766] Helen Nissenbaum, 'Accountability in a Computarized Society' (1996) 2 *Science and Engineering Ethics* 25, 30; McFarland, 'Factors Shaping the Legal Implications of Increasingly Autonomous Military Systems' (n 32) 1339.

[767] Among those states Austria, Belgium, Brazil, European Union, Greece, Holy See, Norway, Pakistan, Spain, Sri Lanka, Switzerland, the Netherlands and the United Kingdom. For the year of 2017, cf <www.unog.ch/80256EE600585943/(httpPages)/F027DAA4966EB9C7C12580CD0039D7B5?OpenDocument>. For the year of 2018, cf <www.unog.ch/80256EE600585943/(httpPages)/7C335E71DFCB29D1C1258243003E8724?OpenDocument>. For the year of 2019, cf <www.unog.ch/80256EE600585943/(httpPages)/5C00FF8E35B6466DC125839B003B62A1?OpenDocument>.

[768] Norway, '2017 Group of Governmental Experts of the High Contracting Parties to the Convention on Prohibitions or Restrictions on the Use of Certain Conventional Weapons Which May Be Deemed to Be Excessively Injurious or to Have Indiscriminate Effects' (2017)

The risk of a possible 'accountability gap' is one of the main arguments of those who advocate putting an 'emergency brake' on the development and acquisition of AWS.[769] The only possible solution would be to call for a pre-emptive ban of AWS, namely by a binding instrument similar to the five Protocols to the CCW.[770]

As will be seen in the first part of this chapter, there is no substantial reason to support the idea of a 'responsibility gap'. The argument that, with the introduction of AWS, there is no human control is simply inaccurate. In order to clarify the position, this section will focus on three different situations, that is, *'malfunctions'*, *'accidents'* and *'errors'*, that could explain violations of IHL caused by AWS. In one way or another, each of these circumstances will represent a challenge for the IHL framework. However, the conclusion is that IHL provides the legal mechanisms to meet every single challenge that 'malfunctions', 'accidents' and 'errors' may pose.

5.1 DO AWS *REQUIRE* A DISTINCT LEVEL OF HUMAN CONTROL?

The term MHC, as far IHL and AWS are concerned, has been used since the debate began and relates to the requirement to maintain MHC at all levels of an attack.[771] Thus, the identification, selection and engagement of military targets – collectively known as 'critical functions' – drive the need for human control to do everything possible to guarantee the lawfulness of an attack. In short, a human is kept in the loop, ensuring the predictability of the outcomes

<www.unog.ch/80256EDD006B8954/(httpAssets)/DF861D82B90F3BF4C125823B00413F73/$file/2017_GGE+LAWS_Statement_Norway.pdf> (our emphasis).

769 Siboni and Eshpar (n 203) 81. cf Chapter 2, Section 2.2.2.

770 Matthias (n 16) 175; Sparrow, 'Robots and Respect: Assessing the Case against Autonomous Weapon Systems' (n 717) 108; Lt Col Alan Schuller, 'Expert Meeting. Autonomous Weapon Systems. Implications of Increasing Autonomy in the Critical Functions of Weapons' (International Committee of the Red Cross 2016) 27; Schuller, 'At the Crossroads of Control: The Intersection of Artificial Intelligence in Autonomous Weapons Systems with International Humanitarian Law' (n 185) 379, 382; Crootof, 'War Torts: Accountability for Autonomous Weapons' (n 316) 1366; Human Rights Watch and International Human Rights Clinic, 'Losing Humanity: The Case against Killer Robots' (n 30) 42; Nehal Bhuta, Susanne Beck and Robin GeiB, 'Present Futures: Concluding Reflections and Open Questions on Autonomous Weapons Systems' in Nehal Bhuta and others (eds), *Autonomous Weapons Systems: Law, Ethics, Policy* (Cambridge University Press 2016) 367; Scharre, *Army of None: Autonomous Weapons and the Future of War* (n 425) 261–263; Watts (n 641) 184–187.

771 UNIDIR, 'The Weaponization of Increasingly Autonomous Technologies: Concerns, Characteristics and Definitional Approaches' (UNIDIR 2017) Nr 6 1–2 <www.unidir.org/publications>.

while also reaffirming the validity of the accountability mechanisms that are in place to deal with unlawful outcomes.[772]

In Chapter 3, it was explained why the term MHC is not helpful in discussion about the legitimacy of AWS. It was also explained that 'human intervention' should be seen as one of many possibilities of exercising human control. The question of 'control' is obviously important in terms of accountability and the aim of this section is, indeed, to clarify that 'control' should not be seen as the possibility of humans intervening at the different stages of the OOSA Loop but rather in the level of trust and confidence in AWS that commanders will develop based on the testing and evaluation of these new weapon systems. In order to explain such a line of thought, it is important, first, to understand why the concept of MHC can be an obstacle in the way of discussion; second, to appreciate the significance of trust and confidence in machine learning algorithms; and finally, to reject the proposition that human control could be replaced by artificial mechanisms of control.

MHC has been interpreted in different ways;[773] important among them is Heather. Roff's observation that MHC 'emerged as one point of coalescence [. . .] however, the particulars of the concept have been left so open as to foster conversation and agreement'.[774] For example, take the 2017 Netherlands statement at the GGE:

> [T]he concept of meaningful human control does not require immediate new or additional legislation, as the concept should be regarded as a standard deriving from existing legislation and practices (such as the targeting process). [. . .] It is not to be expected that autonomous weapon systems will entirely or substantially take over the role of humans on the battlefield.[775]

At the same time, Pakistan takes the view that MHC 'does not provide a solution to the technical, legal, moral and regulatory questions that they [AWS] pose',[776] and the United Kingdom argues that the discussions at the CCW 'should be mindful of unintended consequences [. . .] and that human

772 Roff and Moyes (n 64); Rebecca Crootof, 'The Meaning of "Meaningful Human Control"' (2016) 30 *Temple International & Comparative Law Journal* 53, 55; 'Killing by Machine: Key Issues for Understanding Meaningful Human Control' (n 61).

773 UNIDIR, 'The Weaponization of Increasingly Autonomous Technologies: Considering How Meaningful Human Control Might Move the Discussion Forward' (UNIDIR 2014) Nr 2 2–3 <www.unidir.org/publications>.

774 Roff and Moyes (n 64); Evans and Salmanowitz (n 186).

775 The Netherlands (n 278).

776 '2016 Pakistan Statement on CCW Meetings of Experts on Laws' (n 429).

control is a "key factor" to be discussed'.[777] Finally, Brazil more realistically averred that '[during 2019] we have managed to build consensus on the centrality of the human element, even though this consensus remains *generic in nature and is subject to differing interpretations an terminologies. This emerging consensus must be deepened and reinforced, with a view to concrete decision making.*'[778]

To the doctrinal discussion should be added the fact that states party to the CCW use terms and concepts that contradict their own policies. It is possible to take the United Kingdom as an example. In April 2018, the Foreign & Commonwealth Office submitted a new statement at the CCW, reiterating that autonomous systems '[are] capable of deciding a course of action, from a number of alternatives, *without depending on human oversight and control*, although these might still be present'.[779] The definition was already difficult to follow given that the UK Government has committed itself in Parliament to an agreement that weapons should always remain under human control. It becomes harder to follow when it is stated that 'LAWS do not currently exist, in line with the UK's definition' but no definition of LAWS is given.[780] At the same time, the UK Government announced the deployment, in 2019–

777 '2018 United Kingdom of Great Britain and Northern Ireland. Statement for the General Exchange of Views at the Meeting of the Group of Government Experts on Lethal Autonomous Weapons Systems' (n 284). Similar to the United Kingdom, the statement delivered by the Government of Brazil stated 'We recognize the centrality of the human element, so that all critical decisions, especially target designation and use of force, must be made by humans to ensure accountability under international law (. . .) The human element is the key to consider, understand and regulate the development, deployment and use of weapons systems with autonomous functions.' '2019 Brazil Statement. Agenda Item 5(c): "Further Consideration of the Human Element in the Use of Lethal Force; Aspects of Human Machine Interaction in the Development, Deployment and Use of Emerging Technologies in the Area of Lethal Autonomous Weapons Systems"' (*Reaching Critical Will*, 2019) <https://reachingcriticalwill.org/images/documents/Disarmament-fora/ccw/2019/gge/statements/26March_Brazil5c.pdf>.

778 '2019 Brazil Statement. Agenda Item 5(c): "Further Consideration of the Human Element in the Use of Lethal Force; Aspects of Human Machine Interaction in the Development, Deployment and Use of Emerging Technologies in the Area of Lethal Autonomous Weapons Systems"' (n 777) (our emphasis).

779 '2018 United Kingdom of Great Britain and Northern Ireland. Statement for the General Exchange of Views at the Meeting of the Group of Government Experts on Lethal Autonomous Weapons Systems' (n 284).

780 In 2019, the Government of the United Kingdom stated that 'the UK does not envisage a scenario in which machines with high-order autonomy will exercise complete self-determination: all weapon systems will function because of some human decision to deploy the system in order to achieve a specific outcome'. '2019 United Kingdom of Great Britain and Northern Ireland Statement. Agenda Item 5(b): "Characterization of the Systems under Consideration in Order to Promote a Common Understanding on Concepts and Characteristics Relevant to the Objectives and Purposes of the Convention"' (n 53).

2020, of the 'autonomous warrior'[781] and the 'Taranis' that, according to BAE Systems, 'will also have the capability to make its own informed "decisions" inflight (with assumed ground control operator override)'.[782] The UK Government's mixed definitions and contradictory messages have been noted in recent reports by UNA-UK and by the press in general.[783]

In light of the aforementioned discussion, it is fair to conclude that there is no agreement on whether MHC is a useful concept in the AWS debate or, indeed, what MHC actually means. In this regard, UNIDIR made two important observations. First, in the last thirty years, states have been using warfare systems (AEGIS and Harpy, among others) operating with limited human intervention but there has been very little debate about their acceptability. Thus, it should be asked: why do AWS raise so much concern? Second, MHC, as used by some ban proponents, 'explicitly emphasizes the quality of control ("meaningful") and it implicitly accords responsibility to human agents for decisions concerning each individual attack'.[784] Thus, MHC begs the question of whether AWS will, in fact, necessarily lead to a responsibility vacuum.

Simply put, it is important to ask whether machine learning algorithms would indeed represent a break in the chain of human control over technology. UNIDIR argues that 'it shouldn't be the technology guiding this conversation. We need to shift to a proactive conversation on human control/judgement/intent/responsibility etc. and then apply that to technology.'[785] Technology has offered warfare-efficient solutions throughout the centuries, and has, to date, been adequately regulated by IHL. Never before has it been necessary to invert the order that IHL should set the parameters of what it is permissible to allow technology to do. Thus, machine learning algorithms will only turn out to be 'unlawful' if they encode norms that are not human designed. A number of authors have pointed out the important fact that the debate about AWS should reject any idea of preferring humans operating

781 Mark Lancaster, 'British Army Set to Redefine Warfare with Joint Autonomous Warrior' (*GOV.UK*, 20 June 2018) <www.gov.uk/government/news/british-army-set-to-redefine-warfare-with-joint-autonomous-warrior>.

782 'BAe Systems Taranis Technology Demonstrator/Unmanned Combat Air Vehicle (UCAV)' (*Military Weapons*) <www.militaryfactory.com/aircraft/detail.asp?aircraft_id=986>.

783 United Nations Association-UK, 'Killer Robots: Who Is Making the Decisions? UNA-UK Briefing on Lethal Autonomous Weapons Systems and International Action to Prevent the Threat' (UNA-UK 2018) <www.una.org.uk/sites/default/files/KillerRobots_20180814b.pdf>; Anthony Cuthbertson, 'UK Government Developing Flying "Killer Robots" Investigation Reveals' (*The Independent*, 13 November 2018) <www.independent.co.uk/life-style/gadgets-and-tech/news/drones-robots-uk-autonomous-artificial-intelligence-ministry-defence-a8631211.html>.

784 UNIDIR, 'The Weaponization of Increasingly Autonomous Technologies: Considering How Meaningful Human Control Might Move the Discussion Forward' (n 773) 5, 10.

785 '2016 UNIDIR Statement at CCW Meeting of Experts on LAWS' (n 431) para 5.

machines over autonomous systems of warfare.[786] What is indeed relevant is what can guarantee a better IHL compliance. Another fact that is crucially important to remember is that machines operating without human intervention are not new. Thus, it can be misleading and dangerous to stick that the principle of humanity does not refer primarily *'to the promotion of means and methods of war that best protect humanity within the bounds of war, irrespective of whether the means to that end is human or machine or some combination of the two'*.[787]

A commander, when deciding whether or not to deploy an AWS, needs to have developed a sense of *trust* that should lead him/her to establish what *level of precaution and control* that mission entails. So far, up until the time of writing, the pre-emptive ban campaigners have been unable to provide a convincing argument or to demonstrate a way in which AWS might prevent commanders from exercising their due responsibility to make the required legal assessments, design and program the system in accordance with IHL parameters. Above all, they have failed to show any reason why an AWS should not be capable of completing the tasks delegated to it.[788]

A final question remains to be answered. R. Arkin and others have proposed that some level of control could be delegated to the AWS, through an artificial mechanism known as the *Ethical Governor*. This mechanism would guarantee IHL compliance and, at the same time, turn AWS into self-contained systems, obviating altogether the need to involve human operators.[789]

5.2 AN ARTIFICIAL MECHANISM OF COMPLIANCE AND CONTROL: THE *ETHICAL GOVERNOR*

A full understanding of the technical architecture of the Ethical Governor (hereinafter EG) is beyond the scope of this work because, among other reasons, such a mechanism remains in the world of theoretical possibility. As Arkin stated, most of the coordination functions and sequences underpinning the EG

786 Kenneth Anderson, Daniel Reisner and Mathew C Waxman, 'Adapting the Law of Armed Conflict to Autonomous Weapon Systems' (2014) 90 *International Law Studies* 386, 410.

787 ibid (our emphasis).

788 Davison (n 165) 7; Roff and Danks (n 627) 15.

789 Arkin, *Governing Lethal Behavior in Autonomous Robots* (n 34) 125; Peter Asaro, 'A Body to Kick, but Still No Soul to Damn: Legal Perspectives on Robotics' in Patrick Lin, Keith Abney and George A Bekey (eds), *Robot Ethics: The Ethical and Social Implications of Robotics* (MIT Press 2012) 175 (our emphasis).

remain to be evaluated, and 'control within the Ethical Governor remains an open research question at the time of writing'.[790]

However, an overview of the system might help to illustrate those features that would support 'respect' for IHL. It has been suggested that the EG could be programmed to effectively control and enforce the 'ethical' use of lethal force by an AWS on the battlefield. According to the author, 'when these weaponized autonomous systems appear in the battlefield, they should help to ensure that humanity, proportionality, responsibility, and relative safety are extended during combat not only to friendly forces, but equally to non-combatants and those who are otherwise *hors de combat*'.[791]

Bearing in mind the OOSA Loop structure, it becomes easier to understand the specific function of the EG. First, *Observation* and *Orientation* are represented by perception and the logical assertions that are created to design possible courses of action (r_1; r_2; r_3; r_4). From these hypothetical courses of action an inference is made after the constraints are applied, that is, the customary and conventional norms of IHL and the ROE. According to Arkin, in a situation involving the use of lethal force, the constraints would operate according to the Principle of Double Intent ($C_{obligate}$ + $C_{forbidden}$) that would ensure that more options would be evaluated than would normally be reviewed by 'a typical soldier', leading to the *Selection* of a course of action *P*.[792] It is at this stage that the EG would come into play. Just before an AWS releases a munition, the EG intervenes 'as necessary to prevent an unethical response from occurring'. The EG is, therefore, a self-learning preventive mechanism that only needs to operate when the course of action selected seems to be 'unethical'.[793] In this situation, the system must send 'a notification to the deliberative system in order to permit replanning at either a tactical or mission level as appropriate, and to *advise the operator* of a potential ethical infraction [...] in the ethical constraint set C'.[794]

790 Arkin, *Governing Lethal Behavior in Autonomous Robots* (n 34) 130, 136. The applicability of mechanisms of the Ethical Governor has been developed in other areas, namely between patients with Parkinson' disease and their caregivers. The Ethical Governor would enable a robot to ethically intervene in a situation where patients or caregivers go across accepted ethical boundaries. cf Jaeeun Shim, Ronald C Arkin and Michael Pettinatti, 'An Intervening Ethical Governor for a Robot Mediator in Patient–Caregiver Relationship: Implementation and Evaluation' [2017] *IEEE* 2936; Louise Dennis and Michael Fisher, 'Practical Challenges in Explicit Ethical Machine Reasoning' [2018] *Cornell University Library* 1, 1–2.

791 Arkin, *Governing Lethal Behavior in Autonomous Robots* (n 34) preface XVIII.

792 ibid 48, 132–133.

793 ibid 127.

794 ibid 128.

Finally, another element that requires attention is the *Ethical Adaptor* (hereinafter EA) functionality. Arkin argues that an AWS will not be designed to be perfect, 'but to perform better than human soldiers operating under similar circumstances'. To this end, therefore, the EA will be designed to deal with any 'errors' that the system might cause on the battlefield, on two levels. First, the *after-action reflection* (the review conducted by a human operator after errors have occurred in order to make the constraints more effective for future missions involving lethal force) and, second, the *run-time affective restriction of lethal behaviour* (an internal mechanism of the system capable of developing a sense of guilt – variable V_{guilt} – which would analyse two types of feedback: from the operator and/or from the system itself) so as to eliminate or at least minimise the possibility of future errors occurring.[795]

As interesting as Arkin's proposed EG may sound, the project is still dependent on several '*ifs*', including whether an AWS' 'perceptual' capabilities are likely ever to achieve a sufficiently sophisticated level of autonomous performance. Leaving the technical element to roboticists, it is argued that Arkin's project already raises enough problems to provoke lengthy debate. First, there is a contradiction between the terms used that confuses ethical with lawful behaviour. Second, and more importantly, the author does not exclude human control as far as the after-action reflection is concerned. This model is compatible with a system operating without human intervention. However, 'self-learning preventive mechanisms' and 'run-time affective restriction of lethal behaviour' raise concerns regarding the human role at the time of designing and programming the AWS. It is important to recall that AWS must be designed for specific missions, according to the directions and values chosen by their human operators. They will be regarded as culpable for violations of IHL only if, in the final analysis, a link of causality can be proved between the outcome and the accuracy of the design and programming of the inbuilt algorithms in the system. AWS will never 'decide' for a 'reason', let alone 'for the right reasons' because of the anti-codifiable nature of moral judgement.[796]

The author does not give a definition of AWS and does not mention the nature of the algorithms that would underpin the AWS's lawful lethal behaviour. Only one mention is made in relation to the functionality of the EA. According to the author, AWS 'will never be perfect', and it is intended that

795 ibid 138–143.

796 Sparrow, 'Killer Robots' (n 55) 62; Champagne and Tonkens (n 16) 126–127; Steele and Heinze (n 765) 101; Duncan Purves, Ryan Jenkins and Bradley J Strawser, 'Autonomous Machines, Moral Judgment and Acting for the Right Reasons' (2015) 18 *Ethical Theory and Moral Practice* 851, 860.

the function of the EA will be 'to deal with any errors that the system may possibly make regarding the use of lethal force'.[797] This proposition, nonetheless, should be rejected, as inadmissible. Accountability is the cornerstone of any legal system and the possibility of 'errors' being addressed by that same system could well lead to a progressive decriminalisation of IHL infringements. Actions have to be clearly traceable back to the moment of design and programming and to the human operator who carried out these tasks. This should be the general rule whenever the outcome can be traced to a human operator.

Arkin does not take into consideration the differences between the types of errors that may occur. The author just states that 'responsibility must return to those who designed, deployed and commanded the autonomous agent to act, as they are those who controlled its beliefs'.[798] But is a 'malfunction' an 'error' according to the author? And what is to be made of situations where there is no fault on the part of the programmers and designers, yet the final outcome is unlawful?

In light of the aforementioned discussion, in order to avoid a process of decriminalisation of offences against IHL, it is important to distinguish clearly between the different types of 'error' and the respective legal answers.

5.3 INDIVIDUAL ACCOUNTABILITY AND STATE RESPONSIBILITY

Among governments, NGOs and scholars there is a growing consensus that either the *person(s)* or the *state(s)* involved must be held accountable for violations of IHL caused by AWS.[799] One of the challenges that AWS will

797 Arkin, *Governing Lethal Behavior in Autonomous Robots* (n 34) 138.

798 ibid 44.

799 '2019 Brazil Statement. Agenda Item 5(c): "Further Consideration of the Human Element in the Use of Lethal Force; Aspects of Human Machine Interaction in the Development, Deployment and Use of Emerging Technologies in the Area of Lethal Autonomous Weapons Systems"' (n 777); '2019 EU Statement. 5(a) An Exploration of the Potential Challenges Posed by Emerging Technologies in the Area of Lethal Autonomous Weapons Systems to International Humanitarian Law' (n 15); Curtis EA Karnow, 'Liability for Distributed Artificial Intelligences' (1996) 11 *Berkeley Technology Law Journal* 148, 188–190; Sparrow, 'Robots and Respect: Assessing the Case against Autonomous Weapon Systems' (n 717) 108; Nissenbaum (n 766); Espada and Hortal (n 46) 10; Grove (n 578) 6–7; Michael C Horowitz, 'The Ethics & Morality of Robotic Warfare: Assessing the Debate over Autonomous Weapons' (2016) 145 *Daedalus* 25, 30–31; Hin-Yan Liu, 'Weapons Systems: Autonomy In' in Domonic A Bearfield and Melvin Dubnick (eds), *Encyclopedia of Public Administration and Public Policy* (3rd edn, CRC Press 2015) 1–6, 5 <www.academia.edu/11900030/Autonomy_in_Weapons_Systems>; Paola Gaeta, *Autonomous Weapon Systems and the Alleged Responsibility Gap* (ICRC 2016) 44–45; Crootof, 'The Killer Robots are Here: Legal and Policy Implications' (n 315) 1881–1882; Krupiy (n 31) 59.

represent for international lawyers, as the Norwegian Government stated in 2017, will be that of ensuring that 'individual and state responsibility for unlawful acts in times of armed conflict' is recognised. This 'is a cornerstone of modern international law'.[800] The rules relating to the deployment of AWS in armed conflicts throw up some contentious issues.[801] A number of states (see the Proposals tabled by Austria, Brazil and Chile)[802] and some authors believe there are at present, quite simply, no rules to deal with the challenges presented by AWS.[803] They maintain that if it is necessary to put in place measures to avoid a responsibility vacuum, a new treaty is needed either to establish the level of human intervention required for AWS or to establish 'Tort Law' mechanisms to cover the deployment of AWS.[804]

Ideal as this option would appear, there are some obstacles in the way of its implementation. As was seen at the 2018 meeting of the CCW, the dissent of a minority of states (Australia, Israel, Russian Federation, South Korea and the United States) was enough to pull back discussions about a future ban, although the majority of states representatives present wished the debate to proceed.[805] It is clear that a new binding document would not be welcomed by the main weapons manufacturers, among them the United States, which have long-established programs to develop autonomous warfare technology.[806] Another obstacle concerns *tort responsibility*.[807] Invoking state responsibility,

800 Norway (n 768). In same line of thought, the statements by the Holy See, Sri Lanka, Switzerland and the European Union in 2018. cf Holy See (n 63); Sri Lanka (n 267); '2018 European Union Statement Group of Governmental Experts Lethal Autonomous Weapons Systems Convention on Certain Conventional Weapons' (n 471).

801 Rain Liivoja, 'Why It's so Hard to Reach an International Agreement on Killer Robots' (*The Conversation-Academic Rigour Journalistic Flair*, 12 September 2018) <http://theconversation.com/why-its-so-hard-to-reach-an-international-agreement-on-killer-robots-102637>.

802 Austria, Brazil and Chile (n 63).

803 Asaro, 'On Banning Autonomous Weapon Systems: Human Rights, Automation and the Dehumanization of Lethal Decision Making' (n 29) 707; Rebecca Crootof, 'Autonomous Weapon Systems and the Limits of Analogy' (2018) 9 *Harvard National Security Journal* 51, 59; Crootof, 'The Killer Robots are Here: Legal and Policy Implications' (n 315) 1894–1896.

804 Crootof, 'War Torts: Accountability for Autonomous Weapons' (n 316) 1347; Anderson, Reisner and Waxman (n 786) 406; Wallach, *A Dangerous Master. How to Keep Technology from Slipping Beyond Our Control* (n 97) 230; Haji-Janev and Hristovski (n 4) 336.

805 Dean Balsamini, 'US, Russia Block Formal Discussion on Whether to Ban "Killer Robots"' *New York Post* (New York, 1 September 2018) <https://nypost.com/2018/09/01/us-russia-block-formal-discussion-on-whether-to-ban-killer-robots/>.

806 Matthew Broersma, 'US Military to Spend £1.54 billion on AI Research' (*Silicon*, 11 September 2018) <www.silicon.co.uk/workspace/us-military-to-spend-1-54bn-on-ai-research-236765?inf_by=5b9936e3671db86e488b5491>.

807 Tort is understood as a civil wrong distinguished from the law of contract, the law of restitution and the criminal law. A tort is a breach of a duty and tort law serves to protect a person's interest in his/her bodily security, tangible property, financial resources or

in the case of an internationally wrongful act caused by an AWS, is far from being explored. Not only is it impossible to derive customary rules due to the diversity of state practices, states will always be resistant to a regime of liability for the deployment of legitimate weapons.[808]

Another possible way of dealing with the problem of accountability, proposed by Jack Beard and R. Arkin, is to hold military commanders accountable for whatever violations AWS may cause on the battlefield. This option certainly appears to be more reasonable. However, it can only be applied if the military commander (or any other human operator in charge of the AWS) can be shown to have acted with *dolus* or *negligence* (Article 25(3)(a); Article 28 ICC Statute).[809] For example, if it were proven that the algorithms underpinning the AWS' behaviour had not been properly designed or programmed; the system was not deactivated in due time or the commander did not supervise the AWS' operators as required. However, if the cause of unlawful results cannot be attributed to a human operator, this legal framework could not apply; it would amount to a *scapegoating form of liability* (a case in which a specified person is singled out as liable although there is no mens rea).[810]

Marc Champagne and Ryan Tonkens take, notwithstanding, an opposing point of view. The authors argue that such a situation allows space for a 'responsibility blank check'. A person, such as a military commander or an operator, could accept responsibility for the 'actions of all autonomous robotic devices'.[811] If this

reputation. Interference with one of these interests is redressable by an action for compensation, usually in the form of unliquidated damages. The law of torts aims to restore the injured person to the position he/she was in before the tort was committed. cf Allan Beever, *A Theory of Tort Liability* (Hart 2016) 1–3.

808 Michel Maontjhoie, 'The Concept of Liability in the Absence of an International Wrongful Act' in James Crawford, Alain Pellet and Simon Olleson (eds), *The Law of International Responsibility* (Oxford University Press 2010) 505, 507, 512; Alan Boyle, 'Liability for Injurious Consequences of Acts Not Prohibited by International Law' in James Crawford, Alain Pellet and Simon Olleson (eds), *The Law of International Responsibility* (Oxford University Press 2010) 98.

809 Krupiy (n 31) 68.

810 At the 2019 GGE Meeting the Government of Brazil raised concerns about the proposal that commanders should always 'be ultimately accountable for violations of IHL during military operations under [their] purview (. . . [but] factual responsibility must remain commensurate with legal accountability, otherwise the human commander operator ends up a mere legal scapegoat in case anything goes wrong'. cf Brazil, '2019 GGE on Laws. Challenges to IHL Item 5(a)' (n 267). As T Chengeta argues, 'this idea has the chilling effect of throwing the important element of mens rea out of the window and putting in place some form of "strict criminal liability"'. cf Chengeta, 'Accountability Gap: Autonomous Weapon Systems and Modes of Responsibility in International Law' (n 20) 34.

811 Champagne and Tonkens (n 16) 126. The same perspective is shared by Christopher Toscano arguing for administrative accountability of commanders. Toscano (n 514) 237–238.

non-causal imputation were seen as scapegoating commanders and operators, the authors argue, 'this possibility should not overshadow the fact that, *when informed consent is present, the same mechanism can be used fairly*'.[812] Thus, the 'role responsibility' to which those in charge of an AWS have committed themselves, by virtue of their having accepted their positions of command – which constitutes a form of social contract – would include responsibility for unlawful, unpredictable violations of IHL caused by AWS.[813] This interpretation might be possible, it is argued here, in domestic law, but it is unlikely to be accepted in International Law because in that sphere responsibility is inherently dependent on 'fault'.

In order to throw some light on the accountability question, and thereby facilitate further discussion, it is essential to distinguish individual accountability (e.g. that of operators or military commanders) from state responsibility. Many different aspects of this could be described, but especially important is the difference in nature between these two forms of liability. The primary purpose of state responsibility is to provide reparation when an internationally wrongful act has been committed by the state. International individual responsibility, on the other hand, is punitive in character and attaches criminal liability to the commission of particularly heinous crimes that concern the international community as a whole (Article 1 and 5(1) ICC Statute). Thus, mens rea remains a foundational element of individual responsibility in International Law. Intentionality on the part of the wrongdoer is a prime determinant in establishing individual responsibility for war crimes (Article 8 ICC Statute).[814] By contrast, state responsibility is objective in scope (triggered by a breach of a state's international obligations) and requires no fault to be established, unless fault forms part of the primary obligation which is breached (e.g. obligations which provide for a due diligence standard to be observed by states which, if not met, will require proof of the state's negligence).[815]

On this point, it is important to note that the *International Law Commission's Articles on State Responsibility* (hereinafter ARSIWA) expressly exempt from their scope of application 'any question of the individual responsibility under international law of any person acting on behalf of a State' (Article 58 ARSIWA). Likewise, the ICC Statute provides

812 Champagne and Tonkens (n 16) 127.

813 ibid 133.

814 Rome Statute of the International Criminal Court of 17 July 1998 (Hereinafter ICC Statute). Andrea Bianchi, 'State Responsibility and Criminal Liability of Individuals' in Antonio Cassese (ed), *The Oxford Companion of International Criminal Justice* (Oxford University Press 2009) 18.

815 ibid 18–19; Seixas-Nunes (n 240).

that '[n]o provision in this Statute relating to individual criminal responsibility shall affect the responsibility of States under international law' (Article 25(4) ICC Statute). In short, the 'question of individual responsibility is in principle distinct from the question of state responsibility' but they can overlap, as Article 58 ARSIWA makes clear, stating that 'any person acting on behalf of a state' is not excused from individual criminal responsibility.[816]

Considering the aforementioned discussion, individual and state responsibility can act in 'complementary' ways, although separately, to supplement the effectiveness of ICL in general and IHL in particular.[817] As Elies van Sliedgret emphasises, state conduct can play a role in establishing individual criminal responsibility, because the organised and collective nature of international crimes can indeed reveal states' involvement.[818]

5.3.1 *Individual Responsibility and the Violations of IHL Caused by AWS*

Individual accountability for war crimes is a long and well-established rule of customary and treaty law.[819] However, the first attempt to regulate automated/autonomous decision-making processes was made by the European Parliament when, in February 2017, GDPR was approved, creating a legal-ethical framework according to which robots qualify as 'electronic persons', and transparency and accountability become the governing priorities.[820] Private citizens are seen as having a 'right to be informed' as regards 'automated/autonomous decisions' that may affect them.[821] In spite of GDPR's

816 Crawford, *The International Law Commission's Articles on State Responsibility: Introduction, Text and Commentaries* (n 697) 312–313; Elies van Sliedregt, *Individual Criminal Responsibility in International Law* (Oxford University Press 2012) 5.

817 Bianchi (n 814) 24; Marco Sassoli, 'Humanitarian Law and International Criminal Law' in Antonio Cassese (ed), *The Oxford Companion to International Criminal Justice* (Oxford University Press 2009).

818 Sliedregt (n 816) 5.

819 McFarland, *Autonomous Weapon Systems and the Law of Armed Conflict: Compatibility with International Humanitarian Law* (n 46) 137–138.

820 European Parliament, 'Civil Law Rules on Robotics European Parliament Resolution of 16 February 2017 with Recommendations to the Commission on Civil Law Rules on Robotics (2015/2103(INL))' (n 57).

821 'General Data Protection Regulation' (2017) Articles 13, 14, 22 <https://gdpr-info.eu/>; Wojchiech Samek and Klaus-Robert Muller, 'Towards Explainable Artificial Intelligence' in Wojchiech Samek and others (eds), *Explainable AI: Interpreting, Explaining and Visualizing Deep Learning* (Springer 2019) 9; Sandra Wachter, Brent Mittelstadt and Luciano Floridi, 'Why a Right to Explanation of Automated Decision-Making Does Not Exist in the General Data Protection Regulation' (2017) 7 *International Data Privacy Law* 76; 'A Guide to Using Artificial Intelligence in the Public Sector' (n 151) 13.

importance, the fact is that the 'autonomous decision-making processes' envisaged by the framework do not include 'autonomous outcomes' involving the use of lethal force.[822] The context of an armed conflict raises other questions, but an important point to consider is whether the 'right to be informed' could be extended to those who fall victim to IHL violations caused by AWS, a possibility envisaged by Article 32 API.[823]

As distant as it may seem, the GDPR has initiated an interesting line of enquiry: *might it be possible for algorithms to demonstrate the logic followed to achieve a certain outcome?* In situations involving unlawful outcomes caused by AWS, this would help to restrict the sphere of individual responsibility, establishing where and how an individual might have been the one to *cause* the violations produced by the AWS. The most serious outcome, and the main object of attention in this chapter, is the violation that cannot be tracked to a human operator.

In attending to the individual responsibility framework, it is vitally important to consider that the Nuremberg IMT forcefully affirmed the central role of individual responsibility by stating that '*crimes against international law are committed by men, not by abstract entities, and only by punishing individuals who commit such crimes can the provisions of international law be enforced*'.[824] More recently, the ad hoc Tribunals and the ICC have all demonstrated the continuing importance of establishing individual criminal responsibility as the 'cornerstone of international criminal law'.[825] More specifically, Article 25(1) of the ICC Statute introduced a novel concept when it stated that 'the Court shall have jurisdiction over natural persons pursuant to this Statute', thus restricting the jurisdiction to '*natural persons*',[826] excluding all other possible legal entities.[827]

822 Wachter, Mittelstadt and Floridi, 'Why a Right to Explanation of Automated Decision-Making Does Not Exist in the General Data Protection Regulation' (n 821) 78–79.

823 Article 33 API; Article 138 GC IV; Dapo Akande and Antonios Tzanakopoulos, 'The Crime of Aggression in the ICC and State Responsibility' (2017) 58 *Harvard International Law Journal* 33, 818.

824 The United Nations War Crimes Commission, *Law Reports of Trials of War Criminals. The I.E. Farben and Krupp Trials*, vol 10 (The United Nations War Crimes Commission by His Magesty's Sationary Office 1949) 223.

825 *Prosecutor v Tadić, Opinion and Judgement* (n 700) paras 664–666; Beard (n 59) 642; Sliedregt (n 816) 17.

826 Albin Eser, 'Individual Criminal Responsibility' in Antonio Cassese, Paola Gaeta and John RWD Jones (eds), *The Rome Statute of the International Criminal Court: A Commentary*, vol 1 (Oxford University Press 2002) 776.

827 The possibility of extending individual responsibility beyond 'natural persons' was strongly argued by the French delegation, suggesting the ICC jurisdiction if the 'crimes were committed on behalf of such legal persons or by their agencies or representatives'. However, no consensus was possible and draft provisions to this effect were abandoned by

Some authors have argued that the legal framework is doomed to fail, using this argument in support of 'personhood status for emerging artificial agents'.[828] There has already been an opportunity to address these arguments but at the point at which the problem of accountability is raised, it will be important to ask: how could an AWS be deployed to commit a crime as a self-determined agent? Following this line of thought, Jens D. Ohlin considers that if it is to be used as an instrument of criminality, 'it is largely irrelevant whether the AWS qualifies as an autonomous agent with moral responsibility'.[829] However, if a situation were to arise in which 'an AWS [could] be considered a moral agent', the foundations of international accountability, it is proposed, would crumble.[830]

In the meantime, commanders and other human operators, as moral agents capable of taking decisions per se, are responsible for the deployment of AWS and for the pre-established outcomes of their missions.[831] If any human operating an AWS uses the system with the intention to commit a crime, by designing, programming or activating the system with the intention of achieving an unlawful outcome, there is nothing to distinguish that AWS from any other weapon used for criminal purposes.[832] The responsibility for the war crime rests with the operator(s) responsible for those decisions, as was confirmed by the ICTY in the *Galić Case*: the perpetrator 'must have acted consciously and with intent'.[833] Question: what is to be made of unlawful outcomes that have *not* been consciously and intentionally caused by human operators and

the Working Group. cf William A Schabas, *The International Criminal Court: A Commentary on the Rome Statute* (2nd edn, Oxford University Press 2012) 409–410; Eser (n 826) 778–779; UN General Assembly, 'Ad Hoc Committee on the Establishment of an International Criminal Court' (1995) GAOR, Fiftieth Session, Supplement No 22 (A/50/22) <www.legal-tools.org/doc/b50da8/pdf/>; Chantal Meloni, *Command Responsibility in International Criminal Law* (TMC Asser Press 2010) 26–27.

828 Chapter 3, Section 3.3.1. cf Jain (n 463) 306.

829 Jens David Ohlin, 'The Combatant's Stance: Autonomous Weapons on the Battlefield' (2016) 92 *International Law Studies* 1, 30.

830 It would make applicable the regime provided in Article 25(3) ICC Statute. cf Jain (n 463) 312–313.

831 As M Walzer argues, soldiers will be responsible for what they do on the battlefield, because they cannot be seen as mere technicians. They need to make decisions that are of real significance, and faced with such category of decisions, soldiers have clear obligations. Walzer (n 233) 40, 304; Roff (n 56) 352–364.

832 Alston, 'Lethal Robotic Technologies: The Implications for Human Rights and International Humanitarian Law' (n 37) 51.

833 *Galić Case* (n 713) 54; International Committee of the Red Cross, *Commentary on the Additional Protocols of 8 June 1977 to the Geneva Conventions of 12 August 1949* (n 347) para 3474.

yet, nonetheless, come about as the result of an action undertaken by an AWS?

It is true that, throughout the centuries, legal systems have developed forms of *vicarious responsibility* and, as has been noted, some authors suggest there could be a 'blank check' to cover the 'responsibility role'.[834] However, this way of proceeding would, it is argued here, be unprofitable. Interactions between commander and soldier in the military, in particular, demand a 'special relationship' between two parties based on consent and obedience, and this is not applicable in situations involving AWS.

Another important factor to bear in mind is that ICL holds a military commander responsible for the acts of his/her subordinates only in cases when he/she 'knew' or 'should have known' that a crime was or was about to be committed (Article 28 (a)(i) ICC Statute).

Since it has been established that there is no reason to establish new legal parameters to cover situations in which AWS might be used to commit crimes, it will be interesting and useful to analyse the widely debated question of whether any responsibility can be traced to manufacturers, programmers, designers and/or those in charge of the maintenance of an AWS before and after it is deployed.

5.3.2 *The Liability of AWS Manufacturers, Designers, Programmers and Technicians: A Responsibility Gap?*

Both UN Special Rapporteurs, P. Alston and C. Heyns, have raised the possibility of a form of 'collective responsibility' for the challenges that AWS might represent in terms of accountability. According to that perspective, 'candidates for legal responsibility include the software programmers, those who build or sell hardware, military commanders, subordinates who deploy these systems and political leaders'.[835]

Individual responsibility would constitute only a partial answer, apart from the difficulties of distinguishing and proving the individual contribution of each party to an international crime. In order to answer these urgent questions, four factors need to be considered: (1) the *theory of causation*; (2) how to define and distinguish between '*malfunctions*', '*accidents*' and '*errors*' caused by the

834 Vicarious Responsibility is a form of liability that 'the fault, or other element is ascribed to one party, but liability is ascribed to a different party'. Roff (n 56) 352–362.

835 Alston, 'Report of the Special Rapporteur on Extrajudicial, Summary or Arbitrary Executions, Philip Alston. Addendum -Study on Targeted Killings' (n 247) 17–18; Heyns, 'Report of the Special Rapporteur on Extrajudicial, Summary or Arbitrary Executions, Christof Heyns' (n 10) 77.

system; (3) how to differentiate levels of liability, specifically that known as *strict recklessness*; (4) the possible forms that the liability of manufacturers, programmers and technicians might take.

5.3.2.1 The Theory of Causation

In the realm of Law, the *theory of causation* probes the nexus between the consequences of human behaviour and its legal relevance. Causation is important, among other factors, to establish the facts that make an act/action criminal (actus reus and mens rea).[836] When studying possible forms of liability for violations of IHL caused by AWS, what is important to establish is the *causal nexus* – one that is either direct (by *action*) or indirect (by *omission*) – that, according to legal judgement, is the dominant cause of the unlawful consequences registered on the battlefield.

Considering the aforementioned discussion, it is possible to differentiate two different groups. The first group includes *war crimes*. The term 'war crimes' is used here as an overarching concept to cover all serious violations of IHL, for both international and non-international armed conflicts, recognised by positive International Law.[837] For a crime to be committed, the person must bear some form of culpability for his/her conduct, a certain degree of intentionality (through dolus to recklessness) towards a criminalised outcome.[838] If manufacturers, programmers and technicians fail to satisfy this requirement of mens rea, it will be impossible to attribute responsibility to any of them.[839] The second group includes those violations of IHL that are *faceless*, occurring in circumstances in which it is not possible to establish a chain of human causation. However, even in this group it would be inaccurate to suppose that there would necessarily be a 'responsibility gap' or 'vacuum'. The reality is that although in such a case unlawful unpredictable outcomes cannot be imputed to human operators, the situation is not equivalent to a responsibility vacuum. It is a well-established rule of International Law that states are to be held

836 Léon Castellanos-Jankiewicz, 'Causation and International State Responsibility' [2012] Amsterdam Center for International Law, University of Amsterdam 1, 8.

837 Solis (n 590) 95. For the problem of extending individual criminal responsibility to war crimes committed in non-international armed conflicts, see Charles Garraway, 'War Crimes' in Elizabeth Wilmshurst and Susan Breau (eds), *Perspectives on the ICRC Study on Customary International Humanitarian Law* (Cambridge University Press 2007) 378; *Prosecutor v Duko Tadic, Decision on the Defence Motion for Interlocutory Appeal on Jurisdiction* (n 598) para 129.

838 Jain (n 463) 306; Cryer and others (n 619) 384.

839 Noll (n 105) 91.

accountable for 'international wrongful acts' (Article 2 ARSIWA) for which causation is considered irrelevant.[840]

5.3.2.2 Distinguishing between 'Malfunctions', 'Accidents' and 'Errors'

For decades, different types of algorithms have been used in weapon systems such as drone technology. AI has provided a revolution, for example, in terms of 'battlespace awareness'.[841] Bostrom argues that 'better-engineered systems – that are smarter and have more common sense – [. . .] are less likely to make tragic mistakes'.[842] Nonetheless, it is important to consider the possibility and to distinguish between different types of 'mistakes'.[843]

First, '*malfunctions*'. Until today 'malfunctions' mainly resulted from hardware failures. 'Malfunctions' are technical failures that simply happen, sometimes causing civilian damage (e.g. a bomb is released without human permission because the lock system fails). Malfunctions unfortunately occur, in spite of humans on-the-loop, and cannot necessarily be attributed to any human fault. As Bostrom explains, in cases of 'malfunction', the 'fallout is limited'.[844] A case of 'malfunction' is not a novelty pertaining to AWS alone, but is common to any weapon systems deployed in the battlespace.[845] The problem with 'malfunctions' is that it will always be a matter for a state to admit lack of 'due diligence' or to recognise a breach of the international norm.[846]

A different case would be if an '*accident*' involving AWS caused violations of IHL. The category 'accident' should include those violations that are caused

[840] Castellanos-Jankiewicz (n 836) 11. Along the same lines the EU Statement, at the 2019 GGE Meeting, argued that 'States have a responsibility to ensure that the development, deployment and use of emerging technologies in the area of lethal autonomous weapons systems comply with international law.' '2019 EU Statement. 5(a) An Exploration of the Potential Challenges Posed by Emerging Technologies in the Area of Lethal Autonomous Weapons Systems to International Humanitarian Law' (n 15).

[841] Lewis, Blum and Modirzadeh (n 441) 2–4.

[842] Bostrom (n 103) 143.

[843] For example, in the *Drones Wars UK report*, published in June 2019, it is stated 'that the causes of approximately half of the crashes [involving Drones between 2018-2019] in the dataset are given and include mechanical failure, communications problems ("lost link"), engine failure, weather problems and pilot error'. All these situations, in good legal reasoning, should receive a different legal answer. Chris Cole, 'Accidents Will Happen: A Review of Military Drone Crash Data as the UK Considers Allowing Large Military Drone Flights in Its Airspace' (Drone Wars UK 2019) 5, 11–12 <https://dronewars.net/wp-content/uploads/2019/06/DW-Accidents-WEB.pdf>.

[844] Bostrom (n 103) 146.

[845] Henderson, Keane and Liddy (n 19) 361.

[846] Crootof, 'War Torts: Accountability for Autonomous Weapons' (n 316) 1392; Deeks, Lubell and Murray (n 25) 24.

by poor design, programming or maintenance, that is, due to negligent or reckless behaviour. This last point is crucial to distinguish 'accidents' from crimes which require *dolus directus*.

Either a 'malfunction' or an 'accident' may, potentially, happen during a mission, preventing its pre-established goal from being accomplished. The difference, in the case of an 'accident', is that it is traceable to a human fault, for example a fault on the part of a designer, manufacturer, programmer or technician, and not to a hardware failure.[847] 'Errors', however, are caused by *software failures* (e.g. the missile is not able to adapt to the circumstances of the battlefield, so hits the wrong target; the munition engages the target accurately but causes more damage than initially foreseen; the algorithm for situation management does not function as planned).[848]

AWS will be highly complex systems that will certainly require a higher level of technical knowledge and more human operators in the pre-deployment phase than in automatic or semi-autonomous systems. As McFarland argues, 'unlike manually operated weapons, much of the behaviour of an AWS would be determined by parties other than the individual who employs it on the battlefield. Care must be taken to ensure that the elements of crimes involving the weapon system accurately reflect the involvement of the person who is the perpetrator of the offence.'[849] This is patent in Arkin's preface, where he argues that 'the reality of these systems moving out from their ivy tower laboratories into the real-world military-industrial complex prior to their actual deployment [. . .] forced upon me a further responsibility to inform my colleagues of the consequences of their and our research'.[850] This increased responsibility will be accompanied by a more stringent requirement for accuracy at the crucial moments of manufacturing, designing, programming and maintaining an AWS.[851] The question, however, is whether the categories of *dolus eventualis* and *recklessness* are, or should be, accepted by ICL, other than in cases of command responsibility (Articles 28 and 30 ICC Statute).

847 Hammond (n 764) 665.

848 Much more situations can be envisaged. It is not our purpose to be exhaustive, but to simply make aware that machine learning algorithms learn by trial and error and, therefore, errors are part of the learning process. Thus, the system can be confronted with data on the battlespace that can force to re-program the system but at the same time causing accidents. Matthias (n 16) 175, 183.

849 McFarland, *Autonomous Weapon Systems and the Law of Armed Conflict: Compatibility with International Humanitarian Law* (n 46) 150.

850 Arkin, *Governing Lethal Behavior in Autonomous Robots* (n 34) preface.

851 Scharre, *Army of None: Autonomous Weapons and the Future of War* (n 425) 269–270.

A recent example can be seen in the *William Holbrook v Prodomax Automation Ltd Case*, when in 2015 a technician, Wanda Holbrook, was killed by an allegedly out-of-control robotic machine.[852] The District Court of Michigan came to the conclusion that Prodomax, Lincoln Electrics and others 'owed a duty to Wanda and to the public to properly design, manufacture and test their products, including the robots, robot controllers [. . .] and/or safety devices involved in this case'.[853] Prodomax and others have argued that there were no problems regarding the design and manufacture of the robot.[854] However, the Court came to the conclusion that 'the "100 cell" automation system failed to meet numerous Occupational Safety and Health Administration (OSHA) and Michigan Occupational Safety and Health Administration (MIOSHA) laws and regulations including those regulations pertaining to risk assessment and the control of hazardous energy. All defendants were responsible for these failures.'[855] It is argued here that the same line of reasoning should be adopted in the international forum. Other example are the recent accidents involving the Boeing 737 Max[856] and, more recently, the problems detected with the Boeing 777.[857] In the latter situation, 'metal fatigue in the fan blades of the engines, some of them dating to the mid-1990s' is pointed out as the possible cause for the forced landings registered in January and February 2021.

The concept of '*error*' raises more complex issues. In this type of situation, the system's software is the cause of the violation; it is a *system error*. In this scenario, no human operative can be blamed, and the outcome will in effect be an *inversion* of the original *mission*. As Chengeta argues, in situation of unlawful unpredictable results, 'it is difficult if not impossible to establish a guilty mind, therefore, diminishing the culpability of the individual deploying it'.[858] A source of 'error' might, for example, be a 'biased

852 *William Holbrook v Prodomax Automation Ltd* [2017] US District Court for the Western District of Michigan Case No 17-00219.

853 ibid para 24.

854 ibid 18, 19, 20.

855 ibid 21.

856 A more recent example of an 'accident' is the case regarding the design problems of the Boeing 737 Max. See Jack Nicas and others, 'Boeing Built Deadly Assumptions into 737 Max, Blind to a Late Design Change' *The New York Times* (1 June 2019) <www.nytimes.com/2019/06/01/business/boeing-737-max-crash.html?auth=login-google>; Seixas-Nunes (n 240).

857 Andrew E Kramer, 'Boeing 777 Makes an Emergency Landing in Moscow after Engine Warning' *The New York Times* (26 February 2021) <www.nytimes.com/2021/02/26/world/europe/boeing-777-engine-emergency-landing.html>.

858 Chengeta, 'Accountability Gap: Autonomous Weapon Systems and Modes of Responsibility in International Law' (n 20) 24.

algorithm'.[859] According to the UNIDIR Report *Algorithmic Bias and the Weaponization of Increasingly Autonomous Technologies*, it is urgent to reject the idea that reality (in this case the battlefield) will be analysed objectively by an algorithm. According to this report, *inappropriate data training* (the system was trained according to exemplar data which did not accurately represent the features of the battlefield); *inappropriate focus* (there is incorrect or inappropriate information in the input or training data); and *inappropriate processing data* (when the algorithm employs a statistically biased estimator in order to learn accurate predictive models from small data sets) can lead to illegitimate targeting processes.[860] A biased algorithm can have different sources, but they can all be reduced either to human error (*'accidents'*) or to error on the part of the system itself (*'errors'*).

It is, therefore, important to begin with a distinction between 'malfunctions' and 'errors' since neither involves human fault.[861] First, 'malfunctions' are associated with hardware and 'errors' are associated with software, with the decision-making process of an AWS. Software is to some extent independent of hardware. While the first applies to the algorithms, concepts and mathematical architecture, the latter applies to the material and structures that allow the system to operate in the external world. Simply put, hardware detects the environment; and software makes

859 For different questions regarding 'biased algorithms', cf Matthias Spielkamp, 'Inspecting Algorithms for Bias' (*MIT Technology Review – Business Impact*, 12 June 2017) <www.technologyreview.com/s/607955/inspecting-algorithms-for-bias/>; Deeks, Lubell and Murray (n 25) 13–14; Nareissa Smith, 'The Intelligence Is Artificial. The Bias Isn't' (*Law and AI: A Blog Devoted to Examining the Law of Artificial Intelligence, AI in Law, and AI Policy*, 28 May 2019) <www.lawandai.com/2019/05/28/the-intelligence-is-artificial-the-bias-isnt/>; Phil Muncaster, 'Data Challenges Mean AI Systems Can't Be Trusted' (*Infosecurity*, 4 June 2019) <www.infosecurity-magazine.com/news/infosec19-data-challenges-ai-1/>; Gaon and Stedman (n 21) 1145.

860 UNIDIR, 'Algorithmic Bias and the Weaponization of Increasingly Autonomous Technologies' (UNIDIR 2018) Nr 9 3–5. In reaction to the American AI Initiative some researches have manifest concerns regarding facial recognition software and how it can develop biases against women and minorities. Another example is the reaction of Google employees who forced the company to abandon a partnership with the Pentagon regarding Maven Project. cf Matt Field, 'Trump Orders Some Sort of Vague Action in the AI Arms Race' (*Bulletin of the Atomic Scientists*, 11 February 2019) <https://thebulletin.org/2019/02/trump-orders-some-sort-of-vague-action-in-the-ai-arms-race/>; Scott Shane, Cade Metz and Daisuke Wakabayash, 'How a Pentagon Contract Became an Identity Crisis for Google' *The New York Times* (30 May 2018) <www.nytimes.com/2018/05/30/technology/google-project-maven-pentagon.html>.

861 Neglecting the distinction between 'malfunctions' and 'errors' cf Thomas W Simpson and Vincent C Muller, 'Just War and Robot's Killings' (2016) 66 *Philosophical Quarterly* 302, 6–11.

sense of it.[862] Nonetheless, the category of 'error' should be recognised. As Noll argues, an AWS can become 'co-author itself through its learning capacity, which means that it comes to possess a normativity that can no longer be traced back to any intention originating in a human designer'.[863] Second, 'malfunction' prevents/interrupts a mission from being accomplished, while 'errors' lead the system to *invert the original pre-given mission* and produce a non-programmed outcome. Third, in terms of accountability, the two situations demand different answers. 'Malfunctions' are unforeseeable, while 'errors' should be foreseen when the system is tested and evaluated. The battlefield is unpredictable, but tests and evaluations should create a certain level of trust that the AWS will perform according to the program. Therefore, 'errors' should not lead to the same type of consequences as 'malfunctions'.

Looking now at specific situations of 'error', in Chapter 1, an allusion was made to the distinction between 'semantic errors' and 'syntax errors' identified by Smart, Grim and Hartzog.[864] This classification, however, no longer seems accurate. What were called 'semantic errors' (where the outcome is not as predicted) should be re-named 'technical errors', or simply *malfunctions*. 'Semantic errors', according to the authors, should include those cases that occur because the situation was inadequately translated into software or because it was poorly designed. These should now be called '*accidents*'. Finally, the appropriate term to deal with unlawful unpredictable outcomes produced by an AWS should be 'syntax errors', or simply '*errors*', when the system fails to interpret or to correctly identify the properties of the environment where it is deployed.[865]

862 Jurgen Altmann, *Military Nanotechnology: Potential Applications and Preventive Arms Control* (Routledge 2006) 75–78. Bostrom refers to the difference between programs and computers. Bostrom (n 103) 87–888.

863 Noll (n 105) 93.

864 Smart, Grimm and Hartzog (n 159) 17–19.

865 An interesting case to analyse would be that of the technical failure of the Boeing 737 Max. The situation may be approached in two ways. First, investigators suspected that faulty software (MCAS) was behind the two accidents. If this were the case, it could be argued that the accidents were caused by a program 'error'. Second, there was the possibility that it had been an 'accident'. If Boeing was aware of the 'error' and did not notify the pilots, or withheld vital information pertaining to emergency situations, the cause could be fault on the part of human operatives not having performed with appropriate diligence. cf Dominic Rush, 'Pilots Confronted Boeing with 737 Max Fears after First Fatal Crash, Audio Reveals' *The Guardian* (Brussels, 15 May 2019) <www.theguardian.com/business/2019/may/15/boeing-737-max-pilots-lion-air-ethiopian-airlines-audio>; Reuters, 'Boeing Completes Software Update on 737 Max Planes' *The Guardian* (Brussels, 17 May 2019) <www.theguardian.com/business/2019/may/17/boeing-completes-software-update-on-737-max-planes>; Gwyn Topham, 'BA

Bearing in mind the structure of machine learning algorithms, AWS will operate on probabilities geared towards the optimisation of the *mission* entrusted to the system. Apart from the risks inherent in probabilistic calculations, the *algorithm for the mission* operates inside a 'black box', so human intervention is impossible. However, the state's right to employ AWS, with their new capabilities – but also with their inherent risks – cannot be accepted without corresponding obligations. Distinguishing accurately between different situations and causes of unlawful outcomes is one of them, in order to avoid the possibility of hiding the consequences of human error, or systems' independent action, within the category of 'malfunctions'.

Looking at all the warnings expressed by roboticists regarding the nature of unpredictability, it is possible to imagine a situation, albeit exceptional, in which the system overturns the pre-established mission causing unlawful unpredictable outcomes. As Bostrom states, 'AI is strong enough that human opposition is ineffectual.' It can be argued that the system creates an *original mission* that contravenes what was established by its human operators, causing, eventually, an 'existential catastrophe'. As Bostrom explains, this possibility should not be discounted even if the level of autonomy were so broad as to anticipate outcomes that are far from desirable.[866]

In light of the aforementioned discussion, it can be seen, first, that if distinctions are not properly made and the different cases are subjected to the appropriate legal analysis, the consequence will be that some will postulate a 'responsibility gap' or end up scapegoating commanders and operators. This would contravene IHL values. Second, to state that a system can produce an 'independent action' does not imply that system is inherently an 'independent actor' and, therefore, 'unpredictable' system.[867] It raises the possibility that, in very exceptional circumstances, an AWS may produce an outcome that violates the rules with which the *algorithm for the mission* was programmed.[868]

Following on from the aforementioned discussion, an AWS 'independent action' cannot be considered a *deliberate action* such as an 'attack'. According to Article 49 API, an 'attack' means an 'act of violence against the adversary, whether in offence or in defence'. Even if an 'attack' carried out by an AWS does not correspond, in any way, to what was designed and programmed by those in charge of the system, there are still no grounds to claim that the system

Owner Puts Trust in Boeing with Order for Troubled 737 Max' *The Guardian* (Brussels, 19 June 2019) 35.

866 Treacherous turn, Bostrom (n 103) 144–145.

867 Crootof, 'War Torts: Accountability for Autonomous Weapons' (n 316) 1373–1374.

868 Some authors, in order to address this problem, prefer the terminology of 'war algorithms'. Lewis, Blum and Modirzadeh (n 441).

operated deliberately. Such an assertion would imply that an AWS should be regarded as a moral agent. Thus, if it proves to be impossible to establish a link of causation to an identifiable human fault, the state should be held responsible for any 'unpredictable attack', because of the risk attendant upon deploying an AWS in the battlefield.

The *Petrov Case* can be of some help. In September 1983, Stanislav Petrov was able to deactivate the Russian counter-response system, avoiding a nuclear war.[869] For now it is immaterial whether or not AWS are able to deploy nuclear warheads. The focus should be on two main issues: first, the aforementioned is an example of how, although human operators may not have access to the operational system by direct intervention, they are able to exercise control, deactivating the system and preventing an 'unpredictable attack'. The second point is to examine the 'error'.[870] Explanations were not given about its origin, for example whether it was the result of bad programming or maintenance (an 'accident'), or whether it was an error of the system (a syntax error, or 'error'). Whichever explanation holds, both situations deserve legal answers. In the case of an 'accident', if it can be proven that commanders or technicians acted with *dolus eventualis* or with *recklessness* when establishing the AWS' parameters and codifying IHL and ROE directives into an algorithm, they should be held accountable for the unlawful consequences verified on the battlefield. In the case of an 'error', humans cannot be scapegoated but the deploying state can be held responsible.

5.3.2.3 The Parameters of Individual Responsibility and the Specificities of the Mental Element (mens rea)

The principle *nullum crimen sine lege*, or *principle of legality*, is the cornerstone of ICL, according to which no one may be held criminally liable and punished if, at the moment when he/she performed a certain act, the act was not regarded as a criminal offence by the relevant legal order.[871] This principle was embraced by the ICC Statute in Article 22, which provides the following:

869 Bostrom (n 103) 357, footnote 12.

870 Matthias (n 16) 182.

871 Antonio Cassese (ed), *The Oxford Companion to International Criminal Justice* (Oxford University Press 2009) 438; Cryer and others (n 619) 20. The importance of this was thoroughly debated and embraced by the majority of the state parties during the Travaux Preparatoires of the ICC Statute. cf 'Report of the Preparatory Committee on the Establishment of an International Criminal Court, vol 1 (Proceedings of the Committee of the Preparatory Committee during March–April and August 1996)' (UN General Assembly) Fifty-First Session A/51/52 16, paras 51–52.

1. A person shall not be criminally responsible under this Statute unless the conduct in question constitutes, at the time it takes place, a crime within the jurisdiction of the Court.
2. The definition of a crime shall be strictly construed and shall not be extended by analogy. In case of ambiguity, the definition shall be interpreted in favour of the person being investigated, prosecuted or convicted.
3. This article shall not affect the characterization of any conduct as criminal under international law independent of this Statute.

A reading of Article 22, ICC Statute, makes it clear that extension by analogy is not the only condition forbidden in International Criminal Law; so is 'judicial creativity'. As Judge Geoffrey Robertson stated, in the *Norman Case*, 'what restrains the judges from creating new crimes is the overriding principle of legality, expressed invariably in Latin, *nullem crimen sine lege* – conduct, however awful, is not unlawful unless there is a criminal law against it in force at the time it was committed'.[872] Thus, and this is highly relevant in the case of accountability issues related to the deployment of AWS, no one can be accountable for an act which they have not committed, or in some way participated in, or contributed to.[873] In this regard, the *Tadić Case* is illustrative:

> The basic assumption must be that in international law as much as in national systems, the foundation of criminal responsibility is the principle of personal culpability: nobody may be held criminally responsible for acts or transactions in which he has not personally engaged or in some other way participated (*nulla poena sine culpa*).[874]

A consequence of the principle of legality's specificity is to demand two elements to ensure individual liability: a material element (actus reus) and a mental element (mens rea).[875] Actus reus describes all the external features

[872] Another relevant aspect of the dissenting opinion by Judge Robertson is the recognition of the end of the era of *substantive justice* – the legal order is primarily aimed to protect social values whether or not that conduct has already been legally criminalised at the moment that the conduct took place – to give place to *strict legality* according to which criminal rules only apply to conducts that were already criminalised at the time of commission. *Decision on Preliminary Motion Based on Lack of Jurisdiction (Child Recruitment)* [2004] Special Court for Sierra Leone, Appeal Chamber SCSL-2004-14-AR 72(E)) para 11; Cassese, *The Oxford Companion to International Criminal Justice* (n 871) 438–440.

[873] Antonio Cassese, *International Criminal Law* (Oxford University Press 2003) 136.

[874] *Prosecutor v Duško Tadić, Judgement* [1999] ICTY - Appeals Chamber IT-94-1-A para 186.

[875] The jurisprudence of the tribunals for the former Yugoslavia and Rwanda use the terms actus reus and mens rea to describe the objective and subjective elements of a crime. The ICC

of a crime under International Law committed by action or omission. The mental element refers, rather, to the interior and psychological sphere of the actor (mens rea).[876]

Before the ICC Statute the international jurisprudence had not developed its criteria, on a case-by-case analysis, to provide a general provision on mens rea.[877] Not without controversy and debate, the advent of the ICC Statute, for the first time in the history of International Criminal Law, provides a general definition of the mental element in Article 30.[878] Article 30 (1) stipulates that, for a person to be criminally responsible, '*the material elements are committed with intent and knowledge*'. Thus, in order for an individual to be held accountable, according to the ICC Statute, he/she would have had to have participated, evincing culpable behaviour, in the commission of a crime. The element of necessary culpable behaviour will be vitally important to rule out proposals that suggest holding the commander responsible for all AWS' outcomes in the battlespace or to consider tort responsibility (which seems to be excluded from the ICC Statute). Champagne and Tokens suggest that commanders' consent should carry the implication of an 'overall responsibility' for all outcomes produced by an AWS. However, this understanding confuses the rules of Precaution, namely as they relate to the choice of means and methods of war, with a deliberate action (or omission) undertaken in order to commit a crime.[879] This conclusion should not obscure the possibility of states establishing domestic legal mechanisms for tort responsibility. The problem with this approach is that this is simply not a mechanism recognised by ICL.

Article 30 ICC Statute provides that:

1. Unless otherwise provided, a person shall be criminally responsible and liable for punishment for a crime within the jurisdiction of the Court only if the material elements are committed with intent and knowledge.

Statute opted for more neutral terms (material and mental element) giving a step back from the Anglo-American terminology. Sliedregt (n 816) 4.

876 ibid 39–40; Antonio Vallini, 'Mens Rea' in Antonio Cassese (ed), *The Oxford Companion to International Criminal Justice* (Oxford University Press 2009) 412; Schabas (n 827) 626. For a critique of the term 'mens rea' or 'mental element', cf George P Fletcher, 'The Theory of Criminal Liability and International Criminal Law' (2012) 10 *Journal of International Criminal Justice* 1029, 1037.

877 Sliedregt (n 816) 50.

878 Mohamed Elewa Badar and Sara Porro, 'Article 30: Mental Element' in Mark Klamberg (ed), *Commentary on the Law of the International Criminal Court* (Torkel Opsahl Academic EPublisher 2017) 314; Mohamed Elewa Badar, 'Dolus Eventualis and the Rome Statute without It?' (2009) 12 *New Criminal Review* 433, 438.

879 Cassese, *The Oxford Companion to International Criminal Justice* (n 871) 137; Roff (n 56).

2. For the purposes of this article, a person has intent where:
   (a) in relation to conduct, that person means to engage in the conduct;
   (b) in relation to a consequence, that person means to cause that consequence or is aware that it will occur in the ordinary course of events.
3. For the purposes of this article, 'knowledge' means awareness that a circumstance exists, or a consequence will occur in the ordinary course of events. 'Know' and 'knowingly' shall be construed accordingly.

The difficulty of interpreting Article 30 ICC Statute goes beyond the scope of this work and has, in any case, already been extensively discussed by scholars.[880] What is important to retain here is that the 'material element' germane to an assumption of guilt comprises 'intent' to cause and 'knowledge' of the *circumstances* or *consequences*.[881] In light of this alone, a 'guilty state of mind' in relation to unforeseeable outcomes resulting from the deployment of an AWS cannot be attributed to any of the human operators involved with its design, programming and/or maintenance.

It would be impossible here to develop a fully comprehensive interpretation of Article 30, but paragraph (2)(b) deserves special attention: does it or does it not cover *dolus eventualis/recklessness*? A crime is deemed to be committed with *dolus* when there is *full intent to commit a crime*. This requires that the perpetrator, at the time of the crime, is aware that his/her conduct will purposefully bring about all the material elements of a crime. This requirement would have to be met in the case of commanders, designers, programmers, technicians or any other human operators involved in the deployment of a system for an *intentional* unlawful attack.[882]

The situation is different when the perpetrator realises that unlawful consequences *might occur*, but proceeds in a state of trust that will not happen.[883] At this level it is particularly important to distinguish between *dolus eventualis* and *recklessness*. The dividing line between the two categories is difficult to draw. In this regard, the *Lubanga Case* stated that in situations in which the suspect '(a) is aware of the risk that the objective elements of the crime may result from his or her actions or omissions, and (b) accepts such an outcome by reconciling himself or herself with it or consenting to it (also known as *dolus*

880 Cassese, *The Oxford Companion to International Criminal Justice* (n 871) 159–160; Sliedregt (n 816) 45; Badar and Porro (n 878); Schabas (n 827) 627–630; Badar (n 878) 440–452.

881 Vallini (n 876) 412; Schabas (n 827) 628; *Prosecutor v Thomas Lubanga Dylo* [2009] ICC – Pre-Trial Chamber I ICC-01/04-01/06-803, Decision on the Confirmation of Charges para 356.

882 Cass (n 144) 1058; Schabas (n 827) 629.

883 Sliedregt (n 816) 40–41.

eventualis)', he/she acts with *dolus eventualis*.[884] The Court decided that the distinguishing factor between cases of *dolus eventualis* and those of recklessness was when 'the perpetrator [is] aware of the existence of a risk that the objective elements of the crime may result from his or her actions or omissions, *but does not require that he or she reconcile himself or herself with the result*'.[885]

Finally, there is the situation in which the perpetrator acts *negligently*, in which case there is neither volition nor a cognitive element; a crime would be judged to have been committed because a person had failed to take due care and was ignorant of the circumstances or consequences of his/her omissive behaviour.[886] Thus, such conduct would not be covered by Article 30 ICC Statute, except if it fell under the category of 'unless otherwise provided'.[887] Article 28 ICC Statute is one of those exceptions when it establishes that a military commander can be held accountable for war crimes if he/she *should have known*, or '*consciously disregarded information*'. That these two categories are clearly specified in Article 28 has a bearing on the interpretation of Article 30.[888]

According to some experts, Article 30 does not cover *dolus eventualis*, and there is no help to be found, either, in jurisprudence. In the *Lubanga Case*, for example, the Pre-trial Chamber accepted the category of *dolus eventualis*, stating that 'the above-mentioned volitional element also encompasses other forms of the concept of *dolus* which have already been resorted to by the jurisprudence of the *ad hoc* tribunals, that is [. . .] *dolus eventualis*' while the category of recklessness is not accepted.[889] In September 2008, in the *Katanga and Ngudjolo Chui Case*, the category was avoided and the ICC did not take a position on the matter.[890] In the *Bemba Case*, in 2009, the Pre-trial Chamber argued that the language of Article 30 ICC Statute '[did] not accommodate a lower standard than the one required by *dolus directus in the second degree* (oblique intention)', and that '[t]his standard is undoubtedly higher than the principal standard commonly agreed upon for *dolus eventualis* – namely,

884 *Prosecutor v Thomas Lubanga Dylo* (n 881) para 352.

885 ibid 355, footnote 438. For the full debate concerning Dolus Eventualis and Article 30 ICC Statute, cf Badar and Porro (n 878) 316–318, para 308); Schabas (n 827) 630; Badar (n 878) 444 ff.

886 Sliedregt (n 816) 42.

887 *Prosecutor v Thomas Lubanga Dylo* (n 881) para 355.

888 Badar and Porro (n 878) 315; Schabas (n 827) 631.

889 *Prosecutor v Thomas Lubanga Dylo* (n 881) para 438 (our emphasis); Badar and Porro (n 878) 317; Badar (n 878) 443–444.

890 The Chamber stated that 'there is no need for the present Decision to discuss whether the concept of *dolus eventualis* has a place within the framework of Article 30 of the ICC Statute because the Chamber will not rely on this concept for the mental element in relation to the crimes charged'. *Prosecutor v Germain Katanga and Mathieu Ngdjolo Chui* [2008] Pre-Trial Chamber ICC-01/04-1/07 251, footnote 329; Badar (n 878) 434.

foreseeing the occurrence of the undesired consequences as a mere likelihood or possibility'.[891] This understanding was then later embraced by both the Trial Chamber and the Appeals Chamber in the *Lubanga Case*.[892]

The implicit acceptance of *dolus eventualis* in Article 30 ICC Statute should not be ignored insofar as AWS are concerned. As Ohlin argues, 'international criminal law is ill-suited to prosecuting AWS cases' because the treatment of crimes of *dolus eventualis* is inadequate. However, as the author argues, this problem must be solved before ICL 'can generate a responsible legal regime for holding military commanders responsible for recklessly perpetrating a war crime through an autonomous system'.[893]

All human operators involved in processes and procedures relating to an AWS will be aware of the risks inherent in the deployment of such systems. Take, for example, a case in which an AWS is deployed despite the fact that, at the time of designing/programming, the *level of risk* was perceived to be high (i.e. that it might involve violations of IHL).[894] Excluding the category of *dolus eventualis* would mean a well-covered process of disregard for international values and, eventually, a decriminalisation of IHL. Indeed, in the *Lubanga Case* the Trial Chamber, although rejecting the category of *dolus eventualis*, argued that Article 30 (2)(b) ICC Statute and the corresponding awareness that a consequence 'will occur in the ordinary course of events' 'involves consideration of the concepts of "possibility" and "probability", which are inherent to the notions of "risk" and "danger"'.[895]

Every mission on the battlefield has always involved risk, for many reasons, but until today the use of a weapon and/or the decision to release a munition has been a matter for human judgement, even under the most severe conditions on the battlefield. R. Arkin, although promising that AWS will be more

[891] *Situation in the Central African Republic in the Case of the Prosecutor v Jean-Pierre Bemba Gombo* [2009] ICC ICC-01/05-01/08 362–363. Sharing the understanding of the Court, cf Sliedregt (n 816) 48; Mark A Summers, 'The Problem of Risk in International Criminal Law' (2014) 13 *Washington University Global Studies Law Review* 667, 682.

[892] *Situation in the Democratic Republic of the Congo in the Case of the Prosecutor v Thomas Lubango Dyilo* [2012] ICC- Trial Chamber I ICC-01/04-01/06-2842 para 1011; *Situation in the Democratic Republic of the Congo in the Case of the Prosecutor v Thomas Lubango Dyilo* [2004] ICC-0104-0106 5 (ICC – Appeals Chamber Judgment on the appeal of Mr Thomas Lubanga Dyilo against his conviction) paras 447–448.

[893] Ohlin (n 829) 3.

[894] Liivoja, Leins and McCormack (n 22) 615.

[895] *Situation in the Democratic Republic of the Congo in the Case of the Prosecutor v Thomas Lubango Dyilo* [2012] (n 892) para 1012. This consideration was strongly criticised by Judge A. Fulford in his Separate Opinion (cf ibid para 15; *Situation in the Democratic Republic of the Congo in the Case of the Prosecutor v Thomas Lubango Dyilo* [2004] (n 892) paras 447–449).

efficient than human soldiers, does not exclude the possibility of 'errors' and 'malfunctions' on the part of those systems.[896] Moreover, the author, when explaining the different mechanisms of autonomous control (e.g. constraints such as the EA and the EG), highlights how those mechanisms are dependent on human programming and can, on occasion, cause system failures.[897] Thus, the use of AWS will probably demand more care and attention to the levels of *substantial risk* attendant upon a mission, as the Pre-Trial Chamber argued in the *Lubanga Case*.[898] Another argument is that AWS are not liable because of their lack of moral agency (see the IMT Judgement and Article 25 ICC Statute) in spite of all their new capabilities.[899] Therefore, if an 'accident' is caused by human failure, that is, a failure to take into account potential unlawful consequences, it is reasonable to demand these operators' accountability.[900]

A circumscribed reading of paragraph 2(b) Article 30 would cover only those exceptional situations in which an AWS is used with full intent to commit a war crime. However, according to Gregory McNeal's research, in the operations undertaken by US armed forces in Afghanistan and Iraq, 22 per cent of collateral damage was due to weapons malfunction.[901] McNeal offers no information about the causes of such malfunctions or how the United States has addressed such problems in terms of reparation to the victims. Notwithstanding, what is crucially important is – if the category of *dolus eventualis* is to be excluded from Article 30 ICC Statute – to note that cases involving AWS that are poorly designed, programmed or maintained,

896 Arkin, *Governing Lethal Behavior in Autonomous Robots* (n 34) 41.

897 The author gives the example presented by Sagan. First, a case in which ROE are excessively tight, preventing a commander's operating, second, one in which ROE are so lax that AWS could be used to effect undesirable outcomes. Although the author comments on these two possibilities involving human-written ROE, he fails to explain how the same failures could be avoided by an AWS when all the rules of the mechanisms of control depend on human input. ibid 86–87.

898 *Prosecutor v Thomas Lubanga Dylo* (n 881) para 353.

899 Bartosz Brozek and Marek Jakubiec, 'On the Legal Responsibility of Autonomous Machines' (2017) 25 *Artificial Intelligence Law* 293, s 4; Roff (n 56) 356–357; Cass (n 144) 1057.

900 Asaro, 'Robots and Responsibility from a Legal Perspective' (n 56).

901 The author does not give a definition of malfunction. However, the author explains that when collateral damage happens, in spite of the probabilities given by methodologies such as CDEM, '70% of the time it was due to failed "positive identification" of a target, 22% of the time it was attributable to weapons malfunction, and a mere 8% of the time it was attributable to proportionality balancing'. cf Gregory S McNeal, 'The U.S. Practice of Collateral Damage Estimation and Mitigation' (*Law and Public Policy*, 11 May 2011) <\https://gsmcneal.com/the-u-s-practice-of-collateral-damage-estimation-and-mitigation/>; Neta C Crawford, *Accountability for Killing: Moral Responsibility for Collateral Damage in America's Post-9/11 Wars* (Oxford University Press 2013) 354–356.

and that, as a result, cause 'accidents' on the battlefield, will have no standing in the International Courts. It is true that states can investigate further domestically and decide for themselves whether there is any form of liability to address (Article 1 ICC Statute). However, the values of the international community would be threatened. As Summer rightly notes, ICL should be receptive to crimes that were, at best, 'a risk at the time the defendants entered into plans'.[902]

5.3.2.4 Making Designers, Programmers and Technicians Accountable

The capability of AWS to operate without the need for human intervention can create a challenge because some machines' actions would not fit into any form of international accountability. A. Matthias, among others, is keen to demonstrate that designers, programmers and any other persons involved in the production and set-up stages of an AWS cannot be held accountable for unlawful unforeseeable outcomes. These outcomes fall outside the sphere of human control, giving place to a 'responsibility gap'.[903] This problem has been addressed before, but it is useful to recall some factors that are frequently forgotten.

First, machine learning algorithms are, by definition, less predictable; certainly, they import new risks into the battlespace. However, states have all along insisted on the importance of legal reviews, and of being kept fully informed as to how AWS will operate. Unpredictability can cause violations of IHL that may put the interests of the home state in jeopardy, an eventuality that prompts states to rigorously test the systems. Another factor deserving serious consideration is the 'responsibility gap' that, ostensibly, could exempt states from their duty to respect and to ensure respect for IHL 'in all circumstances' (Article 1 API).[904] Concomitantly, the 'gap' absolves states from responsibility deriving from the international convention that the state is 'responsible for all acts committed by persons forming part of its armed forces' (Article 91 API).

Second, some may argue that many of the personnel involved with manufacturing and programming AWS do not belong to the armed forces of a state and are, therefore, not subject to International Law but 'to domestic tort law'.[905] Apart from this, it is already difficult to make manufacturers and programmers accountable even in a state's internal forum.[906]

[902] Summers (n 891) 690.
[903] Matthias (n 16) 180; Hammond (n 764) 667.
[904] Seixas-Nunes (n 240).
[905] Cass (n 144) 1049.
[906] ibid 1049–1052.

Both considerations are certainly true, as is demonstrated by the *William Holbrook v Prodomax Automation Ltd Case*.[907] Notwithstanding, each AWS, apart from its general design, will be programmed for a specific mission that a commander has entrusted to the system (open delegation). As is clear, and as Arkin underlines, it is inconceivable that an AWS could be deployed without specific ROE and other constraints designed and programmed into it to equip it for a particular mission.[908] Thus designers, programmers, manufacturers and technicians should indeed be seen as part of the military structure (the *integration model*).[909] In this situation, they would be obliged to conduct themselves in accordance with International Law, as would any other participant in the hostilities, as well as being subject to domestic law.

The integration model might not apply in all situations. Very well-established military manufacturers are private, can work for several different states and can hardly be considered part of any one state's armed forces.[910] This fact, however, should not be seen as an obstacle that excludes designers, programmers and manufacturers from compliance with international values. Article 1 ICC Statute (The Court) provides:

> An International Criminal Court ('the Court') is hereby established. It shall be a permanent institution and shall have the power to exercise its jurisdiction over persons for the most serious crimes of international concern, as referred to in this Statute, and shall be complementary to national criminal jurisdictions. The jurisdiction and functioning of the Court shall be governed by the provisions of this Statute.

The ICC Statute establishes the principle of complementarity between international and domestic jurisdiction regarding the international criminalisation of the individual.[911] Thus, there is nothing precluding designers, manufacturers and programmers from being prosecuted at national level by the state

907 *William Holbrook v Prodomax Automation Ltd* (n 852).

908 Arkin, *Governing Lethal Behavior in Autonomous Robots* (n 34) 37–38.

909 US Army War College, *Army Force Management Model. 2019–2020 How the Army Runs* (The United States Army War College 2020) 1–2, 3–2 <https://publications.armywarcollege.edu/pubs/3736.pdf>; US Army War College, *Army Force Management Model. 2015–2016 How the Army Runs* (The United States Army War College 2015) 4–9 <https://apps.dtic.mil/sti/pdfs/AD1001713.pdf>.

910 'AIRBUS' <www.airbus.com/defence.html>; 'BAE Systems' <www.baesystems.com/en/home>; 'Boeing Defense' <www.boeing.com/defense/>.

911 Sliedregt (n 816) 11; William A Schabas, *The International Criminal Court: A Commentary on the Rome Statute* (Oxford University Press 2010) 57–62; Mark Klamberg, 'Article 1: The Court' in Mark klamberg (ed), *Commentary on the Law of the International Criminal Court* (Torkel Opsahl Academic EPublisher 2017).

deploying the AWS 'unless the State is unwilling or unable genuinely to carry out the investigation or prosecution' (Article 17(1)(a) ICC Statute). In this case, ICC will consider the case admissible.[912]

Finally, a third and more contentious issue is that some authors discredit 'negligent behaviour' as an appropriate legal category in cases involving AWS. Crootof argues that although lethal accidents do happen in the battlespace, 'if an individual could be held criminally liable for negligent actions in war and if her commander would be indirectly liable for negligence, every commander would be a war criminal'.[913] Apart from this, admitting negligence would undermine the moral legitimacy of IHL because it would be immoral to hold someone accountable 'for [the] independent and unpredictable actions of autonomous weapons systems'.[914]

It is important to prevent the introduction of any 'scapegoating mechanism' that might be applied to AWS operatives, individuals who could not have been in any position to know of potentially illegal outcomes. However, first, it would be illogical, legally, for there not to be a mechanism to hold individuals accountable for proven conscious behaviour in the design, manufacture, programming or maintenance of an AWS; second, the standard to be applied to AWS' operators should not be that of 'negligence', since such is excluded from Article 30 ICC Statute, but that of *dolus eventualis*.

Crootof argues, it is proper that ICL should prohibit certain behaviours and, therefore, that it does not apply in situations involving AWS since they have no moral agency. Instead, the author suggests, Tort Law (which is focused 'on wrong-doing, fault, and regulation of valuable but sometimes dangerous activities') would facilitate state responsibility by 'delimitating what violations are sufficiently serious to require reparation' and make the state liable for full reparation in cases of injury caused by AWS.[915] What is suggested in this work is to a certain extent parallel. Intentional unlawful conducts involving substantial risk should be forbidden because of the dependence of AWS on their programmers. It has to be said that Crootof's argument relates to unlawful unpredictable outcomes caused by AWS, however, and it would be deficient to qualify as an 'injury' what should be classed as a 'war crime' caused by human failure.

912 Mohamed Abdou and Mark Klamberg, 'Article 17: Issues of Admissibility' in Mark klamberg (ed), *Commentary on the Law of the International Criminal Court* (Torkel Opsahl Academic EPublisher 2017) 206–207. As a clear example, the ICC in the *Katanga Case* had the opportunity to explain the criteria of 'unwilling' and 'unable' for a state to carry out an investigation or a prosecution. *Prosecutor v Germain Katanga and Mathieu Ngdjolo Chui* [2009] Appeal Chamber ICC-01/04-01/07 OA 8 paras 70, 76–78.

913 Crootof, 'War Torts: Accountability for Autonomous Weapons' (n 316) 1384.

914 ibid; Hammond (n 764) 667.

915 Crootof, 'War Torts: Accountability for Autonomous Weapons' (n 316) 1388.

In this regard, it does not seem quite right to follow Daniel Hammond, who considers that the 'negligence approach' has its flaws. The argument is based on the nature of machine learning algorithms. According to the author, as 'AWS learn from their experiences and surroundings, their decisions would depend on much more than the original programming'.[916] However, it cannot be forgotten that the *algorithm for the mission* will 'learn' from the battlespace in order to perform the mission that has been delegated to it. The intentionality is human and an AWS operates towards a human-determined end, the mission.

Generally speaking, mens rea is a problem well covered by the majority of legal systems (i.e. civil and common law systems) but, as the ICTY states in the *Tadić Case*, national legislation can only be taken into consideration if there exists a common understanding of a given concept as reflecting International Customary Law.[917] It is also true that the 'subjective element' will always be an object of debate and reasoning for the International Court, and it will not always be a straightforward interpretation task, as exemplified by the *Genocide Convention Case*, but the *Lubanga Case* has opened a door for *dolus eventualis* to be considered.[918] Thus, if these situations were not covered by ICL, it could well lead to a true 'responsibility vacuum'. The rules of Precaution and the fundamental values of IHL should not be compromised or allowed to become the object of recklessness, nor should a state be held responsible for an 'international wrongful act' when it is not its author.

The foregoing analysis and inclusion of the category of *dolus eventualis* cannot proceed without snags. The possible requirements of measuring and quantifying the level of risk are currently the subject of lively debate.[919] Notwithstanding, if a human operator is aware and conscious of a substantial risk of IHL violation, yet disregards that possibility, he/she should be held accountable because the consequences were so predictable; this was pointed out by the Pre-trial Chamber in the *Lubanga Case*. In the final analysis, an important philosophical question should be put to International Criminal Lawyers: taking into account the nature and features of AWS, should the failure to acknowledge a substantial risk be as blameworthy as the decision to commit a crime? The two situations obviously invoke different levels of culpability, but is it not the case that an outcome caused by *dolus eventualis* has the same causal link as an outcome caused by *dolus directus* conduct, that is, a disregard for the most

916 Hammond (n 764) 667.

917 *Prosecutor v Duško Tadić* (n 874) paras 225–226.

918 *ICJ, Case Concerning Application of the Convention on the Prevention and Punishment of the Crime of Genocide (Bosnia and Herzegovina v Serbia and Montenegro)* paras 187–188.

919 Summers (n 891) 680–681.

important international values?[920] Looking at the concerns expressed by different states at the GGE in connection with accountability, those party to the ICC Statute could exercise their powers to suggest an amendment to the ICC Statute as envisaged in Article 121 of the Statute.

Finally, in the case of an AWS 'accident' it can be difficult to envisage and to identify one, specific, guilty individual. An AWS can be dependent on multiple programmers, designers and technicians or on multiple systems. As Helen Nissenbaum states, 'instead of identifying a single individual whose faulty actions have caused the injuries, we find that we must systematically unravel a messy web of interrelated causes and decisions'.[921] Authors such as Christopher Toscano and Ohlin have contemplated this possibility. According to Toscano:

> Nothing in AWS technology alters the law or negates accountability, whether HRL or IHL. In fact, the role of humans will remain the key factor in this entire debate. Designers, developers, human operators and managers, regulators, and policymakers will set constraints on AWS actions.[922]

The author recognises an inherent uncertainty about the adaptive capabilities of AWS, but holds the view that if any IHL violation were to occur, the military commander, on grounds of the fulfilment of both the objective and subjective elements of a crime, would be held accountable because he/she ordered the system into action.[923] This understanding has already been examined: a military commander's liability cannot be seen as a 'wide umbrella' accommodating 'everyone's' faults. What is troubling is the fact that the author does not seem to recognise that AWS errors might be caused by the unpredictability of the algorithms themselves. The author recognises that tests and evaluations should be undertaken in order to 'minimize the probability and consequence of failures that could lead to unintended engagements or to loss of control of the system'.[924] However, despite this recognition, the author appears to be in favour of applying a legal solution that is, in fact, appropriate only in the case of IHL violations caused by human operators.

In conclusion, AWS may bring a set of new risks to the battlefield. In their case, the concept of human intervention once a system has been activated does not apply. Although a commander may be responsible for the design of the mission, the tasks of re-adapting or re-manufacturing, programming and maintaining the systems may be well out of his/her sphere of control and authority.

920 Fletcher (n 876) 1034–1035.
921 Nissenbaum (n 766) 30.
922 Toscano (n 514) 224.
923 ibid 238.
924 ibid 208; US Department of Defense, 'DoD 3000.09. Autonomy in Weapon Systems' (n 7) 3, 9.

Such situations require not only that the category of *dolus eventualis* be accepted by future international jurisprudence, following the *Lubanga Case*, but also that it should not be assumed that a commander's remit is a 'wide umbrella' protecting operatives – who are responsible for the safe operation of an AWS – about the minutiae of whose performance he/she could not be expected to know.

5.3.3 *The Liability of Military Commanders for IHL Violations Caused by AWS*

Command responsibility, as it stands today, is the product of a long historical process characterised by judicial creationism: the judge enlarging the spectrum of situations covered by the law and applying previous principles and decisions to the circumstances of each new case. This practice is particularly evident in the jurisprudence of the ICTY and ICTR. The ICC Statute, however, changed this situation. Article 28 of the ICC Statute contains a detailed 'definition of the doctrine of superior responsibility for the purpose of the Court which should reduce the need – and opportunity – for judges to develop that doctrine beyond its statutory framework'. This created two forms of liability: one for military commanders (Article 28 (a) ICC Statute) and another for non-military superiors (Article 28 (b) ICC Statute).[925]

In approaching the issue of commanders' responsibility for crimes committed by means of AWS, it is important to remember *DoD 3000.09*. According to the Directive the United States must develop all the tests and evaluations (T&E) to:

> certify that operators of autonomous and semi-autonomous systems have been trained in systems capabilities, doctrine, and TTPs [tactics, techniques, and procedures] in order to exercise appropriate levels of human judgement in the use of force and employ systems with appropriate care and in accordance with the law of war, applicable treaties, weapon system safety rules, and applicable ROE.[926]

Two points here are of particular interest. First, the Directive explicitly states that 'operators of autonomous systems should be trained in systems capabilities', which seems to reinforce the relationship between a commander and all operators under his/her authority. If designers, manufacturers and technicians are to be included as part of the armed forces, all will be included within the military commander's responsibility for the actions of 'the forces under his or her effective

925 Guenael Mettraux, *The Law of Command Responsibility* (Oxford University Press 2009) 12, 25.

926 US Department of Defense, 'DoD 3000.09. Autonomy in Weapon Systems' (n 7) 10–11, para 8(a)(5).

command and control, or effective authority and control' (Article 28 (a) ICC Statute). This question is not itself new. The new element will be that if it is agreed that designers and programmers are part of the armed forces, and if *dolus eventualis* is accepted as a possible criminal state of mind, command responsibility is significantly extended. In short, this is to establish command responsibility for *crimes* and *accidents* caused by his/her subordinates. There are reasons, indeed, to describe this form of liability as *sui generis*, since the responsibility of the commander is *for omission* of his/her duty to supervise and prevent the occurrence of any IHL violations by the forces under his/her control.[927] Thus, in this view, command responsibility is regarded as a *legal umbrella* that covers all necessary procedures in order to ensure that an AWS will perform in accordance with IHL.

The second point of interest is the stipulation that training should be given to prepare operators to 'exercise appropriate levels of human judgement in the use of force', and that human operators shall 'employ systems with appropriate care and in accordance with the law of war [. . .] and applicable ROE'. This seems to reinforce another aspect of a commander's responsibility, that is, to ensure that particular precaution and attention should be given at the moment the *algorithm for the mission* is being designed and programmed. By this, apparently, the responsibility is laid upon commanders to take all precautionary measures in order to avoid 'errors' that might be made by the system. This is, therefore, not a matter of command responsibility but of the individual responsibility of the commander (Articles 25 and 30 ICC Statute; Article 57 API).

5.3.3.1 The Military Commander and Responsibility for Crimes and Accidents Committed by His/Her Subordinates

Article 28 of the ICC Statute stipulates that:

> In addition to other grounds of criminal responsibility under this Statute for crimes within the jurisdiction of the Court:
>
> (a) a military commander or person effectively acting as a military commander shall be criminally responsible for crimes within the

927 *Prosecutor v Halilović (Halilović Trial Judgment)* [2005] ICTY IT-01-48-T 78. *Situation in the Central African Republic in the Case of the Prosecutor v Jean-Pierre Bemba Gombo* (n 891) Decision on the Confirmation of Charges, 15 June 2009, para 405; Schabas (n 827) 457; International Committee of the Red Cross, *Commentary on the Additional Protocols of 8 June 1977 to the Geneva Conventions of 12 August 1949* (n 347) Article 86, paras 3524, 3526); Kai Ambos, 'Superior Responsibility' in Antonio Cassese, Paola Gaeta and John RWD Jones (eds), *The Rome Statute of the International Criminal Court: A Commentary*, vol 3 (Oxford University Press 2002) 851 <https://papers.ssrn.com/sol3/papers.cfm?abstract_id=1972189>; Meloni (n 827) 173.

jurisdiction of the Court committed by forces under his or her effective command and control, or effective authority and control as the case may be, as a result of his or her failure to exercise control properly over such forces, where:

(i) that military commander or person either knew or, owing to the circumstances at the time, should have known that the forces were committing or about to commit such crimes; and

(ii) that military commander or person failed to take all necessary and reasonable measures within his or her power to prevent or repress their commission or to submit the matter to the competent authorities for investigation and prosecution.

(b) With respect to superior and subordinate relationships not described in paragraph (a), a superior shall be criminally responsible for crimes within the jurisdiction of the Court committed by subordinates under his or her effective authority and control, as a result of his or her failure to exercise control properly over such subordinates, where:

(i) the superior either knew, or consciously disregarded information which clearly indicated, that the subordinates were committing or about to commit such crimes;

(ii) the crimes concerned activities that were within the effective responsibility and control of the superior; and

(iii) the superior failed to take all necessary and reasonable measures within his or her power to prevent or repress their commission or to submit the matter to the competent authorities for investigation and prosecution.

The wording of Article 28 ICC Statute reflects in some part the requirements long established by the ad hoc Tribunals. In this connection, the *Celebici Case* was the first to reason extensively on command responsibility. Until the *Celebici Case*, the accused would be charged and convicted for direct participation in crimes under Article 7(1) of the ICTY Statute.[928] However, in the *Celebici Case*, the Trial Chamber formulated two *material elements* (the existence of a *superior–subordinate relationship* and the *failure of the commander to take all necessary measures to prevent* a crime or to punish the perpetrator) and *one subjective element* (the superior *knew or had reason to know* that the subordinate was about to commit, or had intentionally committed a crime).[929] Another material element was then added afterwards by the Trial Chamber in the *Orić Case*: a *base crime* committed by the subordinate.[930]

928 Sliedregt (n 816) 186–187.

929 *Prosecutor v Mucić et al (Celebici Case)* [1998] ICTY (Trial Chamber) IT-96-21-A para 346.

930 *Prosecutor v Naser Oric* [2006] ICTY IT-03-68-T 294.

The introduction of Article 28 ICC Statute added a fourth material element, stipulating that the crime committed by the subordinate must be the '*result* of his or her [the military commander's] failure to exercise control properly over his/her forces'.[931] Not without dispute, especially by the ICTY jurisprudence, this requirement has been interpreted by scholars, and by more recent jurisprudence, as one of the elements to be proved for the purpose of establishing the liability of a military commander.[932] Indeed, in the *Bemba Gombo Case*, the first in which the ICC applied Article 28 ICC Statute, the record states:

> [T]he Chamber therefore considers that the *chapeau* of article 28(a) of the Statute includes an element of causality between a superior's dereliction of duty and the underlying crimes. This interpretation is consistent with the principle of strict construction mirrored in article 22(2) of the Statute which, as a part of the principle *nullum crimen sine lege*, compels the Chamber to interpret this provision strictly.[933]

This leads immediately to the conclusion that a commander cannot be held accountable for processes that are out of his/her control. Thus, in the case of 'malfunctions' and 'errors' for which a chain of causation *human action/outcome* is impossible to establish, no human can be considered liable, let alone the commander. The commander is, therefore, only responsible for crimes committed or about to be committed by his forces (e.g. AWS 'accidents').

In order to complete our summary of the challenges attendant upon command responsibility, an analysis of the final two requirements is called for – *the base crime* and the *command–subordinate relationship* – both vitally important to the deployment of AWS. Looking first at the *base crime*, the first

931 *Situation in the Central African Republic in the Case of the Prosecutor v Jean-Pierre Bemba Gombo* (n 891) para 420 (our emphasis). It is interesting to note the opposite decision in the *Halilović Case*. The trial Chamber found that the requirement of causality 'would change the basis of command responsibility for failure or prevent or punish to the extent that it would practically *require involvement on the part of the commander in the crime* his subordinates committed, thus altering the very nature of the liability imposed under Article 7(3)'. *Prosecutor v Halilović (Halilović Trial Judgment)* (n 927) para 78.

932 Meloni (n 827) 175–176; Schabas (n 827) 461–462; Volker Nerlich, 'Superior Responsibility under Article 28 ICC Statute' (2007) 5 *Journal of International criminal Justice* 665, 673. The ICC in the *Bemba Case* states that 'the Chamber acknowledges that the ad hoc Tribunals do not recognise causality as an element of superior responsibility. However, unlike article 28(a) of the Statute, the relevant provisions on superior responsibility in the Statutes of the ad hoc Tribunals do not expressly require such an element.' *Situation in the Central African Republic in the Case of the Prosecutor v Jean-Pierre Bemba Gombo* (n 891) para 423, footnote 550.

933 *Situation in the Central African Republic in the Case of the Prosecutor v Jean-Pierre Bemba Gombo* (n 891) para 405.

material element common to any form of responsibility is the commission of *a crime* within the jurisdiction of an international Court.[934] Command responsibility has always been differentiated by two types of crime: the *principal crime*, which is committed by subordinates, and the *secondary crime*, which is committed by the military commander in that he/she is found to have failed to prevent the commission of a war crime.[935] The Trial Chamber in the *Orić Case* clearly expresses this understanding, noting that 'the superior cannot be considered as if he had committed the crime himself, but merely for his neglect of duty with regard to crimes committed by subordinates'.[936] The second constitutive element of command responsibility is the existence of a *subordinate relationship* between the military commander and those who committed a criminal offence – a vertical chain of command – such that the accused (as commander) should be able to control his/her *forces* and to prevent or punish their crimes.[937]

Article 28 ICC Statute reflects ICTY jurisprudence, especially insofar as the superior–subordinate relationship includes a military commander (*de jure commander*) or a person 'effectively acting as military commander' (*de facto commander*).[938] The traditional understanding is that the vertical chain of command is, by its nature, an *interpersonal* relationship.[939] The function of the doctrine of commander responsibility would be to establish a criminal link between two individuals: a superior who fails to exercise control and a subordinate who commits a war crime.[940] It would have to be ascertained whether, through his/her role or position, the commander had established a personal relationship of subordination vis-à-vis the perpetrator and that this had been acknowledged by both parties.[941]

As the Appeal Chamber upheld in the *Celebici Case*:

> [T]he necessity to prove that the perpetrator was the 'subordinate' of the accused, [...] mean[s] that the relevant accused is, by virtue of his or her position, senior in some sort of formal or informal hierarchy to the

934 Nerlich (n 932) 668.

935 *Prosecutor v Halilović (Halilović Trial Judgment)* (n 927) para 54; Meloni (n 827) 134–138.

936 *Prosecutor v Naser Oric* (n 930) para 293.

937 Mettraux (n 925) 137.

938 Sliedregt (n 816) 198; Meloni (n 827) 155; *Prosecutor v Limaj* [2005] ICTY IT-03-66-T 515, 522; *Situation in the Central African Republic in the Case of the Prosecutor v Jean-Pierre Bemba Gombo* (n 891) 408–409.

939 Mettraux (n 925) 138.

940 ibid 139; Sliedregt (n 816) 184; Chengeta, 'Accountability Gap: Autonomous Weapon Systems and Modes of Responsibility in International Law' (n 20) 32.

941 The superior has to be aware of his position of authority in relation to any other individual and to have voluntarily accepted that position of authority. Mettraux (n 925) 139.

> perpetrator. *The ability to exercise effective control, in the sense of a material power to prevent or punish, [. . .] will almost invariably not be satisfied unless such a relationship of subordination exists.* [our emphasis][942]

Considering the aforementioned discussion, two very important conclusions have to be drawn. First, in situations where human operators involved with the operationality of an AWS (designers, programmers and technicians, among others), commit a crime with *dolus directus* or *eventualis*, that will be the principal crime. Due to the complexity of the operations in which an AWS might be involved, or the complexity of the *algorithm for the mission*, it would be unrealistic to expect the commander to know all the circumstances pertaining to a crime caused by AWS. In order to hold a commander accountable there must be information available that puts him/her on notice of violations of IHL that may be caused by the AWS and also, as stated by the Appeal Chamber in the *Delalic Case*, the 'material ability to prevent or to punish criminal conduct'.[943]

The second conclusion refers to the nature of the relationship of those involved, which must be interpersonal. In this regard, some authors seem to suggest another theoretical approach. In their view, since the functions of human soldiers are increasingly 'delegated' to autonomous weapon systems, 'it may become appropriate *de lege ferenda* to extend the commander's supervisory duty, *mutatis mutandis* and *by analogy*, also to autonomous weapon systems operating under his direct command and control'.[944] This is indeed

942 *Prosecutor v Mucić et al (Celebici Case)* (n 929) 303. Using the same line of argument in the *Nahimana Appeal Case*, the ICTR has reiterated the *Celebici Case* in the following terms: 'the Appeals Chamber has already recalled the elements which must be proved in order to establish superior responsibility. It has also pointed out that civilian leaders need not be vested with prerogatives similar to those of military commanders in order to incur such responsibility under Article 6(3) of the Statute: it suffices that the superior had effective control of his subordinates, that is, that he had the material capacity to prevent or punish the criminal conduct of subordinates. For the same reasons, it does not have to be established that the civilian superior was vested with "excessive powers" similar to those of public authorities. Moreover, the Appeals Chamber cannot accept the argument that superior responsibility under Article 6(3) of the Statute requires a direct and individualized superior-subordinate relationship.' *Prosecutor v Nahimana* [2007] Appeals Chamber ICTR-99-52-A para 785.

943 Solis (n 590) 392; Sliedregt (n 816) 45–52; *Prosecutor v Delalic et al* [2001] Appeals Chamber IT-95-14-T 300–302. The same reasoning was followed by the ICC in the *Bemba Case*, stating that the commander is to be held accountable if he/she 'fails to take all necessary and reasonable measures within his or her power to prevent or repress their commission, or to submit the matter to the competent authorities for investigation and prosecution'. *Situation in the Central African Republic in the Case of the Prosecutor v Jean-Pierre Bemba Gombo* (n 891) 415, 422.

944 Nikolas Sturchler and Nicholas Siegrist, 'A "Compliance-Based" Approach to Autonomous Weapon Systems' (*EJIL: Talk!*, 1 December 2017) <www.ejiltalk.org/a-compliance-based-approach-to-autonomous-weapon-systems/>.

a perspective worth considering, but there is a question over what is to be understood by an AWS 'operating under his direct command and control'.

Combining the jurisprudence in the *Orić* and *Celebici Cases* and adapting it to apply in a situation involving AWS, *it would be necessary to establish a link of subordination proper to moral agents*. It is the interpersonal structure of command that is unlikely to be reflected in the relation between a commander and an AWS. Aside from the problem of the AWS' status, thoroughly debated in Chapters 2 and 3, extending 'command responsibility' analogically to AWS might import problems rather than provide solutions.

1. The analogy could be accepted only if 'control' were to mean that the commander was responsible for the design and programming of the *algorithm for the mission* or for intervening to deactivate the system. However, for that matter the applicable framework would involve the individual accountability of the commander (Articles 25 and 30 ICC Statute) and not his/her command responsibility (Article 28 ICC Statute).
2. The analogy could work only if one were to accept the existence of a subordinate relationship between the commander and the designers, programmers and technicians. However, it is for the most part understood that AWS are instruments of war, not partners in a military subordinate relationship.
3. An analogy could be accepted as regards the 'information available' to the commander and his power to intervene. The commander, according to the information available, could exercise 'direct command and control' over the system. But this possibility would be at odds with the very definition of AWS.

Autonomous Weapon Systems, for a start, not only do not require but do not *allow for* human intervention. Second, the whole purpose of an AWS is that the system should be able to make sense of data, in both quantity and quality, much faster, more efficiently and accurately than a human operator.[945] This will be the case to the extent that any information about or explanation of the system's functionality (the logic, algorithm structure and planned consequences that inform the decision-making process) will only be available ex ante. At the same time ex post data (rationale, specific circumstances, weighting factors) will be available only after the outcome

945 Simon Chignard and Soizic Penicaud, '"With Great Power Comes Great Responsibility": Keeping Public Sector Algorithms Accountable' (*Le blog d'Etalab*, 11 June 2019) 2 <www.academia.edu/39576180/_With_great_power_comes_great_responsibility_keeping_public_sector_algorithms_accountable?email_work_card=title>.

has been produced.[946] Thus, in spite of all the disadvantages, it might be possible to argue that commanders could be held entirely responsible for all the operations under Article 25 (1) ICC Statute for individual accountability, but certainly not that the stipulations set out in Article 28 apply.

Such an understanding is that chosen by Ohlin. The author argues that the crimes that would give most cause for concern would be those that involved a military commander who had failed, recklessly, to exercise proper control. With reference to the jurisprudence of the ICTY in the Tadić *Case*, the author seeks to establish a parallel between the *Joint Criminal Enterprise* (hereinafter JCE), dubbed JCE III and enshrined in Article 25(3)(a) ICC Statute. This provides that:

> In accordance with this Statute, a person shall be criminally responsible and liable for punishment for a crime within the jurisdiction of the Court if that person:
>
> (a) commits such a crime, whether as an individual, jointly with another or through another person, regardless of whether that other person is criminally responsible.

This provision recognises a form of indirect perpetration (commission through another person) that happens when one person manifestly exercises control over others who carry out the crime. The AWS would in that case be comparable to 'cogs' so integrated in the 'wheel of common design' that it is impossible to individualise guilt for each and every outcome.[947]

Applying this doctrine to the deployment of AWS, there would be a person or persons regarded as the *indirect perpetrator(s)*, the person(s) who gives the order, usually the intellectual force behind the operation, and another regarded as the *direct perpetrator*, the person who executes the crime, in this case an AWS. In order to address the problem of AWS as direct perpetrator, Ohlin elaborates the pragmatic concept – the *combatant's stance* – which recalls the legal theory of Chopra and White with regard to artificial agents.[948] The concept of *combatant's stance* reflects the simple fact that if a combatant were to engage with an AWS, that AWS would be indistinguishable, functionally, from any other combatant. The AWS would be a *combatant simpliciter*, and the military commander the indirect perpetrator who would act, not through another person, *but through an* AWS.[949]

946 Wachter, Mittelstadt and Floridi, 'Why a Right to Explanation of Automated Decision-Making Does Not Exist in the General Data Protection Regulation' (n 821) 6.
947 Ohlin (n 829) 4.
948 Chopra and White (n 528) 170.
949 Ohlin (n 829) 16–20.

The solution for which Ohlin argues is an appealing one, but it fails to address some important issues that have, it is argued, been addressed in this section. The suggestion that an AWS 'is more than a mere machine' falls into a grey area but, at the same time, a framework in which a person is used as an instrument to commit a crime is not relevant. Moreover, any form of JCE requires an interpersonal relationship of subordination which could hardly apply in a situation involving the deployment of an AWS.

Returning to the responsibilities of the commander under Article 28(a)(ii) ICC Statute, the commander has the *duty to submit the case to the competent authorities*. As the Pre-Trial Chamber argued in the *Bemba Gombo Case*, this duty arises after the commission of crimes in cases where commanders lacked the ability to sanction their forces.[950] Indeed, it also emerges when there is no possible chance of *changeability of the outcome*. The duty of *constant care* will demand that not only military commanders but also all who are involved in military operations become more closely engaged with the performance of AWS.[951] If a human operative is found not to have performed his/her duties satisfactorily, the commander has a duty to notify the authorities and, equally, he/she is obliged to report to the authorities if the performance of an AWS calls into question the predictability of the system (Article 28 (a)(ii); (b)(iii) ICC Statute). The measures that the authorities take towards reparation in such a case might constitute an argument for state responsibility.

To conclude, commanders can only be held accountable when they have the power to effectively control the acts of their subordinates, who may include designers, manufacturers and technicians, and in so doing avoid the commission of a crime carried out with *dolus directus* or *dolus eventualis*. The individual responsibility of the commander for matters of precaution is another matter.

5.3.3.2 Military Commanders' Responsibility to Take All Precautionary Measures

The Trial Chamber in the *Orić Case* upheld the claim:

> The capacity to sign orders is an indicator of effective control, provided that the signature on a document is not purely formal or merely aimed at

950 *Situation in the Central African Republic in the Case of the Prosecutor v Jean-Pierre Bemba Gombo* (n 891) 440.

951 Noam Neuman, 'A Precautionary Tale: The Theory and Practice of Precaution in Attack' (2018) 48 *IsraelYearbook on Human Rights* 19, 28; William Boothby, *The Law of Targeting* (Oxford University Press 2012) 72.

> implementing a decision made by others, but that the *indicated power is supported by the substance of the document.*[952]

From this statement it can be concluded that the orders given by the commander circumscribe his/her responsibility. Although the capacity to sign orders is addressed in *Orić* as matter of command responsibility, it can also provide information as to what the precautionary measures taken by the commander were before deploying the AWS, also contributing to the matter of the commander's mens rea since orders might well reflect the commander's intentionality.[953] The matter under scrutiny in this section is that of 'accidents' that happen as a result of the commander's failure in responsibility, and much of what was covered in the earlier discussion of 'accidents' has direct application here.

As Nissenbaum clearly explains, a standard of care, a higher level of precaution as regards autonomous systems, would be a truer reflection of how a system of accountability should be regulated. Such a standard would offer a way of distinguishing between those 'accidents' that are the result of a failure in duty of control on the part of the commander and those that occur in spite of a programmer's or designer's best efforts.[954] Therefore, for the foreseeable future, it is assumed that preventive and precautionary measures will fall within the remit of commanders as part of their responsibility for planning how and when to deploy an AWS on the battlefield.[955] The disadvantage here, one that is common in 'accidents', is that *dolus eventualis* is not applicable to commanders acting in their *individual capacity*.

5.4 STATE RESPONSIBILITY FOR UNPREDICTABLE VIOLATIONS OF IHL

The problem of accountability is certainly one of the most widely discussed topics in debates about AWS and, for some, it has proved impossible to resolve.[956] In previous sections it has been shown that there is no reason that would justify an *accountability vacuum* as far as 'accidents' are concerned.[957]

952 *Prosecutor v Naser Oric* (n 930) para 312 (our emphasis).

953 The difficulties that documentary evidence might entail are not ignored here, for example the lack of documentary evidence in the case of unlawful orders. This issue will be addressed in Section 5.4.5. Carsten Stahn, *A Critical Introduction to International Criminal Law* (Cambridge University Press 2019) 337.

954 Nissenbaum (n 766) 37.

955 Anderson, Reisner and Waxman (n 786) 404.

956 Henderson, Keane and Liddy (n 19) 357.

957 Anderson and Waxman, 'Debating Autonomous Weapon Systems, Their Ethics, and Their Regulation Under International Law' (n 4) 1099.

Two situations, however, remain to be examined: situations involving 'malfunctions' and, above all, those involving 'errors'.

Both 'malfunctions' and 'errors' cover situations in which violations of IHL occur for unexpected and unpredictable reasons. In the former case, for example, the system causes civilian damage because of a hardware malfunction that prevents mission completion. In the latter, the system overrides the *algorithm for the mission*, in the process creating a 'new mission'. It is clear that the distinction between 'malfunctions' and 'errors' can be difficult to make, and this difficulty is not without consequences.

Example: on the 2 of May 2011, Osama bin Laden was captured during the campaign code-named *Operation Neptune's Spear*. It was a difficult and lengthy operation owing to the fact that bin Laden was thought to be hiding in a remote region between Afghanistan and Pakistan. However, instead, it transpired that he was hidden in Pakistan, in Abbottabad, north of Islamabad.[958] This operation involved data orientation, deliberations about the correct method of attack and consideration of the rules of Distinction and Proportionality, among other factors. As an exercise, imagining that *Operation Neptune's Spear* was a task entrusted to an AWS, the capture of bin Laden would have been the aim of the *algorithm for the mission*. Restricting the enquiry only to questions about identification of the target, three scenarios deserve attention:

a) At the moment of the attack, due to the dusty environment, the *sensors* do not work properly, and X is targeted instead of bin Laden;
b) Bin Laden and X present similar biometric data and the system selects X instead of O, bin Laden;
c) The system, when optimising the best course of action, receives new data from the battlefield, misinterprets it, and selects X as the target instead of bin Laden.

In none of these situations is bin Laden targeted. Clearly (a) is a case of hardware malfunction, (b) is a case of poor design and (c) is a case of 'error'. If X were also a legitimate target, his/her targeting would not be a violation of IHL; but if X is a civilian, a member of the community of Abbottabad, accountability problems immediately arise. Indeed, the only possibility of avoiding this confusion would be to have access to the 'facts' considered by the algorithm for situation management, in order to distinguish one situation from another.

As will be explained further on, no satisfactory solution has been found to deal with unlawful unpredictable outcomes caused by AWS, aside from the

958 Neuman (n 951) 19; David A Wallace, 'Operation Neptune's Spear: The Lawful Killing of Osama Bin Laden' (2012) 45 *Israel Law Review* 367–369.

call for a ban. Although a number of authors have pointed out the 'unpredictable nature' of AWS, few have considered situations in which systems invert the plans with which they were originally programmed. The aim of the following sections is to provide some clarification on this matter and highlight the problems that should be addressed.

5.4.1 *Systems' Errors: Legal Implications*

Paul Scharre provides a considerable list of recent systems' malfunctions and errors that caused terrible consequences, such as the US Patriot system that shot down two British Aircraft in 2003,[959] Air France Flight 447 in 2009,[960] the Fukushima Daiichi meltdown in 2011[961] and the 2015 AC-130 bombing in Afghanistan,[962] among others.[963] The most important point to note is the author's observation that 'malfunctions, errors, accidents are inevitable'.[964] The four examples just mentioned could have been prevented if the risks involved had been anticipated, but they were not. Human fault? The design, programming and maintenance of these systems are entrusted to highly qualified engineers and technicians who aim, surely, for safety and predictability. Nonetheless, despite the high level of expertise on the part of engineers and programmers, in all the aforementioned examples the undesired outcomes resulted from a combination of systems.[965] The examples given by the author, however important, do not

959 Michael Smith, 'US "Clears" Crew Who Shot Down Tornado' *The Telegraph* (London, 16 July 2003) <www.telegraph.co.uk/news/worldnews/northamerica/usa/1436240/US-clears-crew-who-shot-down-Tornado.html>.

960 William Langewiesche, 'The Human Factor' (*Vanity Fair*, 2014) <www.vanityfair.com/news/business/2014/10/air-france-flight-447-crash>.

961 'Fukushima Daiichi Accident' (*World Nuclear Association*, June 2018) <www.world-nuclear.org/information-library/safety-and-security/safety-of-plants/fukushima-accident.aspx>.

962 Alissa J Rubin, 'Airstrike Hits Doctors without Borders Hospital in Afghanistan' *The New York Times* (3 October 2015) <www.nytimes.com/2015/10/04/world/asia/afghanistan-bombing-hospital-doctors-without-borders-kunduz.html>; US Central Command, 'Investigation Report of the Airstrike on the Medecins Sans Frontieres I Doctors without Borders Trauma Center in Kunduz, Afghanistan on 3 October 2015' (2015) USFOR-A CDR 52–56 <http://fpp.cc/wp-content/uploads/01.-AR-15-6-Inv-Rpt-Doctors-Without-Borders-3-Oct-15_CLEAR.pdf>.

963 Scharre, 'Autonomous Weapons and Operational Risk: Ethical Autonomy Project' (n 230) 14, 29–30; Cole (n 843); Oliver Wyman, 'Why the Use of Drones Still Faces Big Regulatory Hurdles' (*Forbes*, 10 September 2018) <www.forbes.com/sites/oliverwyman/2018/09/10/why-the-use-of-drones-still-faces-big-regulatory-hurdles/#4f24e83c1c0d>.

964 Scharre, 'Autonomous Weapons and Operational Risk: Ethical Autonomy Project' (n 230) 13–15.

965 ibid 14–37. DoD 3000.09 addresses this problem by insisting on the responsibility of 'certify-[ing] that operators of autonomous and semi-autonomous weapon systems have been trained in system capabilities, doctrines and TTPs in order to exercise appropriate levels of human judgement in the use of force and employ systems with appropriate care in accordance with

involve AWS, and only one of the situations, the AC-130 bombing, happened in the context of an armed conflict and was due to human fault. AWS will be a radical innovation and bring their own challenges.

The whole discussion about AWS is still shrouded in the mystery of the unknown. If, in the past few years, the world has witnessed a tremendous breakthrough in AI in different areas of technology, as far as we are concerned now, the operationality of AWS will always be dependent on whether technology can indeed deliver weapon systems able to operate lawfully and autonomously throughout the OOSA Loop. The future remains unknown, but the onus is on scientists and robotics engineers to ensure that it does.

Despite the uncertainty of the future, it is important to make a clear distinction between 'malfunctions' and 'errors', because they will be subject to different forms of liability. As some authors have had occasion to argue, 'malfunctions' and 'errors' can cause death, injury and damage to protected persons or objects. However, as the authors note, while a case of 'malfunction' 'is unlikely to be considered a war crime as it is highly unlikely to [be] seen as a wilful act', in the case of 'errors in programming [...] [the flaws] should be identified and resolved'.[966] Regarding the second category, the authors distinguish 'accidents' attributed to a human operator from those due to a failure in program operationality, observing that 'if the error cannot be resolved, or if the error is known but ignored, then further use of the AWS may breach Article 57 API'.[967]

Scharre proposes instead an analysis of 'damage potential', alluding to 'the amount of damage an autonomous system could do, if it failed to perform appropriately, before a human operator could take corrective action'.[968] However, this concept raises some problems. First, the commander is only responsible for *measuring foreseeable risks* associated with a mission and choosing, accordingly, the appropriate weapon system to meet the situation (Article 57(2)(a)(ii) API). Second, if machine learning algorithms can cause unlawful unpredictable outcomes, it will be impossible to know in advance what damage and how much of it they might cause if there were no human supervisor overseeing their operations.

The aforementioned authors seem to imply that 'errors' should be met with the same legal response as 'malfunctions', that is, no one can be held accountable owing to the absence of human intentionality. Following that argument, the solution offered is to acknowledge that a 'responsibility gap' is inevitable in

the law of war [...] and applicable ROE'. US Department of Defense, 'DoD 3000.09. Autonomy in Weapon Systems' (n 7) 11.

966 Henderson, Keane and Liddy (n 19) 361.

967 ibid 361–362.

968 Scharre, 'Autonomous Weapons and Operational Risk: Ethical Autonomy Project' (n 230) 10.

cases of 'error'. This, it is argued here, would lead progressively to a *decriminalisation of contraventions of IHL*. Simply put, under the present accountability mechanisms 'errors' resulting in breaches of IHL would not be covered. This situation cannot be accepted.

In light of the aforementioned discussion, it is evident that individual accountability cannot be applied when 'errors' occur, because there is no link of causation between the outcome and a human operator. This should not lull international lawyers into accepting easily that 'errors' are merely unavoidable hazards of warfare technology. Such an argument would indeed be a reason to support a total ban as the only legal mechanism to deal with AWS. As Anderson and Waxman have argued:

> Treating criminal liability as the presumptive mechanism of accountability risks blocking the development of machine systems that might, if successful, overall reduce actual harms on the battlefield [...] simply in order to satisfy an *a priori* principle that there will always be a human to hold accountable.[969]

The recognised danger of a 'responsibility gap' should not persuade international lawyers to stretch the principle of individual accountability to cover unlawful situations that are unforeseeable as far as commanders or human operators are concerned.[970]

The insistence of some authors on individual accountability has led to postulations that are full of contradictions. Thurnher, for example, regards the rules of targeting as inherently subjective, noting that 'it is the human, not the autonomous system, who makes the qualitative and subjective choices'.[971] If human operators were able to provide all the answers in advance, it would indeed be fair to conclude that 'operational commanders would be wise to plan carefully for how and when to use such systems', and commanders could be held fully responsible.[972] However, the author, at the end, also argues that 'machine learning computers will be likely help future LARs attain the necessary behaviours to make critical decisions about whether and how to engage and destroy a target'.[973]

969 Anderson and Waxman, 'Debating Autonomous Weapon Systems, Their Ethics, and Their Regulation Under International Law' (n 4) 1111; Dickinson (n 471) 4.

970 Crootof, 'War Torts: Accountability for Autonomous Weapons' (n 316) 1364.

971 Thurnher, 'Examining Autonomous Weapon Systems from a Law of Armed Conflict Perspective' (n 23).

972 Jeffrey S Thurnher, 'Legal Implications of Fully Autonomous Targeting' [2012] *Joint Force Quarterly* 77, 82 <http://ndupress.ndu.edu/Portals/68/Documents/jfq/jfq-67/JFQ-67_77-84_Thurnher.pdf>.

973 ibid 79; Thurnher, 'Examining Autonomous Weapon Systems from a Law of Armed Conflict Perspective' (n 23) 220.

With the introduction of machine learning algorithms, the situation is radically different: the risk in deploying an AWS is that the system might not perform according to its design.[974] As the 2018 GGE Final Report clearly states:

> Technical characteristics related to self-learning (without externally-fed training data) and self-evolution (without human design inputs) have to be further studied. Similarly, attempting to define a general threshold level of autonomy based on technical criteria alone could pose difficulty as autonomy is a spectrum, its understanding changes with shifts in the technology frontier, and different functions of a weapon system could have different degrees of autonomy.[975]

The Report, however, does not take a clear position regarding accountability. It states that 'in crafting potential policy measures, emerging technologies in the area of lethal autonomous weapons systems should not be anthropomorphized', and that 'human responsibility for decisions on the use of weapons systems must be retained [. . .] across the entire life cycle of the weapons system'.[976] It is urgent, therefore, to look at the specificities of machine learning algorithms, trying not to apply the traditional paradigm of deterministic algorithms or the model of individual accountability.

Machine learning algorithms will present their own problems, such as statistical bias, inappropriate data training or focus and misinterpretation of reality, and operators will not have any opportunity to intervene once the AWS is activated. In situations in which human operators are not able to deactivate the system in due time, the breaches of IHL caused by the system's errors will have to be legally addressed.

5.4.2 *State Responsibility for AWS' Unpredictable Outcomes: Difficulties*

At the CCW GGE meetings in Geneva, Brazil, the European Union, the Holy See, Norway, Pakistan, Sri Lanka, Switzerland and Turkey delegates have expressed their concern regarding accountability problems, citing the difficulty, if not impossibility, of enforcing state responsibility. In contrast, states in support of the development of AWS have not raised accountability as a major concern. Looking, for example, at *DoD 3000.09*, no direct

974 Scharre, 'Autonomous Weapons and Operational Risk: Ethical Autonomy Project' (n 230) 8.

975 'Report of the 2018 Session of the Group of Governmental Experts on Emerging Technologies in the Area of Lethal Autonomous Weapons Systems' (n 193) para 27 (C).

976 ibid para 26 (C) and (H).

guidelines are given except that the Under Secretary of Defence for Policy shall provide 'oversight responsibility' regarding the development and employment of AWS. At the same time, it is acknowledged that AWS will operate without the level of predictability characteristic of deterministic algorithms.[977]

A more conservative position is taken by the United Kingdom. The United Kingdom is not supportive of a pre-emptive ban of AWS, but it rejects, at the same time, the possibility of authorising attacks without human permission or supervision, stating that 'predictability is likely to be inversely proportional to mission and environmental complexity'.[978] Thus, fully autonomous systems shall not be deployed by the United Kingdom and 'civil and criminal accountability may lie with the government, the chain of command and with the last person to issue the command authorising a specific activity'.[979] Aside from the ambiguity of UK policy, *JDP 0–30.2* considers governmental responsibility for weapons systems to be a possible form of liability.

A legal answer to the problem of how to deal with unpredictable outcomes will always be complex. Delegations to the CCW have suggested different approaches, among them are a legally binding instrument, a political declaration or more 'clarity on the implementation of existing obligations under international law, in particular IHL'.[980] The problems associated with a new treaty or a political declaration have already been addressed, but the third suggestion deserves attention. Machine learning algorithms clearly represent a challenge on a double front, not only in terms of accountability but also, first and foremost, in terms of transparency. The term 'transparency' needs to be applied not only to the specific way algorithms operate (within the 'black box') but also to how states develop their practices and policies in relation to the acquisition and development of new technology of warfare.[981] Both dimensions are relevant to the debate about how AWS would actually operate in the battlespace.

Article 36 API imposes on states the obligation to carry out legal reviews of new weapons, but states' practices are very far from being consistent.[982] Canada, among others, raised this concern at the 2018 GGE, stating that it is 'supportive

977 US Department of Defense, 'DoD 3000.09. Autonomy in Weapon Systems' (n 7) 9.

978 UK Ministry of Defence, 'Joint Doctrine Publication 0–30.2 Unmanned Aircraft Systems' (n 7) para 4.19.

979 ibid 41–43, paras 4.14, 4.16, 4.18.

980 'Report of the 2018 Session of the Group of Governmental Experts on Emerging Technologies in the Area of Lethal Autonomous Weapons Systems' (n 193) para 33. cf Chapter 2, Sections 2.1 and 2.4.1 regarding the viability of legally binding declarations.

981 Scharre, 'Autonomous Weapons and Operational Risk: Ethical Autonomy Project' (n 230) 15.

982 Anderson and Waxman, 'Debating Autonomous Weapon Systems, Their Ethics, and Their Regulation Under International Law' (n 4) 1103.

of developing key transparency and confidence-building measures'.[983] However, as many scholars rightly note, secrecy has ever been a feature in weapons development and, although Article 36 API is considered by many to be customary law, it is hard to find support for an obligation to release legal reviews publicly.[984] Furthermore, the difficulties are not exclusively confined to the 'legal reviews'; there is also the difficulty of gaining access to the data, that is, to the post-assessment. There are different ways of dealing with investigations of IHL violations. As far as UK policy is concerned, investigations have become independent from the military chain of command to ensure that they are genuinely independent. The United States has adopted a contrasting policy, basing the investigations on command orientation and, as Sean Watts observes, are not immune to 'command abuse'.[985]

Many other difficulties could be pointed out, such as the fact that not all the states have signed up to API and APII, and there is the well-known discrepancy regarding the content and interpretation of international customary rules, among other disparities. But all these challenges can be interpreted as arguments in support of the proposition that state responsibility is the appropriate form of international liability for unlawful unpredictable outcomes.[986]

5.4.3 *Features of International State Responsibility: Attribution and Causation*

As the International Law Commission (hereinafter ILC) notes, it is important to distinguish the primary rules – rules that define the international

983 '2018 Canada Opening Statement at GGE on Lethal Autonomous Weapons' (2018) <www.unog.ch/80256EDD006B8954/(httpAssets)/86612887B010EB33C12582720056F0C6/$file/2018_LAWSGeneralExchange_Canada.pdf>. Expressing similar concerns, 2019 Brazil Statement, Brazil, '2019 GGE on Laws. Challenges to IHL Item 5(a)' (n 267). cf The 2019 Netherlands Statement '2019 Statement of the Netherlands. Agenda Item 5(a): An Exploration of the Potential Challenges Posed by Emerging Technologies in the Area of Lethal Autonomous Weapons Systems to International Humanitarian Law' (2019) <www.unog.ch/80256EDD006B8954/(httpAssets)/A2E0497EE93C232AC12583CB0037813B/$file/5a+NL+Statement+Legal+Challenges-final.pdf>; '2019 EU Statement. 5(a) An Exploration of the Potential Challenges Posed by Emerging Technologies in the Area of Lethal Autonomous Weapons Systems to International Humanitarian Law' (n 15).

984 Knuckey (n 324) 176–177; Deeks, Lubell and Murray (n 25) 19–20.

985 Interview with Sean Watts and Charles Garraway, 'Accountability for Violations of the Laws of Armed Conflict: A Duty to Investigate and Prosecute?' (Chatham House 5 July 2012) 4–5 <www.chathamhouse.org/sites/default/files/public/Research/International%20Law/050712summary.pdf>. For the specific situation of the United Kingdom, Mark Lattimer, 'The Duty to Investigate Civilian Deaths in Armed Conflict: Looking Beyond Criminal Investigations' (*EJIL: Talk!*, 22 October 2018) <www.ejiltalk.org/the-duty-to-investigate-civilian-deaths-in-armed-conflict-looking-beyond-criminal-investigations/>.

986 Hammond (n 764) 668–669.

obligations of a state – from secondary rules that are activated when one of those rules is violated. Thus, the term 'international responsibility' refers to the new set of *obligations* that arise as a result of the international wrongful act.[987]

While the secondary rules concern themselves with the framework for state responsibility, the primary rules of IHL, concerning the substantive obligations of a state, have long been explicitly set out in IHL treaties and in Customary International Law, and are continually in a state of further development.[988] As regards some of the most relevant rules, the Fourth Hague Convention decrees that a belligerent party 'shall be responsible for all the acts committed by persons forming part of its armed forces' (Article 3). Common Article 1 of the Geneva Conventions outlines the general duty of states party to treaties to 'respect and to ensure respect' for those treaties '*in all circumstances*'. Additional Protocol I includes an identical duty and repeats the Hague formulation concerning responsibility for breaches (Articles 1(1) and 91 API), by referring to a 'party to the conflict'. The ICJ, in the 1996 *Advisory Opinion*, stated that 'many rules of humanitarian law applicable in armed conflict are so fundamental' that those 'rules are to be observed by all States whether or not they have ratified the Conventions that contain them'.[989] Further, in the *Nicaragua v United States of America Case*, the Court took the opportunity of clarifying that the obligation of states to respect and ensure respect for IHL 'in all circumstances' derives 'not only from the Conventions themselves, but from the general principles of humanitarian law to which the Conventions merely give specific expression'.[990]

The duty of states to ensure respect for IHL 'in all circumstances' is in accordance with the doctrine of state responsibility, that is, that the rules of IHL must be respected both by its organs and by other entities under its jurisdiction, especially when acting on behalf of a state in the territory of another state; otherwise the state will be held accountable for unlawful acts on the battlefield.[991]

A state is a corporate entity that necessarily implements rights and obligations in the international arena through its agents. The ILC has, therefore, developed a *theory of agency* (and not a *causal analysis*) according to which an

987 Gill and Fleck (n 146) 560, para 30.01.

988 James Crawford, *State Responsibility: The General Part* (Cambridge University Press 2014) 65.

989 *ICJ*, *Legality of the Threat or Use of Nuclear Weapons, Advisory Opinion* (n 673) para 79.

990 *Military and Paramilitary Activities in and against Nicaragua (Nicaragua v United States of America)* (n 241) para 220.

991 Laurence Boisson Chazournes and Luigi Condorelli, 'Common Article 1of the Geneva Conventions Revisited: Protecting Collective Interests' (2000) 82 *International Review of the Red Cross* 67, 72.

international wrongful act is attributed to the state if it arises from acts or omissions of its organs and agents.[992] Accordingly, in the *Armed Activities Case*, the Court stated that '*according to a well-established rule of customary rule of a customary nature, [. . .] a party to an armed conflict shall be responsible for all acts by persons forming part of its armed forces*'.[993]

It is clear that only actors with recognised International Legal Personality can be held internationally responsible. AWS cannot be regarded as members of states' armed forces, let alone be held accountable for 'errors', for the reasons outlined in this study.

However, this begs the question of what the status of an AWS should be when it causes unlawful unpredictable results. States act through individuals and organs which *act* on behalf of the state. If an 'error' occurs, however, an AWS may produce outcomes that are beyond human control. Should the deploying state be held responsible for 'erroneous outcomes'? According to India, at the 2019 GGE Meeting, '*the responsibility for development, production and deployment of LAWS, should rest with the concerned State. The associated risks as regards proliferation (including to non-state actors) need to be covered under dual responsibility of the State and by strengthening international regulations*'.[994]

This is the type of situation that prompts international experts to call the attention of the public to the risks of developing ever more sophisticated AI, and scholars to argue that it has become problematic to establish a distinction between combatants and weapons.[995] The argument that there is a risk that the distinction between combatants and weapons may become blurred is to assume that AWS will outgrow their status as 'weapons systems' and acquire some level of 'agency'. Such an eventuality would contradict the arguments developed throughout this work.[996] However, the argument that AWS are just more sophisticated instruments of warfare than those encountered to date raises the problem of whether 'errors' are to be regarded as 'malfunctions', despite the risk of

992 Castellanos-Jankiewicz (n 836) 18; Crawford, *The International Law Commission's Articles on State Responsibility: Introduction, Text and Commentaries* (n 697) 91–92; James Crawford (ed), *Brownlie's Principles of Public International Law* (8th edn, Oxford University Press 2012) 542; Crawford, *State Responsibility. The General Part* (n 988) 113.

993 *Case Concerning Armed Activities on the Territory of the Congo (Democratic Republic of Congo v Uganda)* (ICJ, Judgement) 214.

994 '2019 Statement by India: An Exploration of the Potential Challenges Posed by Emerging Technologies in the Area of Lethal Autonomous Weapons Systems to International Humanitarian Law' (n 657).

995 Chapter 1, Section 1.2 and Chapter 2, Section 2.4.1.

996 Chapter 3, Section 3.5.1.

decriminalising IHL violations.[997] Thus, the important question to ask is: how can 'error' be attributed to the deploying state?

5.4.4 *Responsibility of the State for* Unlawful Unpredictable Outcomes

It is at this point that the state responsibility framework deserves serious attention and research. A combined reading of Articles 1, 85 and 91 API and Article 25 (4) ICC Statute makes it clear that the state is *the* international actor responsible for ensuring respect for IHL. As Major Kathleen McKendrick argues, 'first and foremost, [. . .] states must take responsibility for applying their already existing international legal and ethical obligations in the development and use of new weapons technology'.[998]

This section will be divided in two. First, an analysis of arguments advanced by scholars for state responsibility and, second, a proposed new model to clarify the function of state responsibility for the deployment of AWS.

5.4.4.1 Arguments Advanced by Scholars for State Responsibility

Among the views of those authors who discuss state responsibility can be found opposing interpretations of its significance. Keely Cass, although agreeing that it is appropriate that the state be held accountable, finds that 'holding [the State] solely responsible is problematic because reparation may not be seen as a harsh enough punishment'.[999] At the other extreme, Hammond argues that the state is not only responsible for legal reviews of weapons destined to be used in armed conflict, it is also the beneficiary of the use of those weapons. Therefore, if the state takes the decision to employ weapons such as AWS, it 'renders the State more culpable in a moral sense than the producers, who merely respond to a demand created by the State, and the commanders who merely carry out the policy decision the State made'.[1000] Notwithstanding these considerations, neither author offers any further development or analysis of the questions attendant upon their premises. These include: why should errors be attributed to states? And, if errors are not attributed to states, what is the appropriate form of liability?

997 Crootof, 'War Torts: Accountability for Autonomous Weapons' (n 316) 1366.

998 McKendrick (n 143); cf Chengeta, 'Accountability Gap: Autonomous Weapon Systems and Modes of Responsibility in International Law' (n 20) 4.

999 Cass (n 144) 1053–1054.

1000 Hammond (n 764) 652, 670.

Crootof offers a detailed consideration of state responsibility for unpredictable results. The author argues that the state is in the best position to ensure that AWS will comply with IHL. States will have 'pockets deep enough to adequately compensate victims for their actions' and, finally, state responsibility may operate as a more effective restraint vis-à-vis violations of IHL than any form of individual liability.[1001] The author proposes the concept of 'war torts' to identify 'serious violations of international humanitarian law that give rise to state responsibility'.[1002] This concept would include all types of violations of IHL 'where there is fault, regardless of whether or not there is also guilt', in this guaranteeing a mechanism of 'compensatory "corrective justice"'.[1003]

A different approach is suggested by Laura Dickinson. Dickinson proposes, as a way of addressing the problem of unlawful unpredictable results, a system of 'administrative accountability'.[1004] This is characterised by the fact that it is a domestic, rather than an international process, and could also serve as an intermediate stage. Dickinson recognises the potential limits of her proposal, noting that it will depend entirely on states' willingness to comply, but argues for a domestic mechanism that

> [i]ncludes multiple administrative procedures, inquiries, sanctions, and reforms [...] [and] can be deployed within the military or the administrative State more broadly to respond to an incident in which violations of IHL/LOAC may have occurred.[1005]

Looking at the obligations that customary and conventional international law impose on states to ensure respect for, and prevent any violation of IHL, and at the mechanisms of administrative accountability that some countries already have (e.g. Australia, Canada, the United Kingdom and the United States), Dickinson believes this would be an appropriate process to provide oversight of violations of IHL which would not, in her account, constitute war crimes.[1006]

Considering the deployment of AWS in the battlespace, Crootof and Dickinson agree that states, as the main actors in the international community, are at the same time the agents primarily responsible for the protection of their values. Nonetheless, it seems, on the one hand, that Crootof does not take into account the mechanisms already available to implement state

1001 Crootof, 'War Torts: Accountability for Autonomous Weapons' (n 316) 1390.
1002 ibid 1386; Dickinson (n 471) 24.
1003 Crootof, 'War Torts: Accountability for Autonomous Weapons' (n 316) 1386–1387.
1004 Dickinson (n 471) 5.
1005 ibid.
1006 ibid 34–41.

responsibility and, on the other hand, Dickinson seems to overlook the importance of international values and the obligations enshrined in the ARSIWA. Also, as the author explains, 'administrative accountability' would work only in the case of lesser violations of IHL.[1007]

5.4.4.2 Understanding State Responsibility for Errors

The way in which state responsibility works can be described as a 'process by which international law establishes whether the conduct of a natural person or other such intermediary can be considered an "act of state", and thus be capable of giving rise to state responsibility'.[1008] The ARSIWA stipulates that 'every internationally wrongful act of a State entails the international responsibility of that State' (Article 1 ARSIWA) and, according to Article 2 ARSIWA, a state engages in an 'internationally wrongful act' when 'its conduct, consisting of an act or omission: (a) is attributable to the State under international law; and (b) constitutes a breach of an international obligation of the State'. Attribution of a wrongful act to the state requires that the act (action or omission) is considered an act of the state: this argument is supported because the state is responsible for the conduct of all the organs, instrumentalities and officials which form part of its organisation.[1009]

Article 4 ARSIWA enshrines one of the hard-core norms for the doctrine of attribution, establishing that the state is responsible for the actions of its organs. Article 4 provides:

1. The conduct of any state organ shall be considered an act of that state under international law, whether the organ exercises legislative, executive, judicial or any other functions, whatever position it holds in the

1007 The author does not explicitly define 'administrative accountability' but rather prefers to explain its features. In order to provide some more clarity to the term, 'administrative accountability' should be understood as 'all forms of investigations that are not criminal in nature. They are one way in which States can fulfil their obligation to suppress violations of international humanitarian law. This type of proceeding can be conducted prior to, in parallel with, or following a criminal investigation, in order to, for example, address issues linked to an incident that are not of a criminal, but of an operational, policy, or disciplinary character.' cf Noam Lubell, Jelena Pejic and Claire Simmons, 'Guidelines on Investigating Violations of International Humanitarian Law: Law, Policy and Good Practice' (The Geneva Academy of International Humanitarian Law and Human Rights, International Committee of the Red Cross September 2019) paras 158–159 <www.icrc.org/en/document/guidelines-investigating-violations-ihl-law-policy-and-good-practice>; Dickinson (n 471) 26.

1008 Crawford, *State Responsibility: The General Part* (n 988) 113.

1009 Crawford, *The International Law Commission's Articles on State Responsibility: Introduction, Text and Commentaries* (n 697) 92–93, paras 5–7; Lewis, Blum and Modirzadeh (n 441) 52–54.

organisation of the state, and whatever its character as an organ of the central government or of a territorial unit of the state.

2. An organ includes any person or entity which has that status in accordance with the internal law of the state.

As James Crawford explains, executive governments are the most direct manifestation of state authority and 'the most obvious executive manifestations are the actions of the armed forces, which in the context of armed conflict are in all cases attributable to and engage the international responsibility of the state in question'.[1010]

The precise implication of the direct link between the acts of the armed forces and state responsibility is that all acts of designing, programming, maintaining and activating/deactivating an AWS are attributable, *ratione materiae*, to the deploying state. This is true even when the organs of a state act in excess of authority or contrary to orders or instructions received. As the ICJ found, in the *Armed Activities Case*, 'it is furthermore irrelevant for the attribution of their conduct to Uganda whether the UPDF personnel acted contrary to the instructions given or exceeded their authority'.[1011]

In light of the aforementioned discussion, AWS cannot be considered 'organs of the State'; nonetheless the decision to activate/deactivate a system belongs to an organ of the state. Furthermore, the decision whether or not to deploy an AWS is also the decision of a state's government: as *JDP 0–30.2* stipulates, governmental responsibility is to be considered to apply as far as military activities are concerned.[1012]

The nature of AWS is not to be underestimated. Anderson and Waxman point out that what makes a system autonomous is not only a matter of whether a human operator would *realistically* be able to override the AWS once activated, but the capability of the system to select among possible targets.[1013] The fact that an AWS *should* operate in accordance with the *algorithm for the mission* does not preclude the possibility of its selecting an unlawful course of action due to some unexpected circumstances. As can be readily understood, programmers and designers cannot program what they

1010 Crawford, *State Responsibility: The General Part* (n 988) 116–119.

1011 ibid 136–140; *Case Concerning Armed Activities on the Territory of the Congo (Democratic Republic of Congo v Uganda)* (n 993) paras 214, 243; Crawford, *The International Law Commission's Articles on State Responsibility: Introduction, Text and Commentaries* (n 697) 106–107, paras 3–4.

1012 UK Ministry of Defence, 'Joint Doctrine Publication 0–30.2 Unmanned Aircraft Systems' (n 7) para 4.19.

1013 Anderson and Waxman, 'Debating Autonomous Weapon Systems, Their Ethics, and Their Regulation Under International Law' (n 4) 1100–1101 (our emphasis).

do not know. As such, 'malfunctions' and 'errors' can simply happen and collide with the correct operationality of the *algorithm for the mission*.[1014]

'Malfunctions' may happen however diligent the state or human operators have been and do not, therefore, qualify as wilful acts that merit some form of accountability. This situation does not exclude situations of compensation ex gratia, without any admission of responsibility. The *Iran Flight 655 Case* exemplifies this perfectly.[1015]

The same cannot be said for cases of 'error'. In deploying AWS, a state opts not to have human operators on-the-loop, accepting that the operation will be dependent on the discretionary capabilities of an AWS to select and adapt to optimise the outcome. The fact that these new systems of warfare can cause unlawful unpredictable outcomes does not exclude states from their responsibility. As the ICJ argues in the 1996 Advisory Opinion, IHL applies to '*all forms of warfare and to all kinds of weapons*, those of the past, those of the present *and those of the future*'.[1016]

The nature of AWS, being systems whose operations will be based on probabilities and not on pre-given deterministic data, demands an implicit acceptance of the inherent risk that devolves upon the deploying state, a point which the Indian Government highlighted at the GGE.[1017] The challenge that 'foreseeability' presents is that it requires the state to accept responsibility for a less direct or proximate act than it has had to do before.[1018] It is possible to

1014 Henderson, Keane and Liddy (n 19) 361.

1015 A settlement agreement was obtained between Iran and the United States with the latter stating that 'the United States recognised the aerial accident of 3 July 1988 as a terrible human tragedy and expressed regret over the loss of lives caused by the incident', agreeing to pay compensation directly to the victims but not the Iranian Government since, according to the United States, both countries were involved in an armed conflict and IHL should be the applicable law. Crawford, *The International Law Commission's Articles on State Responsibility: Introduction, Text and Commentaries* (n 697) 222, paras 11–12; 'Case Concerning the Aerial Incident of 3 July 1988 (Flight 655) Memorial Submitted by the Islamic Republic of Iran' (1990) paras 4.73–4.74 <www.icj-cij.org/en/case/79/written-proceedings>; 'Case Concerning the Aerial Incident of 3 July 1988 (Flight 655) Preliminary Objections Submitted by the United States of America' (1991) 4–5 <www.icj-cij.org/files/case-related/79/6639.pdf>; 'Settlement Agreement, Arrangement Amiable. Case Concerning the Aerial Incident 3 July 1988' (1996) 1 and para 6 <www.icj-cij.org/files/case-related/79/11131.pdf>.

1016 *ICJ, Advisory Opinion on the Legality of the Threat and Use of Nuclear Weapons, Judgment* (n 265) para 86.

1017 '2019 Statement by India: An Exploration of the Potential Challenges Posed by Emerging Technologies in the Area of Lethal Autonomous Weapons Systems to International Humanitarian Law' (n 657). With a similar perspective, cf '2019 EU Statement. 5(a) An Exploration of the Potential Challenges Posed by Emerging Technologies in the Area of Lethal Autonomous Weapons Systems to International Humanitarian Law' (n 15).

1018 Emmanuela-Chiara Gillard, 'Some Reflections on the "Incidental Harm" Side of Proportionality Assessments' (2018) 51 *Vanderbilt Journal of Transnational Law* 827, 833; Crawford, *State Responsibility: The General Part* (n 988) 492–494.

find many arguments in support of responsibility for 'indirect' or 'remote' damage. It could be argued that Article 31 ARSIWA would not, in fact, admit such an interpretation.

Article 31 provides that:

1. The responsible state is under an obligation to make full reparation for the injury caused by the internationally wrongful act.
2. 'Injury' includes any damage, whether material or moral, caused by the internationally wrongful act of a state.

It could be argued that Article 31 (2) demands a sufficient or direct causal link between the unlawful consequences and the wrongful act.[1019] However, that is not the interpretation of the ILC commentary on state responsibility. Indeed, the ILC commentary states that causality is necessary, but it is not a sufficient condition to warrant reparation since, in some situations, the criterion of 'foreseeability' can be used. An example is the *Nauliaa Case* in which the Tribunal considered that the idea of 'foreseeability', as a source of state responsibility, can arise either in terms of the scope of the actions or in terms 'of the extent of damages to be said to flow from an attributed act'.[1020] On another front, the Arms Trade Treaty also establishes 'the responsibility of all States, in accordance with their respective international obligations, to effectively regulate the international trade in conventional arms, and to prevent their diversion, as well as the primary responsibility of all States in establishing and implementing their respective national control systems'.[1021] In light of these considerations, states' responsibility for weaponry under their control is clearly recognised.

Some authors have suggested that the 'law should not impose a higher standard upon an AWS simply because of the absence of a human operator'.[1022] Since machine algorithms learn by trial and error, damages, should they occur, 'should be identified and resolved [...] [and] if the error cannot be resolved, or if the error is known but ignored, then further use of the AWS may breach Article 57 [API]'.[1023] This line of argument is, nonetheless, difficult to accept.

1019 David D Caron, 'The Basis of Responsibility: Attribution and Other Transubstantive Rules of State Responsibility' in Richard B Lillich and Daniel B Magraw (eds), *The Iran United States Claims Tribunal: Its Contribution to the Law of State Responsibility* (Brill–Nijhoff 1998) 153–154.

1020 ibid 154, footnote 136; Crawford, *State Responsibility: The General Part* (n 988) 204–205, para 10.

1021 'Arms Trade Treaty' (n 631) principles.

1022 Henderson, Keane and Liddy (n 19) 361.

1023 ibid 361–362.

The fact that one situation 'error' could be accepted without legal consequences is to compare situations involving 'error' with those involving 'malfunctions'. The reality, however, is that cases of 'error' are in a different category and should be addressed accordingly. First, from the IHL point of view, customary and conventional international law demand that states respect IHL 'in all circumstances' (Article 1 API), and this norm does not seem to take into account any kind of exception.[1024] Second, Conventional Law and Jurisprudence have already recognised that level of state responsibility. Third, although 'errors' cannot be considered 'war crimes', the interpretation of Article 8 Rome Statute ('War Crimes') is that the seriousness of an IHL violation should not be scaled according to the number of unlawful acts or the number of victims.[1025] The fact that an AWS might violate IHL as a result of its own 'error' should be considered serious enough, in itself, to compel due consideration. Simply put, 'errors', in spite of their remoteness, must be deemed to confer direct liability onto the deploying state.

The aforementioned observations should not be a surprise or seem too broad or vague. In 2010, NATO issued a set of non-binding guidelines, establishing mechanisms of compensation for civilian casualties in Afghanistan.[1026] These guidelines consist of nine paragraphs, of which four are particularly relevant here:

1. Promptly acknowledge combat-related cases of civilian casualties or damage to civilian property.
2. Continue to fully implement the ISAF standard operating procedures for investigating possible cases of civilian casualties, or damage to civilian property, and endeavour to provide the necessary information to the ISAF civilian casualties tracking cell.

[...]

8. The system by which payments are determined and made should be as simple, prompt and transparent as possible and involve the affected civilians at all points feasible.
9. Payments are made, and in-kind assistance is provided without reference to the question of legal liability.

1024 ICRC, 'Rule 144: Ensuring Respect for International Humanitarian Law Erga Omnes' (*IHL Database Customary IHL*, 2005) <https://ihl-databases.icrc.org/customary-ihl/eng/docs/v1_rul_rule144>.

1025 Schabas (n 827) 226.

1026 'NATO Nations Approve Civilian Casualty Guidelines' <www.nato.int/cps/en/natohq/official_texts_65114.htm?selectedLocale=en>.

Although these guidelines do not specifically refer to situations involving 'error', they do not exclude response and compensation for malfunctions of weapons. In fact, the importance of Paragraph 2 is precisely that it establishes a duty to investigate violations of IHL committed 'by [the State's] nationals or armed forces'; this is considered to be a well-established norm of International Customary Law.[1027] Rule 158 of the ICRC Study states:

> States must investigate war crimes allegedly committed by their nationals or armed forces, or on their territory, and, if appropriate, prosecute the suspects. They must also investigate other war crimes over which they have jurisdiction and, if appropriate, prosecute the suspects.

The fact that AWS, as such, are listed in none of the categories enumerated in Rule 158 does not absolve the state from a duty to investigate violations committed by its weapon systems (although the NATO Guidelines do seem to bear an implication to this effect as regards 'malfunctions'). While Paragraph 8 establishes the intention that the compensation process should be transparent, Paragraphs 1 and 9, although excluding strict liability, illustrate that responsibility for civilian casualties, even when they result from lawful activities, is gaining more acceptance among states.[1028] As will be explained next, there is no reason to exclude a state deploying AWS from any of these obligations. The distinction is that even if the state cannot be held responsible internationally for collateral damage, a situation involving damage caused by an 'error' on the part of an AWS should entail direct responsibility on the part of the state to proceed with the mechanisms of reparation.

The concept of direct state responsibility for unpredictable outcomes is not new. As long ago as 1972, the *Convention on International Liability for Damage Caused by Space Objects* ruled that 'notwithstanding the precautionary measures to be taken by states and international intergovernmental organizations involved in the launching of space objects, damage may on occasion be caused by such objects' and, therefore, that 'a launching State shall be absolutely liable to pay compensation for damage caused by its space object on the surface of the Earth or to aircraft in flight' (Article 2).[1029] This *Convention* is an important legal precedent through which responsibility for damage caused

1027 ICRC, 'Rule 158: Prosecution of War Crimes' (*IHL Database Customary IHL*, 2005) <https://ihl-databases.icrc.org/customary-ihl/eng/docs/v1_rul_rule158>.

1028 Crawford, *Accountability for Killing: Moral Responsibility for Collateral Damage in America's Post-9/11 Wars* (n 901) 372–381.

1029 'Convention on International Liability for Damage Caused by Space Objects' (1972) <www.unoosa.org/oosa/en/ourwork/spacelaw/treaties/introliability-convention.html>; Dinstein and Dahl (n 80) Rule 5.

by the unpredictable actions of an AWS could be determined in International Law.[1030]

Finally, the authors' observation that 'if the error is known but ignored' further use of the AWS may breach Article 57 API deserves careful consideration.[1031] It seems that this solution would be insufficient in situations involving 'malfunction' and clearly it is not applicable to 'errors'. Deploying an AWS that was known to malfunction would not only be in breach of the commander's duty to 'take all feasible precautions in the choice of means and methods of attack'. It would also be to act in complete disregard of the commander's individual responsibility (see Articles 25(3)(a) and 30 ICC Statute) if committed with knowledge or 'command responsibility', or if the commander 'knew or should have known' that the forces under his/her control were using or were about to use AWS that did not operate in compliance with IHL standards (Article 28 (a)(i)(ii) ICC Statute). Aside from individual responsibility, both types of malfunction would entail state responsibility for 'the entire time during which the act continues and remains not in conformity with the international obligations' (Article 14(2) ARSIWA), because Article 30 ARSIWA demands from a state the cessation of the wrongful conduct and the offer of insurances and guarantees of non-repetition by the deploying (responsible) state.[1032]

In conclusion, it is possible to find supportive arguments to explain why a case of AWS 'error' should be distinguished from that of a malfunctioning weapon system. In the case of 'errors', violations are committed by the system itself, and for these the state is responsible. The question that it is now important to answer is, in practice, *how will such distinctions be made* in order to ensure that the appropriate form of liability applies?

5.4.5 *Explaining AWS' modus operandi: Demanding 'Factual Algorithms' as Digital Evidence for War Crimes Prosecutions*

An armed conflict has always an intrinsic complexity and, therefore, criminal investigations and prosecutions for IHL violations will demand not only admissible but also *reliable* evidence (Article 64(1) RPE;[1033] Article 64(9)(a)

1030 Gill and Fleck (n 146) 561, paras 30.01–30.0; Steven Freeland, 'There's Satellite in My Backyard! – Mir and the Convention on International Liability for Damage Caused by Space Objects' (2001) 24 *UNSW Law Journal* 462, 471, 484.

1031 Henderson, Keane and Liddy (n 19) 361–362.

1032 Crawford, *The International Law Commission's Articles on State Responsibility: Introduction, Text and Commentaries* (n 697) 196–197.

1033 'Rules of Procedure and Evidence of the International Criminal Court' (hereinafter RPE).

ICC Statute). This can represent a challenge for the *Office of the Prosecutor* (hereinafter OTP), and some reasons spring to the forefront. First, the limited access to relevant evidence, especially when states refuse to collaborate in an investigation. Second, the opposite problem, that is, the multiplication of evidence-gathering, which will necessitate lengthy operations to gather all the evidence relevant to the prosecution.

The aforementioned difficulties have led some authors, among them Peter Margulies, to suggest a *dialogic model between commanders and machines*. Qualified as 'dynamic diligence', such a model would require continuous assessment of the AWS's compliance with IHL and, more importantly, programme flexibility to allow interpretation of the AWS's outputs.[1034] This, however, begs the question of why the system should be called 'autonomous' in the first place; the defining feature of an AWS is supposed to be its ability to operate by means of its embedded machine learning algorithms alone, without the need for human intervention. Thus, requiring adjudgments, assessments or any other dialogic mechanism of interrogating the 'autonomous' decision-making process, before the AWS engages a target, seems to be at odds with the whole *ethos* of machine learning algorithms and autonomous systems.[1035] This understanding could be helpful in preventing situations of 'error' but would not offer any useful data as far as the role of human operators in 'accidents' is concerned.

Margulies' perspective is close to that adopted by the 2016 draft Report of the European Parliament's Committee on Legal Affairs (JURI), *Civil Law Rules on Robotics*, in which a Charter on Robotics is proposed.[1036] According to this report a code for ethical conduct should be written for robotics engineers, designed in a way that 'allows individual adjustments to be made on a case-by-case basis in order to assess whether a given behaviour is right or wrong in a given situation and to take decisions in accordance with a pre-set hierarchy of values'.[1037] However, first the European Parliament has not only excluded AWS from their project but also approved, in September 2018, a resolution calling for an all-out pre-emptive ban on offensive AWS,[1038] and, second,

1034 Margulies (n 390) 406–407.

1035 Sandra Wachter, Brent Mittelstadt and Luciano Floridi, 'Transparent, Explainable, and Accountable AI for Robotics' (2017) 2 *Science Robotics* 1–6; Dickinson (n 471) 14.

1036 European Parliament Committee on Legal Affairs (n 547).

1037 ibid 14–15.

1038 European Parliament, 'European Parliament Resolution of 12 September 2018 on Autonomous Weapon Systems' (2018) 2018/2752 (RSP) B, paras 3–4 <www.europarl.europa.eu/sides/getDoc.do?pubRef=-//EP//NONSGML+TA+P8-TA-2018-0341+0+DOC+PDF+V0//EN>.

systems that operate inside a 'black box' do not seem to be compatible with a *dialogic model*.[1039]

Taking into account the difficulties discussed earlier, the perspective chosen here is to reject the suggestion that human operators should engage in dialogue with systems that are *functionally autonomous*. Instead, human operators should be able to demand that AWS produce '*factual algorithms*' as a way of addressing problems concerning the relevance and reliability of evidence.

The leading argument is that state empowerment, through the deployment of AWS, demands transparency and accountability for every hypothetical scenario that might involve violations of IHL. This argument is even more pertinent when the philosophy underpinning ICL, and the ICC in particular, is that the 'most serious crimes of concern to the international community as a whole must not go unpunished and that their effective prosecution should be ensured by taking measures at the national level and by enhancing international cooperation'.[1040] In order to guarantee this *ethos*, it would be necessary to have access to the *digital evidence* that shows exactly how the *algorithm for the mission*, that is, the algorithm for *situation management*, operated once the AWS was activated.

This possibility is not itself new, since 'digital evidence' has been accepted both at national and international level.[1041] The ICTY, the ICTR, the ICC and the Special Tribunal for Lebanon (hereinafter STL) have all considered digital evidence to be admissible, and, in the specific case of the ICC Statute, 'the court may rule on the relevance or admissibility of any evidence, taking into account, *inter alia*, the probative value of the evidence and any prejudice that such evidence may cause to a fair trial or to a fair evaluation of the testimony of a witness, in accordance with the

1039 cf Chapter 1, Section 1.3.2.

1040 Preamble of the Rome Statute of International Criminal Court. cf Gus Waschefort, 'Gravity as a Requirement in International Criminal Prosecutions: Implications for South African Courts' (2014) 47 *The Comparative and International Law Journal of Southern Africa* 38, 42–43.

1041 'Digital Evidence' is information stored or transmitted in binary form that may be relied upon in a judicial dispute. It can be found on a computer hard drive, a mobile phone, a personal digital assistant (PDA), a CD and a flash card in a digital camera, among other places. Digital evidence is commonly associated with electronic crime, or e-crime. However, digital evidence is now used to prosecute all types of crimes, not just e-crime. In the specific case of AWS, it will refer to the data relevant to an investigation that is *observed, oriented and selected* by the computerised system of an AWS, in order to carry out a targeting process during an international or non-international armed conflict. cf US National Institute of Justice, 'Digital Evidence and Forensics' (2016) <https://nij.ojp.gov/digital-evidence-and-forensics>.

Rules of Procedure and Evidence' (Article 69(4) ICC Statute).[1042] Thus, it seems to be generally accepted that *factual algorithms* provide reliable and admissible evidence.

The proposal that the *algorithm for the mission* can be regarded as evidence requires some clarification. First, Chopra and White support the argument that an 'artificial agent' should and could always be verified by a human operator.[1043] However, this interpretation faces some difficulties. As has been explained, an AWS' operational algorithms will operate inside a 'black box', so it might be impossible to access information that shows how the system's algorithms operated in action. The third-person verification would be reduced to a mere acknowledgement that violations of IHL had been caused by the AWS but would not be sufficient to explain the cause. Second, the inherent complexity of machine learning algorithms might create insurmountable difficulties for 'third persons' attempting to verify them, especially for those in charge of investigating and prosecuting war crimes, who may lack technical knowledge. As Lindsay Freeman points out, digital information is changing the landscape of evidence but 'prosecutors, investigators, defense attorneys, and judges all need to be prepared'.[1044] Third, in the case of AWS, digital evidence requires particular expertise. The wrong interpretation or evaluation of digital evidence could result in an undesirable legal situation in which human operators could be scapegoated, or violations of IHL decriminalised, in spite of their gravity.[1045] As such, the path ahead should actually be the opposite of that proposed by Chopra and White: a way must be found to enable *the system to demonstrate the logic* that led to the engagement of the selected targets, that is, *the 'DNA' of a targeting process*. For this purpose, AWS should include embedded self-explanatory mechanisms, instead of relying on their programmers, except in the eventuality that the system is destroyed and therefore unable to do it. This proposal finds support in two cases. The first is that of Malaysia Airlines Flight MH17 that crashed in Eastern Ukraine, and the second the *Prosecutor v Salim Jamil Ayyash, Mustafa Amine Badreddine, Habib Merhi, Hussein Hassan Oneissi and Assad Hassan Sabra Case* (hereinafter the *Ayyash et al. Case*) held before the STL.[1046]

1042 For several cases in which International Tribunals made use of 'digital evidence', cf Stahn (n 953) 337–339; Lindsay Freeman, 'Digital Evidence and War Crimes Prosecutions: The Impact of Digital Technologies on International Criminal Investigations and Trials' (2018) 41 *Fordham International Law Journal* 283, 287–290.

1043 cf Chapter 3, Section 3.6.2; Chopra and White (n 528) 129.

1044 Freeman (n 1042) 329.

1045 ibid 297.

1046 Catherine Schoichet and Ashley Fantz, 'U.S. Official: Missile Shot Down Malaysia Airlines Plane' (CCN *Europe*, 18 July 2014) <http://edition.cnn.com/2014/07/17/world/europe/ukrai

Starting with the first case: on 27 July 2014, a Buk Antiaircraft Missile shot down Malaysian Airlines Flight MH17 over a war zone in Ukraine, causing the death of 298 victims. Five countries involved in the targeting operation – Australia, Belgium, Malaysia, the Netherlands and Ukraine – created a *Joint Investigative Team* (hereinafter a JIT) to look into the 6,000 kilos of detritus and identify those criminally responsible for the crash.[1047] The JIT, in spite of all difficulties, came to the conclusion that the attack had been carried out by Russia's 53rd Antiaircraft Missile Brigade.[1048] Although the Russian Federation has refused to participate in any way, international prosecutors have indicted four individuals who are believed to have ties with Russian intelligence.[1049]

The second case is that of the attack in Beirut on 14 February 2005 that killed the former Lebanese Prime Minister Rafik Hariri and 21 others, and injured 226 more.[1050] Four individuals were charged with conspiracy to commit a terrorist act, along with several other related charges. During the investigation, Wissam Eid, a computer engineer allowed access by a judge to the Lebanon's main cell phone companies, designed an algorithm to make sense of the cell phones' metadata, and this was considered to be crucial material evidence.[1051]

These two situations offer some help towards understanding not only the role of the investigators, but also how algorithms can become a source of evidence explaining the relevant facts of a war crime. In the first situation no evidence was available because the MH17 was destroyed, and it was equally impossible to gain access to the decision-making processes of the Buk Missile. Although the JIT was created and there was plenty of digital evidence, the team of investigators ran into several problems. As one of the investigators on the Dutch Safety Board stated, 'we have nothing of which we know for sure

ne-malaysia-airlines-crash/index.html>; *Prosecutor v Ayyash et al Decision to Hold Trial in Absentia* [2012] Special Tribunal for Lebanon STL-11-01/I/TC, R109799.

1047 Joint Investigation Team, 'MH17: Six Aspects of the Criminal Investigation Explained' (June 2016) <www.om.nl/mh17-ezine-juni2016/e-zine-en.html>.

1048 ibid Section Investigation into the Weapon System.

1049 Andrew E Kramer, 'Four to Face Murder Charges in Downing of Malaysia Airlines Flight 17' *The New York Times* (19 June 2019) <www.nytimes.com/2019/06/19/world/europe/mh17-ukraine-russia-suspects.html>; 'Investigators: Buk Missile from Russian Antiaircraft Brigade Downed MH17' (*Radio Free Europe Radio Liberty*, 24 May 2018) <www.rferl.org/a/mh17-criminal-probe-to-appeal-to-the-public-for-help/29246988.html>; 'MH17 Ukraine Plane Crash: What We Know' (*BBC News World*, 19 June 2019) <www.bbc.co.uk/news/world-europe-28357880>.

1050 For the background of the *Ayyash Case, Prosecutor v Ayyash et al Decision to Hold Trial in Absentia* (n 1046) paras 4–13.

1051 ibid paras 1, 4, 31, 105–111; Freeman (n 1042) 307–309.

whether it is true and genuine. After all, we are dealing with a conflict involving several parties. These parties may have an interest in manipulating or contaminating material.'[1052] Looking to scenarios involving AWS, it is self-evident that an investigating team will encounter limitations, especially when the investigators have 'to verify if self-appointed experts are indeed experts, rather than amateurs'.[1053] The *Ayyash et al. Case*, on the other hand, shows how an algorithm can efficiently organise a huge volume of digital evidence and, at the same time, prove to be a reliable source of evidence that is able to provide data and information patterns that illuminate the underlying causes of unlawful outcomes.

Some could argue that, in spite of the value of digital evidence, algorithms can be tampered with and/or manipulated and that, therefore, they should not be regarded as reliable and admissible sources of evidence. Two observations are important here, before proceeding with the main argument. First, the concept of 'factual algorithms' is coherent with recent developments in machine learning, which have shown that explanatory dialogues between embedded algorithms and the final user (known as *Explainable Artificial Intelligence*, or XAI)[1054] are possible. Second, the concept is not entirely new; in the EU legal context, a number of scholars, in response to the challenges posed by GDPR, have suggested the operationality of *counterfactual algorithms* to obtain explanations from machine learning algorithms without having to deal with 'black boxes'.[1055] Counterfactual algorithms would assume the form of structural equations in execution by identifying alterations to pre-given variables.[1056] In short, 'counterfactual explanations' would inform an enquirer how the outcome came to be *x* and not *y*.[1057] For the same reason, and taking into account the specificities of AWS, the model adopted should be one of *factual demonstration*. In armed conflict, context is not relevant to the establishment of counterfactual explanations (e.g. if *x* were

1052 Joint Investigation Team (n 1047) Section Investigation into a Weapon System.

1053 ibid; Luke Harding, 'Q&A: What We Know and Don't Know about the Downing of MH17' *The Guardian* (Brussels, 24 May 2018) <www.theguardian.com/world/2018/may/24/qa-mh17-investigation-russian-missile-aircraft-ukraine>.

1054 Chapter 4, Section 4.5.3, footnote 716.

1055 Sandra Wachter, Brent Mittelstadt and Chris Russell, 'Counterfactual Explanations without Opening the Black Box: Automated Decisions and the GDPR' (2018) 31 *Harvard Journal of Law & Technology* 842. For another perspective of *counterfactual algorithms*, Chris Russell, 'Efficient Search for Diverse Coherent Explanations' [2019] *Proceedings on the Conference on Fairness, Accountability, and Transparency* 20, 22.

1056 Wachter, Mittelstadt and Russell (n 1055) 848; Russell, 'Efficient Search for Diverse Coherent Explanations' (n 1055) 1.

1057 Wachter, Mittelstadt and Russell (n 1055) 859.

a civilian, he/she would not have been targeted). The point is, rather, that the algorithms would identify the facts that were selected and considered by the AWS in the process of determining that *x* was a legitimate target.

It should not be assumed that factual algorithms will be able to provide exhaustive detail that reveals every single step taken by the *algorithm for the mission*, but they should be able to trace the constitutive steps of the set of algorithms that integrate the *algorithm for the mission* with the different layers of the OOSA Loop. Thus, the *relevant data* will correspond with the outcome of the *algorithm for situation assessment* (Observation and Orientation of data); *course selection* will correspond with the aim of the *selection algorithm*, at which stage possible courses of action are pondered; finally, the *engagement process* should yield all the relevant data collected from the battlespace after the AWS was activated, and reveal the logic behind the targeting process – which is the purpose of the *algorithm for situation management*. Access to this information will not open the door to understanding exactly what the cause of the action that violated IHL was – a 'malfunction', an 'accident', an 'error' or a combination of any or all of those events – but also would provide investigators with a higher level of certainty since an algorithm, as a set of rules, follows a determined order of events. Manipulation or exploitation of the vulnerabilities of algorithms, such as hacked or biased algorithms, will be easier to detect.

An explanation of algorithms as admissible evidence is now required. It is clear that all International Criminal Tribunals were created to answer to the most serious crimes committed during an armed conflict.[1058] This is particularly relevant since the ICC will have jurisdiction over crimes committed after its ratification, and over the deployment of AWS in future armed conflicts. According to Gus Waschefort, 'gravity, as a foundational philosophy for the actual establishment of the ICC [...] exists to give legitimacy to the existence of the Court, it is not an admissibility, jurisdictional, or substantive requirement or threshold' but rather the fact that *gravity* is an element of the crime.[1059] As such, war crimes caused by algorithms cannot be excluded and the 'broad discretionary power [that is] granted to the International Prosecutor in selecting the targets for prosecution' (Article 53(1) ICC Statute) should be applicable to computerised AWS.[1060] Thus, the OTP can apply the rules for admissibility of evidence to autonomous systems (as clarified by the Trial Chamber in the *Bemba Case* and enshrined in Article 64, ICC Statute). Accordingly, the

1058 Waschefort (n 1040) 43.
1059 ibid 43, 49–50.
1060 ibid 45; Stahn (n 953) 343–345.

> Chamber recalls [. . .] for any tendered item to be admitted into evidence, it must satisfy a three-part admissibility test. Under this test, the Chamber will examine, on a preliminary basis, whether the submitted materials (i) are relevant to the case; (ii) have probative value; and (iii) are sufficiently relevant and probative to outweigh any prejudicial effect that could be caused by their admission.[1061]

As such, it can be concluded that the rules enshrined in Article 64 ICC Statute are a guarantee because the Chamber will have to inquire about the reliability of the algorithm and whether the probative value of the algorithm could cause, in any circumstance, an unfair trial.[1062] As the Chamber has explained, when an item of evidence is challenged (e.g. a *factual algorithm*), 'the burden rests on the party seeking the item's admission to demonstrate its admissibility', and when it is not contested, 'the Chamber may equally exclude the item if one or more of the requirements of the three-pronged test are clearly not met'.[1063] This legal framework would prevent algorithms from being manipulated since an unlawful outcome would obey a certain code which, if changed, would most certainly have led to an outcome other than the one produced. Thus, there are no reasons to believe that factual algorithms cannot be as reliable (if not more reliable) than more traditional sources of evidence.

Finally, it can be argued that factual algorithms will not solve any problems in cases of states being involved in the commission of war crimes; witness Russia's refusal to collaborate in the investigation of the crash of Flight MH17. This problem is not specific to factual algorithms but applies to any source of evidence. However, as already seen, the International Tribunal has found that digital evidence can prove to be a reliable source of substantiation, for example when the accused are in absentia.[1064] Another point worthy of consideration is that, taking into account the nature of AWS, a state may be interested in proving that a violation of IHL was caused by a 'malfunction' or 'accident', and not by an 'error', for which the latter state would be the only responsible agent.

It has been noted that 'errors' are, in fact, the only category that would involve state responsibility exclusively. As such, it is important at this point to recall that another general obligation incumbent upon the state is 'to make full reparation

1061 *Prosecutor v Jean-Pierre Bemba Public Redacted Version of 'Decision on the Prosecution's Application for Admission of Materials into Evidence Pursuant to Article 64(9) of the Rome Statute' of 6 September 2012* [2012] ICC ICC-01/05-01/08 para 7.

1062 ibid para 8; Freeman (n 1042) 295.

1063 *Prosecutor v Jean-Pierre Bemba Public Redacted Version of 'Decision on the Prosecution's Application for Admission of Materials into Evidence Pursuant to Article 64(9) of the Rome Statute' of 6 September 2012* (n 1061) para 10.

1064 *Prosecutor v Ayyash et al Decision to Hold Trial in Absentia* (n 1046).

for the injury caused by the internationally wrongful act' (Article 31 ARSIWA),[1065] in order *to restore the international legal order*.[1066] The question now is: how is the obligation on states to provide access to factual algorithms to be implemented?

Crootof notes that a *legally binding treaty*, establishing the principles of Tort Law for state responsibility, would adequately cover cases resulting in unpredictable outcomes.[1067] However, judging from states' declarations at the CCW, it is difficult to envisage a protocol that is likely to be agreed and signed. First, the states that are the most prominent manufacturers of weaponry have vehemently rejected the idea of a pre-emptive ban and, indeed, of treating AWS differently from any other weapon system. Second, states have long refused to accept *objective responsibility* in any form for hazardous activities, and it seems far too complex and unreal to demand that states establish compensatory limits for violations of IHL.[1068] Third, as Hammond suggests, tort liability faces another difficulty: what International Court would be considered legitimate to adjudicate in the case of 'war torts'?[1069] Crootof highlights the problems inherent in the ICC and ICJ statutes owing to the fact that their jurisdiction is dependent on states' consent. With this in mind, the author suggests that a workable path to take might be to establish 'a carefully tailored independent tribunal' that would charge 'independent prosecutorial-like actors – call them International Representative Plaintiffs – with bringing war torts suits against states on behalf of harmed individuals'.[1070]

Considering the aforementioned discussion, it is difficult to see why a new Court, as suggested by Crootof, would offer any advantage over the existing jurisdictional organs. Another obstacle is that the ICJ, in the *Jurisdictional Immunities Case*, argued that:

> [c]ustomary international law continues *to require that a State be accorded immunity in proceedings for torts allegedly committed on the territory of another State* by its armed forces and other organs of State in the course of conducting an armed conflict. That conclusion is confirmed also by judgments of the European Court of Human Rights.[1071]

1065 Crawford, *The International Law Commission's Articles on State Responsibility: Introduction, Text and Commentaries* (n 697) 201.

1066 Castellanos-Jankiewicz (n 836) 1, 12–13, 16.

1067 Crootof, 'War Torts: Accountability for Autonomous Weapons' (n 316) 1386, 1396–1400.

1068 Boyle (n 808) 96–98.

1069 Hammond (n 764) 683.

1070 Crootof, 'War Torts: Accountability for Autonomous Weapons' (n 316) 1397–1398.

1071 *Jurisdictional Immunities of the State (Germany v Italy v Greece intervening)* (ICJ) para 78 (our emphasis).

Thus, it seems unlikely that the idea of 'International Representative Plaintiffs' would be accepted without going against established Customary International Law and the current jurisprudence of the International Courts.

Attempts to introduce new enforcement mechanisms tend to be susceptible to failure, and IHL already has legal mechanisms to ensure that states are accountable for military operations performed by AWS. Investigatory obligations exist in IHL, both in the law protecting the victims of armed conflict and in that governing the conduct of hostilities. The Conventions and their Additional Protocols of 1977 include extensive obligations on all parties to a conflict to account for the dead and the missing, prompted mainly, according to Article 32 API, 'by the right of families to know the fate of their relatives' (a rare case of a reference to rights held by natural persons and, moreover, civilians).[1072] Further, the ICRC Study (Rule 158) provides that 'States must investigate war crimes allegedly committed by their nationals or armed forces, or on their territory, and, if appropriate, prosecute the suspects. They must also investigate other war crimes over which they have jurisdiction and, if appropriate, prosecute the suspects.'[1073]

Elizabeth Wilmshurst and Susan Breau raise some legitimate concerns regarding the formulation of Rule 158 of the ICRC Study, in particular where it states that the duty to prosecute is dependent on 'appropriateness'.[1074] However, first, as the authors argue, the term 'appropriate' should not be taken as carte blanche to avoid prosecutions brought about for political reasons; as regards 'errors', it would not be 'appropriate' to prosecute states when they cannot be considered agents of international crimes.[1075] Second, states can discharge their obligations in relation to the investigation and prosecution of war crimes by establishing international tribunals or commission to do the work. For that reason, it would seem superfluous to establish a new and special Court just for dealing with situations involving AWS. The *Panel of Experts on Accountability in Sri Lanka* endorsed the prudence of adhering to Customary International Law when, in

1072 Lattimer (n 985); Lubell, Pejic and Simmons (n 1007) paras 147–149.

1073 ICRC, 'Rule 158: Prosecution of War Crimes' (n 1027); Ian Park, 'Joint Series on International Law and Armed Conflict: The Obligation to Investigate Violations of IHL' (*EJIL: Talk!*, 30 September 2016) <www.ejiltalk.org/joint-series-on-international-law-and-armed-conflict-the-obligation-to-investigate-violations-of-ihl/>; Chengeta, 'Accountability Gap: Autonomous Weapon Systems and Modes of Responsibility in International Law' (n 20) 7.

1074 Elizabeth Wilmshurst and Susan Breau, *Perspectives on the ICRC Study on Customary International Humanitarian Law* (Cambridge University Press 2007) 391–392.

1075 For the difficulties inherent to make States accountable for international crimes, cf Jorgensen (n 264) 69–79.

2011, they pointed out that it already includes obligations to investigate and prosecute serious violations of IHL, and that achieving accountability involves, among other things, the right to the truth.[1076]

In light of the aforementioned discussion, AWS may well represent an improvement in terms of international accountability vis-à-vis IHL. States need significant resources to proceed with prosecutions for war crimes, and it can prove difficult to gain access to evidence if it is located in the territory of another state.[1077] Although there are no hard and fast rules regarding the practical conduct of such investigations, it is commonly agreed that they should be independent, effective and objective, taking into account the context and the circumstances prevailing at the time.[1078] Since the *algorithm for the mission* has to operate based on objective and codified criteria, the introduction of factual algorithms could guarantee that level of required objectivity necessary for an investigation of the reasons behind violations of IHL.

1076 'Report of the Secretary-General's Panel of Experts on Accountability in Sri Lanka' (2011) II–III.

1077 Park (n 1073); Wilmshurst and Breau (n 1074) 393.

1078 Park (n 1073).

Final Conclusion

The fact that it is now known that roboticists and engineers will, before long, have the capacity to design and build weapon systems that are autonomous and can 'think for themselves' has set the stage for an overwhelming mass of speculation about the status, capability and legitimacy of AWS under the IHL framework. Conscious that there are still many legal questions to be answered and technological challenges to be overcome, the first aim of this thesis was to survey the virtual forest of terms coined in the course of discussion, debate and speculation, organise them, analyse them and establish a clear definition of what an AWS actually *is*.

It is the – by no means easy – role of international lawyers to look at every aspect of what is known about new weapons and interpret it according to the applicable legal framework, and AWS are no exception. It is impossible to conjecture exactly what the future is likely to hold while AWS are still in the realm of hypothesis, so the perspective chosen for this research was to investigate the current stage of development of AI, the better to understand how AWS will actually operate. One conclusion is clear: AWS will be designed by human operators, and programmed in order to accomplish a pre-given military mission without requiring human intervention. This innovation, this possibility of fielding weapon systems capable of operating without human intervention, is at the root of all the emergent problems besetting research into and further development of AWS.

The advent of weapon systems able to operate without human supervision is possible because machine learning algorithms are now a reality. These algorithms are programmed to learn and to adapt to the multifarious and fast-moving circumstances of the battlefield, collecting and processing data faster and more precisely than a human operative. In the same way that AWS are activated (the first level of human control), they are designed and programmed (the second level of human control) to be deactivated when they are no longer required (the third level of human control). Because the level of human control is considered sufficient and appropriate in respect of a particular mission, further human intervention is not required. This should be considered the gist of the concept of 'autonomy' as it applies to weapon systems.

The next point to understand is that the 'mission' will pre-determine the 'autonomy' of a weapon system. AWS will in fact be programmed with a 'dependent autonomy', designed in accordance with and circumscribed by the '*algorithm for the mission*', which will follow the principle of the OOSA Loop. It is the complexity of this algorithm that facilitates its capacity to perform all the stages of the OOSA Loop in autonomous mode. In order to illustrate how the selection-making process works, it is helpful to divide the '*algorithm for the mission*' into three sub-dependent algorithms, each responsible for a specific stage of the Loop. First, the algorithm for 'situation-assessment' will govern the observation and orientation of data collected from the battlespace. Once the system has 'made sense' of its surroundings, the 'selection-algorithm' can be activated in order to select the course of action most likely to lead to the pre-established outcome. Finally, the algorithm for 'situation-management' will adapt the performance of the system to the supervenient circumstances of the battlefield and govern the stage of 'engagement'.

Noting the above observations, it seems there is no argument that supports the claim that AWS call into question, or somehow blur the distinction between 'weapons' and 'combatants'. The aim of this investigation is to establish whether the AWS project announced by military manufacturers and roboticists is capable of compliance with the long- and well-established principles of IHL. Up until the date of writing there have appeared to be unsurmountable obstacles in the way of ensuring that AWS comply with the rules of Distinction and Proportionality. This is not so much because of technical difficulty in encoding such rules, but more because, despite their many debates, experts and states' representatives have so far failed to reach a satisfactory agreement as to how the rules apply in circumstances involving AWS. It seems that significantly greater responsibility will devolve upon commanders, who will be tasked with ensuring that precautionary measures are in place to guarantee, according to all the information available from the system and the battlespace, that an AWS will operate according to the *algorithm for the mission* as planned, and do so in such a way as to comply with IHL regulations in every respect.

Unfortunately, it is inevitable that any weapon system, be it ever more sophisticated, may fail in its operationality, resulting in disastrous and perhaps unlawful unpredictable outcomes. In the case of 'autonomous' weaponry, it has been posited that a 'responsibility vacuum' might ensue there being no human operative to hold accountable for engagements that end in violations of IHL. This is a serious and pertinent consideration, and it is imperative that it be resolved. For the purposes of discussion, such failures will be called 'malfunctions' – unhappily, well recognised for causing civilian damage in the arena of war. However, it has been impossible, throughout this study, to identify a single argument that would justify treating AWS' malfunctions any differently, under the law, from those of any other weapons hitherto. Such occurrences are, regrettably, accepted as the inevitable consequences of war for which no one can be held accountable.

The same cannot be said of contraventions of IHL resulting from 'accidents', that is, machine failures that are traceable to human fault. Faults in the design, programming, maintenance and manufacturing of AWS demand more attention. ICL, jurisprudence and doctrine have been shown to be reluctant to accept *dolus eventualis* as a valid category in terms of individual international accountability. Nonetheless, the deployment of AWS is not compatible with accepting human negligent behaviour for a number of reasons, but above all because human intervention will not be possible during the *algorithm for the mission*.

Another vitally important factor is 'error', that is, cases of mission failure that are not caused by mistakes made by human designers or programmers but by errors on the part of the program itself. They will take place when/if the '*algorithm for the mission*' misinterprets incoming data and inverts the intended, pre-programmed mission, and will certainly result in unpredictable outcomes. However, such occurrences do not place these outcomes beyond the reach of the law. They are, rather, occasions upon which the responsibility of the state for 'wrongful international acts caused by weapons deployed by the state' is brought into play.

The thesis ends with a challenge for roboticists. The only possible way to distinguish between these categories of accident is for the algorithms to provide factual information regarding the AWS' selection-making process. In parallel with counterfactual algorithms, factual algorithms could provide data that would make it relatively straightforward to draw a distinction between events that should be considered the unfortunate consequences of war, those due to human error and those having their origin in the operationality of the AWS itself.

Any solution will always depend on the goodwill of intervenient parties to an armed conflict but in no way should the rules of transparency be compromised. The risk of accepting that all violations of IHL caused by AWS are 'malfunctions' due to their very autonomy could give rise to either a very dangerous process of decriminalisation of IHL values or to humanity's being deprived of a mechanism of war that could, in the final analysis, ensure more respect for the principle of humanity.

Index

Printed in the United Kingdom by TJ Clays Ltd.